Afric

Africa ...
natio ...
cuttin ...
the b ... at in-depth, an.
wide-ranging in its scope, Africa Now engages with the critical political,
economic, sociological and development debates affecting the continent,
shedding new light on pressing concerns.

Nordic Africa Institute

The Nordic Africa Institute (Nordiska Afrikainstitutet) is a centre for
research, documentation and information on modern Africa. Based in
Uppsala, Sweden, the Institute is dedicated to providing timely, critical
and alternative research and analysis of Africa and to co-operation with
African researchers. As a hub and a meeting place for a growing field of
research and analysis, the Institute strives to put knowledge of African
issues within reach of scholars, policy makers, politicians, media,
students and the general public. The Institute is financed jointly by the
Nordic countries (Denmark, Finland, Iceland, Norway and Sweden).

www.nai.uu.se

Forthcoming titles

Margaret C. Lee (ed.), *Africa's World Trade*

Mary Njeri Kinyanjui, *Women and the Informal Economy in Urban Africa*

Karuti Kanyinga, Duncan Okello and Anders Sjögren (eds), *Kenya: The Struggle for a New Constitutional Order*

Thiven Reddy, *South Africa: Beyond Apartheid and Liberal Democracy*

Anders Themner (ed.), *Warlord Democrats in Africa*

Titles already published

Fantu Cheru and Cyril Obi (eds), *The Rise of China and India in Africa*

Ilda Lindell (ed.), *Africa's Informal Workers*

Iman Hashim and Dorte Thorsen, *Child Migration in Africa*

Prosper B. Matondi, Kjell Havnevik and Atakilte Beyene (eds), *Biofuels, Land Grabbing and Food Security in Africa*

Cyril Obi and Siri Aas Rustad (eds), *Oil and Insurgency in the Niger Delta*

Mats Utas (ed.), *African Conflicts and Informal Power*

Prosper B. Matondi, *Zimbabwe's Fast Track Land Reform*

Maria Eriksson Baaz and Maria Stern, *Sexual Violence as a Weapon of War?*

Fantu Cheru and Renu Modi (eds), *Agricultural Development and Food Security in Africa*

About the editor

Amanda Hammar is research professor at the Centre
of African Studies, Copenhagen University. She has
researched and published on agrarian change, local
government, state-making, sovereignty, displacement
and crisis in southern Africa, with a special focus
on Zimbabwe and, less so, on Mozambique. She
co-edited *Zimbabwe's Unfinished Business: Rethinking
Land, State and Nation in the Context of Crisis* (Weaver
Press, 2003) and two journal special issues related to
political economies of displacement in southern Africa
(*Journal of Contemporary African Studies*, 2008; *Journal
of Southern African Studies*, 2010). Her current work is
focused on changing modes of urban governance and
citizenship in times of crisis and displacement.

Displacement economies in Africa

Paradoxes of crisis and creativity

edited by Amanda Hammar

Nordiska Afrikainstitutet
The Nordic Africa Institute

Zed Books
LONDON | NEW YORK

Displacement Economies in Africa was first published in association with
the Nordic Africa Institute, PO Box 1703, SE-751 47 Uppsala, Sweden in 2014
by Zed Books Ltd, 7 Cynthia Street, London N1 9JF, UK and Room 400,
175 Fifth Avenue, New York, NY 10010, USA

www.zedbooks.co.uk
www.nai.uu.se

Set in OurType Arnhem, Monotype Gill Sans Heavy by Ewan Smith
Index: ed.emery@thefreeuniversity.net
Cover design: www.roguefour.co.uk
Printed and bound in Great Britain by TJ International Ltd. Padstow, Cornwall

Distributed in the USA exclusively by Palgrave Macmillan, a division of
St Martin's Press, LLC, 175 Fifth Avenue, New York, NY 10010, USA

A catalogue record for this book is available from the British Library
Library of Congress Cataloging in Publication Data available

ISBN 978-1-78032-489-0 hb
ISBN 978-1-78032-488-3 pb

MIX
Paper from
responsible sources
FSC   FSC® C013056
www.fsc.org

Contents

Figure and tables

Figure

Tables

Introduction

1 | Displacement economies: paradoxes of crisis and creativity in Africa[1]

Amanda Hammar

An insistent presence

Finding a name for something that is viscerally 'there' but is still undefined provokes a creative frustration. This something 'insists upon its presence' as a problematic (Thompson 1978, cited in Guyer 2002: ix), prompting a productive search for analytical terms with which to counter this absence in a meaningful way. This is a search often enriched by a collective rather than an individual endeavour. Such creative frustration occurred in the 2000s during my engagement with contexts of violent crisis and displacement and their continuities in southern Africa, and specifically in Zimbabwe. Through this, what came to light repeatedly were the *paradoxes* of displacement: openings occurring as well as closures; dislocation and movement at the same time as confinement and 'stuckness'; creation as well as destruction; wealth accumulation alongside impoverishment. Inevitably, these are experienced unevenly by those affected by or effecting forms of displacement. What seemed increasingly evident, however, was not only that there were complex historical and contemporary conditions that generated displacement in its various manifestations: that is, one-off acts of mass dislocation, for example, or longer-term, cumulative forms of chronic dislodging. In addition, one could observe the emergence of, and articulation between, a range of new physical, social, economic and political spaces, relations, systems and practices that displacement itself was *producing*.

Witnessing these compelling paradoxes of displacement, there seemed to be no existing conceptual framework or language at the time with which to investigate and make sense of their curious simultaneities, their multi-actor, multi-sited and multi-temporal dimensions, and their complex relational manifestations and implications. Even if there were some promising leads to pursue, there was no single theoretical approach or disciplinary perspective or field of study that was encompassing enough on its own. The rich literatures related to refugee studies, for example, with few exceptions, were barely paying attention to questions of political economy and the shifting economic dynamics that displacement was linked to. The focus of migration studies of various shades, while certainly inclusive of various economic perspectives, was not concerned with the enforced, violent dimensions of movement which are

3

core aspects of displacement. And the growing scholarship on shadow or war economies on the one hand and underground or informal economies on the other, while relevant on many levels, did not have a focus on displacement as such at their centre. So even while all these continue to be resonant and inspiring fields of knowledge, each in themselves has been unable to grasp what was emerging but was as yet unnamed.

It was this frustration which prompted a search for more appropriate ways of thinking and speaking about displacement. This volume is one of the collective outcomes of that ongoing search, itself merely a starting point rather than an endpoint in this enterprise. This introductory chapter aims to unfold key steps in the journey thus far which have led to the development of an approach to (not a theory of) displacement that focuses on the relational qualities and the paradoxes of displacement in general, and on both what produces displacement and what it in turn produces. This approach has been applied in this volume to what we call here *displacement economies*, entailing theoretical and analytical engagement with a selection of empirically situated displacement contexts.

Importantly, the focus on displacement economies does not simply concern classic notions of 'the economy' as such, or simply 'economic' elements. The approach developed within this volume – often combining various political economy and cultural politics sensibilities – engages with a series of dynamic questions that cut across sociocultural, political and economic spheres.[2] These questions, not all of which are addressed equally or directly in this collection, include the following: How does the value (commodification and consumption) of things, bodies, spaces, natural resources and even money itself change (or continue) in times of severe and sustained crisis and displacement, and with what effects? Under such conditions, how do the spaces, forms and dynamics of production alter, and with what effects? What new forms and dynamics of accumulation, distribution and exchange emerge under such conditions, and with what effects? How do notions and experiences of time change and, in so doing, affect economic and social practices? How do both formal and informal economies and the articulations between them – contested as their distinctions or boundaries are – get altered in such times, and with what effects? Additional related questions arise such as: How do social relations as well as forms and sites of social reproduction get reshaped in contexts of crisis and displacement? And how do political spaces and practices in such contexts generate, and also get altered by, changes in economic dynamics?

Conceptualizing displacement

Displacement – read broadly as constituting an act, experience and/or effect of some form of forced dislocation, or confinement – is as old and continuous as human history. When have there not been periods or places

4

marked by violent conquest or occupation; enclosure or enslavement, dispossession, removal or forced resettlement, with their profound individual as well as collective material and symbolic effects? Albeit with a much shorter provenance, displacement as a *concept* or object of study[3] also has a history, while a quite different if related intellectual and practical history has evolved concerning intervention in displacement contexts. This section discusses the ways in which 'displacement' evolved initially as an *operational* concept within a post-Second World War global humanitarian framework. It then moves on to discuss displacement as a *relational* concept, which is what underpins the approach in this volume.

Displacement as an operational concept Displacement – often also termed forced displacement or forced migration – developed as an operational concept most notably in the aftermath of the Second World War. It became prevalent within international humanitarian circles concerned with mass dislocations precipitated by the war. The first formal instrument put in place to address this phenomenon was the 1951 United Nations Convention Relating to the Status of Refugees, later supplemented by the 1967 Protocol. The Convention defines a refugee as follows:

> A person who owing to a well-founded fear of being persecuted for reasons of race, religion, nationality, membership of a particular social group or political opinion, is outside the country of his nationality and is unable or, owing to such fear, is unwilling to avail himself of the protection of that country; or who, not having a nationality and being outside the country of his former habitual residence as a result of such events, is unable or, owing to such fear, is unwilling to return to it ...[4]

The focus specifically on refugeehood to the exclusion of other dimensions of displacement laid the basis for conceptualizing and responding to displacement institutionally, primarily and rather narrowly in terms of an international legal predicament, reflecting certain anxieties about international border-crossing.[5] Furthermore, it privileged and prioritized refugees as a category of forced migrant that was to make invisible a much wider range of others affected by, and implicated in, processes of displacement. For example, it excluded recognition of forms of physical dislocation or forced (re)settlement generated not by wars or persecution but primarily by the political-economic interests and projects of states or private corporations. In 1969 the Organization of African Unity (OAU) added an external dimension to the primarily internal threats identified in the UN Convention, reflecting continental realities and the anti-colonial, nationalist politics of the times.[6] The OAU resolved that the term 'refugee', besides encompassing the Convention definition, should 'also apply to every person who, *owing to external aggression, occupation, foreign domination* or events seriously disturbing public order in either part or the whole of his country of origin or nationality', was forced to 'seek refuge in another place outside his country of origin or nationality' (emphasis added).[7] In addition, while the 1951 Convention recognized the right of refugees to return to their places of origin, the OAU explicitly stressed that repatriation had to be voluntary.

A related but rather different institutional regime came into play some three decades later with respect to the formal recognition of those dislocated and relocated within their own borders. They would eventually come to be labelled internally displaced persons (IDPs). Historically, the empirical reality of internal displacement had been widespread in many contexts. In some cases it was prompted by violent internal social conflicts such as civil wars. In others, it resulted from politically and/or economically driven state projects of 'development' or 'modernization' (Scott 1998). Often these entailed mass forced removals and resettlement, as with the creation of the 'homelands' in apartheid South Africa (Platzky and Walker 1985) or through large-scale dam development (Colson 1971; Roy 1999; Oliver-Smith 2010). In such situations those subjected to such violent dislocation were not classified in any institutionally standardized way. It was only in 1998 that the United Nations developed its Guiding Principles on Internal Displacement, in which IDPs were described as:

> persons or groups of persons who have been forced or obliged to flee or to leave their homes or places of habitual residence, in particular as a result of or in order to avoid the effects of armed conflict, situations of generalised violence, violations of human rights or natural or human-made disasters, and who have not crossed an internationally recognised State border.[8]

The IDP framework drew more broadly from international human rights norms and standards than from the established refugee paradigm. Linked to this in part, the international legal status of IDPs, and the instruments available to advocates, governments and international organizations to address internal displacement, have evolved quite differently – and less forcefully, one might suggest – from those developed for refugees. Certainly, the emergence of a more formalized 'IDP regime' has made the overall phenomenon more visible and generated more serious attention. However, it has tended towards homogenizing the ways in which displacement within states is recognized and addressed, especially in operational terms, much as has been so within the refugee regime. Increasingly in the past few decades, large multinational institutions like the World Bank have recognized (internal) displacement as a key effect of development programmes and projects – including some of their own – and developed measures to address, compensate for or pre-empt these (Christensen and Harild 2009: 4).[9] Yet, as with the older refugee focus, certain global-technocratic discourses have tended to dominate the operational framing of displacement as a whole (even while critical scholarship has challenged this: see, for example, Turton 2003; Bakewell 2008). Focusing on typologies of causes, and forms of physical dislocation or removal, relocation and resettlement, an entire humanitarian regime has come into being aimed at protecting or assisting those categorized within this framework (Harrell-Bond 1986).

International but also national institutions, laws, labels and procedures have helped to define, identify and validate who, what and where are included within the operational field of displacement. The emphasis on population rather than process has contributed to this limited and limiting perspective (Lubkemann 2010). Terms like refugee, IDP (internally displaced person), asylum seeker or returnee are among the most common and familiar labels in the dominant lexicon. This corresponds with the excessive focus on formally recognized spaces and experiences of physical dislocation – which are often linked simultaneously to, or become themselves, places of confinement. This includes refugee camps or IDP camps, asylum or detention centres, or resettlement areas. People's internment within formal camps is commonly justified as being for their own 'protection'. At the same time it involves measures to contain – or constrain – the displaced within given boundaries that seemingly separate them from those threatening them or from other legally emplaced or entitled citizens (Bøås and Bjørkhaug, this volume).

There is continued emphasis, operationally, on those documented and encamped. This is despite the fact that self-settled displacees in both rural and increasingly urban areas constitute a substantial majority of forced migrants (Raeymaekers, this volume). Their presence in these new and often already pressured spaces has significant effects both for themselves and for the physical, social, economic and political environments into which they have moved.

More generally, the persistent and rather static focus in operational contexts on the formally displaced – who are primarily viewed through a lens of 'victimhood', 'protection' and 'management' – tends to leave other actors and dynamics still largely unseen and unnamed. Yet as noted by Lubkemann (2010) and Polzer and Hammond (2008), there has been a growing scholarship in recent years critiquing various invisibilities created by such a framework, and attending to more complex and layered dynamics among displaced communities, camped or uncamped. This has brought greater attention to, for example, self-settlement in various contexts (Malkki 1995; Bascom 1998; Bakewell 2000; Raeymaekers, this volume); to internally displaced persons more generally (Dubernet 2001; Murray 2005; Bøås and Bjørkhaug, this volume), and to the density of difference and politics inside camps themselves (Turner 2010). It has highlighted those involuntarily immobilized or displaced-in-place (Lubkemann 2008a; Magaramombe 2010; Jones 2010 and this volume), as well as exploring the effects of displacement on host communities (Gebre 2003; Rodgers 2008; Evans, Rodrigues, and Raeymaekers, this volume). More attention has been given to refugee women, especially in urban settings (Roque 2008; Abusharaf 2009, Elliott, this volume), and also to the relationship between religion and displacement (Lauterbach 2014), as well as to the diversity and dynamics of new and expanding diasporas (Koser 2003; McGregor and Primorac 2010; Hansen, this volume). And there has been a growing focus too on the relationship between displacement and state-making (Hammar 2008; Landau and Monson 2008).

The displacement economies approach pushes the boundaries of the above-mentioned perspectives, extending well beyond the refugee and/or IDP arenas and humanitarian orientation more generally. It includes but moves beyond established insights into those directly if differentially dislocated. Through its specific focus on the paradoxically productive dynamics of displacement, it brings attention in new ways to people more *indirectly* affected by displacement, such as those left behind or confined, as well as those hosting displacees, be they familiar or unfamiliar, family members or strangers, officially recognized or not. It also considers the complex and shifting political economies under-pinning or sustaining displacement, which might include the interests of central states, municipalities, military, rebel movements, private companies or development agencies, either alone or in alliance with one another. Addition-ally, the approach takes into account those benefiting directly or indirectly from displacement and how they affect both informal and formal economies. This may include political parties, state agents, new and old entrepreneurs and investors, new and old gatekeepers or brokers, as well as those among the displaced who might, in fact, find ways to benefit differentially from the condition of displacement. Finally, it is interested in locating the interests and effects of those 'managing' the displaced, such as state agencies, donor agencies, non-governmental organizations, church organizations, border agen-cies, and so on.

The approach furthermore moves beyond the usual system of often de-historicized, oversimplified and often policy-oriented categorizing of types of displacement and 'the displaced', reinforced by popular and iconic media images and narratives.[10] Together, such labels, narratives and images have naturalized the association between displacement and violence, emergency, chaos, loss and victimhood. In addition, they often imply absolute vulnerability and passivity of the displaced, reinforced by an implied gratitude for being helped or saved. All this fuels the largely unquestioned, normative humanitar-ian discourses and systems established to 'manage' the misplaced, with all the large-scale human, legal, political, structural and environmental challenges this implies. Such hegemonic representations of displacement are not 'untrue' or inaccurate in their totality. However, they clearly reflect only a partial perspec-tive of what displacement can and does entail in terms of enforced material, spatial, social and symbolic changes. They systematically leave out the full range of relevant people and processes involved, as well as the diverse effects displacement produces. In doing so, as already suggested, they leave much and many hidden or unnoticed.[11] Such analytical blind spots generate (contradictory) political-administrative regimes of recognition of place, personhood and practices. These in turn (re)produce logics of belonging, entitlement and exclusion within and across space which reinforce regimes of management to control things, bodies and borders (see, for example, Vigneswaran et al. 2010; Raeymaekers 2010).

The chapters in this collection importantly demonstrate what and who else one sees through using a wider and more inclusive analytical lens, which we have defined under the term displacement economies. This approach does not underestimate the concrete, lived realities and effects of forced dislocation or confinement on those subjected to such conditions: far from it. Nor does it dismiss the need for effective systems of assistance that address the immense scale and depth of disruption and suffering caused by all forms of enforced movement or enclosure. These situations of violent crisis and displacement are endemic in today's world. On the African continent, as elsewhere, they result from wars and other forms of political violence; from agrarian land reforms, urban 'renewal' programmes and other forms of dispossession or forced resettlement; from various combinations of man-made and natural environmental disasters, such as oil or chemical spills or nuclear fallout, or droughts, floods and famines; or from development-enforced[12] or corporate-induced displacements such as mega-dam construction, mining operations or conservation.[13] The displacement economies approach or framework investigates such situations from an open-ended, multidimensional, multidisciplinary perspective that recognizes the profoundly relational qualities of displacement.

Defining a relational concept of displacement What, then, does this mean for a relational (rather than operational) definition of displacement? Among the contributors in this volume, there is no formally agreed upon, unified definition of displacement per se. However, there is a broad concurrence with the definition outlined below, which has evolved organically through my own empirical and conceptual encounters with displacement over many years[14] and which has been positively reinforced by engaging with the scholarship here and elsewhere.

I define displacement as *enforced changes in interweaving spatial, social and symbolic conditions and relations*. Each of the key words in this definition – enforced, spatial, social, symbolic – is intended to act precisely as a metaphorical key to open up a series of reflections or questions. The notion of *enforced*, which even if obvious is not always fully analysed, necessarily leads one to ask open-ended yet relational questions about who and what has compelled changes, affecting whom and in what ways. It requires an analytic lens that reflects on relations and practices of power, sovereignty and authority in terms of both the capacities and legitimations underpinning modes of force and those precipitating or implementing them. In addition, it prompts one to examine and make visible both the positionalities and counter-agency of those being compelled.

The *spatial* is a necessary but not isolated element of this process. Space in itself always matters (Massey 2005) and is always relational (see Evans but also Behrends, and Raeymaekers, this volume). In this regard, it matters in terms of attention to actual and symbolic locations or places, including those from which people are forced to move and those they move to. One needs to consider what such interconnected places/spaces mean in terms of the distances/proximities between them, what they respectively contain or promise with respect to resources, and how they are desired, occupied, used, controlled and reconstituted and by whom (Behrends, Elliott, Hansen, and Rodrigues, this volume). At the same time, not all displacement involves physical re-moval or forced movement away from a particular place. For some it may mean various forms of what Lubkemann (2008a) calls 'involuntary immobility'. This may entail being forced to remain behind, as in 'displacement-in-place' (Magaramombe 2010; Jones, this volume); or forced confinement such as in the IDP camps in northern Uganda (Finnström 2008; Bøås and Bjørkhaug, this volume); or simply abandonment and having no means to move (Solidarity Peace Trust 2009; Lubkemann 2008b).

The relationship of a given group of people to a familiar place is always internally differentiated in complex and dynamic ways. Such differentiation and complexity necessarily change under conditions of crisis (Jones, Hammar, Bracking, this volume; but also Guyer 2002). This is even more the case when people are forced to move to a new place through violence and other kinds of disruption, loss and unpredictability. On the other hand, certain patterns may also persist and get replayed in new places (Raeymaekers, Evans, this volume). Such conditions of displacement profoundly affect individuals' and groups' *social* relationships to space and to one another in the very broadest senses, affecting physical, temporal, economic, political and cultural dynamics and sensibilities. This cannot be separated from their *symbolic* relationships to place, personhood and possibilities. Displacement may, for example, touch on and alter both personal and political senses and expressions of belonging, be this to a given social group (as defined by kin, class, gender, ethnicity, religion, and so on), or to an actual locality, or to 'the nation'. These will all have material as well as social consequences. Displacement may also precipitate a changed relationship to time: to the past, and even more so to the future, each affecting relationships with the present (Jones, this volume, and Vigh 2008).

Considering displacement economies in Africa

Displacement is neither a generically African experience or condition, nor only a contemporary one. It features everywhere and throughout historical eras. One may consider the transatlantic slave trade or colonial encounters globally as well as post-colonial conflicts for a start. With respect to the present-day, conservative global figures provided by the Office of the United Nations Commissioner for Refugees (UNHCR) estimate that there are close to forty million displaced people worldwide, notably referring to both IDPs and refugees. Sub-Saharan Africa (SSA) is consistently cited as the region most affected. Of the 10.4 million currently estimated 'persons of concern' to UNHCR globally, 28 per cent (around 2.9 million) are located in SSA, whereas out of an estimated 28.8 million IDPs worldwide, 10.4 million (again, close to 28 per cent) are in SSA, with the figure having increased by 7.5 per cent from the previous year.[15] Yet these figures represent only one source, and a certain mode, of 'calculating' a particular if primary dimension of displacement: namely its physical manifestations in terms of formally documented dislocated populations. As already noted, this is a very partial view of those actually displaced, or affected by displacement. The wider intention here, however, is to underscore the overall scale and significance of the combined phenomena, experiences and effects of displacement on and for the continent (Lubkemann 2010).

As has been argued already, displacement is not simply about the technocratic or political counting of those forcibly dislocated or confined and what needs to be done to assist, protect, manage, integrate, repatriate or resettle them. Nor is it only about the various longer- and shorter-term causes of displacement, although these are a crucial aspect of the relational layers of an overall displacement context, as most chapters in this volume emphasize. Given the scale of physical, demographic and spatial disruption alone associated with specific displacement contexts, there is clearly a great deal being generated under such conditions of turbulence. The key concern here is especially with *what displacement generates* in terms of new economies and political economies, which remain remarkably under-studied.

As Jacobsen and Landau (2003: 186), among others, have noted, 'almost no economics research has been published in refugee studies'. A start has been made in some relevant directions (see Harrell-Bond 1986; Mazur 1989; Jacobsen 2002 and 2005 within a refugee-centric approach; but Hammar and Rodgers 2008 and Hammar et al. 2010 from a broader displacement perspective).[16] However, the displacement economies approach explicitly aims to address this deficit. It raises questions, some of which have previously been flagged, about: what new forms of commodification and value are produced; how both old and new resource regimes (such as those related to land, minerals, forests or even finance itself) are reordered; in what ways patterns of access, ownership, labour, production, distribution, exchange, accumulation and differentiation change or persist; and how such conditions affect the dynamic articulation between official or so-called 'formal' economies and alternative or 'informal' economies.

This focus does not assume a privileged place for displacement economies in the analysis of the changing social and material fabric of African lives and possibilities. It fully acknowledges that there are already many 'telling challenges' that have long been confronting and reshaping Africa's economies, which others continue to address (Verran 2007; Guyer 2004). The intensification of globalization, structural adjustment and liberalization, while fuelling pockets of wealth and elite accumulation, has arguably increased rather than decreased the continent's marginalization within the global economy (Ferguson 2006). This has been exacerbated by burgeoning national debts linked partly to induced deregulation of economies and declining levels of production, but also to internal political crises and severe governance failures. Even so, some sectors are booming, such as mobile phones and minerals. The expanded extraction of lucrative natural resources alongside unequal resource access and distribution has generated new patterns of differentiation and deepening poverty at local levels, including new forms of personal debt and obligation. Linked to some of these more contemporary processes, although with much longer histories, are persistent as well as new violent conflicts across all regions of the continent, primarily within but also between countries. Compounding these trends are continuing high rates of HIV/AIDS. Yet in addition to and combined with all this, there is little doubt that displacement itself, in its multiple dimensions, is profoundly affecting African economies, as this volume begins to reveal.

Connecting economies of violence, uncertainty and displacement In a more general sense, there are various overlapping ways in which Africa's 'economy' has been portrayed (often in the singular): from assertions of 'its' historical and continued marginalization and 'failure' (Van de Walle 2001); to culturalist representations of a socially embedded 'moral economy' of different shades (Olivier de Sardan 1999), marked not least by pervasive neo-patrimonialism (Chabal and Daloz 1999; Kelsall 2008); to images of a continent whose economic form and fate are largely defined by violence, war, chaos and criminalization (Bayart et al. 1999); to the recent more optimistic soundbites of 'Africa rising'[17] and its new value in the global economy linked especially to growth in (China-led) demands for natural resources and (more generally) for land for biofuel and food production (Cheru and Obi 2010). Whichever reading one adopts, either of 'the' economy or of diverse economies in Africa, it is reasonable to suggest that little systematic attention has been paid to the specific significance of displacement within and for economic domains at micro and macro levels.

This collection is an important contribution to the project of orienting and sharpening the analytic gaze in this direction. However, it does so with the benefit of insights from other relevant bodies of scholarship related to what we might generically term here *alternative* economies. This refers to economies shaped in one way or another by conditions of crisis, violence or uncertainty, including displacement. Rich bodies of empirically grounded work have been produced by different sets of scholars in relation to what have been variously (and sometimes simultaneously) termed 'war economies' (Richards 1996; Keen 2000; Goodhand 2003; Cramer 2006; Raeymaekers 2010), 'shadow economies' (Nordstrom 2004, 2007; Schneider and Enste 2002; Bracking, this volume), 'underground economies' (Venkatesh 2006; Smith 2002; Jones, this volume), 'real economies' (MacGaffey 1991; Roitman 2004), and even 'stateless economies' (Little 2003). These differ from yet resonate with an older and broader literature on 'informal economies' (Hart 2006; Meagher 2010) or 'popular economies' (Guyer 2002). While these latter may have evolved under less overtly violent conditions in general, they represent responses, over many decades, to chronic economic and political uncertainties (Vigh 2008) which continue to intensify in scale and complexity across the continent. Yet as Bracking (this volume) asserts, 'traditional literature on the informal sector does not adequately explain informalization in the context of displacement economies wrought in crisis and violence'.

Without emphasizing any of these realms in particular, what I wish to highlight here is their collective influence on ways of revealing and analysing economic logics, systems, practices and practitioners that elude the categories of classic economic theory (Verran 2007). They provide us with alternative ways of asking questions and imagining answers about African economies in particular and political economies in general. Many of the studies in these respective fields aim to examine what lies 'behind the surface' of official façades or within messy, illicit entanglements. Yet even though such work often and importantly focuses on or exposes what is considered 'illegal' – such as illicit trade and smuggling, or formally unregulated markets – this is only one side of things. These economies do not preclude legal economic practices. At the same time, they also often exhibit highly routinized forms of organizing, albeit under less formal regimes of authority (Lindell 2008). Much as a growing scholarship on 'real states' in Africa is posing challenges to classic theories of the state (Hagmann and Péclard 2010; Bierschenk and Olivier de Sardan forthcoming), this critical engagement with alternative economies – and their articulations with official economies – is challenging 'conventional ideas about economy, politics and social order' (Little 2003: 1) that have been 'based on Western experience and institutions' (Guyer 2004: 172, cited in Verran 2007: 164). At the same time, this kind of research is helping to make visible in concrete ways the empirical complexities and contingencies of African social, political and economic realities in times of crisis, violence and uncertainty.

The following section provides an introduction to some of the elements that are beginning to characterize the emerging displacement economies approach. The discussion draws extensively although not solely on the work brought together in this collection.

Elements of an approach: conceptual arenas and themes

The elements mapped below are intended to define and expand upon some of the working themes and conceptual parameters of a displacement economies approach. Given that economies in general are understood here in a socially related sense, not all these elements are explicitly or specifically 'economic', but all have implications for the ways economies work and might be understood.

Enforcement, movement, mobility Force is central to displacement, and clearly sets it apart from more voluntaristic notions such as migration, transnationalism or mobility more generally (De Bruijn et al. 2001). Yet this raises the challenge of defining what might be included under the term 'force'. We need to consider what it may include in more subtle and invisible senses, beyond the most obvious and overt forms of physical violence or threats to life and survival of targeted 'populations' that compel flight or enclosure, be this from wars or state practices associated with removal, resettlement, repatriation or confinement. At the same time, who might be identified as responsible for and/or benefiting from such force? To what extent does one include economic or environmental violence where often causality or intentionality is harder to pinpoint directly? The notion of scale and duration of what and when counts as 'force' are at the core of defining the formal 'status' of different categories of displacees, both within humanitarian regimes and among sovereign states with regard to the terms under which people are provided with protection or not. The approach taken here, while acknowledging the effects of such technocratic assessments, considers scale and degrees of intensity, and temporality itself, in more open-ended ways.

The displacement economies approach maintains a broad and inclusive understanding of force that allows for an open reading of situated empirical contexts, from which one might then generate theoretical insights about modes and patterns of compulsion and responses to it. The approach considers as significant psychological dimensions associated with force (such as fear or hopelessness) as much as direct or indirect political, economic, social, cultural or environmental factors which compel people to do what they would not otherwise have willingly chosen to do. But this does not imply a lack of agency among those on the receiving end of force. *How* people respond to enforcement in its various forms is, of course, an expression of their own agency, and a key consideration in the recognition and analysis of specific displacement economies.

The compelled movements – and/or immobility – that characterize displacement are of different kinds and durations, with highly diverse and relational effects on demographics, physical and social environments, and economies. They have implications as well for social mobility or immobility (Hammar, Jones, this volume) as well as for the movement – or blockage – of material assets, including money (Bracking, this volume). What this points to is the importance of taking for granted neither flow nor fixity of either people or things when studying displacement. Nor should one assume anything predictable about the direction or endpoint of enforced movement or its degree of permanence. Physical dislocation, for example, may occur many times, over time, from or between multiple sites. It may entail permanent or temporary relocation or resettlement, at closer or longer distances from places of origin, each context in turn having particular effects on social, political and economic realities. And it may include actual return – voluntary or otherwise – or at least the prospect of return (what I would call returnability), while in some cases return may never be an option.[18] As the cases in this volume and elsewhere illustrate, the specificities of each context affect the conditions of possibility for lives and livelihoods, for patterns of inclusion and exclusion, and for loss and accumulation of those who are displaced as well as others related in various ways to their displacement.

Spatiality and agency To (re)state the obvious, movement in any direction, or in no direction (stuckness), is always necessarily spatial. It occurs in and through space and is often also specifically *about* space in terms of economic, political or social territorialization, the respatializing of bodies and belonging, and the changing uses or 're-purposing'[19] of space itself. The enforced changes in and of one's spatial world in contexts of displacement inevitably alter actors' relationships to old and new places in terms of the loss of former social and material grounding, and subsequent repositioning and struggle for recognition and new terms of belonging. Those actively dispossessed (who in some cases might remain physically 'in place'), or physically dislocated, often lose not only physical place and property and the means of production or livelihood, but also a sense of their 'proper' place in the world (Jones, this volume; see also Roque 2008). At the same time there are others who gain materially or in terms of status and authority in each displacement context. This can be through replacing the displaced, or making use of the opportunities that, paradoxically, displacement generates, as many chapters here illustrate (see Behrends, Bracking, Evans, Hammar, Hansen).

Again, as the evidence in this volume demonstrates, these kinds of dynamics are at play whether displacement entails departures of different forms and duration (Behrends, Evans, Elliott, Hammar, Raeymakers, Rodrigues), or staying (Jones, Hammar), or direct confinement (Bøås and Bjørkhaug), or whether it includes various kinds of return (Evans, Hansen, Rodrigues) or combinations of these (Behrends, Evans). At the same time, enforced changes in relation to space/place and being in the world manifest and unfold in particular ways in different socio-spatial locations. As such, it matters to some extent whether the displacement context is overtly or primarily rural (Bøås and Bjørkhaug, Evans), or urban (Hammar, Hansen, Jones, Rodrigues), or involves formal camps (Bøås and Bjørkhaug) or versions of self-settlement (Behrends, Elliott, Evans, Raeymakers). It matters whether it includes border zones (Behrends, Evans, Raeymakers) or offshore 'security jurisdictions' and cyberspace (Bracking). Each context in turn has its own combination of histories, resources, populations and polities that affect the parameters of the possible.

While taking loss and suffering seriously, the rather persistent stereotype of 'the displaced' as passive victims is far from accurate or helpful in excavating the many dimensions of what actually occurs within a displacement context, not least in terms of concrete and differentiated losses and gains. It is clear that even when subjected to and diminished by dislocating force, 'one moves in not on space'[20] as an *active agent*, occupying and remaking space through the best use of available if highly circumscribed resources, networks and capacities. Displacement contexts are constantly being remade through complex strategies and tactics of presence and absence, visibility and invisibility, inclusion and exclusion. The possibilities are, however, far from infinite. As many of the chapters illustrate, they are constrained, as much as opened up, by the specific geographical, historical, social and political-economic realities of each context.

Relationality, scale, temporality As stated, displacement contexts are multidimensional and relational. First, they exhibit both causes and effects of displacement in multiple sites, and do so simultaneously and/or over time. Secondly, displacement always has both localized and much larger scales of significance that are interconnected socially, economically and politically. In other words, displacement patterns within given historical and spatial con-junctures need to be analysed in relation to locally situated expressions, and memories, of often much older and larger processes, all of which are infused with complex power relations. Here one might consider the contemporary manifestations of historical dispossessions, dislocations and enclosures. Forced labour, colonialism, globalization and 'development', as well as various wars, all have had long-lasting imprints on local, national and regional geographies and political economies (Arrighi et al. 2010).

Overlaying these historical processes are the effects of more recent (often violent) processes, such as post-colonial agrarian reforms (Alexander 2006; Hammar, this volume) and increased transnational land deals or 'grabbing' (Makki and Geisler 2011). Also coming increasingly into play are 'discoveries' of concentrated natural resources and the expansion of both state and trans-national corporate extractive practices (Watts 2004; Rodrigues, this volume).

In some places linked to this are both new and sustained wars (Cramer 2006; Kaldor 2007 [1998]; and Behrends, Bøås and Bjørkhaug, Elliott, Evans, Raeymaekers, and Rodrigues, this volume). To some extent these situations have generated new patterns of both legal and illicit trade and investment (MacGaffey 1991; Roitman 2004; Nordstrom 2004; Elliott, Hansen, this volume). Added to this mix are the effects of wide-scale urbanization, structural adjustment and informalization (Guyer 2002; Jones, this volume). With all this in mind, adopting a regional or international focus while keeping track of multi-sited national arenas is highly productive, even necessary, I would argue, for understanding displacement contexts and especially displacement economies (Hammar et al. 2010).

Similarly, displacement contexts and their economies need to be considered through a multi-temporal lens. On the one hand, this means thinking of displacement as a series of processes (as opposed to simply events) that unfold over time and that may be replayed but also overlaid in different eras and of varying durations (Rodrigues, Evans, this volume). On the other hand, the notion of multiple temporalities here also refers to *meanings* and expectations of time and time horizons, which quite clearly change under conditions of displacement and sustained crisis, and affect the visions and directions that shape possibilities and choices (Guyer 2002; Jones, this volume). Especially when life and livelihood trajectories and hope more widely are radically curtailed, and when formerly more predictable trajectories alter radically, the 'future' takes on substantially different meanings (see especially Bøås and Bjørkhaug, Jones, Raeymaekers, this volume, and Bracking, this volume, more specifically on how this translates into financial savings and 'futures').

Disruption, disorder and differentiation Among its many effects, displacement disrupts and dislodges not only people but social orders, physical infrastructure, ecosystems, political and administrative systems, and economic relations and practices, while at the same time generating new ones on different terms. Displacement contexts – and the displacement economies they generate or reflect – entail (and reveal) both continuities and reconfigurations of relationships between people, things, space and time. We know from our own and others' research that in multiple sites and circumstances, displacement alters 'patterns of power, exclusion, production, exchange, accumulation and transformation' (Hammar and Rodgers 2008: 366). This differentially affects the full spectrum of actors who populate such contexts: those directly displaced as well as those abandoned or forced to remain behind; those who precipitate or perpetuate displacement, 'legitimately' or through 'informal' channels of violence; those who broker or benefit from displacement; those who host or in other ways accommodate the displaced; those who manage and often manipulate the sites and subjects of displacement.

Within the various empirical communities of the displaced (or immobilized or confined), there is no fixed pattern or possible prediction as to who may retain or lose former positions of privilege, as extensive or marginal as these may have been. At the same time, pre-existing hierarchies of power and patterns of vulnerability with respect to any particular socially differentiated group (be this in terms of class, race, gender, generation, ethnicity, religion and so on) are already part of a displacement context and are likely to be reinforced. Yet sometimes the position of individuals or groups can shift, intentionally (as, for example, in Zimbabwe's targeted land reforms) or not. Specific outcomes are a matter of empirical investigation. Across this collection we see examples from different settings of how generation (Jones, Raeymaekers), gender (Behrends, Bøås and Bjørkhaug, Elliott, Hansen) and class positions (Bracking, Evans, Hammar, Rodrigues) in particular – but sometimes also race, ethnicity, clan or kinship hierarchies – are challenged or reconstituted to varying degrees. In other cases, even simultaneously in the same setting, old patterns of social differentiation between but also within certain groups are reproduced or deepened, albeit under new and unfamiliar conditions. These emerging patterns, and the networks and alliances that form or break as a result, have implications for the ways in which economic opportunities open and close for different actors under conditions of displacement.

Displacement economies in practice

This section briefly presents the book's chapters, each of which provides insights into the messy yet revealing realities of different displacement economies in practice. They include cases from specific settings in most regions of the continent, and draw on theoretical and methodological approaches from diverse disciplines (anthropology, political economy, geography, political science, development studies). The research included in this volume was not selected on any comparative grounds. Rather, in its breadth of coverage it has been a way to introduce, evoke, illustrate and address, where possible, the kinds of key questions that underpin a displacement economies approach. In this sense, all the chapters are connected to each other by a number of common interests and concerns, even if treated differently. At the same time, certain kinds of issues appear more salient for some than others. Consequently, the chapters have been grouped into three analytically suggestive themes that highlight selected dimensions of displacement. This is not intended as a way of introducing any kind of typology of displacement economies by the back door (a rejection of typologies has already been pointed out). Instead, it illustrates the diversity and complexity of displacement contexts, while homing in on some of the key dynamics and conditions that generate particular displacement economies. The hope here is that more work in this general direction will be added to this early mapping of a growing field.

The three working themes, and respective authors, are: 'Economies of rupture and repositioning' (Behrends, Evans, Hammar); 'Reshaping economic sectors, markets and investment' (Rodrigues, Elliott, Hansen, Bracking); and 'Confinement and economies of loss and hope' (Bøås and Bjørkhaug, Jones, Raeymaekers).

Economies of rupture and repositioning Andrea Behrends situates us in the volatile displacement context of the Sudan (Darfur)–Chad borderlands. She provides insights into changing economic strategies and practices that have occurred here in more recent years but which are layered upon long histories of recurring violence, dislocation and chronic instability. War, displacement and rebellion have been an integral part of this border area for more than a century, with chance on the one hand, and dire necessity on the other, prompting yet circumscribing people's survival 'options'. Over time, such conditions have affected, among other things, the nature, location and longevity of markets and lines of trade; land access and labour conditions; and shifting patterns of accumulation. The years of recent conflict (2003–8) in Darfur have been particularly severe, in turn generating extraordinary scales of humanitarian aid. This period has prompted new uncertainties and hardships as well as opportunities on the Chadian side of the border for local residents and Sudanese camp refugees alike. Through biographical sketches linked to four different but interconnected sites in the area, Behrends reveals how, in turbulent times, different actors work the opportunities and limitations to survive the present and secure future livelihoods. This includes, for example, rural families dividing themselves between highly insecure rural villages and the relative safety of town so as to retain their land in the former and generate cash income for food and crucial supplies in the latter. We also see how the growth of the aid industry, while assisting many displacees, temporarily boosts and reshapes local economies. This in itself adds to the complexities – including new forms of violence and differentiation – of interweaving displacement economies in the area. Behrends's cases, as do others in this volume, help illustrate the paradoxes of crisis and creativity in contexts of violence and displacement, and reinforce the need to ask who profits and who loses under such conditions.

Martin Evans focuses on a conflict and border zone in a quite different setting. Drawing on over a decade of fieldwork on the border between Senegal's Casamance area and northern districts of Guinea-Bissau, he considers the relationship between displacement, return and shifting economies in the context of West Africa's longest-running civil conflict. Following protracted dislocation over relatively short distances from Casamance into Guinea-Bissau in the 1990s, the 2000s saw an increasingly sustained dynamic of return to border areas within Casamance. This was driven by economic and social desperation among the displaced, improved security conditions at home, and the provision of international aid for reconstruction. However, return, like displacement, is characterized by complex dynamics. The reoccupation and exploitation by returnees of both living and cultivation spaces has had to accommodate ongoing security concerns (risks of attack, robbery and landmines), new and contested patterns of land tenure, an overgrown landscape, and wrecked infrastructure. At the same time, returnees have increasingly focused on combining rural and urban livelihoods, aimed at minimizing economic and security risks. The re-established physical presence as well as changed expectations of returnees after years away, together with other dynamics of social change linked partly to a younger local demographic, has further impacted on village life. In addition, the return process has contributed to the reconfiguration of political structures from sub-village up to regional level. In some cases, ambitious entrepreneurs have sought to take advantage of the opportunities provided by return (including uncertain land tenure regimes and access to international aid) not only to accumulate wealth but also to reshape political space in their favour.

Amanda Hammar engages with the paradoxes of class repositioning in post-2000 Zimbabwe, an era marked by persistently dramatic displays of political and structural violence that generated both large-scale dislocation and displacement-in-place. She draws on various studies in Zimbabwe during the 2000s to reflect on the ways in which differentiation and new landscapes of inclusion and exclusion have unfolded in this context. These changes have included a radical reconfiguration of agrarian systems of settlement, tenure, labour, and land access and use, as well as other livelihood possibilities and practices. Similarly, in urban areas, hyperinflation and wide-scale business closures created mass unemployment, undermining the financial rewards and status of formal sector jobs. But even the mushrooming informal sector came under attack by the state and ruling party. Consequently, for both the working and middle classes, social mobility has been substantially interrupted and even for many reversed. Overall, new logics of accumulation and dispossession have emerged, intensifying the divide between a small elite and an impoverished and marginalized majority. For the latter, whether at home or in the ever-expanding diaspora, new ways have had to be found to reorient their modes of being in the world, with respect to their relationships to space and time, to belonging and citizenship, to money and things, to themselves and others. While distinctions of race, gender, age and political loyalty are also important in this context, Hammar argues here that class provides a particularly useful lens for mapping the political economies and paradoxes of displacement.

Reshaping economic sectors, markets and investment Cristina Udelsmann Rodrigues examines the long history of multiple displacements and changing economic landscapes within Angola's Lundas diamond provinces, from colonial times to the present. She traces several cycles and types of

enforced movement and confinement over time that began with labour being brought forcibly to work in the mines during colonial corporate rule (up
until 1975). This practice had ceased by the time of independence. However,
the area was subsequently transformed by various kinds of displacement-
induced demographic shifts after independence associated with Angola's civil
war (from 1975 to 2002), as well as by the adaptive strategies that were a
response to such conditions. She identifies four main groups displaced (or
confined) during this period: first, military personnel, both government troops
and Unita guerrillas, forced to stay for long stretches in the Lundas, far from
their places of origin; secondly, those fleeing from war who were compelled
to move to safer places, a large majority moving to Luanda or other coastal
cities, while others remained in government-controlled Lundas cities; thirdly,
those mineworkers and their families forced by the guerrillas to remain to
work in the mines or as other forms of labour for the guerrillas; fourthly,
those fleeing from war in the Democratic Republic of Congo (DRC), especially
from 1998 to 2003. The end of the civil war brought further changes linked to
territorial control and economic management of the diamond sector, including
surveillance and control of informal mining activities, as well as more active
urban administration and development. This chapter provides an important
historical overview of the changing conditions, new or differently positioned
actors, and alternative forms of economic activity and opportunity generated by
war, displacement and then peace that have shaped Angola's evolving diamond
economy and local forms of urban settlement in the Lundas. It provides an
important perspective on the longevity and interweaving layers over time of
certain displacement economies.

Hannah Elliott explores the effects of various contexts of Somali displacement on the camel milk economy in Kenya. Forced migration from war-torn
Somalia and pastoralist sedentarization in Kenya, together with urban opportunities, have brought Somalis from diverse backgrounds across the Somali
regions and the global diaspora to Nairobi's Eastleigh estate, which is today
strongly associated with the Somali community in Kenya. A vibrant trade in
camel milk has accompanied Eastleigh's rapid growth in response to new
demand. The chapter seeks to elucidate the shifting relations of production,
exchange and consumption behind the milk market's boom by tracing camel
milk's 'life history' and trajectories in relation to the Eastleigh market. It finds
that mass displacement from Somalia has in turn induced the transformation
of the camel milk economy linked to the Kenyan Somali pastoralist communities, who themselves have experienced dislocation through sedentarization and
loss of economic opportunities. Camel milk trade has become a vehicle for
social and economic integration for poor 'ex-pastoralist' Kenyan Somali women
and, increasingly, for refugee women from Somalia, in Nairobi. Commercial
production of milk is a means through which Kenyan Somali pastoralists can

diversify their livelihoods and remain with herds in the face of threats to subsistence pastoralism. For consumers, drinking camel milk brings 'home' in the *badia* (countryside) to Eastleigh and is a way of 'being Somali' in exile. Central to these shifts in relations is the forging of a common 'Somali' identity through which diverse Somalis cope with the parallel displacement crises afflicting the heterogeneous and dispersed Somali population in Kenya.

Peter Hansen reveals how members of the Somaliland diaspora look upon post-conflict Somaliland as an opportunity for private sector investments. Contrary to the fighting that continues to characterize south-central Somalia, Somaliland – not yet formally recognized as a state – is relatively peaceful and has a thriving private sector. In the eyes of its diaspora, because of the destruction caused by the civil war and the numerous gaps to be filled structurally and economically, Somaliland represents a place of socio-economic opportunity. With very little competition and barely any market regulation, this makes it relatively easy for the diaspora to invest in Somaliland: all that is required is capital, and local knowledge and connections. The chapter shows how individual investments and hopes for socio-economic advancement and recognition are linked to a belief in the future of Somaliland as a prosperous, *de jure* nation-state. It argues that ongoing transnational practices, originating in war displacement but now characterized by strategies of circular migration to and from Somaliland, are critical for individual economic and social investment in Somaliland. For example, migration to the West gives access to Western passports, employment opportunities, socio-economic security and bank credits. Diaspora investments are increasingly intended to replace the flow of remittances, and are linked to a long-term strategy of return. Hansen argues that such strategic investments are tied to a particular form of adaptive place-making that echoes historical Somali nomadic practices, identities and territorialities. However, these are equally layered in the present with histories of civil war and large-scale displacement.

Sarah Bracking brings into view some of the hidden dimensions of financial structures and transactions that are not an unusual feature of many displacement economies, and in which, as she notes for post-2000 Zimbabwe, parts of the economy itself get displaced. In her chapter, she explores the processes of relocation and externalization of people, money and non-monetary assets resulting from political violence, dispossession and displacement in Zimbabwe from the first violent election of June 2000 up to the installation of the Government of National Unity in late 2008. The channels by which money and other assets move around, between and over national economies – and how these are stored through both formal and informal 'secrecy jurisdictions' – change radically in times of crisis. New distal, transnationalized and electronic banking structures emerge, as do other informal modes and spaces of asset transfer and saving. Interestingly, such practices are not limited to the wealthy, as even medium to small-scale in-country entrepreneurs and traders keep 'offshore' bank accounts and hold their money or physical assets in neighbouring territories. In fact there is an odd synergy between institutions built up to meet the needs of elites to move assets offshore, and those built up by smaller players. At the same time, from external locations the actions of diaspora remitters open new avenues for vertical delivery of finance, puncturing the national level while not necessarily being an official part of it. What Bracking also importantly exposes are the ways in which licit and illicit economic practices constantly cross between formal and informal economic sectors. More broadly she points to how official and unofficial economies in themselves interweave and reinforce one another, contributing to the continuation of Zimbabwe's far-reaching displacement economy.

Confinement and economies of loss and hope Morten Bøås and Ingunn Bjørkhaug provide an extreme case of a displacement economy defined by violence-induced confinement and closure in northern Uganda. Drawing on data gathered in 2005 and 2007, they describe a context in which almost the entire 1.3 million rural population of Gulu, Kitgum and Pader districts were forcibly settled and more or less interned by the Ugandan army in IDP camps, for 'their own protection' from the Lord's Resistance Army (LRA). The authors refer to the conditions under which people were forced to function as a 'prison economy'. The camps themselves were often only a short distance from people's former homesteads and fields. But strongly enforced if haphazard security regulations, and fear of LRA attacks or abductions, prevented most from cultivating their lands, although some did access plots within the security zone for small-scale market gardening. Overall, living conditions in the camps were dire, with extreme levels of poverty and overcrowding that was both physically and socially hazardous.[21] Cash income opportunities in the camps were minimal, almost no credit was available, and very few people received remittances from relatives outside of the war zone. The consequence, according to Bøås and Bjørkhaug, was 'a violent life-world of inactivity', forcing people to make a living at the very margins of existence: trading, bartering, begging, or waiting for what few material goods, food aid or money might come their way. Peace would eventually come to northern Uganda; however, the seeming endlessness of war and apparent permanence of their condition of displacement and enclosure 'removed people's aspirations for the future'.

Jeremy Jones addresses a different form of confinement, enforced less through physical violence and policing than by structural violence and the conditions of impossibility for young urban men generated by Zimbabwe's by now chronic economic and political crisis.[22] Here it is not bodies but livelihoods, and futures, which have been displaced in a context of hyperinflation, mass unemployment and extreme material shortage, where former economic strategies 'that were once feasible, if not totally dependable, became entirely ineffective'. This not only undermined young men's ability to fulfil needs and obligations let alone desires in the present, but severely diminished their avenues to a meaningful future. Jones defines this kind of existential as well as material confinement or 'stuckness' as a form of 'displacement-in-place', yet in its own way it is, paradoxically, an *active* world of constantly seeking or creating opportunities within highly circumscribed time-space. This is illustrated through close ethnographic attention to one young 'township' man's daily 'hustling' to make ends meet. Yet his attempts to do so 'properly' are within a framework in which there was 'no longer a set route to occupy a proper place in the economy, and as such, he was confined to precarious living in the here and now'. Jones uses this case for a wider interrogation of the idea of economic 'place' and to argue for a more subtle conceptualization of the economic 'ground' on which livelihoods are built in times of crisis and displacement. This helps illuminate the seemingly contradictory pairing of force and closure on the one hand, and agency and opportunity on the other, that constitutes the reality of economic action under such conditions.

Timothy Raeymaekers echoes the concern with precarity and closure in relation to current and future economic lives and broader life courses, although in a context involving physical movement rather than confinement: specifically, circular, war-generated dislocation of rural youth in the eastern part of the DRC. This is the site of recurring mass population displacement from persistent civil conflict. Over two million IDPs have been estimated in this area alone, of which only 5.5 per cent are formally recognized. The rest are mainly self-settled in various 'spontaneous' sites, including abandoned buildings or forests, or with host families for whom this adds increasing strains on already poverty-stricken households. Raeymaekers focuses especially on *unarmed* and dislocated youth, a somewhat analytically and practically neglected constituency in war zones. He homes in on 'immigrant' rural youth in the town of Butembo. Displaced, vulnerable and poor, with unstable networks, they are confronted with ethnicized and elite-controlled markets and, where work is found, subjected to abusive labour conditions. He investigates how, in the face of radical 'economic restructuring' precipitated by war and displacement, his subjects – young men and women moving between rural home areas and urban spaces not yet their own – try to manage the tension between dispersed and diminished livelihood opportunities and maintaining affective relations.[23] How, he asks, in this war-torn environment, do they reconcile their daily need to make a living with their aspirations for making a better life?

Conclusion

The focus on displacement economies – as both object of study, and approach – has emerged out of necessity. Particularly as an approach, it arose out of the need to find a productive vantage point and a conceptual language with which to analyse a range of clearly present yet largely unrevealed or under-explained dimensions and dynamics of displacement. Among the occlusions that the displacement economies framework aims to counter are, first, the many paradoxes of displacement. These include the simultaneities of dislocation and confinement, order and disorder, loss and gain, impossibility and opportunity, rupture and chronicity, distance and proximity, nothingness and hope, destruction and creativity. Secondly, there has been limited attention to historicizing and more broadly contextualizing displacement, with a tendency to view 'it' as an event or inevitability rather than as a complex, relational process linked to and through multiple temporalities – where, for example, 'the future' unpredictably opens and closes – and a combination of political economies and spatial and cultural politics.

Thirdly, and particularly fuelled by technocratic and humanitarian practices of labelling, far too few of the extensive range of relevant actors beyond simply 'the displaced' have been included in analyses of displacement. The approach here makes visible a much wider diversity of 'uninhabitants'[24] who inhabit the multiple sites and processes of displacement. This includes those connected to the state, the private sector and the development industry at different levels. Nor has there been much attention to the ways in which actors in displacement contexts are recurringly repositioned, economically and socially, through shifting patterns of dispossession and differentiation, access and accumulation. In addition, 'the displaced' themselves have largely been read and represented through a lens of victimhood and passivity, rather than as resilient and active agents engaged in the complex processes of remaking their own lives under highly uncertain conditions.

Fourthly, there has been little explicit attention to date to the relationship between displacement and the disruption and/or reproduction of structures of authority. Displacement is frequently linked to political upheaval of some kind, and is even precipitated at times by state or party–state projects or by other kinds of contestations. Under such conditions, hierarchies of authority get undermined and institutional fragmentation arises wherein sovereignties multiply and change face without warning. Eventually a different 'order' may get constituted, and in the process the once seemingly ordinary work of being and becoming is turned upside down by changing boundaries of citizenship and belonging. The approach here, however, keeps open the question of what happens to forms and practices of authority and of citizenship, when bodies, things and ideas get displaced, and 'the economy' gets redefined in new ways.

Finally, while existing work on displacement often exposes some of the causes and manifestations of specific acts of dispossession, dislocation or enclosure, it rarely asks the question: what (more) does displacement *produce*? In a sense this is at the heart of the displacement economies approach. It is a generative question in itself that prompts a series of other questions, some already noted elsewhere in this chapter, and addressed to varying degrees in this volume: questions concerning, for example, the changing value and modes of exchange of things; shifts in forms of production, labour, accumulation, distribution; new relationships between alternative and official economies; changes in social identities and relations and forms and sites of social re-production; and reshaped political and administrative spaces and practices.

In summary, the displacement economies approach insists on seeing beyond displacement as simply an event or 'natural fallout' of other processes, or as a moral or management problem. Instead, it brings into view the relational spaces and overlapping histories, politics and political economies shaping and shaped by particular displacement contexts. And it helps to reveal both the intended and unexpected – and paradoxical – material and symbolic effects that displacement in practice produces.

Notes

1 I would like to express my deep appreciation to all the contributors to this volume whose work has helped significantly to shape the displacement economies framework in general. In addition I am particularly grateful to Graeme Rodgers and an independent reviewer for their extensive and astute comments on this chapter. I also thank the Nordic Africa Institute in Uppsala for its wider support for my programme on Political Economies of Displacement in Southern Africa (2006–10), which was an initial laboratory for these ideas, and for funding the workshop that first brought together many of the authors for this volume. Some who attended this event with papers were subsequently unable to be part of the book project itself, but their contributions to the early discussions were extremely valuable. These include Sverker Finnstrom, Graeme Rodgers and Henrik Vigh. I would also like to thank other colleagues who contributed insightfully to discussions of working drafts at the workshop: Michael Barrett, Mirjam de Bruijn, Ilda Lindell, Mats Utas and Wolfgang Zeller. Also, thanks to Oliver Bakewell, Finn Stepputat and Bjørn Møller, who commented on versions of some chapters presented at various conferences. Some additional chapters for the book were subsequently solicited from authors whose work clearly spoke to the notion of displacement economies, and which has greatly enhanced our collective endeavour. Finally, many thanks to Ken Barlow at Zed Books for his positive support and especially for his immense patience.

2 There has long been a recognition that 'the economy' or economics 'is not a separate or separable sphere of social life' (Lee et al. 2008). Key to this perspective is Polanyi (1944), who established the substantivist school with a more cultural approach to economics. However, this drew on early economic anthropologists such as Malinowski and Mauss, who addressed, among other things, patterns of exchange outside of classic market definitions. Various strands of social science have continued within these broad traditions, especially in contemporary economic anthropology and sociology, and economic and human geography (such as Jane Guyer, Keith Hart and David Harvey). For recent critical scholarship challenging the false divide between 'the economy' and other social domains from a more post-structuralist perspective, see Timothy Mitchell (1998, 2008), who additionally examines 'economics' both as a discipline and a disciplining project.

3 See Colson (2007 [2004]: 113–14) for

a brief overview of the belated attention by anthropology to the study of displacement.

4 See www.unhcr.org/pages/49da0e466.html, accessed 29 March 2013. While important, this does not have the same weight as a Convention.

5 Many thanks to Graeme Rodgers for pointing this out.

6 This is one example of several regional instruments that adapted the Convention definition to more localized conditions. Others include the Cartagena Declaration of 1984, which emerged from some specific Central American concerns.

7 See the OAU's 1969 Convention Governing the Specific Aspects of Refugee Problems in Africa at: www.unhcr-centraleurope.org/pdf/resources/legal-documents/international-refugee-law/1969-organization-of-african-unity-convention-governing-the-specific-aspects-of-refugee-problems-in-africa.html, accessed 29 March 2013.

8 See www.internal-displacement.org/8025708F004D404D/(httpPages)/CC32D8C34EF93C88802570F800517610?OpenDocument, accessed 29 March 2013.

9 As early as the 1970s, the World Bank commissioned expert advice on the effects of dam displacement (see Oliver-Smith 2010).

10 David Turton (2003) refers to such categories or labels as 'artefacts of policy concerns rather than of empirical observation and scientific enquiry'. See also Zetter (2007) on labelling of refugees. There is in fact a much older history of ideas about the sociological categorization of social types. Georg Simmel was foundational in this regard, with his work on 'the stranger' and 'the poor' in the early 1900s. Well ahead of his time, he talked of how certain social types become so not by virtue of their membership of a given social group but 'by the collective attitude which society as a whole adopts toward it' (Simmel in Simmel and Jacobsen 1965: 139). This would later be echoed in more contemporary ideas such as 'the constitutive outside' (see Mouffe 2000).

This speaks to relevant concerns related to the politics and political economy of 'helping' and 'doing good', for which there is no space here, but see, for example, Gronemayer (1992).

11 For a valuable discussion of invisibilities in relation to displacement in general, see Polzer and Hammond (2008). See also Bakewell (2008) on the need for research on forced migration beyond policy categories in order to counter empirical and conceptual invisibilities.

12 See Oliver-Smith (2010) on the preferred use of the term 'displacement-enforced' rather than 'displacement-induced' to emphasize the actual extent of force involved in many such contexts.

13 Nixon (2011: 152) talks of the 'poignantly paradoxical figure' of the 'developmental refugee' (a term coined by Thayer Scudder) in the sense of development implying 'positive growth' while refugee implies 'flight from a grave threat – in this case, the threat of development-inflicted destitution'.

14 I outlined this more fully in a lecture at the Nordic Africa Institute in November 2010, entitled 'The Concept and Paradoxes of Displacement'.

15 Updated UNHCR figures can be found at: www.unhcr.org/pages/49c3646c11.html. These here were accessed on 23 May 2013. However, figures are far from stable given constant crises that prompt mass displacements. Most recent increases in SSA are from the Democratic Republic of Congo and Sudan, while North Africa and the Middle East, especially Syria most recently, have necessarily seen major increases in the past few years. But see Hammar and Rodgers (2008: 358) on the problem of numbers: their variability from source to source, depending on 'who is counting, what criteria are used for counting, and for what purpose'.

16 See many of the contributions to two edited special journal issues: *Journal of Contemporary African Studies*, 26(4) (co-edited by Hammar and Rodgers), focused on 'Political economies of displacement in southern Africa'; and *Journal of*

Southern African Studies, 36(2) (co-edited by Hammar, McGregor and Landau), on 'The Zimbabwe crisis through the lens of displacement'. These collections are both forerunners to the development of the present volume.

17 *The Economist* (2 March 2013) projects that 'Over the next decade its GDP is expected to rise by an average of 6% a year, not least thanks to foreign direct investment. FDI has gone from $15 billion in 2002 to $37 billion in 2006 and $46 billion in 2012.' It does note, however, that 'Africa is too big to follow one script, so its countries are taking different routes to becoming better places'. See www.economist.com/news/special-report/21572377-african-lives-have-already-greatly-improved-over-past-decade-says-oliver-august, accessed 23 May 2013.

18 Returnability can be read both subjectively and objectively, giving it a highly contested 'value'. For example, considering debates around the UNHCR's invocation of the 'cessation clause' for Rwandan refugees worldwide, while global technocrats and the Rwandan authorities have deemed it safe for all Rwandans to return, many refugees claim it will never be safe for them to return. Many thanks to Graeme Rodgers for raising this point. In other cases, as with the flooding of the Zambezi Valley to build Kariba Dam (Colson 1971), there was no physical place to return to. See Hammond (2004) in relation to the experience of Ethiopian repatriation.

19 This evocative term was mentioned by Erin Collins at a conference on 'Property and citizenship in developing societies' in Copenhagen, May 2013.

20 This was a phrase used by Henrik Vigh in the book's initial workshop in Uppsala, April 2010.

21 See also Finnström (2008).

22 See also Kamete (2012). These urban conditions contrast with many rural environments where many inhabitants of all ages experienced direct physical violence and dislocation in the cauldron of political conflict, as well as economic devastation, forcing hundreds of thousands to flee either to towns or across borders.

23 Compare with Filip de Boeck's (forthcoming) examination of the political critiques and moral claims of urban youth, 'displaced-in-place' in DRC's capital city, Kinshasa.

24 This is a term coined by Rebecca Solnit (2000) cited in Nixon (2011: 313), underlining a 'restorative ambition' to repopulate 'places of cultural and imaginative evacuation'. The displacement economies approach similarly aims to make visible the 'uninhabitants', as well as other hidden dimensions and connections, that are also part of a displacement context but which are not fully recognized owing to certain theoretical, political or technocratic 'evacuations'.

References

Abusharaf, R. (2009) *Transforming Displaced Women in the Sudan: Politics and the Body in a Squatter Settlement*, Chicago, IL: University of Chicago Press.

Alexander, J. (2006) *The Unsettled Land. State-making and the Politics of Land in Zimbabwe 1983–2003*, Oxford/Harare/Athens: James Currey/Weaver Press/Ohio University Press.

Arrighi, G., N. Aschoff and B. Scully (2010) 'Accumulation by dispossession and its limits: the southern Africa paradigm revisited', *Studies in Comparative International Development*, 45: 410–38.

Bakewell, O. (2000) 'Repatriation and self-settled refugees in Zambia: bringing solutions to the wrong problems', *Journal of Refugee Studies*, 13(4): 356–73.

— (2008) 'Research beyond categories: the importance of policy irrelevant research into forced migration', *Journal of Refugee Studies*, 21(4): 432–53.

Bascom, J. (1998) *Losing Place: Refugees and Rural Transformations in East Africa*, New York: Berghahn.

Bayart, J. F., S. Ellis and B. Hibou (eds) (1999) *The Criminalization of the State in Africa*, Oxford: James Currey.

Bierschenk, T. and J.-P. Olivier de Sardan (eds) (forthcoming) *States at Work. Dynamics of African Bureaucracies*, Leiden: Brill.

Chabal, P. and J.-P. Daloz (1999) *Africa Works: Disorder as Political Instrument*, Oxford: James Currey.

Cheru, F. and C. Obi (eds) (2010) *The Rise of China and India in Africa: Challenges, Opportunities and Critical Interventions*, London/Uppsala: Zed Books/Nordiska Afrikainstitutet.

Christensen, A. and N. Harild (2009) *Forced Displacement – the Development Challenge*, Washington, DC: World Bank (Social Development Department).

Colson, E. (1971) *The Social Consequences of Resettlement*, Manchester: Manchester University Press.

— (2007 [2004]) 'Displacement', in D. Nugent and J. Vincent (eds), *A Companion to the Anthropology of Politics*, Malden, MA, Oxford and Carlton, Australia: Blackwell, pp. 107–20.

Cramer, C. (2006) *Civil War is Not a Stupid Thing: Accounting for Violence in Developing Countries*, London: Hurst & Co.

De Boeck, F. (forthcoming) 'Corpus Vile: Death and expendable youth in urban Congo', in V. Das and C. Han (eds), *An Anthropology of Living and Dying in the Contemporary World*, Berkeley: University of California Press.

De Bruijn, M., R. van Dijk and D. Foeken (eds) (2001) *Mobile Africa: Changing Patterns of Movement in Africa and Beyond*, Leiden, Boston, MA, and Cologne: Brill.

De Wet, C. (ed.) (2006) *Development-Induced Displacement: Problems, Programs and People*, New York: Berghahn.

Dubernet, C. (2001) *The International Containment of Displaced Persons*, Burlington, VT: Ashgate.

Ferguson, J. (2006) *Global Shadows: Africa in the Neo-Liberal World Order*, Durham, NC, and London: Duke University Press.

Finnström, S. (2008) *Living with Bad Surroundings: War, History and Everyday Moments in Northern Uganda*, Durham, NC: Duke University Press.

Gebre, Y. (2003) 'Resettlement and the unnoticed losers: impoverishment disasters among the Gumz hosts in Ethiopia', *Human Organization*, 62(1): 50–61.

Goodhand, J. (2003) 'From war economy to peace economy?', LSE Online Conference Paper, London, eprints.lse.ac.uk/28364/.

Gronemayer, M. (1992) 'Helping', in W. Sachs (ed.), *Development Dictionary: A Guide to Knowledge as Power*, London: Zed Books, pp. 53–69.

Guyer, J. I. (2002) 'Preface', in J. I. Guyer, L. Denzer and A. Agbaje (eds), *Money Struggles and City Life. Devaluation in Ibadan and Other Urban Centres in Southern Nigeria, 1986–1996*, Portsmouth, NH: Heinemann, pp. x–xvi.

— (2004) *Marginal Gains. Monetary Transactions in Atlantic Africa*, Chicago, IL: University of Chicago Press.

Hagmann, T. and D. Péclard (2010) 'Negotiating statehood: dynamics of power and domination in Africa', *Development and Change*, 41(4): 539–62.

Hammar, A. (2008) 'In the name of sovereignty: displacement and state making in post-independence Zimbabwe', *Journal of Contemporary African Studies*, 26(4): 417–34.

— (forthcoming) 'The concept and paradoxes of displacement', in T. Virtanen and K. Havnevik (eds), *Challenging Concepts*, London/Uppsala: Zed Books/Nordiska Afrikainstitutet.

Hammar, A. and G. Rodgers (2008) 'Introduction: Notes on political economies of displacement in southern Africa', *Journal of Contemporary African Studies*, 26(4): 355–70.

Hammar, A., J. McGregor and L. Landau (2010) 'Introduction: Displacing Zimbabwe: crisis and construction in southern Africa', *Journal of Southern African Studies*, 26(2): 263–83.

Hammond, L. C. (2004) *This Place Will Become Home: Refugee Repatriation to*

Ethiopia, Ithaca, NY: Cornell University Press.

Hansen, A. (1982) 'Self-settled rural refugees in Africa: the case of Angolans in Zambian villages', in A. Hansen and A. Oliver-Smith (eds), *Involuntary Migration and Resettlement*, Boulder, CO: Westview Press.

Harrell-Bond, B. (1986) *Imposing Aid: Emergency Assistance to Refugees*, Oxford: Oxford University Press.

Hart, K. (2006) 'Bureaucratic form and the informal economy', in B. Guha-Khasnobis, R. Kanbur and E. Ostrom (eds), *Linking the Formal and Informal Economy. Concepts and Policies*, UNU-WIDER Studies in Development Economics, Oxford: Oxford University Press, pp. 21–35.

Jacobsen, K. (2002) 'Can refugees benefit the state? Refugee resources and African statebuilding', *Journal of Modern African Studies*, 40(4): 577–96.

— (2005) *The Economic Life of Refugees*, Bloomfield, CT: Kumarian Press.

Jacobsen, K. and L. Landau (2003) 'The dual imperative in refugee research: some methodological and ethical considerations in social science research on forced migration', *Disasters*, 27(3): 185–206.

Jones, J. (2010) '"Nothing is straight in Zimbabwe": the rise of the Kukiya-kiya economy 2000–2008', *Journal of Southern African Studies*, 36(2): 285–99.

Kaldor, M. (2007 [1998]) *New and Old Wars*, 2nd edn, Stanford, CA: Stanford University Press.

Kamete, A. Y. (2012) 'Not exactly like the phoenix – but rising all the same: reconstructing displaced livelihoods in post-cleanup Harare', *Environment and Planning D: Society and Space*, 30(2): 243–61.

Keen, D. (2000) 'War, crime and access to resources', in R. Väyrynen, E. W. Nafziger and F. Stewart (eds), *War, Hunger and Displacement: The Origins of Humanitarian Emergencies*, New York: Oxford University Press, pp. 283–304.

Kelsall, T. (2008) 'Going with the grain in African development?', *Development Policy Review*, 26(6): 627–55.

Koser, K. (ed.) (2003) *New African Diasporas*, London: Routledge.

Landau, L. and T. Monson (2008) 'Displacement, estrangement and sovereignty: reconfiguring state power in urban South Africa', *Government and Opposition*, 43(2): 315–36.

Lauterbach, K. (2014) 'Spiritual gifts and relations of exchange among Congolese in Kampala, Uganda', in T. Sundnes Drønen (ed.), *Religion and Development – Nordic Perspectives on Involvement in Africa*, New York: Peter Lang, pp. 75–86.

Lee, R., A. Leyshone and A. Smith (2008) 'Rethinking economies/economic geographies', *Geoforum*, 39(3): 1111–15.

Lindell, I. (2008) 'The multiple sites of urban governance. Insights from an African city', *Urban Studies*, 45(9): 1879–98.

Little, P. D. (2003) *Somalia: Economy without a State*, Oxford/Bloomington and Indianapolis/Btec: James Currey/Indiana University Press/Hargeisa.

Lubkemann, S. C. (2008a) 'Involuntary immobility: on a theoretical invisibility in forced migration studies', *Journal of Refugee Studies*, 21(4): 454–75.

— (2008b) *Culture in Chaos. An Anthropology of the Social Condition in War*, Chicago, IL, and London: University of Chicago Press.

— (2010) 'Past directions and future possibilities in the study of African displacement', Unpublished manuscript prepared for the Nordic Africa Institute, Uppsala.

MacGaffey, J. (ed.) (1991) *The Real Economy of Zaire. The Contribution of Smuggling and Other Unofficial Activities to National Wealth*, London: University of Pennsylvania Press.

Magaramombe, G. (2010) 'Agrarian displacements, replacements and resettlement: "displaced in place" farm workers in Mazowe District', *Journal of Southern African Studies*, 36(2): 361–75.

Makki, F. and C. Geisler (2011) 'Development by dispossession: land grabbing as new enclosures in contemporary Ethiopia', Paper presented at the International Conference on Global Land Grabbing, 6–8 April, Institute of Development Studies, University of Sussex.

Malkki, L. (1995) *Purity and Exile: Violence, Memory and National Cosmology Among Hutu Refugees in Tanzania*, Chicago, IL: University of Chicago Press.

Massey, D. (2005) *For Space*, Thousand Oaks, CA, London and New Delhi: Sage Publications.

Mazur, R. E. (1989) 'The political economy of refugee creation in southern Africa: micro and macro issues in sociological perspective', *Journal of Refugee Studies*, 2(4): 441–67.

McGregor, J. and R. Primorac (eds) (2010) *Zimbabwe's New Diaspora. Displacement and the Cultural Politics of Survival*, New York and Oxford: Berghahn.

Meagher, K. (2010) *Identity Economics. Social Networks and the Informal Economy in Nigeria*, Woodbridge and Rochester, NY/Ibadan: James Currey/HEBN.

Mitchell, T. (1998) 'Fixing the economy', *Cultural Studies*, 12(1): 82–101.

— (2008) 'Rethinking economy', *Geoforum*, 39(3): 1116–21.

Mouffe, C. (2000) *The Democratic Paradox*, London and New York: Verso.

Murray, R. (2005) 'Refugees and internally displaced persons and human rights: the African system', *Refugee Studies Quarterly*, 24(2): 55–66.

Nixon, R. (2011) *Slow Violence and the Environmentalism of the Poor*, Cambridge, MA, and London: Harvard University Press.

Nordstrom, C. (2004) *Shadows of War. Violence, Power, and International Profiteering in the Twenty-first Century*, Berkeley: University of California Press.

— (2007) *Global Outlaws: Crime, Money, and Power in the Contemporary World*, Berkeley and Los Angeles: University of California Press.

Oliver-Smith, A. (2010) *Defying Displace-ment: Grassroots Resistance and the Critique of Development*, Austin: University of Texas Press.

Olivier de Sardan, J.-P. (1999) 'The moral economy of corruption?', *Journal of Modern Africa Studies*, 37(1): 25–52.

Platzky, L. and C. Walker (1985) *The Surplus People: Forced Removals in South Africa*, Johannesburg: Ravan Press.

Polanyi, K. (1944) *The Great Transformation*, New York: Farrar and Rinehart.

Polzer, T. and L. Hammond (2008) 'Invisible displacement (editorial introduction)', *Journal of Refugee Studies*, 21(4): 417–31.

Raeymaekers, T. (2010) 'Protection for sale? War and the transformation of regulation on the Congo–Ugandan border', *Development and Change*, 41(4): 563–87.

Richards, P. (1996) *Fighting for the Rain Forest: War, Youth, and Resources in Sierra Leone*, Oxford: James Currey.

Rodgers, G. (2002) *When Refugees Don't Go Home: Post-war Mozambican Settlement across the Border with South Africa*, PhD thesis, Faculty of Arts, University of the Witwatersrand, Johannesburg.

— (2008) 'Everyday life and the political economy of displacement on the Mozambique–South Africa border', *Journal of Contemporary African Studies*, 26(4): 385–99.

Roitman, J. (2004) 'Productivity in the margins. The reconstitution of state power in the Chad Basin', in V. Das and D. Poole (eds), *Anthropology in the Margins of the State*, Sante Fe, NM/Oxford: School of American Research Press/James Currey, pp. 191–224.

Roque, S. (2008) 'Manuela: a social biography of war displacement and change in Angola', *Journal of Contemporary African Studies*, 26(4): 371–84.

Roy, A. (1999) *The Greater Common Good*, Bombay: India Book Distributor.

Schneider, F. and D. H. Enste (2002) *The Shadow Economy: An International Survey*, Cambridge: Cambridge University Press.

Scott, J. C. (1998) *Seeing Like a State: How*

Certain Schemes to Improve the Human Condition Have Failed, New Haven, CT: Yale University Press.

Simmel, G. and C. Jacobsen (1965) 'The poor', *Social Problems*, 13(2): 118–40.

Smith, R. S. (2002) 'The underground economy: guidance for policy makers?', *Canadian Tax Journal*, 50(5): 1155–61.

Solidarity Peace Trust (2009) *'Gone to Egoli'; Economic Survival Strategies in Matabeleland: A preliminary study*, Port Shepstone: Solidarity Peace Trust.

Solnit, R. (2000) *Savage Dreams: A Journey into the Landscape Wars of the American West*, Berkeley: University of California Press.

Thompson, E. P. (1978) *The Poverty of Theory: Or an Orrery of Errors*, London: Merlin Press.

Turner, S. (2010) *Politics of Innocence: Hutu Identity, Conflict, and Camp Life*, New York, Berghahn.

Turton, D. (2003) 'Refugees and "other forced migrants"', Refugee Studies Centre Working Paper no. 13, Queen Elizabeth House, International Development Centre, University of Oxford.

Vandergeest, P., P. Idahosa and P. S. Bose (eds) (2007) *Development's Displacements. Ecologies, Economies, and Cultures at Risk*, Vancouver and Toronto: UBC Press.

Van de Walle, N. (2001) *African Economies and the Politics of Permanent Crisis, 1979–1999*, Cambridge: Cambridge University Press.

Venkatesh, S. A. (2006) *Off the Books. The Underground Economy of the Urban Poor*, Boston, MA: Harvard University Press.

Verran, H. (2007) 'The telling challenges of Africa's economies', *African Studies Review*, 50(2): 163–82.

Vigh, H. (2008) 'Crisis and chronicity: anthropological perspectives on continuous conflict and decline', *Ethnos*, 73(1): 5–24.

Vigneswaran, D. with T. Araia, C. Hoag and X. Tshabalala (2010) 'Criminality or monopoly? Informal enforcement in South Africa', *Journal of Southern African Studies*, 26(2): 465–81.

Watts, M. (2004) 'Resource curse? Governmentality, oil and power in the Niger Delta, Nigeria', *Geopolitics*, 9(1): 50–80.

Yarrow, T. (2011) *Development beyond Politics. Aid, Activism and NGOs in Ghana*, Basingstoke and New York: Palgrave Macmillan.

Zetter, R. (2007) 'More labels, fewer refugees: remaking the refugee label in an era of globalization', *Journal of Refugee Studies*, 20(2): 172–92.

PART I

Economies of rupture and repositioning

2 | Securing livelihoods: economic practice in the Darfur–Chad borderlands

Andrea Behrends[1]

Introduction

When I returned to the Darfur border in 2007, I found Hashaba, the Chadian village in which I had lived six years before, emptied of nearly all its inhabitants. A few old people had remained there. They lived off wild berries that they found in the bush. 'In normal times, this is children's food,' one old man told me, 'and they eat it when they play in the bush. Now we don't have anything else.' I knew the old man whom they called Daldoum from my previous visits, although I hardly recognized him this time as the active and vivid man he used to be. He was very skinny and his clothes were dirty and torn.

He and his wife Mariam had come to Hashaba from a Sudanese village eight years before, escaping the violence that was spreading on the other side of the border. Now the violence had arrived in Chad, but they did not want to leave this place, where distant relatives had given them somewhere to stay and a piece of land to cultivate. Daldoum had been the chief of the Sudanese refugees in the village of Hashaba. A year ago, he said, all the others had left for Adré, with its approximately 13,000 inhabitants the largest town in the region, and the last border post on the way to Darfur in Sudan. The same had happened in the villages around Hashaba, with more than ten thousand people having moved to the outskirts of Adré to live there in shacks built from straw, only after some time to be replaced by more permanent houses constructed with wood, mud bricks and straw. They had all felt threatened by the violence that had spread from across the border. Had they stayed, they feared that the rebels and the militias would have destroyed everything and killed them. And indeed, at the time of my visit in 2007, the militias did come to the village almost every day. Daldoum said that they would sit under the village's largest tree and throw stones at them, yelling, 'We will kill you and take your land!', but then they would leave them alone. Daldoum and the others are few and old and have nothing to lose, since all houses and fields around them have long been dismantled by their former owners or destroyed by the militias.

Their daughter Ashta is among those who had left for Adré. She lives in the outskirts of town in Hille Djidíde, which means New Town. There, she built a hut for herself and the children. She earned a bit of money by working on other people's fields and by helping out in the production of mud bricks, carrying them to and from the ovens in which they are burnt.[2] That way she has managed to survive and even buy her twenty-year-old son a horse carriage. He now earns a bit of money himself, carrying people and market goods; and he shares his income with his mother and his young wife. Ashta says that by leaving her parents in the village, they could keep the land while she and the children are gone. By her doing so, she hoped, the land could not be lost or given to someone else. She went to see her parents from time to time, walking on foot the eight kilometres of sandy tracks, to bring them food and to help farming around their house. In 2011, when I last visited Ashta and her parents, she still lived in Hille Djidíde and her parents were still in the village. One year later, in 2012, international aid agencies replaced her makeshift home with a house built of solid bricks. But other villagers had started to return temporarily to the village and to farm the land around their former houses.

Particularly notable among people farming in Hashaba are those who now live in one of the twelve refugee camps that the United Nations High Commissioner for Refugees (UNHCR) had built in 2003. There, they have no access to farming land, and they come to the village and stay during the farming season. In fact I found one of the villages close to Hashaba full of people – but hardly any of them were the village's former inhabitants: 'These are the refugees from the Farchana refugee camp,' Daldoum told me. 'They live and work on the land that others have left behind, and then they return to the camps after their harvests.'[3] As he has remained in Hashaba village, Daldoum was now in a position to distribute land, since he and his wife had been there to guard it while the others were gone.

To maintain access to and ownership of land is at the foreground of economic planning and practice during their sustained displacement for Daldoum and his daughter Ashta. Similarly, access to farmland, even if only temporary, has been critical for those refugees who came from farming communities in Sudan and now live in one of the refugee camps. For many, it is a means to partly regain autonomy and to escape the dependence on aid and provisions within the camp. For Daldoum and Ashta, it is a strategy to secure (future) livelihoods throughout turbulent times. *Securing livelihoods* serves as my basic definition for their economic practice during their sustained displacement. It denotes those processes by which people make use of or translate into their respective contexts internationally devised aid infrastructures in order to produce security. This notion follows Thomas Eriksen's (2010) understanding of 'human security'. He starts from the assumption that it takes 'hard work' to 'create secure lives in a complex and turbulent world' (ibid.: 5). He maintains that the term 'human security' may be vague and wide ranging, but that it does allow for an orientation along the lines of social cohesion, integration, stability and collective identity. By asking what renders people secure and what insecure, it is possible to study the patterns and regularities of their actions on various levels of interaction.[4]

Focusing on economic practices to secure livelihoods also links up with the intention of building a better future as a strongly compelling factor for those dealing with an uncertain and disrupted present. Daldoum and his daughter Ashta provide one example of such rigorous future orientation. By physically remaining in a potentially mortal war zone, the old man not only stubbornly resists the constant threats of expulsion and death and the seemingly more secure situation within a refugee camp. He also foresees a way of ensuring that his family can regain the land, and with the land the livelihoods they had to leave behind owing to the war. He does so with the help of his daughter, who – although distantly relocated – risks regularly walking the 16 kilometres from Adré to the village and back in rebel and militia territory to support her parents by bringing them occasional provisions of food and other necessities, such as blankets, pots or soap. To Daldoum and Ashta, *risk* is a necessary factor in securing their livelihood during wartimes.

In this contribution I compare different situations in which people try to find and, if possible, remain in a condition of security in moments of insecurity and disruption. Here, the relational concept of displacement economies, laid out in the introduction to this volume by Amanda Hammar, perfectly fits the way different actors engage in historically entangled boundary crossing. Furthermore, it speaks to the creative mixing of economic survival strategies that I encountered in the Darfur–Chad borderlands. Indeed, one essential element of Ashta's and Daldoum's activities is firmly economic: their daily focus is on the necessity of getting at least a minimum (cash) income to be able to buy food to feed their family or for medical help, transport or other needs. Ashta and Daldoum do so by building upon the knowledge of their neighbours and other villagers in dealing with a crisis, which nonetheless also means having to put up with remaining risks and dangers. Others rely on systems of survival created through foreign interpretations of the crisis situation, as in the case of international models of emergency assistance and development aid. International models might provide for higher security from violence, for instance in the guarded surroundings of a refugee camp. But they also bear the risk of disconnecting people from local opportunities to access land and, thus, from the opportunity to build up an independent future security that comes close to what they had to leave behind in the war.[5]

To compare different situations, I refer to constraints and possibilities for economic strategies within four distinct yet interconnected socio-spatial sites that are part of what constitutes the broader displacement context of this borderland region: 1) the village of Hashaba, where Daldoum and his daughter have lived and from which most people have fled; 2) the town of Adré, where internally displaced people live largely without assistance from international aid agencies; 3) Abéché, the major city in eastern Chad with a current population of about 200,000 and the initial aid hub for the large number of aid organizations operating in the region; and 4) the refugee camp of Farchana, one of twelve such camps, in each of which between 20,000 and over 40,000 refugees currently live. The latter are assisted by international organizations like the United Nations High Commissioner for Refugees (UNHCR) or the World Food Programme (WFP), plus a large number of governmental and non-governmental organizations which take up different tasks within the camp. By comparing these sites and their actors, this chapter aims to show that the options open to each group are not unlimited: they are spatially and historically bound by the particularities of the respective contexts the actors find themselves in. The question guiding the presentation below of the region's background is therefore: how did the events of rebellion and counter-insurgency in the Darfur–Chad border region affect the specific economies of actors in these different contexts? And how does living in one of the four displacement sites I describe shape the definition of livelihood security? In all four sites, not only the present but also relevant past events, political loyalties and personal experiences will enter the analysis.

'Displacement economy' as a socio-spatial analytical frame

Apart from the example of Daldoum and his daughter Ashta, who are associated, respectively, with two of the above-mentioned sites – namely the village of Hashaba and the group of internally displaced people living in Adré – I introduce below two more individuals who act as case examples to illustrate the third and fourth sites. The third example is that of Cheikh Moussa, a Sudanese refugee who moved from a border village close to Hashaba to the Farchana refugee camp. He receives aid from international programmes and is confronted with constraints to his mobility, since he still does not consider returning to Sudan a safe option. The fourth example is that of Brahim, who grew up in Adré. Today he lives in the vicinity of the Farchana refugee camp, where he works for an international NGO. He and his relatives profited financially from the international presence that followed the war along the international border with Sudan. Brahim and his family represent a group of better-off inhabitants of Abéché and Adré who, historically, held a privileged position in the region. They are among those who have remained more or less neutral and thus little affected by the conflicts in Darfur and across the border in Chad. I will argue that in all four cases, different but historically contingent practices to generate livelihood security under conditions of war and displacement prove to be successful. The question, then, will be to see which specific factors become important in such situations of war and displacement, and in which ways do the actors in all four sites relate to these factors differently in the process of producing livelihood security.

To compare and analyse strategies to secure livelihoods, I draw on this volume's key notion of 'displacement economy' primarily with regard to its socio-spatial qualities – that is, as the larger space in which economically oriented interaction takes place. In my reading, the 'displacement economies' concept reflects a particular focus on what could more generally be termed 'arena'. In Anselm Strauss's (1978) understanding of an arena, individual actors compose 'social worlds', but they are committed to participating in a broader arena. Within the arena, 'they commonly act as representatives of their social worlds, performing their collective identities' (Klapp 1972, cited in Clarke and Star 2008: 120). The complexity and flexibility of entangled histories, actors and sites which figure prominently in Hammar's definition of 'displacement economies' also echo in Clarke and Star's (2008) expansion on Strauss's original definition of an arena. They explain that an arena could, in fact, be understood as encompassing a multitude of social worlds, criss-crossed with 'conflicts, different sorts of careers, viewpoints, funding sources, and so on' (ibid.: 113). Using this framework opens up perspectives on 'situatedness and contingency, history and fluidity, commitment and change' (ibid.) within particular situations.

With this more general approach to arenas in mind, I adhere to the concept of a 'displacement economy' in relation to the overall space in which actors within and across each of the four sites interact. I abstain, however, from delineating fixed territories and boundaries as I consider the four sites to be both wider than and at the same time inclusive of particular places. For this study, I will refer to the conflict and displacement zone of the Darfur–Chad borderlands as a set of interconnected, flexible and varying sites that make up an encompassing displacement economy. This context includes different (collective) actors and institutions that apply particular strategies of survival. I refer to their strategic actions as a set of partly standardized yet very flexible practices. Following Thévenot (1984), such practices would have developed over time until they turned into shared 'forms' of activity to access resources, and common ideologies on how to achieve common or individual goals. These broadly shared knowledge systems can nonetheless be amended and changed, depending on the respective actors involved and the situations in which they are evoked.

Daldoum and Ashta, for instance, from their respective sites of displacement, are concerned with access to land and the chance to farm. Through this they can secure their future livelihoods, according to the practices they know and which have been developed during recurring droughts, war and displacement. The international experts who are responsible for running the refugee camps such as Farchana, and who are engaged in establishing entitlements and distributing and controlling the provision of aid, are informed by practices assembled in the UNHCR headquarters in Geneva and which are adapted by being used over and over again. They are connected to the overall logic of providing emergency aid, protection and development (Li 2007; Escobar 1995, 2006; Fassin and Pandolfi 2010). However, within any displacement economy, practices of securing livelihoods do not follow one stable pathway, nor do they remain fixed as if handed down as an immutable model. Instead, as 'travelling models', practices change according to each new application and according to each new actor or group of actors within a given context (Behrends et al. forthcoming; Lewis and Mosse 2006; Mosse 2008; Rottenburg 2009). And while some practices may have become obsolete others may be reinvigorated. Creativity, as Hammar explains in the Introduction, is thus co-produced with loss and destruction in the interplay of various actors in their quest for security and future stability, and according to the avenues open to them (see also Berk and Galvan 2009).

The larger context of rebellion and displacement in Chad

As most of its neighbouring countries do, Chad produces oil. Oil revenues fuel the government's acquisition of arms, patronage-supported contracts linked to white elephant construction projects and distribution of money, and inscrutable contracting among the president's family and close followers. Quite evidently, these revenues are not channelled into alleviating the population's extreme poverty. Although democratic by name, elections have not been transparent, and succession into office has followed military coups since the country's independence in 1960. Terrorist networks do not seem to be significantly active in Chad, which might also be due to US counter-insurgency measures in the country's north. Still, the members of President Déby's wider family enjoy impunity and cause widespread insecurity, appropriating what they like, threatening and killing members of other ethnic groups and, occasionally, each other. The Darfur crisis in neighbouring Sudan and the events in Chad leading to the 2008 attempt at overthrowing the current president, as well as all attempts at securing livelihoods within the larger context of displacement in eastern Chad, have to be understood in light of this background.

In 2003 the existing tensions within the country very noticeably increased. In February of that year, conflicts in Darfur suddenly turned extremely violent. Widely covered by international media, this war soon came to be characterized as the new millennium's first genocide (Prunier 2005; Mamdani 2009). Two rebel groups, the Justice and Equality Movement (JEM) and the Sudan Liberation Army/Movement (SLA/M), opposed the government of Sudan's president Omar al-Bashir.[6] The government's reaction was immediate. By both bombarding the area and unleashing local militias (the infamous Janjawid) against the unarmed rural population, villages were burnt, men, women and children killed, and hundreds of thousands were displaced inside Darfur and across the border in Chad.

40

In this situation, the humanitarian aid machinery, first slow in reacting to the crisis, was soon in full swing. While there had been one UNHCR officer to deal with the smaller number of about ten thousand spontaneously settled refugees in border villages before this war, the number of aid agencies now increased exponentially. Starting in 2003, more than 280,000 refugees have been counted as having crossed the border into Chad and an estimated 180,000 people were displaced inside the country. At the peak of the conflict, more than one hundred national and international organizations operated in the area under the auspices of the UNHCR and coordinated by the Office for the Coordination of Humanitarian Affairs (OCHA). This was to have its own effects on the displacement economy under examination here.

In May 2004, rebellion against President Déby started in Chad. At first sight, this looked like a repeat pattern of *coups d'état* from inside the circles of power in Chad's turbulent history (Buijtenhuijs 1978, 1987; Reyna 1990; Burr and Collins 1999). While this is certainly true, there are several particular interpretations of this rebellion's outbreak and its location in the border region (Marchal 2006; Behrends 2008; Tubiana 2008a, 2008b). Among the most common of these is that the relatives of President Déby, who live on both sides of the Darfur–Chad border, were heavily targeted and involved in the Darfur war. Initially, Déby tried to stay out of the war and to maintain peaceful relations with the government of Sudan. However, by 2004, in the midst of the ongoing Darfur war and the aid operations centred in eastern Chad, some of the president's closest men took this 'neutrality' and inaction as a reason to launch a rebellion against him. After the first defections of high-ranking army officers and others within the president's inner circle, hundreds followed and the newly founded movements retreated into the war zone along the border.

There was also a connection to Chadian oil production, which started in 2003. The twin brothers Tom and Timan Erdimi, who led the rebellion, are President Déby's own nephews. One had formerly been in charge of the presidential cabinet and the other was responsible for all oil operations in the country. Their uncle's reluctance to help his relatives, combined with the manner in which President Déby handled the new oil revenues, were cited as their main motive for rebelling (Basedau 2006). When in 2006 the president single-handedly changed the country's constitution to prolong his original presidential terms, army defections escalated.

Weapons were easy to find and rebel fighters easy to recruit in the disorder that ensued after the initial attacks within the eastern region. The international community put pressure on Déby to allow European Union and later UN troops into the country. Meanwhile, President Omar al-Bashir of Sudan had begun to openly support the Chadian rebellion and thus the aim of ousting Déby. To him, the Chadian president's willingness to allow foreign troops and humanitarian aid into the border region posed a clear risk to his brutal stand against the Darfurian insurgency. After two (unsuccessful) coup attempts against him, President Déby changed his course of action and also started to openly support the Sudanese rebels against al-Bashir. In 2007, I saw Sudanese rebels move freely within Chadian territory. I heard people calling them *Toroboro* after the former mountainous hideout of Osama bin Laden, a role model for rebels in both Chad and Sudan.

Increasing and decreasing numbers of actors in different displacement sites

During this phase of increasing tensions and intervention, one feature appears to have had a marked influence on all four sites of the displacement economy under scrutiny here: namely that during the war, the sheer number of actors significantly increased. With this, the overall risk factor inevitably also significantly increased. The advent of more and more aid organizations, for instance, caused a higher number of rebel/militia attacks on aid workers, and the aid agencies' four-wheel-drive vehicles became one of the rebels' most targeted items. The increase of internally displaced people went hand in hand with increasing tensions between refugees and host societies over access to land and to aid resources. This was additionally aggravated by a divide-and-rule strategy adopted by the Chadian president, in which he armed local groups against each other and thus, for a while, successfully turned their attention away from attacking the capital (Jánszky and Pawlitzky 2008; Weissman 2008). With Sudanese refugees, internally displaced Chadians, Sudanese and Chadian rebels, the Chadian army, and international as well as Chadian aid workers, the larger arena started to be quite crowded. In 2007, the number of actors mounted further when the UN Security Council passed Resolution 1778 to send around five thousand UN peace troops to Chad, to be based around the refugee camps. With rising numbers of attacks on aid convoys, rebel recruitment inside the camps, and the overall presence of rebel fighters, the troops' mandate was to secure aid operations, personnel and refugee camps. The UN soldiers were to be preceded by a European force (EUFOR Chad), based in the region's capital city, Abéché, to prepare the ground for the later UN intervention (Berg 2009).

Apart from this increase in actual actors and the possible consequences it had for rebels, aid workers, refugees and the local population, the announcement of the impending arrival of several thousand international soldiers caused disruption on another level. By March 2008 the installation of 3,700 EUFOR troops in Abéché was due to be completed. But a month earlier, in February 2008, the Chadian capital N'Djamena came under heavy attack from a united Chadian rebel front. This attack and its aftermath marked the climax and turning point both for the rebellion against President Déby (which, for the time being, has subsided), and for the particular conjuncture of actors and events in the border region. The rebels lost the war in N'Djamena. Although they attacked with more than two thousand men, supported by the Sudanese regime, they could not defeat Déby's arsenal of tanks and heavy artillery, boosted by the country's recent oil gains. After this event, Déby's government used the argument of 'proper development' and 'cleaning up the city' to legitimize mass urban displacement, and destroying people's livelihoods, houses and shops in the capital, thus forcing them to retreat to the rural areas (Amnesty International 2009, 2010).

This event decisively affected the aid machinery in eastern Chad. Soon after the 2008 attack on N'Djamena, international EUFOR troops and, one year later, the UN Mission in the Central African Republic and Chad (MINURCAT) were stationed in Abéché and around the refugee camps. Their mandate was to protect refugees and humanitarian aid workers and to enable reconciliation. But their actual tasks came down to providing training for a Chadian special security police force – the Détachement Intégré de Sécurité (DIS) – and to accompanying aid convoys to protect humanitarian and development aid staff from car theft and the increasing threat of abduction. When in early 2010 Déby and al-Bashir signed a peace agreement, the two governments installed a mixed Chadian–Sudanese force in the border region, replacing the international UN soldiers, who were asked to leave the country before the end of their mission. From that moment on, the number of international actors inside the broad displacement arena started to decrease dramatically. The advent of the mixed forces and the cessation of support from the Sudanese government meant that the Chadian rebels disappeared.

These events form the background for the borderland's four different sites that I selected for analysis in relation to the overlapping economies that emerge in contexts of displacement. Thinking in terms of the crisis-and-creativity paradox that Hammar develops in the Introduction, I look at the factors of *risk* and *opportunity* as they open up to different actors living in one of the borderland's four displacement sites. Thus, I found the dynamically increasing and subsequently decreasing number of external actors to be inversely linked to livelihood security, meaning that high numbers of external actors pose a larger risk than lower numbers. To some individuals, however, one of whom I portray in the following section, this inverse connection signifies something else: as a secondary effect, and only for a smaller number of people, new opportunities arose in relation to the rising number of actors and then fell as this number decreased.

While all villages, soon after the conflict's escalation in 2003, were nearly emptied of their inhabitants, the population numbers in the town of Adré and the city of Abéché increased substantially. Adré grew owing to the arrival of displaced villagers, rebel groups and Chadian military forces. The number of inhabitants in Abéché grew owing to the large influx of aid agencies, which for a time boosted the city's economy to unforeseen heights. It became a magnet for migrants from other parts of the country hoping to find work with the well-paying international agencies. But the real economic winners of this phase were construction companies contracted for luxury housing, offices and storage buildings, generating rents of up to several thousand US dollars per month. The service sector also increased, as did the local trade and the new transport system of rickshaws imported via Sudan and Libya from India. Owing to its close proximity to the Sudanese border, the town of Adré was considered too 'unsafe' for large-scale international intervention and thus did not directly benefit from the international presence. It did, however, profit indirectly from those businessmen, contractors or aid workers who lived in Abéché or around the refugee camps, who invested in the border market of Adré. The latter's closeness to Sudan has made it an important economic hub, whether in peaceful times owing to better prices on the legal market, or during wartimes owing to illegal contraband.

I will return later to the question of risk and opportunity. First I discuss below the two additional cases mentioned previously, namely those of Cheikh Moussa, an inhabitant of Farchana refugee camp, and of Brahim, a local aid worker from Adré.

Refugee economies in the camp – the case of Cheikh Moussa

The war left most of the villagers without access to their land or at least without the possibility of working their land and harvesting. In the villages their insecurity increased to the point of their having to leave, owing first to the Sudanese militias' cross-border raids and later to the omnipresence of Chadian and Sudanese rebel groups. Before the 2003 escalation of violence, however, the villages' population sizes – and the economic opportunities for its inhabitants – initially increased owing to the spontaneous settlement of Sudanese refugees like Moussa. When Moussa Mahamad Saleh Youssouf first came to Chad in 1998, he settled in the vicinity of Wandalou, another small village on the border with Sudan. Wandalou had a medical station financed by the Catholic development organization Secours Catholique et Développement (SECADEV) that was active in the region. What distinguished Wandalou from Hashaba, however, was the fact that the refugees living there remained largely outside the actual village community. While the refugees in Hashaba built their houses next to the villagers, the people of Wandalou decided not to integrate the refugees into their settlement site. As a reason, they remarked that the number of refugees to Wandalou was higher than the number of those who had gone to Hashaba, and they feared being swamped by outsiders. In addition, they had come from farther away from the border and did not have any previous relationships with the villagers – unlike in Hashaba, where some of the refugees had relatives on whom they could rely.

44

However, the influx of refugees and the need to find meat for them to eat contributed to the village's rise as a local market town. As the village chief remembers, it came to be the 'largest camel market in the whole region, even larger than El Geneina [the regional capital of West Darfur in Sudan] itself'.[7] When the region's administration started taxing traders and thus interfered in the free trade that had developed in Wandalou, the market's success soon decreased and eventually stopped altogether. Moussa, at that time, was part of a small group of refugees who were given a piece of land on which to settle. The villagers also gave them farming land, but it was very far outside the village and thus difficult to cultivate.

As a teacher and political activist, Moussa had been threatened by the rising tensions in Darfur. After some minor attacks on his village and warning messages from friends that he might be targeted by government repression, he and the people from his village left for Chad. At that time, they were given some land to settle close to an existing Masalit village, but without the influence of relatives or other acquaintances in the village, they were not given good land to farm. Consequently, they came to rely on donor help, which in 2000 – when I first met Moussa – was managed by SECADEV on behalf of the UNHCR. After an initial phase of emergency aid, the NGOs started a development phase. The ultimate aim of this kind of assistance was to integrate refugees into existing village communities and to render these communities more profit oriented, working through cooperatives on communal land and investing the surplus for the benefit of the whole village. But the refugees interpreted this new kind of aid in a different way: to them, the transition from emergency aid to development aid meant that all provisions of food, blankets, soap and so on stopped and that they would be left 'alone' to cater for their needs. It turned out that the formation of cooperatives was complicated, as the villagers denied the better farming land to the refugees and demanded development aid for themselves with the argument that their resources were also strained by the refugees' presence. In this regard, Moussa's situation was significantly different from that of Daldoum and Ashta, who had integrated into the village of Hashaba, while Moussa and his people remained outsiders, regarded by the villagers with a mixture of suspicion and envy.

Today Moussa lives in the refugee camp of Farchana. With the difficulties encountered in Wandalou – being denied access to good land or to the possibility of finding work as a teacher in the Chadian border villages – he saw no option other than to leave together with the other refugees and to move into one of the UNHCR refugee camps. He selected Farchana because other people from his home in Sudan had started to go there when tensions exploded into open conflict in Darfur. In Farchana his education and former status had greater value than in Wandalou, and he became the elected chief of more than twenty thousand refugees. After being formally registered as refugees,

Moussa and his people were entitled to different kinds of aid, depending on their status as 'vulnerable' (elderly people, single mothers, children) or normal refugees. But after several years in the camp, Moussa today complains that the situation is still not easy for them. They lack precisely the future perspective that Daldoum and Ashta try to maintain by staying close to their village land.

As the refugees' chief, Moussa was part of an uproar that followed the UNHCR refugee policy to encourage the formation of cooperatives. Given what some refugees had experienced in the villages, particularly those around Moussa who had come from Wandalou, they translated this initiative as the imminent end of aid. In this logic it was vital, if they wanted to continue receiving help, not to be obliged to form cooperatives. After a series of negotiations with aid officials, Moussa, at a certain point, changed his attitude and started to promote some of the aid organizations' proposals, for instance the idea of the refugees helping to reforest the area for better access to firewood. But the people in the camp took his move as switching sides, and one day he was severely beaten up by a group of angry camp dwellers. After that he withdrew from all efforts at mediating between the refugees and the organizations and gave up his position as chief.

Now Moussa mainly takes care of his own life. He does not feel safe enough to return to Sudan. When I met him in 2011, one of his sons had just been killed in a counter-insurgency attack by the Sudanese government. He had been a rebel fighter. Moussa grieved deeply over this loss. He fell ill and became one of the 'vulnerable' inside the camp. People within this category are entitled to higher rations of food aid and they are provided with new shelter. In the courtyard of his new house, he has begun to raise sheep to eventually sell in case he urgently needs money. Like many of the other refugees in the camp, he also occasionally travels the 50 kilometres to the international border to farm peanuts in those fields left by Masalit farmers who – like Ashta – had themselves become internally displaced. His brother, who had been in the camp but whom Moussa had helped attain resettlement in the United States, adds another form of income to his portfolio. With his occasional remittances of about US$100 at a time, Moussa can afford to buy new clothes and his beloved alcohol. In this situation, he remains dependent on the aid he receives in the camp.

He explains to me that there is not enough land for the large number of refugees who live there. As insecurity is still high in Sudan, they can neither return to their land nor integrate in Chad as long as they have no access to farmland. The vegetable farming encouraged by the UNHCR is not sufficient for their survival and does not provide enough money to buy the millet that would feed a family throughout the year. Moussa mentions that there are three ways of making a living in the camp: to be a trader selling goods from Sudan, to work on other people's farms and sell the produce across the border to Sudan, or to get one of the salaried jobs such as a teacher, electrician or builder inside the camp. Schools inside the camp educate the refugees to learn these professions, and, being a former teacher, Moussa also teaches some classes. Normally, however, when it comes to hiring people for construction work, or as electricians, tailors or nurses, it is not the refugees who are hired but people from outside the camp in the neighbouring areas.

This issue of labour – that is, the employment opportunities for host communities – points to another layer of economic activity generated through conditions of displacement. The final case study of Brahim will address this issue.

New economic opportunities generated by displacement – the case of Brahim

The only original Chadian among the four examples, Brahim, is from Adré, a son of the first settlers who were Maba from around Abéché. His father migrated to Adré to work as a translator for the French colonial regime. Later he opened up a border hostel for religious pilgrims and migrants, a business that made him moderately wealthy and allowed him to educate all his children, who are all girls except for Brahim. He died when Brahim was still a teenager. Brahim had to stop his education since his mother, who has worked as a midwife into her old age, could not support all their children's school education. In the border town of Adré, Brahim had seen war since his early youth. He lived through two consecutive *coups d'état* that were orchestrated from within this area in 1979 and 1990. Since he did not properly finish his school education, Brahim worked as an assistant teacher when I first met him in 2001. In 2006 he got married to Suleikha, a Maba girl from Adré. In 2007, a well-to-do relative paid for a course in accounting, which he attended in N'Djamena. But instead of staying in the capital, Brahim decided to move back closer to his home town. His eldest sister works for the UNHCR in Farchana, and she helped him to find work with a Christian NGO that constructs houses and market stalls inside Farchana camp. Here, he earns about 250 euros per month, a salary that allows him to rent a house and invest in constructing a larger place in Adré, where he eventually wants to return as a shopowner or owner of an internet café. Suleikha takes care of their four sons and has started an education as a seamstress in one of the refugee camp's vocational schools that are supported by international development agencies.

Brahim has not been formally displaced himself, but like that of many others his career is an integral part of the borderland's displacement economy. His position is one which bridges several of the displacement sites described so far. Being from Adré, where his family is well settled and highly respected, he is very familiar with the people from Hille Djidíde, the new part of Adré mostly settled by internally displaced people (IDPs). His mother had grown up in a village on the Sudanese side of the border and some of her former neighbours came to Chad during the 1980s. Brahim often accompanied her when she was called to the villages as a midwife, and from that time on, people referred to him as the son of Izze (his mother's name). Still, he is clearly not part of the internally displaced community of Hille Djidíde that Ashta belongs to. Neither does he share their economic distress. His family members live in well-built houses, and they own market stalls and shops and several plots of building land and farmland around the town. Many of the family's senior members are well placed in public administration or as *marabous*, religious specialists who are often called upon to mediate in conflict or perform traditional forms of jurisdiction.

Brahim's current economic practice is based on access to the humanitarian and development aid context, which provides a direct link to the aid hub of Abéché where originally all aid agencies had their headquarters. The well-to-do relative who lives in Abéché and who had paid for his education in the Chadian capital provides another link. But although he makes more money than any of the above-mentioned, Brahim's access to all forms of economic endeavour is still precarious. Each year the NGO for which he works depends on the head office's new budget, and each year Brahim fears for his contract. So far he has been lucky and has not been affected by budget cuts, unlike some of his colleagues. For the last couple of years, he has been quite well off, providing his family with what they needed plus some luxury objects such as a motorbike, a satellite dish and TV set, several mobile phones, a computer, and household items such as curtains, furniture and kitchenware. Even if he were to lose his job, in contrast to Moussa, he seems to be in a position to use his gains to save for a future outside the context of humanitarian aid.

Recently, however, this plan has fallen through, owing not to his losing his job but to the overall situation of insecurity and impunity still prevalent particularly in this area of the country. One might also say that he fell victim to someone else's economic opportunity generated under conditions of displacement. In December 2011, Brahim was imprisoned without trial because the telephone number of a former soldier's fugitive wife was found on his mobile phone (and his number on hers). Although he claims that she was only a friend he had met during his studies in N'Djamena, the former soldier's relatedness to the Chadian president left Brahim with no credibility before local law. Not until his wife had sold all their belongings, and his relatives had collected the incredible amount of 15,000 euros, was he released after three months. He managed to keep his job, but for now his plans for future security lie in tatters. In a later reflection on what had happened to him, he told me that it was his and his sister's incomes and humble economic rise due to their work with aid agencies in the refugee camp that had caused jealousies among those in power in the borderlands.

Assessing crisis and creativity within the displacement economy's four sites

The four borderland displacement sites interconnect the village of Hashaba, the town of Adré, the city of Abéché and the refugee camp of Farchana. Together they combine one case of outmigration or flight (the village of Hashaba), and three places of rapidly increasing population numbers owing to in-migration, refuge and the international presence of aid machinery and military. Looking at the four individual cases discussed – Daldoum, Ashta, Moussa and Brahim – each chose a different path to secure their own and their family's livelihoods and to render their futures as secure as possible. As part of the same displacement economy, they each came to make their decisions according to a mixture of known, established practices and new openings that emerged in the wider context of change. Such changes occurred in their respective local communities through the decisions and actions of representatives of the country's government or international agencies or rebel groups or others.

In the following discussion, I will reconsider the four sites – now in their more current conditions – and explore some of the ways in which they confine (or structure) people's economic decision-making processes regarding their (creative) livelihood practices. As already noted earlier in the chapter, I consider risk and opportunity to be of particular significance for the options and choices made in relation to livelihood security. Both risk and opportunity are connected to the (limited) options for making a living in the overall displacement economy under consideration. This has included finding paid work, receiving aid, having access to farmland or criminal activities connected to oppression and rebellion. In the various crisis periods discussed, increasing and decreasing numbers of actors have affected these possibilities. As combined displacement sites I discuss below first the aid hub in Abéché in connection to the refugee camp of Farchana, and then the village of Hashaba in connection to the border town of Adré. The major distinguishing factor between these two interconnected displacement contexts is the relative presence and relative absence of aid agencies in the two areas, respectively.

Abéché and Farchana The city of Abéché, as a temporary aid hub during the wars in Darfur and Chad, was strongly affected by the failed 2008 *coup d'état* in N'Djamena, which prompted the above-mentioned turning point in government policy. Abéché suffered from the fact that in 2010 the UNHCR closed down its headquarters to replace it with a decentralized system of smaller offices in the direct vicinity of the refugee camps, including Farchana. The number of refugees and internally displaced persons had not at the time – nor has it yet – declined, and UNHCR does not see a fast solution to the refugee situation.[8] With a budget of US$176.9 million, the security of refugees and the provision of basic needs continue to be its main concerns. Yet the decision to focus aid on the immediate surroundings of camps inevitably generated key changes in the economies of both Abéché and Farchana. With the departure from Abéché of UNHCR as the flagship, nearly all other aid organizations followed suit. Consequently, the city, which had been flourishing with restaurants, transport, housing and markets – predominantly directed towards the foreigners present during the peak of the war – returned to being the much quieter place it had been before the war, albeit with an extensive territory of luxury hotels and villas that are now vacant. By contrast, as Abéché's aid-related economy declined, the tables turned positively for Farchana and the other refugee camps in the area.

Farchana refugee camp is named after the small village located on the road between Adré and Abéché, about fifty kilometres away from the Sudanese border. It was built in an area with scarce settlement so that enough space could be given to refugees. Situated on the main (dirt) road connecting Abéché (and, farther away, the national capital N'Djamena) to Sudan, it had previously been a small place with a handful of shops for those driving through, and a weekly market. When the UNHCR left Abéché, Farchana started to boom. Its population increased not only because of the 20,000 refugees who have lived in the camp since 2003. Owing to the relocation of the aid agencies' offices and their staff, security police were stationed in its vicinity, and the airstrip that was built by UN international forces now sees two flights per day.

Like Abéché earlier, Farchana has now become a point of in-migration, with people looking for employment and business opportunities in trade, transport and services. The village market and the roadside shops have greatly expanded. Houses are being built for those who want to find work with the aid agencies, and rents as well as the prices for food are rising. A second market within the refugee camp itself is open every day, which makes it attractive for both villagers and refugees to buy and sell here. To those in the hinterland rural areas around the refugee camps, the boom displays similar traits to that in Abéché five years before, although of course on a smaller scale. Several shops for mobile phones and others for the basic necessities have been established. For the poorer population these changes often mean that they have to move farther away from town to escape the rise in prices, while others are attracted to the place hoping to find work.

The changing economic fortunes of both Abéché and Farchana are clearly affected by the opportunities (lost and gained) that have resulted from external funding and employment generated by the presence of international agencies and NGOs. Their presence in turn is linked to conditions of ongoing crisis, violence and displacement.

Hashaba and Adré While the influx of aid personnel, migrants, rebels, army and business people had temporarily strengthened the economies first of

Abéché and then Farchana, the rural areas of Hashaba and the border town of Adré experienced rather different trajectories. As already noted, Hashaba's village economy is based on access to farmland, but such access has never been undisputed. Hashaba and the villages around it lie on the land that the Masalit consider to be traditionally theirs. In 1921 the colonial border divided the Chadian part of Dar Masalit (in Arabic: the land of the Masalit) from the seat of the Masalit sultan as well as the larger part of Masalit territory, which were situated on the Sudanese side of the border (Kapteijns 1985). On a more general level, the question of land is an open one. Legally, all formally unclaimed and unregistered land belongs to the state, but informally, traditional legal systems that run parallel to the official legal structures of the state attribute landownership. The Masalit's agricultural economy is based on millet and cultivating seasonal vegetables and fruits like melons, tomatoes, peanuts or okra in the *wadis* (river beds that dry out after the rainy season).

For the last six decades, so-called Arab families have also moved into the area with their herds of cattle and camels. The Arabs live in *ferigs*, small dwellings outside the Masalit villages. Although economic relations exist between the two groups, the tensions that escalated during the Darfur war and the rebellion in Chad have left them on two different sides of the fighting. While nearly all Masalit left their villages, the Arabs remained in place, continued herding and trading and only relocated their animals across the border into Sudan (see Yalçin-Heckmann et al. 2003).

Without access to schooling or other professional training, the people in the villages, both Masalit and Arabs, have few opportunities except to focus their local economic activities mainly on subsistence farming and barter. Some sell their products in the markets. Thus, at least for the farmers, the villages have become a place for those who cannot afford life in a town or city, because of the difficulty of earning enough money to support a family. Divorced women from urban areas, for instance, often have to retreat to living in a village where they can fall back on their neighbours' support, and where money is not absolutely needed to survive. The town of Adré has constantly grown since French colonial troops founded it as a garrison in the early 1920s. Its population originates from very different places. In Adré's central area live well-to-do Maba whose older fathers – like the father of Brahim – accompanied the first French battalions to work for the colonial administration. Until today, the Maba population of Adré, which also constitutes the core of the formerly powerful Sultanate of Wadai (1635–1912), has maintained its pre-eminent role. When, in 2005, Ashta and the other villagers took refuge in Adré's new part of Hille Djidíde, their former economic practices were no longer an option. Exchanging farm produce for other goods such as soap, sugar or tea was no longer possible. Instead, in a money-based economy many services that had been free in the village, such as access to water, now had to be paid for in cash.

Although aid was offered by international agencies in the camps, these were about fifty kilometres away from where they live, and they decided not to move there. Instead, Daldoum in Hashaba and Ashta in Adré chose to remain in a risky area where they were able to maintain a certain control over accessing their land and farms. As former villagers without formal school education or skills, they neither had the opportunity to work for the international agencies nor the capital to start a business selling, for instance, mobile phones.

Conclusion

When connecting the various sites and actors of this borderland displacement economy with their respective historical backgrounds and the familiar models that inform their practices, it is possible to understand the sometimes surprising outcomes of their choices. To sum up in brief: all four sites provide opportunities to creatively engage in emerging economic activities, and simultaneously contain risks of losing more than could be gained. This means that different actors can flexibly adjust their practices to what surrounds them. Daldoum, who stayed in the village, seems to have taken the greatest risk, facing militias and rebels roaming in the area who constantly threaten his and his wife's lives. For him, the opportunity lies in the future livelihood security related to being able to keep his own land, and save the land of his daughter Ashta from being taken by other returning refugees.

Ashta, who decided to go away from the village and stay close to the town of Adré, risked not finding the money to feed her children and herself every day. She depended on finding day-to-day piece jobs such as carrying bricks and helping out on other people's fields. Her vulnerability lay in the danger that things would fall apart if she fell ill and could not perform these daily tasks. For her, seemingly the only opportunity or benefit was in having saved her life. Yet looking more closely, she was able to establish a small business for her son, who continues to provide for his mother as well. She went through hard times, but if she stays in town and works on her village fields in more peaceful times, she will have the advantage of providing her children with the town's better possibilities for school education and health services and living independently of aid.

In the refugee camp, Moussa risks his future independence since he will not get access to a sufficiently large piece of land while remaining there. While it seemed that he had little choice but to go into the camp, he actually already counted mainly on aid and development assistance even when still living in the spontaneous settlement outside the village of Wandalou. His opportunities are restricted to what the refugee camp provides and what his brother sends him from abroad. This might be more than what Ashta or Daldoum ever receive, but his future livelihood security depends on the provision of aid, at least as long as he cannot return to his original village in Sudan.

Most surprising is the situation of Brahim. His context seemed to entail the least risk, with the opportunity of being supported by his well-to-do family and finding work with the aid agencies. The situation provided him with more opportunities than any of the other persons introduced here: he could keep what he had in Adré and add to it by working for the NGOs that provide aid to the refugees. But ironically, owing to the political dangers inherent in the wider context, he was forced into a precarious situation when brought to prison. As a result, he temporarily lost as much as – or more than – the other three: all his belongings and savings went into the hands of one powerful individual, leaving Brahim with large debts to a great number of his family members. Yet as already mentioned above, the individual who placed Brahim in this precarious position can also be viewed as making use of the creative opportunities generated by the Darfur–Chad borderland's displacement economy.

Similarly counter-intuitive, but contributing to Hammar's 'crisis and creativity' assumption, is the fact that large-scale humanitarian aid, as in the case of eastern Chad, also contributes to the economy of rebel groups. We have seen this through the 'provision' of four-wheel-drive vehicles being frequently targeted for theft (which in turn has led to the partial deterrent strategy of aid agencies colouring their vehicles bright yellow to render them less attractive). Besides this, it was not intended that the presence of aid agencies would contribute to the economic opportunities of a much wider community than those directly targeted to receive aid.

In mid-2012, the displaced people of Hille Djidíde in Adré were newly targeted by international aid agencies, as they had been previously in Hashaba and other villages before the peak years of the war (2003–08). Their houses have been improved and they have been included in a large agricultural programme. This might be connected to the aid agencies' desire to maintain their presence in the area (with economic considerations in their own right!), particularly in the face of ongoing decreases in numbers of actors. For example, many of the former rebel fighters and militias have moved into Sudan to take part in the gold rush that has been occurring there for the last two to three years. However, it also demonstrates another point: that within the wider displacement economy, no practice is independent of the events unfolding in each of the sites depicted here.

With this contribution I have tried to demonstrate that those in all four sites of the borderland displacement economy in eastern Chad, although connected, display particular economic strategies and context-contingent ways of remaining resilient in the face of turbulence and disorder. Alongside the attributes identified by Eriksen (2010) in relation to human security – social cohesion, integration, stability and collective identity – the people living here make use of survival practices and experiences of displacement to creatively adapt to their respective situations. They do so by using what is available to them or what makes sense in their daily practice, moving beyond categories like local resident, refugee, rebel, internally displaced or aid worker.

Such practices can be understood as an established way to interpret and deal with a challenging situation or an institutionalized form (Thévenot 1984). Many of these practices have grown out of history and they are connected to ethnic, religious, political and, evidently, economic circumstances. But, as I demonstrate, they are in no way fixed procedures or unchanging courses of action. On the contrary, in each new situation these practices are newly adapted. Models from elsewhere, introduced for instance by international development agencies, may be adapted to, mixed with, added to or rejected, with respect to existing procedures (Rottenburg 2002, 2009; Lewis and Mosse 2006; Behrends et al. forthcoming). This approach allows for cautious generalization. The village of Hashaba, for instance, displays similar patterns to those observed in the other villages in this particular displacement economy; and the refugee camp of Farchana is an example of the other eleven refugee camps around it, which have their particularities but also great similarities. Looking at the economy that develops around displacement and livelihood strategies allows for a dynamic unfolding through time of the relationship between space, experience and practice that enhances the explanatory and analytical scope of the notion of displacement economies.

Notes

1 Research for this article has been funded by the Max Planck Institute for Social Anthropology, the Volkswagen Foundation and the German Research Foundation (DFG). I furthermore wish to thank Amanda Hammar and the participants of the Uppsala Workshop on 'Displacement Economies' as well as the members of Richard Rottenburg's LOST group for their extremely valuable comments on earlier drafts of this chapter.

2 Mud bricks are needed for the new construction sites outside Adré. These bricks are locally produced during the dry season in ovens that are constructed close to the earth that is used for them in the seasonally dried out river beds (Arab.: wadis).

3 In 2010, many of the farmers started to sell part of their harvest to the herders on the other side of the border. Because so many of the farmers had left Darfur, the region was suffering food shortages.

Idriss Saleh Adjidey, head of a Catholic NGO, saw this as a first sign of reconciliation between the rival groups (interview in Adré, 21 September 2010).

4 'Human security' was first introduced in the 1994 United Nations Development Programme (UNDP) Annual Report as an applied social term, intended to 'humanize' strategic (military) studies, to anchor development research in locally experienced realities and to offer a tool to gauge the ways societies function from the perspective of their inhabitants.

5 See, for the differences between spontaneously settled refugees and refugee camps, the critical works of Allen (1996); De Waal (1989); Malkki (1995); Spittler (1989).

6 This is a very brief summary of the events during the Darfur war. For further reference see, among others, Harir (1994); De Waal (2004); Flint and De Waal (2005, 2008); Jungstand (2005); Prunier (2005);

Behrends (2007); Lanz (2009); Reyna (2010).

7 Interview with the chief of Wandalou, 13 November 2001.

8 UNHCR Global Appeal 2012–13.

References

Allen, T. (ed) (1996) *In Search of Cool Ground. War, Flight and Homecoming in Northeast Africa*, London: James Currey.

Amnesty International (2009) *Broken Homes, Broken Lives and Forced Evictions in Chad*, London.

— (2010) *We Too Deserve Protection*, London.

Basedau, M. (2006) 'Politische Krise und Erdöl im Tschad – ein "Modell" am Ende?', *GIGA Focus*, 3: 1–8.

Behrends, A. (2007) 'The Darfur conflict and the Chad/Sudan border – regional context and local re-configurations', *Sociologus*, 57(1): 99–131.

— (2008), 'Fighting for oil when there is no oil yet. The case of the Chad–Sudan border', *Focaal*, 52: 39–56.

Behrends, A., S. J. Park and R. Rottenburg (eds) (forthcoming) *Travelling Models in African Conflict Management. Translating Technologies of Social Ordering*, Leiden: Brill AEGIS.

Berg, P. (2009) 'EUFOR Tchad/RCA: the EU serving French interests', in M. Asseburg and R. Kempin (eds), *The EU as a Strategic Actor in the Realm of Security and Defence? A Systematic Assessment of ESDP Missions and Operations*, Berlin: SWP, pp. 57–69.

Berk, G. and D. Galvan (2009) 'How people experience and change institutions: a field guide to creative syncretism', *Theory and Society*, 38: 543–80.

Buijtenhuijs, R. (1978) *Le Frolinat et les révoltes populaires du Tchad, 1965–1976*, The Hague and New York: Mouton Publishers.

— (1987) *Le Frolinat et les guerres civiles du Tchad (1977–1984): la révolution introuvable*, Paris: Karthala.

Burr, J. M. and R. O. Collins (1999) *Africa's Thirty Years War. Libya, Chad, and the Sudan 1963–1993*, Boulder, CO: Westview Press.

Clarke, A. E. and S. L. Star (2008) 'The social worlds framework: a theory/methods package', in E. J. Hackett, O. Amsterdamska, M. Lynch and J. Wajcman (eds), *The Handbook of Science and Technology Studies*, Cambridge, MA: MIT Press, pp. 113–37.

De Waal, A. (1989) *Famine that Kills. Darfur, Sudan, 1984–1985*, Oxford: Clarendon Press.

— (2004) 'Counter-insurgency on the cheap', *London Review of Books*, 26(15): 1–8.

Eriksen, T. H. (2010) 'Human security and social anthropology', in T. H. Eriksen, E. Bal and O. Salemink (eds), *A World of Insecurity. Anthropological perspectives on human security*, London and New York: Pluto Press, pp. 1–19.

Escobar, A. (1995) *Encountering Development: The making and unmaking of the Third World*, Princeton, NJ: Princeton University Press.

— (2006) 'The making and unmaking of the Third World through development', in M. Rahnema and V. Bawtree (eds), *The Post-Development Reader*, London: Zed Books, pp. 85–93.

Fassin, D. and M. Pandolfi (2010) *Contemporary States of Emergency: The politics of military and humanitarian interventions*, New York and Cambridge, MA: Zone Books.

Flint, J. and A. de Waal (2005) *Darfur: A short history of a long war*, London and New York: Zed Books.

— (2008) *Darfur: A new history of a long war*, London and New York: Zed Books.

Harir, S. (1994) '"Arab Belt" versus "African Belt". Ethno-political conflict in Dar Fur and the regional cultural factors', in S. Harir and T. Tvedt (eds), *Shortcut to Decay. The Case of the Sudan*, Uppsala: Nordiska Afrikainstitutet, pp. 144–85.

Jánszky, B. and C. Pawlitzky (2008) *Sources of Violence, Conflict Mediation and Reconciliation: A socio-anthropological* study on Dar Sila, N'Djamena: European Commission.

Jungstand, G. (2005) 'Etude sur les relations entre les populations locales et les réfugiés du Darfour dans la région du Ouaddaï', in *Programme de Développement rural décentralisé d'Assoungha – Biltine – Ouara*.

Kapteijns, L. (1985) *Mahdist Faith and Sudanic Tradition. The History of the Masalit Sultanate 1870–1930*, London: Routledge and Kegan Paul.

Lanz, D. (2009) 'Save Dafur: a movement and its discontents', Unpublished manuscript.

Lewis, D. and D. Mosse (2006) *Development Brokers and Translators: The ethnography of aid and agencies*, Bloomfield, CT: Kumarian Press.

Li, T. (2007) *The Will to Improve: Governmentality, development, and the practice of politics*, Durham, NC: Duke University Press.

Malkki, L. H. (1995) *Purity and Exile. Violence, Memory, and National Cosmology among Hutu Refugees in Tanzania*, Chicago, IL: University of Chicago Press.

Mamdani, M. (2009) *Saviors and Survivors: Darfur, politics, and the war on terror*, New York: Pantheon Books.

Marchal, R. (2006) 'Chad/Darfur: how two crises merge', *Review of African Political Economy*, 109: 467–82.

Mosse, D. (2008) 'International policy, development expertise, and anthropology', *Focaal*, 52: 119–26.

Prunier, G. (2005) *Darfur: The ambiguous genocide*, Ithaca, NY: Cornell University Press.

Reyna, S. P. (1990) *Wars without End. The Political Economy of a Precolonial African State*, Hanover, NH: University Press of New England.

— (2010) 'The disasters of war in Darfur, 1950–2004', *Third World Quarterly*, 31(8): 24.

Rottenburg, R. (2002) *Weit hergeholte Fakten: eine Parabel der Entwicklungshilfe*, Stuttgart: Lucius & Lucius.

— (2009) *Far-fetched Facts: A parable of development aid*, Cambridge, MA: MIT Press.

Rottenburg, R. et al. (2008) 'Nomadic–sedentary relations and failing state institutions in Darfur and Kordofan (Sudan)', *Orientwissenschaftliche Hefte*, 26, Halle/Saale.

Spittler, G. (1989) *Handeln in einer Hungerkrise: Tuaregnomaden und die grosse Dürre von 1984*, Opladen: Westdeutscher Verlag.

Strauss, A. L. (1978) 'A social world perspective', in N. K. Denzin (ed.), *Studies in Symbolic Interaction 1*, Greewnwich, CT: JAI Press, pp. 119–28.

Thévenot, L. (1984) 'Rules and implements: investment in forms', *Social Science Information*, 23(1): 1–45.

Tubiana, J. (2008a) *The Chad–Sudan Proxy War and the 'Darfurization' of Chad: Myths and Reality*, Geneva: Small Arms Survey, Graduate Institute of International Studies.

— (2008b) 'Echo effects: Chadian instability and the Darfur conflict', Sudan Issue Brief no. 9.

Weissman, F. (2008) *Humanitarian Dilemmas in Darfur*, Fondation Médecins sans Frontières/Centre de Réflexion sur l'action et les savoirs humanitaires.

Yalçin-Heckmann, L. et al. (2003) *Property Regimes in the Context of War and Displacement: Chad, Croatia and Azerbaijan in comparison*, Halle/Saale: Max Planck Institute for Social Anthropology.

3 | Contested spaces, new opportunities: displacement, return and the rural economy in Casamance, Senegal

Martin Evans[1]

Introduction

Casamance is the south-westernmost part of Senegal, largely separated from the rest of the country by The Gambia to the north and bordering Guinea-Bissau to the south. As the scene of West Africa's longest-running civil conflict, now some thirty years old, Casamance provides a case of displacement economies on a relatively small scale but of long duration. The focus here is on human displacement, understood as the enforced physical dislocation of people, the dynamics of their return and resettlement, and the economic, political and social effects related to these processes. Much of the long-term human displacement in the conflict has occurred in the relatively narrow band of territory between the south bank of the Casamance river and northern border districts of Guinea-Bissau. Following flight and protracted exile from this border area in the 1990s, however, the 2000s and beyond have mostly seen people return, driven by economic and social desperation coupled with generally improved (though still at times volatile) security conditions, and supported by international aid for reconstruction.

Building on field research conducted over twelve years, the chapter considers the emergent economic and political landscape of the border area. It shows how this landscape is the result of layers of displacement over two decades, situated within a deeper historical context of migration. Among other issues, the chapter examines the dynamics of return and reconstruction in the border area, paying particular attention to key economic and social issues and their spatial dimensions. It also engages with another important dynamic shaping and shaped by this emerging displacement economy, namely the reconfiguration of political structures at different levels. Here, in some cases, entrepreneurs seek to take advantage of opportunities provided by displacement and the vagaries of international aid to reshape political space in their favour. From a theoretical perspective, it seeks to understand these dynamics through the concept of 'relational space', formulated in human geography and beginning to be used, if not always explicitly, in studies of displacement.

Displacement and relational space

Space matters, and at the smallest scale; but from a theoretical perspective, it is sometimes all too apparent that different disciplines talk about space in different ways. The analysis presented here takes from human geography the notion of 'relational space' in the sense suggested by David Harvey (2005) and Doreen Massey (2005). This is space constituting and constitutive of social relationships. As Harvey explains, '[p]rocesses do not occur *in* space but define their own spatial frame. The concept of space is embedded in or internal to process' (2005: 273; emphasis in original). While proponents of relational space (as analytical tool) admit that it is difficult to work with, and impossible to 'map' in any Cartesian or absolute sense, they argue that it is, as social reality, the space in which all people actually operate. Massey (2005: 9) describes this

> ... space as the product of interrelations; as constituted through interactions, from the immensity of the global to the intimately tiny ... space as always under construction. Precisely because space on this reading is a product of relations-between, relations which are necessarily embedded material practices which have to be carried out, it is always in the process of being made ... Perhaps we could imagine space as a simultaneity of stories-so-far.

This highlights two further points about how the concept of relational space works in real contexts. The first is exactly that, its essential link with the real and material: relationality begets action and meaning only through the material world. Harvey underlines the dangers of conceptualizing space in too-abstruse terms; whereas '[i]t is only when relationality connects to the absolute spaces and times of social and material life that politics comes alive' (2005: 293). The second point is how the concept can help understand linkages between processes at different scales. Much is said about relationships between the global and the local but this is, again, often vague (ibid.): linkages are presumed but real articulations between different spatial scales of social and material relations are brushed over. The risk is that 'global forces' thus become a lazy trope to explain, inadequately, what is happening locally, while local dynamics in their own right are understated or ignored.

Human displacement, as defined above, is an inherently spatial process, lending itself naturally to the idea that relational space is constantly being 'made'. Relational understandings of space are indeed increasingly applied in displacement settings even if such studies are not always explicitly framed in these terms theoretically. This approach reflects the broader, contemporary 'spatial turn' in the humanities and social sciences beyond geography and thus increasingly evident in African studies (for example, Engel and Nugent 2010a). Two fields in which ideas akin to human-geographic conceptualizations of relationality emerge most strongly are studies of borderlands and mobility in Africa. This comes with the admission that 'social processes of bordering'

58

(Engel and Nugent 2010b: 4) – in a relational sense, how space is 'made' by cross-border practices – remain under-researched. Still, good examples can be found: in the Angola–Zambia borderlands, Barrett (2009) applies the notion of 'hodological space', from the Greek *hodos*, meaning 'path', to understand the lived reality of moving between two points. The socially constructed nature of pathways in contexts of mobility (forced or voluntary) is also explored by Lindley (2009) for Somalia; and by Schapendonk (2010) for stepwise migration from sub-Saharan Africa northwards into the Maghreb and beyond. Mobility provides the focus for a recent conceptualization of cross-border space in the Sahel, too (Retaillé and Walther 2011). Other authors explore how displaced people, specifically, use cross-border practices to their economic and social advantage, for example the Fula across the Sierra Leone/Guinea-Conakry border (Gale 2006) and the Diola across the Senegal/Gambia border (Evans and Ray 2013). For internally displaced persons (IDPs), studies of spatial practices and their social meaning can similarly be found. The role of insecurity in shaping the spatial behaviour of displaced populations is described, for example, for child 'night commuters' in northern Uganda (Dunn 2007). Outside of Africa but certainly applicable therein, Oslender's (2008) novel conceptions of 'geographies of terror' and 'spaces of confinement' are applied in his study of black communities in Colombia subject to violence and displacement by state actors with economic motivations.

Another way to view the relational spaces of people affected by displacement comes from studies of land tenure, which naturally point to the very local character of such dynamics and, importantly, the ways in which people's relationships to land in Africa are ingrained in local histories (Englund 1996, 1999). Some research on the self-settled displaced in Africa – the single largest group of IDPs and refugees on the continent (UNHCR 2011) – concerns how individuals or households create habitable and productive spaces in reception areas. In a study of unusual depth, Black and Sessay (1997) analyse land use change in parts of south-east Guinea-Conakry that received large influxes of Liberian and Sierra Leonean refugees. Highlighting the importance of local institutions and how they adapt, the authors show how land requirements from refugees were accommodated. Rather than becoming a burden on reception areas, refugees were often an asset, valorizing fallows and working existing productive land more intensively, enhancing production. Similar accommodation is seen in a few other studies, notably that of Leach (1992) on Liberian refugees in Sierra Leone; and of Black and Sessay (1998) again, this time on Mauritanian refugees in the Senegal river valley. If and when people go home, return and reconstruction also involve complex and very local processes: 'rebuilding' communities can in reality involve significant reconfigurations of local economic and political space compared with the pre-displacement condition. This has long been the subject of research, again focused on issues of land tenure and natural resource access, in 'post-conflict' settings in Mozambique and elsewhere (McGregor 1997, 1998; Unruh 1998; Unruh and Bailey 2009; Unruh et al. 2003). More recently interest in land tenure in conflict/post-conflict settings has been boosted by recognition of its importance by the humanitarian community (see, for example, Pantuliano 2009).

A further key aspect of relational space is the way in which external (including international) influences shape local political space in Africa, a subject on which relatively little published research exists despite the long history of such processes (Howard 2010). In an intriguing comment in his classic study of Haalpulaar villages in Senegal, Schmitz (1994: 429) notes how territory has been '*déstructuré*' (destructured) over time by outmigration. The growing economic significance of the diaspora in remitting money for livelihoods and development in the village has rendered its relationships with its neighbours less important, making each village increasingly autonomous. In Nigeria, Van den Bersselaar (2005) also observes the role of the diasporic community in shaping the spatial form of the village, a process similarly noted in neighbouring Cameroon down to sub-village level (Evans 2010). Beyond the diaspora, however, less consideration is given to the role of external forces in local politico-spatial dynamics as such. On the other hand, research has clearly shown the influence of the international development industry on local associational and community life in Africa (among others, Mercer 2002; Kelsall and Mercer 2003; Fanthorpe and Maconachie 2010).

In sum, the close-grained studies identified, particularly from meso-level down to micro-level relationships, for example within a village – tending towards Massey's 'intimately tiny' scale – show how space is made, in a relational sense, in displacement settings in Africa. The processes involved in human displacement are experienced by most people at a local level and play out at a local scale, albeit within larger political and economic spaces and under external, sometimes global influences. The chapter now turns to an account of the case study in question and its geographies of displacement.

The Casamance conflict

Originally one region, Casamance today comprises three administrative regions: Ziguinchor, Sédhiou and Kolda, named for their respective capitals. Casamance was divided into Ziguinchor and Kolda regions in 1984, and Sédhiou region formed out of part of Kolda region in 2008. In popular parlance, and particularly in relation to the conflict, though, 'Casamance' is still described as one territorial unit. The contemporary violence there originated in Casamançais discontent with the Senegalese administration in the 1970s and early 1980s (Evans 2004), culminating in the Mouvement des forces démocratiques de la Casamance (MFDC) demanding independence for Casamance from Senegal. The MFDC has since continued to make this demand on the basis of essentially the same grievances. These include poor governance from Dakar (the national capital, situated in northern Senegal), purported deliberate under-development of Casamance, and high-handedness and abuses by northern Senegalese administrators and traders (referred to pejoratively as '*nordistes*') operating there. The latter behaviour is related partly to cultural differences between Casamance and the north. Crucially, the separatists also make the still-disputed claim that Casamance had full political autonomy during colonial times. In their view, the incorporation of Casamance into the independent Republic of Senegal in 1960 is thereby open to legal challenge.

In 1982 and 1983, this discontent was mobilized in protest marches in Zigu-inchor, capital of the then-unified Casamance region. Though largely peaceful in intent, the marches prompted increasingly oppressive and violent reactions from the Senegalese authorities. There were over a hundred arrests following the first march in 1982. At the second in 1983, Senegalese forces fired on protest-ers with live rounds, killing between 50 and 200 people; they then pursued, arrested and harassed many other marchers and their associates. These actions drove the MFDC underground and, faced with ongoing government oppres-sion and seeing no political solution, it procured firearms and launched an insurgency against Senegalese forces in Casamance in 1990. The deployment of the Senegalese army in response led to full-scale militarization of the con-flict. The consequences have included an estimated 3,000–5,000 combat-related deaths, human rights abuses by both sides, and displacement of more than 60,000 people, the majority as IDPs and others as refugees in The Gambia or Guinea-Bissau. The latter country, particularly, has also hosted rear bases for MFDC guerrillas. The conflict has brought severe livelihood problems to many Casamançais as important economic sectors (agriculture, fishing and tourism) have been damaged by the conflict, indeed sometimes deliberately targeted, while foreign aid and investment have at times been withdrawn.

From late 2000 security conditions in Casamance generally improved and continued to do so for much of the following decade. The reasons include greater cooperation from Guinea-Bissau with Senegal vis-à-vis hardline MFDC guerrillas using the former country's territory; re-established if deeply troubled negotiations; exhaustion among the guerrillas; and a huge grassroots desire for peace among Casamançais. However, progress in resolving the conflict as such has proved elusive. The most recent accord between elements of the MFDC and the Senegalese government was signed in December 2004, although this was arguably a public relations exercise to encourage further donor aid while masking structural problems in the peace process. Negotiations between the government and multiple MFDC elements, envisaged in the 2004 accord, stalled after initial talks in 2005. Only piecemeal contacts continued between the government, in the person of President Abdoulaye Wade or his emissaries, and self-appointed interlocutors for particular MFDC factions. The election of Macky Sall to the Senegalese presidency in March 2012 has brought a different approach to the conflict, but it remains to be seen to what extent this translates into changes on the ground. In the meantime, the 2004 accord has not brought a sustainable peace, much like other failed ceasefires and agreements in the 1990s, and sporadic violence continues at the time of writing.

Geographies of displacement in the Guinea-Bissau border zone

Most of Ziguinchor region, the westernmost part of Casamance and original epicentre of the rebellion, has been affected by the conflict in some way, and from the mid-1990s onwards the violence spread eastward into areas of what is now Sédhiou region. There have, broadly speaking, been marked differences between the dynamics north and south of the Casamance river. In the 1990s, districts south of the river – the focus of the chapter – were most heavily affected by violence and displacement, particularly rural areas along the Guinea-Bissau border and extending to outer suburbs and satellite villages of Ziguinchor, situated on the river's south bank (Evans 2005, 2007). Much of this violence was perpetrated by MFDC guerrillas of the Front Sud acting from their rear bases in Guinea-Bissau, with various motives. First, they aimed to extend their territorial control into Casamance for political purposes and to be in a stronger position to attack Senegalese forces. Secondly, violence was used as a terror tactic against civilians who refused to participate in or otherwise support the rebellion. And thirdly, it was used for economic purposes: while not a primary motivation, emptying villages of their populations enabled guerrillas to take the belongings and livestock of the displaced, and in the longer term to harvest their orchard crops, all of which they could consume, sell or exchange to support their livelihoods and war effort (Evans 2003a). By contrast, north of the Casamance river, again in Ziguinchor region and certain neighbouring parts of Sédhiou region, a different but no less troubled history has unfolded. This is not considered here beyond noting that violence in the area in the 2000s and into the 2010s has periodically displaced rural people into The Gambia. This physical dislocation has mostly been temporary in character although recent years have seen a trend towards more permanent settlement by refugees (Evans and Ray 2013).

Long-term human displacement in Casamance shows various characteristics (Evans 2007). First, in terms of scale, any figures can only be approximate but a census carried out in 1998 by Caritas gave a total of over 62,000 IDPs and refugees. Figures specifically for refugees (in Guinea-Bissau and The Gambia) have tended to gravitate around ten thousand, indicating that most displacement has been internal. Secondly, displacement has shown a clear spatial concentration related to the geography of the conflict. Ziguinchor region (unsurprisingly as the main area affected by violence) accounts for around 70 per cent of the Caritas figure, but the great majority of this (63 per cent of the total) is in Ziguinchor department,[2] lying between the Casamance river and the Guinea-Bissau border in south-eastern Ziguinchor region. Most of the remaining 30 per cent has been displaced from the contiguous part of The Guinea-Bissau border area in what is now Sédhiou region. Other data indicate that displacement in the border area, while it took place over a number of years, was mostly the result of a few events that displaced people (often whole village populations) en masse. Fighting that took place in 1992 may alone have displaced tens of thousands. For example, one rural community[3] in Ziguinchor department ultimately saw some 60 per cent of its total population of 7,000 displaced, mostly in that one year (Evans 2007).

A third important feature of displacement in Casamance is that people have often moved only short distances: into larger towns along the south bank of the river, across borders into neighbouring areas of Guinea-Bissau and The Gambia, or even into the more secure cores of villages from peripheral quarters (Evans 2005, 2007). Many refugees in The Gambia, in particular, situate themselves sufficiently close to their home areas so that they can 'commute' across the border to maintain farms and social relations in Casamance (Evans and Ray 2013). Fourthly, while reception centres and camps have received IDPs and refugees, the vast majority of those displaced in Casamance have self-settled, often with kinsfolk at least in the first instance (Evans 2007; Evans and Ray 2013). Overall, then, the dynamics of displacement reflect the confined area in which the conflict has unfolded, its complex local geographies, and the social relations of those affected within Casamance and across its borders (Evans 2003b; Foucher 2007).

These geographies continue to evolve. The Guinea-Bissau border zone was generally calmer in the 2000s, although not immune to attacks, sometimes particularly brutal, against soldiers and civilians. These have mostly been attributed to (relatively rare) breakdowns in communication between returning civilian populations, the bodies facilitating return (the army, rural councils and local NGOs) and MFDC guerrillas operating in the area. However, more serious violence between the Senegalese army and MFDC guerrillas broke out in the border area in August 2009, eventually reaching the environs of Ziguinchor itself. By September the fighting had prompted the displacement of hundreds of civilians, who sought refuge mostly in the town's interior. Many of those affected returned home after a few days or weeks but others took longer (IRIN 2010), despite the army eventually, in early 2010, dislodging the guerrilla elements concerned. These events were significant in that they caused the first new human displacement south of the Casamance river in over a decade, and underlined the death of the peace process as such. The run-up to presidential elections in Senegal in early 2012 again saw violence flare up across Ziguinchor region (IRIN 2012).

The extent to which the renewed violence of recent years may slow return to the Guinea-Bissau border zone is unclear. However, it seems unlikely that it will do so in the longer term, given the considerable momentum that has built up over the past decade, and that earlier occasional attacks in the area had little lasting effect. From a situation of protracted displacement in the 1990s, the 2000s saw an initially tentative but increasingly sustained dynamic of return, which still continues.

Return in the border zone

Various dimensions of the return dynamic are now discussed in terms of the relational spaces produced. Considered first is how the reoccupation and exploitation by villagers of habitable and agricultural lands have had to accommodate ongoing security concerns (risks of attack, robbery and landmines) as well as an overgrown landscape and wrecked infrastructure. Secondly, and related, how new patterns of land tenure are constructed and contested in the return setting. Thirdly, how the relationship between rural and urban livelihoods is developing, a product of current strategies among returnees aimed at minimizing economic and security risks and of a longer history of rural–urban migration in the area. And fourthly, how the spaces of village life are affected by social change, driven by an apparently younger demographic among returnees after years away.

Security, insecurity and new patterns of settlement Return in the border zone has, like displacement, been characterized by complex dynamics operating across relatively confined areas. In 2001, the process saw a small but symbolically important start when IDPs displaced in 1997 from Kandialan Diola, a peripheral suburb of Ziguinchor, began to return there from their places of refuge in safer quarters of the town (Evans 2005). This process continued, with a 'return frontier' (Evans 2009: 514) moving outward into rural areas. Initially it covered other relatively secure settings along the western stretch of the Ziguinchor–Kolda road, which follows the south bank of the Casamance river, with return then extending southward to zones of previous large-scale displacement closer to the Guinea-Bissau border. The lead taken by particular displaced families or whole village communities was copied, and return accelerated. If given the opportunity, most IDPs in Ziguinchor or elsewhere in Casamance, and many refugees in neighbouring countries, are keen to quit the economic and social struggles of life in exile and return to their villages (Evans 2007). Again, it is difficult to quantify the scale of return to date but it has probably involved a few tens of thousands of displaced people (augmented by demographic growth in exile), with flows maybe peaking in the mid-2000s. In several cases observed it is notable that, as with their original flight, the majority of the village population has returned more or less together (Evans 2009).

The material landscape faced by returnees is daunting, however. Their villages have all but disappeared into dense forest regrowth. Infrastructure is absent or inadequate, and the local economy remains depressed because of ongoing insecurity, depopulation and difficulties in reopening productive lands and marketing crops. In addition, landmines and guerrillas may still pose deadly hazards. Still, with generally reduced violence in the border zone, several multilateral and bilateral donors and international NGOs began funding reconstruction programmes in Casamance as the 2000s progressed. Some aid is channelled through government bodies and local NGOs, providing roofing materials and sometimes doors and shutters for houses rebuilt mainly by returnees themselves. Aid also funds construction of village amenities including wells, schools, clinics and community centres, as well as other infrastructure including roads, barrages to improve lowland rice cultivation, and farm tracks to facilitate marketing of produce. Yet contrary to the credit taken by the aid community, the return and reconstruction process is still primarily endogenous, with the drive and resources coming mostly from displaced communities themselves (ibid.). Aid usually follows rather than leads the process, although it may still have important instrumental effects on political space.

Reconstruction and rehabilitation of the material landscape take place amid a still-erratic and spatially uneven security environment, despite general improvements over the past decade or so. As in earlier, more difficult times, people's livelihood activities and problems – their relational economic space – reflect complex local articulations between insecurity and other factors, including isolation and environmental and social change (Evans 2005). Two security issues stand out. The first is the ongoing risk of attack or robbery by MFDC guerrillas, as noted above. The second is the risk posed by landmines: in some cases, only villages and their immediate environs are swept for mines prior to return and reconstruction. Outlying areas, including productive lands such as orchards, are left pending more comprehensive demining efforts, although even state authorities now admit that the mine risk in the border zone looks to have been overestimated.[4] Combined with effective 'mine education', this means that the average annual number of casualties has fallen to near-zero in recent years. Still, a few mine accidents have occurred around return villages during this period, and concerns about mines, however exaggerated, understandably continue to define in part people's local space.

The effects of this security environment are most visible in changes in settlement layout in the border zone (Evans 2009). Typically, villages where the population was entirely displaced have adopted more compact shapes (compared with their pre-displacement forms) on return. This is in the interests of collective security against possible attack and to avoid perceived landmine risks in outlying areas. At least one village (Niabina) has been relocated over a short distance to put it more squarely on a road, again for security reasons.

Consolidation has itself been a problematic process, both from the perspective of land tenure and, among certain ethnic groups, in changing long-standing habits of wide separation between houses. In a relational sense, this is not just a simple matter of settlement layout; it is about quotidian spatial activity, whether in interactions with neighbours or in valorizing (or not) agricultural land. Returnees to the village of Mandina Mancagne (close to Ziguinchor), for example, had previously lived in a more dispersed settlement style, where greater separation from their neighbours had allowed them to use surrounding land for toilet purposes. Now they have had to construct pit latrines for their new houses (ibid.). In villages where only part of the population was displaced, and in other relatively more secure settings, different dynamics can be observed. In certain villages, notably Boutoupa-Camaracounda, close to the border in an area heavily affected by the conflict, the opposite to consolidation is occurring. There is notable decompression of village cores in which the population took refuge during the worst of the violence, with people now moving back into previously abandoned peripheral quarters (ibid.).

A sense of liminality is also often evident in return villages in the spatial disjuncture, with economic consequences, between usable land and no-go areas (perceived or real). At Mpak, for example, farming activity around the new quarter to which people returned was at first severely constrained by a very real risk of landmines, with two mine-related deaths of returnees there. On a field visit in 2006, the cultivated area on the quarter's eastern edge stopped abruptly and the field beyond was overgrown; the orchards visible a short distance behind that were similarly inaccessible, much to the frustration of those seeking to derive a livelihood from them (ibid.).

In such contexts, where memories of former violence and ongoing insecurity still haunt the landscape, villagers often gain a sense of collective security from returning as a group. This reflects how the community has often maintained some measure of contact and cohesion even amid the dispersal and stresses of exile. Returnees are sometimes further emboldened by courageous village leadership and moral support from other social structures and mechanisms, including their families and youth associations. Not all the villages studied have shown such solidarities, however, and while in this 'post-conflict' setting people are reluctant to talk about intra-community division, making it difficult to research, it is evident on the ground. Divisions in communities engendered by the conflict itself may create spatial separation on return. The village of Bambadinka, a significant battleground during the 1990s, is noteworthy for the way in which groups of returnees seem to have sought distance from each other and, in some cases, from the army camp there. Disagreements over resources for reconstruction are also sometimes reflected in how people live apart in the return setting. In all these cases, security dynamics (broadly defined) inform the physical shape of settlements and productive lands, which are in turn intimately tied to the relational spaces of economic and social activity.

Land tenure regimes and wrangles Land tenure is also crucial in the return process. Land disputes, while not the root cause of the conflict, formed a major locus for unrest preceding the outbreak of the rebellion in 1982. With this history and amid growing rancorous land disputes across Senegal today, tenure remains an acutely sensitive matter in Casamance. Echoing concerns expressed by the humanitarian community elsewhere, resolving such issues is regarded as key to peace-building (IRIN 2008; Pantuliano 2009). Land disputes are most visible in urban and peri-urban areas of Casamance. The outskirts of Ziguinchor, particularly Kandialan, have proved a contentious area as people return, partly because of already acute competition for farming land in the relatively secure environment provided by the town (Evans 2007) and the livelihood opportunities such spaces offer through 'commuting'.

In the rural setting of the border zone, too, land tenure often proves problematic. In situations where villages were formerly displaced in their entirety and people have now largely returned to their original holdings, or where there have been few supply constraints on customary authorities granting alternative plots to returnees, few problems seem to have arisen. By contrast, cases of village consolidation have necessitated considerable reorganization of holdings. A common pattern observed is where returnees with original holdings in central parts of a village cede plots to those who lived on the outskirts: because outlying areas cannot be accessed owing to landmines or are otherwise deemed insecure, the latter group now needs to construct homes in the centre. This is in practice a challenging scenario: in Mandina Mancagne, for example, the resulting disputes nearly derailed the whole return process and only firm leadership kept it on track (Evans 2009). In villages where only some of the population fled, further problems have arisen when returnees have found that, in their absence, their holdings have been reallocated by the chieftaincy to other villagers or outsiders (ibid.). In rarer cases, people seem less attached to their land. The displaced inhabitants of the village of Saliot, in the Balantacounda area of the border zone of Sédhiou region, are mostly ensconced in their refuges in the nearby town of Djibanar. The Saliot leadership, at least, has no wish to return and indeed has asked for land to be granted to the villagers nearby, from the town's holdings.[5] This reflects a historically shallow association with their original village, the land for which was given to them only in the 1940s, also by the leadership of Djibanar.

Land tenure thus remains a source of local tensions for returnees and again shapes their economic and social spaces: where and how they use their habitable and productive lands. These are not merely technical problems but concern much deeper psychological and social issues and their economic and spatial dimensions. This is relational space writ large by the dynamics of community, history and memory (Massey 2005).

Hedging their bets: evolving urban–rural linkages Other changes in relational space appear in the evolving urban–rural linkages of the return setting. Many returnees keep footholds both in their places of refuge and their home villages, sometimes to maintain ongoing livelihood activities in the former while trying to reconstruct their houses and restart agricultural activities in the latter. In other cases security informs such behaviour: while hoping for continued improvement, returnees are ready for possible deterioration, too. This is evinced by the curious sight of numbers of newly reconstructed but largely unused houses in some return villages (Evans 2009).

Given that very few returnees have their own transport (except maybe bicycles), distance is important in shaping the spaces of such relationships. Where the place of refuge is relatively close to the village of origin, some of the displaced can 'commute', walking to former homes and productive lands by day but returning to safety by nightfall – a widely observed phenomenon in Casamance (Evans 2003b, 2005) as in other situations of insecurity (for example, Dunn 2007). This is particularly evident where IDPs are returning to peripheral quarters from village cores, or to villages from nearby urban centres such as Ziguinchor. In relational terms, 'commuting' means that use of space is subject to particular (usually diurnal) temporalities, again with economic consequences. In earlier fieldwork in Boutoupa-Camaracounda, when it was one of the few villages left occupied in its rural community, use of agricultural land was paradoxically restricted by the presence of the army camp, as soldiers imposed a dusk-to-dawn curfew in the surrounding area. This limited access time to fields and orchards, particularly for the displaced former residents of an outlying quarter, now living in the village centre but still 'commuting' to their lands about two kilometres away during the day. The curfew made it impossible, for example, for farmers to maintain surveillance at times when monkeys were likely to eat crops (Evans 2005). The 'path space' (Barrett 2009) for 'commuters' may itself be insecure, with their journeys entailing risks of unwanted encounters with rebels, soldiers or bandits. Still, this does not prevent some from taking economic advantage of the return setting: in several return villages, even where people are only just starting to 'commute' to open up their lands, the resulting short-term bonanzas of firewood and charcoal are being taken to urban markets by whatever means available (often bicycles again, or hand-pulled carts) as an opportunistic livelihood activity (Evans 2009).

The situation is different in more rural areas of the border zone, farther from any town and where typically several neighbouring villages have been wholly emptied and little is left standing of any of them. Under circumstances where distance renders 'commuting' difficult or to give themselves more cover, time and energy during reconstruction, some returnees construct temporary shelters of wood and leaves, although in a few villages more substantive structures have been provided as part of international aid projects. Returnees visit and even sleep in these so that they can start clearing and revalorizing their lands and rebuilding their houses, despite poor living conditions. Those sleeping in shelters are exposed to the elements, insects and snakes, and the supply of food and water is problematic.

But the longer-term question of how returnees navigate the relationship between town and village life encompasses more than these immediate concerns of security, livelihoods and house construction. It relates to deeper issues, long rehearsed in African studies, about the more fundamental economic and social relationship between the urban and the rural, and what this means for people's sense of 'home' (Mercer et al. 2008). Many of the displaced have a deep-seated sense of affection and belonging in relation to their home villages, perhaps enhanced through years of exile, often in economically and socially desperate circumstances. Yet like many from Casamance, with its history of economic migration to Dakar and other urban centres in northern Senegal and The Gambia, returnees continue to live with the social contradictions and tensions created by longer-distance rural–urban linkages (Foucher 2002; Lambert 2002). Such relationality has long been conceptualized through understandings of multilocal households, with family members dispersed across space but still functioning to some extent within one social unit (Murray 1981). This in turn problematizes the notion of 'displacement' as being a function of conflict alone, or as a one-off occurrence: at the time of such an event (specifically the physical dislocation of people and loss of their houses, lands and other property), many 'villagers' may not have been at home anyway (Evans 2007) and may continue to be absent, as outmigrants, from the return setting in the interests of making a living. 'Displacement' as defined here is thus not happening in isolation, as an aberration in an otherwise sedentary and stable life for those affected. Rather it is situated in more complex, multilayered spaces of mobility, and immobility.

Demographic change and youth opportunity A related issue is demographic change amid displacement and return. It is widely claimed among the displaced that a significant number of older people have died prematurely because of the original displacement event itself or, more commonly, the stresses of exile (Evans 2003b). This is a difficult claim to test, however. Numerous cases of deaths of displaced elders are certainly cited, and the returning population is predominantly a young one, creating pressures on the provision of school services in the reconstruction process in the border zone (Evans 2009). But this must be situated in a demographic context (for Senegal and sub-Saharan Africa more generally) of relatively early death in general and a burgeoning youth population. The UNDP (2013) gives average life expectancy at birth in Senegal at only 59.6 years, while the 2002 national census put 54.9 per cent of the population at less than twenty years old (République du Sénégal 2006). Analytically isolating a 'mortality crisis' due to displacement is therefore hard, although this is not to deny that premature deaths may well have occurred.

Whatever the true demographic situation, the role of youth in the return and reconstruction process is crucial. 'Youth', in Casamance as elsewhere in Africa, is a socially constructed category related not just to biological age but to factors such as marital status, initiation, residency and economic dependency/independence. The picture is complex and fluid, therefore. In Lower Casamance, for example, men typically begin to marry in their mid-thirties (women considerably younger), but in some cases they may still be defined as youth (*jeunes*) for some years while they establish their own households (Evans 2003b). For the purposes of discussion, the term is here used more inductively, in the sense of members of near-ubiquitous village youth associations, which show various degrees of organization, whether formally registered or not. In some villages, youth have been the main drivers of return, partly to help their parents escape the difficult situations of exile, perhaps partly to avoid those situations themselves as they grow up. At times they are certainly also trying to access the benefits of international aid but, while such external forces may be influential (as in other post-conflict settings; see Fanthorpe and Maconachie 2010), interviews also point to the sincere desire of youth to help their communities rebuild. In a context of widespread youth under- and unemployment, a desire for funded development projects and livelihoods is anyway legitimate enough. With only their own resources, youth associations have mobilized to help return through work parties – for example, clearing bush and building houses – and through lobbying the authorities for other support (official approvals, security and logistics).

Yet returning youth populations themselves face particular challenges. Those who fled as children with their parents, or who were born in exile and grew up in town, sometimes struggle in returning to a village that they never knew or scarcely remember, and are reluctant to abandon urban life and amenities. The relationship of youth with the spaces of return is thus different from that of their parents, and their aspirations can reflect this. The need for social activity is evinced in some return villages by the efforts that youth put into carving football pitches out of dense forest regrowth or desires, expressed in interviews, for the construction of youth centres. Such activity is not trivial. The social space of the border zone has been fragmented by displacement: depopulation, isolation of remaining and returning villages, overgrown roads and in some cases continuing security concerns all serve to disconnect communities from each other and reduce opportunities for social as well as economic engagement. Even the local NGO Enfance et Paix, whose projects support children and youth, speaks in terms echoing Schmitz (1994) of zones '*destructurées*' by the conflict: a word suggesting social destabilization and break-up as well as physical loss of infrastructure and services.[6] In this setting, inter-village football tournaments and dances, for example, help form linkages and mobility between youth groups of different villages. This in turn rebuilds confidence, breaking out of Oslender's (2008) 'spaces of confinement', and may lay foundations for future economic and political relationships across the zone. As well as keeping youth entertained and thereby engaged with wider village life, social interaction can help remake relational space across the border zone as it repopulates.

The remaking of political space and its discontents

The chapter now addresses another important dynamic related to the return process in Casamance, namely the remaking of local political space and boundaries. The political and the economic interlink closely and the politico-spatial changes discussed here have material consequences in the border zone. These changes take different forms at different levels and in some cases are subtle and not immediately visible. In some places, they directly reflect new administrative divisions. Elsewhere, instances are found where the relational spaces of real economic, social and political life in the context of displacement do not fit tidily into normative administrative territory, or bear little practical relation to it, or are even in conflict with it. The drivers for reconfigurations of political space are similarly complex. In some cases, long-term political projects underlie this process of remaking. In others, political entrepreneurs (in the sense of creative individuals who broker development and other projects with a mixture of political and economic goals; see Hüsken 2010) seek to take advantage of opportunities provided by return, reconstruction and international aid to reshape space in their favour.

At village level, a striking example of such a process is seen in Mpak, south of Ziguinchor on the Guinea-Bissau border (Evans 2009). The village population was partially displaced and those concerned – mostly living as refugees in Guinea-Bissau – returned to a new, consolidated quarter bringing together people from two formerly displaced ones. Reconstruction, while ultimately successful, was blighted by jealousies and resentment from those who had stayed put in the rump of the village, with little support, against those now coming back with the benefits of international aid. But at local political level, the main issue was that the return quarter established itself as a largely autonomous unit and accessed aid directly, without passing through the village chieftaincy. This quarter gives the strong impression of a village apart. It is geographically separate from the rump of the village and about a kilometre away from the main village square. It manages its own affairs and has direct relationships with NGOs bringing development projects. While the chief of Mpak and some local NGOs involved with the original return project have tried, in interviews, to downplay this autonomy, it is noteworthy that in local government circles in Ziguinchor, the return quarter is spoken of quite openly as a separate village, not as part of Mpak.

Further reconfiguration of local polities is found farther east, in the Balanta-counda area.[7] To understand this process, the original division of Casamance, in 1984, needs to be revisited. This was widely seen as gerrymandering by then-President Abdou Diouf in an attempt to 'isolate' the rebellion in its western epicentre, from where the majority of the MFDC membership – mainly of the Diola ethnic group – was derived; and to undermine separatist claims to whole-Casamance nationalism. Lower Casamance became Ziguinchor region, while Middle and Upper Casamance became Kolda region. Middle Casamance thus remained a neglected space, affected badly by violence at times from the mid-1990s onwards (Evans 2004) but falling outside of the area in which the conflict has been more formally recognized and managed, and to which reconstruction aid has therefore more recently been given. Middle Casamance also remained as one department, Sédhiou, named for its chief town, lying on the north bank of the Casamance river. For people in the Balantacounda and elsewhere in the Guinea-Bissau border zone of the department, this made access to their departmental capital difficult as it involved crossing the river, wide and treacherous in these middle reaches. Many preferred to go to Ziguinchor, more easily accessible via public transport even on the badly degraded main road and much closer than their own regional capital (Kolda). For purposes of public administration, the relational spaces of Balantacounda inhabitants simply did not fit formal political territory.

Becoming a department in its own right was therefore a long-standing political project for the Balantacounda, to give better access to state services and resources and to recognize the area's particular identity. The call for this new department was also possibly driven by the stresses of the conflict, par-ticularly those placed on its largest town, Goudomp. Fieldwork in 2001 found the town cramped and under-resourced for its population, which was swollen with IDPs (Evans 2003b). In 2008, the Balantacounda achieved its long-desired status when Sédhiou department became a region in its own right, between Ziguinchor region and (the now reduced) Kolda region. Within Sédhiou region, new departments were created, including that of Goudomp, effectively a de-partment of the Balantacounda. This was an evident source of pride to the people of Sédhiou town[8] while Goudomp is slowly upgrading its administrative and commercial services in line with its new status as departmental capital. Rural communities in the Balantacounda were also reconfigured, with one rural council's seat moved from Diattacounda – now given urban municipal-ity status – to Simbandi Balante. Rural dwellers in the Balantacounda seem largely pleased with this arrangement as it greatly improves their access to state services south of the river, in Goudomp, Simbandi Balante and nearby Djibanar (the latter is the seat of another rural community). There is also a feeling that local identity – a sense of the Balantacounda as a distinct space – is better recognized.

Not everyone likes the new administrative set-up, however. In Safane, a village in the interior of the Balantacounda, the leadership feels affronted by the move of the seat of their rural community from Diattacounda to Simbandi Balante, on the main Ziguinchor–Kolda road, and not to their village. This is partly rooted in Safane's perceived historical right to this status because it was, in colonial times, a centre of French governance. This is also an unusually well-educated, organized and connected village for the Balantacounda. It has managed to access international aid projects, still sparse in the area, and plans to build a secondary school with support from its home-town association in Paris. But its ambitions to be the seat of the rural community were never going to be realized. Experiences farther west in Ziguinchor region, where such seats have been attacked and staff displaced (Evans 2005), should be acknowledged. As noted above, the village of Boutoupa-Camaracounda, close to the border, is still under army protection and the president of its rural council remains in exile in Ziguinchor, although administrative business is increasingly moving back to the village. In the Balantacounda, moving the seat of a rural community from the main road down to Safane, on the edge of a large forest on the Guinea-Bissau border – regardless of the village's strong identity and sense of manifest destiny – would be risky. However implicitly, the relational spaces of insecurity in the border zone still inform the map of administrative territory.

Other political discontents include those in the MFDC, which contests the new administrative divisions more widely. Separatists more generally point to and play on the extent to which the territorial limits and administrative status of Casamance and political units within it have always been mired in controversy (Diatta 2008). Elements of the MFDC political wing[9] complained that the new Sédhiou region was further 'Balkanization' of Casamance, seeing it as another attempt to wipe the name 'Casamance' from the map and stymie construction of a Casamance national identity. This is perhaps ironic in that, for the MFDC, its own constituency has tended to be a greater problem than the administrative map as such: it has always struggled to escape from being labelled as a predominantly Lower Casamance, Diola movement. But the contestation here represents a further case of how reconfiguration of administrative territory clashes with the separatists' very different understanding of political space, including the historical status of Casamance itself.

The role of global forces in relation to these new administrative divisions is also ambiguous, as these forces may in turn be instrumentalized by local interests for material benefit. In the case of Sédhiou region, another benefit (if not necessarily a driver) of the new administrative set-up may be *coopération decentralisée* (decentralized development aid). In certain western European countries such as France, Spain and Italy, some bilateral aid has been devolved from central government, with regional and sometimes other layers of their local government system giving aid directly to regional and local governments in developing countries. This is quite visible in Casamance, and the ability to access such aid, as well as state resources in general, puts a further premium on a territory being defined as a region or department, a point exploited by political entrepreneurs. One of the architects of Sédhiou region[10] notes that its status provides the juridical basis for it now to canvass for decentralized aid.

The situations considered show how new political spaces may be shaped by relationships at various scales, domestic and external. At Mpak, a new village has been created not by official statute but through a remaking of political structures under the combined influence of local ambition and international aid. It shows how a relational construction of space clashes with normative administrative territory but (in this case) reflects local reality more closely and has clear material consequences. In Middle Casamance, meanwhile, a different process is occurring as administrative territory is being more closely aligned with the realities of relational space, but again with possible benefits from international aid. While Sédhiou region and Goudomp department may bring better access to domestic patronage and external resources, it is important nonetheless to add that recognition of such political spaces in itself has profound symbolic value, especially in a long-neglected area like this.

Conclusion

The lens of relational space (as concept) shows how the Guinea-Bissau border zone of Casamance is constantly being remade. The area is characterized by fewer if more densely populated settlements than before, and poorer social linkages between and sometimes within them. In addition, it exhibits under-valorization of productive resources and patchy political engagement at all levels with and within returning populations. Yet in other ways the situation of returnees shows continuities with the past. In simple physical space, it is mostly existing village sites, fields and orchards which are being opened up by communities that have maintained some social cohesion even during exile. The ongoing adaptability that returnees show in resuming old economic activities and taking up new ones also represents more of a continuum than a break with their previous states, during exile as well as before displacement (Evans 2009). While such activities often occur amid particularly tight constraints in the border zone today, rural livelihoods were never easy and people have to show the same resourcefulness as before.

The border zone furthermore illustrates how contestations, both violent and non-violent, shape space itself, rather than space being a neutral vessel in which they happen. The ever-shifting landscapes of economic, social and political communities observed, and the complexities and ambiguities of history and memory, figure here as they do in other situations of displacement. This messiness and eternal incompleteness is, as Massey (2005) explains, in the very nature of relational space. The case explored also shows the relationships between normative perspectives on displacement and local understandings. Even the large displacement flows that catch the attention of international agencies are still the product of complex articulations between people, their resources (material and social) and the broader context (Lindley 2009) – in Massey's terms again, the sum of many local 'stories-so-far'. The overlaps and mismatches between real, dynamic, lived space and normative political territory are also highlighted here, as they are elsewhere (Retaillé and Walther 2011), when such situations are considered in relational terms. A logic of access to external resources, including state and international aid, may in turn shape political and economic space, from regional down to very local level, as the cases of Sédhiou region and Mpak respectively show. Relationality – stepping outside of the fixed box of physical space – helps us to understand the linkages between the local and the global in these contexts. However, the analysis here shows how the local must also be understood in its own terms – for example, in the sense of local identity seen in the Balantacounda; global forces do not explain everything.

The displacement economies of the area thus reflect complex tensions between fragmentation and new solidarities, and between rupture with the past and evident continuities. They represent an ever-unfolding response to political and social crisis, clearly linked to the Casamance conflict but also not restricted to that dynamic alone, in space or time. And they demonstrate the importance of the local and the contingent: particular historical trajectories matter, as do individuals and their projects, whether courageous, visionary, entrepreneurial, self-serving or everyday. It is all these people's actions, as well as external forces, which continue to remake local space in Senegal's southern borderlands.

Notes

1 The author warmly thanks the many Casamançais who participated in the research. Fieldwork would also not have been possible without the author's assistant, Oumar Badiane, and staff of the local NGO APRAN. The most recent phase of research was kindly funded by a Small Research Grant from the British Academy. The chapter has benefited greatly from feedback from participants at a workshop at the Nordic Africa Institute, Uppsala, in 2009, and from further discussion at the Fourth European Conference on African Studies, also in Uppsala, in 2011. The insightful comments of the editor of this volume, Amanda Hammar, have been greatly valued throughout the writing process. The input of colleagues at the University of Chester, particularly Brenda Garvey and Chris Ribchester, and of Ben

Page at University College London, are also gratefully acknowledged.

2 Following the French model, a department is an administrative division within a region.

3 An administrative division comprising a collection of neighbouring villages and run by a rural council.

4 Interview with an officer of the national demining agency, Ziguinchor, 3 August 2009.

5 Interview, Djibanar, 14 July 2009.

6 Garvey, personal communication, 9 August 2010.

7 Much of this discussion is based on interviews conducted during fieldwork in the Balantacounda in July 2009, unless otherwise indicated.

8 Garvey (who was conducting fieldwork in Sédhiou town at the time), personal communication, 11 June 2009.

9 Interview, Ziguinchor, 31 July 2009.

10 Interview, Ziguinchor, 18 July 2010.

References

Barrett, M. (2009) 'The social significance of crossing state borders: home, mobility and life paths in the Angolan–Zambian borderland', in S. Jansen and S. Löfving (eds), *Struggles for Home: Violence, Hope and the Movement of People*, Oxford: Berghahn, pp. 85–108.

Black, R. and M. Sessay (1997) 'Forced migration, land-use change and political economy in the forest region of Guinea', *African Affairs*, 96(385): 587–605.

— (1998) 'Forced migration, natural resource use and environmental change: the case of the Senegal River Valley', *International Journal of Population Geography*, 4(1): 31–47.

Diatta, O. (2008) *La Casamance: essai sur le destin tumultueux d'une région*, Paris: Harmattan.

Dunn, K. C. (2007) 'Uganda: the Lord's Resistance Army', in M. Bøås and K. C. Dunn (eds), *African Guerrillas: Raging against the Machine*, London: Lynne Rienner, pp. 131–49.

Engel, U. and P. Nugent (eds) (2010a) *Respacing Africa*, Leiden: Brill.

— (2010b) 'Introduction: the spatial turn in African Studies', in U. Engel and P. Nugent (eds), *Respacing Africa*, Leiden: Brill, pp. 1–9.

Englund, H. (1996) 'Waiting for the Portuguese: nostalgia, exploitation and the meaning of land in the Malawi–Mozambique borderland', *Journal of Contemporary African Studies*, 14(2): 157–72.

— (1999) 'The self in self-interest: land, labour and temporalities in Malawi's agrarian change', *Africa*, 69(1): 139–59.

Evans, M. (2003a) 'Ni paix ni guerre: the political economy of low-level conflict in the Casamance', in S. Collinson (ed.), *Power, Livelihoods and Conflict: Case Studies in Political Economy Analysis for Humanitarian Action*, Humanitarian Policy Group Report no. 13, London: Overseas Development Institute, pp. 37–52.

— (2003b) 'The Casamance, Senegal: "war economy" or business as usual?', Unpublished PhD thesis, King's College, University of London.

— (2004) 'Senegal: Mouvement des forces démocratiques de la Casamance (MFDC)', Africa Programme Armed Non-State Actors Project Briefing Paper no. 2, London: Chatham House.

— (2005) 'Insecurity or isolation? Natural resources and livelihoods in Lower Casamance', *Canadian Journal of African Studies*, 39(2): 282–312.

— (2007) '"The suffering is too great": urban internally displaced persons in the Casamance conflict, Senegal', *Journal of Refugee Studies*, 20(1): 60–85.

— (2009) 'Flexibility in return, reconstruction and livelihoods in displaced villages in Casamance, Senegal', *GeoJournal*, 74(6): 507–24.

— (2010) 'Primary patriotism, shifting identity: hometown associations in Manyu division, South West Cameroon', *Africa*, 80(3): 397–425.

Evans, M. and C. Ray (2013) 'Uncertain ground: The Gambia and the Casamance conflict', in A. Saine, E. Ceesay and E. Sall (eds), *State and Society in The Gambia since Independence*, Trenton, NJ: Africa World Press, pp. 247–87.

Fanthorpe, R. and R. Maconachie (2010) 'Beyond the "crisis of youth"? Mining, farming, and civil society in post-war Sierra Leone', *African Affairs*, 109(435): 251–72.

Foucher, V. (2002) 'Les "évolués", la migration, l'école: pour une nouvelle interprétation de la naissance du nationalisme casamançais', in M. C. Diop (ed.), *Le Sénégal Contemporain*, Paris: Karthala, pp. 375–424.

— (2007) 'The resilient weakness of Casamançais separatists', in M. Bøås and K. C. Dunn (eds), *African Guerrillas: Raging against the Machine*, London: Lynne Rienner, pp. 171–97.

Gale, L. A. (2006) 'Sustaining relationships across borders: gendered livelihoods and mobility among Sierra Leonean refugees', *Refugee Survey Quarterly*, 25(2): 69–80.

Harvey, D. (2005) 'Space as a keyword', in N. Castree and D. Gregory (eds), *David Harvey: A Critical Reader*, Oxford: Blackwell, pp. 270–93.

Howard, A. M. (2010) 'Actors, places, regions, and global forces: an essay on the spatial history of Africa since 1700', in U. Engel and P. Nugent (eds), *Respacing Africa*, Leiden: Brill, pp. 11–44.

Hüsken, T. (2010) 'The neo-tribal competitive order in the borderland of Libya and Egypt', in U. Engel and P. Nugent (eds), *Respacing Africa*, Leiden: Brill, pp. 170–205.

IRIN (2008) 'Finding incentives for peace in Casamance', Integrated Regional Information Networks, United Nations Agency for the Co-ordination of Humanitarian Affairs, 25 June, www.irinnews.org/Report.aspx?ReportId=78944.

— (2009) 'Analysis: Closer to war than to peace in Casamance?', Integrated Regional Information Networks, United Nations Agency for the Co-ordination of Humanitarian Affairs, 18 September, www.irinnews.org/Report.aspx?ReportId=86217.

— (2010) 'Ousmane Goudiaby, "Even if one is afraid, one has no choice"', Integrated Regional Information Networks, United Nations Agency for the Coordination of Humanitarian Affairs, 3 February, www.irinnews.org/HOVReport.aspx?ReportId=87984.

— (2012) 'No end in sight to Casamance conflict', Integrated Regional Information Networks, United Nations Agency for the Coordination of Humanitarian Affairs, 17 February, www.irinnews.org/Report.aspx?ReportId=94895.

Kelsall, T. and C. Mercer (2003) 'Empowering people? World Vision and "transformatory development" in Tanzania', *Review of African Political Economy*, 30(96): 293–304.

Lambert, M. C. (2002) *Longing for Exile: Migration and the making of a translocal community in Senegal, West Africa*, Portsmouth, NH: Heinemann.

Leach, M. (1992) *Dealing with Displacement: Refugee–host relations, food and forest resources in Sierra Leonean Mende communities during the Liberian influx, 1990–91*, Brighton: Institute of Development Studies.

Lindley, A. (2009) 'Leaving Mogadishu: the war on terror and displacement dynamics in the Somali regions', *A Micro Level Analysis of Violent Conflict*, MICROCON Research Working Paper no. 15, Brighton: Institute of Development Studies.

Massey, D. (2005) *For Space*, London: Sage.

McGregor, J. (1997) 'Staking their claims: land disputes in southern Mozambique', Land Tenure Center Paper no. 158, Madison: University of Wisconsin.

— (1998) 'Violence and social change in a border economy: war in the Maputo hinterland, 1984–1992', *Journal of Southern African Studies*, 24(1): 37–60.

Mercer, C. (2002) 'Deconstructing development: the discourse of Maendeleo and the politics of women's participation on Mount Kilimanjaro', *Development and Change*, 33(1): 101–27.

Mercer, C., B. Page and M. Evans (2008) *Development and the African Diaspora: Place and the politics of home*, London: Zed Books.

Murray, C. (1981) *Families Divided: The impact of migrant labour in Lesotho*, Cambridge: Cambridge University Press.

Oslender, U. (2008) 'Another history of violence: the production of "geographies of terror" in Colombia's Pacific Coast Region', *Latin American Perspectives*, 35(5): 77–102.

Pantuliano, S. (ed.) (2009) *Uncharted Territory: Land, conflict and humanitarian action*, Rugby: Practical Action in association with the Overseas Development Institute, London.

République du Sénégal (2006) *Résultats du troisième recensement général de la population et de l'habitat du Sénégal (RGPHIII) 2002: rapport national de présentation*, Dakar: Agence Nationale de la Statistique et de la Démographie.

Retaillé, D. and O. Walther (2011) 'Spaces of uncertainty: a model of mobile space in the Sahel', *Singapore Journal of Tropical Geography*, 32(1): 85–101.

Schapendonk, J. (2010) 'Staying put in moving sands: the stepwise migration process of sub-Saharan African migrants heading north', in U. Engel and P. Nugent (eds), *Respacing Africa*, Leiden: Brill, pp. 113–38.

Schmitz, J. (1994) 'Cités noires: les républiques villageoises du Fuuta Tooro (Vallée du fleuve Sénégal)', *Cahiers d'Études africaines*, 133–5(XXXIV/1–3): 419–60.

UNDP (2013) *Human Development Report 2013. The rise of the south: human progress in a diverse world*, New York: United Nations Development Programme.

UNHCR (2011) *Global Trends 2010*, Geneva: United Nations High Commissioner for Refugees.

Unruh, J. D. (1998) 'Land tenure and identity change in postwar Mozambique', *GeoJournal*, 46(2): 89–100.

Unruh, J. D. and J. Bailey (2009) 'Management of spatially extensive natural resources in postwar contexts: working with the peace process', *GeoJournal*, 74(2): 159–73.

Unruh, J. D., N. C. Heynen and P. Hossler (2003) 'The political ecology of recovery from armed conflict: the case of landmines in Mozambique', *Political Geography*, 22(8): 841–62.

Van den Bersselaar, D. (2005) 'Imagining home: migration and the Igbo village in colonial Nigeria', *Journal of African History*, 46(1): 51–73.

4 | The paradoxes of class: crisis, displacement and repositioning in post-2000 Zimbabwe

Amanda Hammar

Introduction[1]

Zimbabwe's independence in 1980 introduced important if limited openings for racial repositioning and class restructuring. At the same time, in the decades leading up to 2000, increasing austerity that followed the introduction of structural adjustment in 1990, and growing political competition, generated a range of contestations in both rural and urban areas. These were related to new dynamics of exclusion and narrowing access to social, economic, political and symbolic resources. Since the early 2000s, a combination of party-political violence (primarily but not exclusively by ZANU-PF), targeted mass physical removals in both rural and urban areas (much of it state generated), 'indigenization' policies and the broader dislocating effects of structural violence, have dramatically altered 'the economy'. Formal and informal, licit and illicit: economic spheres at national, local, household and individual levels have all been affected in often paradoxical ways. Among other things, 'class' itself has been remade in the furnace of sustained crisis, displacement and uncertainty, which conditions have simultaneously generated new forms and spaces of opportunity.

Severe economic decline in the 2000s, closely linked to the violent and partisan politics of exclusion during this period, led to estimations of formal unemployment having reached over 90 per cent in 2009. Even if more recent estimates are around 70 per cent,[2] the 'working class' – in the classic sense of formally employed factory workers, mineworkers, agricultural labour, transport workers and so on – has notably diminished. This is not the same as saying the majority are 'not working', only that formally waged labour has declined significantly. Informal and often unpredictable work, particularly in urban areas, is how a large majority of Zimbabweans at home have continued to survive, although remittances have played an important if uneven part too for many (Tevera et al. 2010). Millions of others who have crossed the borders survive 'informally' too in neighbouring countries (see, for example, Derman and Kaarhus 2013). This, together with other political factors, has affected labour organizing and the trade union movement more generally.[3]

At the same time, the once-high social value and real financial advantages associated with having a formal sector job have been superseded by the growing status of successful 'wheeler-dealers' working the shift-shaping spaces of an ever-widening shadow economy (Jones 2010; Musoni 2010; Kamete 2012). In turn, many of those (black and white) previously occupying the now shrinking middle class saw their savings vanish as well as their skills and other assets dwindle in value, turning daily life for many, particularly the elderly, into a noticeable struggle. But particularly as the crisis worsened in the mid-2000s, many white-collar professionals such as teachers, nurses and other civil servants – whose children may once have had opportunities to reach university – were forced to become cross-border traders or sex workers to keep families fed. Those professionals who could find formal jobs elsewhere (or even those who couldn't) left and joined a burgeoning diaspora across the globe (McGregor and Primorac 2010). Yet there have been signs of some (uneven) regeneration for professionals at least in certain spaces and sectors (Chagonda 2012), especially since 'dollarization' of the economy in 2009.[4]

Specifically in rural areas, there have been radical changes to the composition and status of those occupying and/or working the land, and to wealth and property distribution overall. The land invasions and subsequent reform process initiated in the early 2000s physically dislocated thousands of white commercial farmers and hundreds of thousands of black farm workers. At the same time they produced new patterns of redistribution and settlement, reversing a historically white-dominated commercial farming monopoly and replacing it with a much more varied spread of primarily black farmers: with 70 per cent of the former commercial farming land now being farmed by small-scale farmers, 13 per cent by middle-scale farmers and 11 per cent by large farms and estates (Moyo 2011, cited in Solidarity Peace Trust 2013).[5] Many of the evicted white commercial farmers – of diverse socio-economic status, despite being viewed generically as occupying the upper echelons of the 'landowning' classes – had to remake themselves in countless new guises and localities. Often they had to start again from scratch either in Zimbabwe or elsewhere (see, for example, Hammar 2010, 2013; Mustapha 2011; Sjaastad et al. 2013).

In other spheres, the increasing absence or deliberate blurring of enforceable regulations post-2000 turned some illegal gold panners and foreign currency dealers – and later, diamond miners – into multiple car and home owners almost overnight (see, for example, Mawowa and Matongo 2010).[6] ZANU-PF party loyalists in particular benefited from a combination of new indigenization rules on the one hand, and the disregard of existing laws and business ethics on the other, joining a small yet growing wealthy elite. All this provides a spotlight on new alignments of class with politics, *contra* earlier eras when overlaps between class and race were more significant.

This chapter draws on various studies in Zimbabwe during the 2000s to reflect on the ways in which differentiation is unfolding more broadly in the context of displacement and chronic crisis, and what this means for old and new forms of resource access, livelihood and accumulation.

Logics of accumulation and dispossession

In February 2010, BBC journalist Sue Lloyd-Roberts visited Philip Chiyangwa, Zimbabwean millionaire businessman and nephew of Robert Mugabe, in his opulent mansion in Harare.[7] In a videoed interview, Mr Chiyangwa talked confidently of owning over two thousand companies, and noted how well he had done 'without having to leave Zimbabwe'. This was a clear reference to the contentious 'targeted sanctions' imposed by the British and American governments and the European Union on President Mugabe and many of his close party and business allies. The regime used this to blame 'the West' more widely for the country's deep economic crisis and continued impoverishment.[8] Later in the same news video we see Lloyd-Roberts being shown around the family's collection of cars by Mrs Chiyangwa. We see a Bentley, a Rolls-Royce, a Mercedes and various sports cars, all with personalized number plates.

With studied neutrality Lloyd-Roberts asks Mrs Chiyangwa whether she's comfortable with all this wealth while there are so many people starving in the country. Mrs Chiyangwa replies with the conviction and gratitude of a born-again Christian: 'These things are God-given blessings,' she says. 'So that if God blesses you with something, you have to be grateful. I know there are people starving, but these are the blessings from God. And I do appreciate what God has done for us.' Yet these were far from generally blessed times in Zimbabwe. One might wonder, then, who constituted 'God' in this not uncommon narrative of benefaction among those of Zimbabwe's ruling elite who have remained conscientiously loyal to Robert Mugabe, who has led both ZANU-PF and the country since independence in 1980.[9] Within this same metaphor, one might equally wonder whether this could be the same God that, by contrast, *failed* to bless many millions of displaced Zimbabweans both inside and outside its borders, struggling daily with poverty and various forms of violence, vulnerability, dislocation or immobility.[10]

Such musings among Zimbabwe's new elite about godly magnanimity might well aim to deflect more critical analyses of the extreme unevenness in asset and wealth accumulation since 2000. Yet they provide one entry point into reflecting upon the reshaping of class in this paradoxical era of simultaneous wealth destruction and creation. Somewhat perversely, these references to 'God-given blessings' evoke questions about the *logics of accumulation* more generally in contemporary Zimbabwe. These are counterposed with (and often legitimized by) *logics of dispossession and exclusion*.[11] Of course, this mutually constitutive pairing of logics has a much older provenance. It long underpinned legitimations of forced removals and the appropriation of land and other resources by colonizers and settler minorities (Alexander 2006), as well as by the post-independence state (Hammar 2001). Numerous displacement-inducing projects by consecutive state authorities in Zimbabwe, as elsewhere, have been represented as being in the service of 'progress' and 'development', or of political sovereignty, while often masking far narrower projects of partisan and private accumulation (Hammar 2008a).

In post-2000 Zimbabwe, these patterns have been played out most explicitly through populist nationalist rhetoric employed by ZANU-PF and its allies inside and outside the state. National liberation discourses have been used effectively to explain and justify the 'reclaiming of lost lands' from white commercial farmers, albeit with mass dislocating effects for the majority of black farm workers (Sachikonye 2003; Magaramombe 2010). They have also been used to legitimize moves to 'indigenize' businesses more widely. This policy, informed by 'black/indigenous empowerment' principles, not only aims explicitly to exclude white Zimbabweans but (less explicitly) opposition supporters. In effect it has frightened off at least some major investors. Similarly, the extensive political violence meted out by ZANU-PF loyalists and state security agents with impunity against actual or suspected opposition supporters has been cast in terms of an anti-imperialist purge of 'enemies' of the nation (read enemies of ZANU-PF). Such practices were only marginally reduced after the formation of the Government of National Unity in 2009. This political persecution, together with sustained structural violence, compelled millions of rural and urban Zimbabweans to move across the borders for longer or shorter periods (Hammar et al. 2010).

Sometimes, somewhat ironically, notions of maintaining law and order have been employed by the ZANU-PF-dominated party-state to obscure partisan logics of accumulation and dislocation (Hammar 2008b). Thus, for example, discourses of illegality and of dirt and disease were used in 2005 to legitimize mass physical urban evictions (Vambe 2010; Harris 2008). These evictions were widely interpreted as retaliatory against the urban opposition vote against ZANU-PF in the 2005 parliamentary elections. However, the wider campaign included 'confiscating' money and goods, as well as appropriating spaces of mostly informal production and trade from local entrepreneurs (Bratton and Masunungure 2007; Musoni 2010; Mawowa and Matongo 2010).

Within the post-2000 discursive framings of belonging to the 'new' Zimbabwe, race, political loyalty and sometimes class have been key and often overlapping markers used to distinguish between different (unofficial) categories of citizen. These have ranged from super-citizen to non-citizen (Hammar 2003). In the wake of the 2013 elections, newly re-elected President Mugabe implied that those in urban areas who had voted for the opposition were in fact not included as national citizens entitled to the provisions and protections of the national state, but rather (outcast) urban citizens who should turn to their 'own' political parties for their needs. Such partisan politicized categorizing, sometimes literally through violent markings on the bodies of the unwanted, has had very real material effects. For some it has generated preferential access to the means of livelihood and accumulation, and the selective exclusion and dispossession of others.

Among the major effects of this evolving regime of distinction has been the emergence of new and closely protected enclaves of excessive wealth on the one hand (Davies 2004), and wide-scale impoverishment on the other.[12] Yet between the most absolute extremes lies a diverse majority faced with radical changes and chronically unpredictable shifts in almost all spheres of their lives. For those caught in this fluid environment where no foothold is certain for long, an uneven and fairly unstable remix of class positions is being generated, alongside redefinitions of age, gender and race (Jones 2010 and this volume). Yet under such fractured conditions, former social dynamics, identities and relations do not disappear entirely. Indeed, maintaining if not reinforcing them may be crucial to sustaining basic survival in some cases or opening new doors in others. But for the overwhelming majority of Zimbabweans, whether at home or in the ever-expanding diaspora, new ways have had to be found to generate livelihoods while trying to establish some level of belonging and security.[13]

Elsewhere I have discussed aspects of the party-state's political project of asserting hegemony and sovereign power in which, I have argued, state-generated displacement has been central (Hammar 2008b).[14] In the present discussion I am concerned primarily with what Chris Cramer (2006) terms 'trajectories of accumulation', and the relationship these have to altering class positions in a context of displacement and chronic crisis such as characterizes contemporary Zimbabwe. Clearly, actors at all levels are always engaged in some way with processes of accumulation from 'above' or 'below', be these business elites, political parties, military officers, emerging farmers, teachers, bureaucrats or informal urban entrepreneurs. Yet what we have seen since 2000 are dramatic changes in *patterns and practices* of access, distribution and exclusion that have affected both individual and collective trajectories of accumulation, and investment. I argue here that the relationship between changing trajectories and practices of accumulation, and class repositionings, is both shaped by and implicated in not only the targeted mass removals – whether termed 'land reform' or 'urban clean-up' – but also the chronic forms of structural and symbolic displacements since 2000.

Thinking about class and capital in the 'new' Zimbabwe

For the purposes of this discussion, I am using a very broad sociological notion of social class: as that which distinguishes structurally as well as symbolically differentiated positions, and dispositions, of particular socio-economic groups.[15] There is no intention here to revisit old debates on class,[16] either sociological or political, or to pit structuralist against post-structuralist thinking. Both have valuable insights to offer on questions of social and economic distinction and differentiation and consequent modes of exclusion. Rather, the aim is to explore how a broad notion of class might help us think about the ways in which conditions of crisis and displacement alter different actors' relationships to ownership or control of resources, their access to the means of livelihood and security, and their respective abilities (and space) to actively create and lay claim to the future. Among other things, class acts as a prompt for some fundamental questions about who has lost and gained what during this period of crisis and displacement in Zimbabwe. It helps investigate who has *replaced* those displaced, and how, where and why has this been possible; and what are the key effects for social and economic life at different scales of these shifts in position/disposition.

While thinking about class, however, one is drawn to reflect to some extent on capital, capital accumulation and even capitalism. In relation to the emergence of an excessively wealthy, mostly partisan elite in the post-2000 era, Rob Davies (2004) makes a critical distinction between a process of 'capitalist accumulation' and what he calls 'simple private wealth accumulation'. Had the former occurred as such, he suggests, this would have signified the development of a new capitalist class in Zimbabwe, interested in economic growth more generally. However, it is the latter, he argues (and bemoans), which largely characterizes the form of 'unproductive' accumulation among the newly enriched in the post-2000 context of crisis. While the classic idea of capitalist accumulation is associated with a certain modernist tale of 'progress', the dominant pattern of simple wealth accumulation Davies observed implies a somewhat different relationship of this new owning/acquisitive class to ideas of and investments in 'the future'.

In a related vein, Dawson and Kelsall (2011) identify the present era in Zimbabwe as one of 'anti-developmental patrimonialism'. This speaks to the relationship between forms of state-facilitated rent acquisition and management, modes of governance, and economic growth. They identify a range of actors – including business elites, the military leadership, war veterans, bureaucrats and ordinary citizens – who they claim have manipulated and gained access to resources by making particular use of the chaos of crisis, and of the speculative opportunities it has afforded (see also Bracking, this volume). This occurs, they suggest, alongside preferential treatment through combined ZANU-PF-party and state patronage networks. To be sure, many of the deals and dynamics exhibited in the recent past were already nascent in the early years after independence, intensifying in the 1990s after the introduction of structural adjustment. However, the crudest and most excessive forms of 'unproductive', 'simple wealth accumulation' (Dawson and Kelsall 2011) were largely kept in check – at least up until the mid-1990s – by a fading yet still significant developmentalist policy agenda.[17]

Echoing Davies, Dawson and Kelsall give the impression of an almost wholesale disappearance of productive capital accumulation in the post-2000 period. They talk somewhat simplistically of a 'parasitic' elite accumulating their wealth through crude forms of 'predatory asset-stripping', with little concern for long-term growth let alone shorter-term national development concerns (ibid.). According to their assessment, accumulation through 'rent management'

> is focused on maximum enrichment and regime survival over the short-term. With hyper-inflation, expropriations, and severe property rights instability, it is difficult to imagine a less propitious environment for long-term invest-ment and growth. Regime supporters may currently be able to profit through consumption of natural resource rents, monopoly trading rights, and black marketeering, but these income flows are not sustainable, let alone expanding. (Ibid.: 27)[18]

While these kinds of characterizations of a significant portion of the new elite are hard to dispute, the picture is rather more complex and varied than this. One cannot argue, for example, that all those in ZANU-PF or among the new party-affiliated elite subscribe to the same principles of (coercive) accumulation (Sachikonye 2011). In fact part of the tension within the party is linked to contesting factions that at times have seemed to represent quite different logics and trajectories of accumulation. Alongside an observed trend of 'accumulation without production', or a short-term interest in 'regime main-tenance', one faction could be said to have more classic 'capitalist' inclinations and hence an interest in an environment that supports 'progress', production and secure investment (Dawson and Kelsall 2011). This latter orientation is often set against the highly influential indigenization position. At times this has manifested itself in public disagreements over the imagined or actual place of white Zimbabweans – and most overtly, white commercial farmers – in Zimbabwe's economic development.[19]

To focus briefly on class distinctions more broadly, one might argue that before 2000 class positions in Zimbabwe were to some degree quite clearly defined. One could talk meaningfully, for example, of a formal, waged 'labour force' in both urban and rural settings. Rural labour refers primarily to agri-cultural farm workers, who were unevenly unionized. One should also note, however, that class differentiation cut across both the communal and old resettlement areas, as well as between these and the historically black small-scale commercial farming areas, the former Native Purchase Areas. Prior to 2000, urban labour in particular was well organized.[20] Although initially bound to the ruling ZANU-PF in the early 1980s, the Zimbabwe Congress of Trade Unions (ZCTU) subsequently asserted its independence from the party and developed stridently into the most significant opposition force prior to the formation of the MDC in 1999. The MDC itself rested on the back of the ZCTU and the then closely allied National Constitutional Assembly (NCA), among other key civic organizations. However, with the decimation of much of the formal economy from 2000 onwards and its intensive informalization, not only did formal sector workers lose jobs, security and status, they also largely lost their labour rights as union members.

At the other end of the spectrum, prior to 2000 one could quite easily identify a class of 'property owners': commercial farmers/landowners, factory owners, mine owners, and so on. Much of this structure had been defined by a colonially inherited nexus of race–class–gender–generation, and this persisted to a large extent well beyond independence. The racialized dimensions of exclusion were challenged with partial success in various sectors in the 1990s through the emergence of a strong and increasingly well-organized indigeniza-tion lobby, in which the aforementioned Philip Chiyangwa played a key role. However, partnership/ownership patterns in many sectors began to change dramatically during the 2000s, and by the end of the decade the landscape had altered radically in favour of black political, military and business elites (Dawson and Kelsall 2011).[21]

With regard to the middle class (in its broadest sense), prior to 2000 there was a noticeable flourishing of white-collar professionals, including bureau-crats, teachers, nurses, doctors, lawyers, engineers, academics, and so on.[22] This was the group that arguably grew the most overtly and organically after independence, linked both to the 'Africanization' of the civil service (in both central and local government spheres) and the expansion and relatively high quality of education at all levels. It was here perhaps most of all that both race and gender patterns were significantly altered, as formerly white and/or male-dominated employment domains were gradually reconstituted by the entry of and eventual dominance by black men and women. By the time the crisis in Zimbabwe reached its peak in 2008, with hyperinflation calculated at sextillion per cent (ibid.), alongside other manifestations of sustained structural decline, not only workers but even those in middle-class professions such as teachers were literally unable to afford to get to work at all (Chagonda 2012).[23] The only alternative for many was to join the informal sector. This may have brought a certain degree of new-found freedom for some, especially women. However, for countless others, especially men in general and older men in particular, it implied not only the loss of financial stability but also of the respectability and standing that formal sector middle-class jobs had provided or promised.

Following independence in 1980, despite the inherited racial–class structure, the pathways to progress were not entirely rigid. For example, with the expan-sion of free education, the children of factory workers, bus drivers, domestic workers, policemen or even farm workers *could* and did become educated in ways that weren't possible for their parents, and could be upwardly mobile up to a point. But after 2000, a double-sided process began to occur that altered the former avenues to 'a better life'. On the one hand, as already noted, there was an intense narrowing and foreshortening of the routes to wealth accumulation among a relatively small partisan elite closely associated with ZANU-PF – and arguably, since 2009, also associated to some extent with the opposition parties (two MDCs) forming part of the Government of National Unity. On the other hand, new and extreme levels of displacement and impoverishment affected an ever-widening range of ordinary Zimbabweans, not just those already poor and reliant on the informal sector. The inability to make ends meet cut across the full spectrum of those *formally* employed, from factory workers to civil service clerks, to municipal technicians, to teachers, medical personnel, engineers, managers in commerce and industry and so on. Pensioners in particular were badly affected.

All this introduced a degree of socio-economic levelling, including a shared suffering among the (former) middle class, not least across racial divides.[24] This included the shared experience of what Jane Guyer (2007: 409) has described for a quite different setting (the USA) as 'a strange evacuation of the temporal frame of the "near future"'. This is a frame that would 'normally' include

> the reach of thought and imagination, of planning and hoping, of tracing out mutual influences, of engaging in struggles for specific goals, in short, of the process of implicating oneself in the ongoing life of the social and material world that used to be encompassed under an expansively inclusive concept of 'reasoning'. (Ibid.)

Indeed, this sense of evacuation of normality is commonly expressed by Zimbabweans across the board. Experiences of selectively targeted or sustained social and structural displacements, alongside the unravelling of former or expected frameworks of order and predictability, have radically affected not only the actual conditions of the present but the substantive and imaginable terms of 'the future'. Yet, as the following section indicates, general conditions in pre-2000 Zimbabwe had already begun to alter both the assumed and actual trajectories of 'progress' for different social classes.

The political economy of decline in Zimbabwe

The severity and complexity of Zimbabwe's post-2000 political and economic crisis is indisputable. It reached its most intense levels to date in mid to late 2008, when hyperinflation was at its worst and political violence had reached unprecedented extremes. The formal introduction of 'dollarization' in early 2009,[25] accompanying the signing of the Global Political Agreement between ZANU-PF and the two MDC factions, marked a critical turning point, though not an end, to the continuum of crisis.[26]

Yet the patterns of decline at both macro and micro levels were in evidence long before the constitutional referendum in February 2000, commonly recognized as marking the start of 'the crisis'.[27] The decline began at least at the start of the 1990s with the introduction of the Economic Structural Adjustment Programme (ESAP). This heralded a dramatic rise in poverty levels and a general drop in the standard of living for most social classes in Zimbabwe (Gibbon 1995). Many talked sardonically of being 'esapped', while a well-placed few made money out of the shortages or by having access to limited foreign currency including donor finance. Already, the once much-aspired-to government jobs were losing their lustre. The declining value of public sector salaries forced people to moonlight at best or, if necessary, abuse their positions to gain private access to public resources.

This was a period in which public financing was substantially reduced and public services such as health, education and infrastructure declined. There were numerous labour strikes around 1996 and 1997, including strikes by public servants, as well as food riots. The situation worsened in 1997 when Mugabe was compelled by veterans of the national liberation war – a key ZANU-PF constituency, central to the party's political legitimacy – to agree to massive and unaffordable payments of gratuities. Added to this, Zimbabwe entered the war in the Democratic Republic of Congo (DRC) in 1998, costing the country daily fortunes in US dollars that it couldn't afford. External debt rose substantially; this could not be serviced and would later result in Zimbabwe being excluded from access to IMF and other loans.[28]

Inevitably, as already noted, it was also a period in which informalization intensified on many levels. This was particularly notable in areas such as urban housing and in the spaces and forms of work and trade, as well as in ways of doing business in government.[29] At the time, the ZANU-PF party-state allowed and even encouraged informal self-provisioning of housing in the high-density areas, aware that it couldn't fulfil its obligations to provide for its citizens. This would be reversed after 2000. Accusations of violations of formal housing regulations and registration, along with claims of criminality and unsanitary conditions, were used systematically as a pretext for the mass urban eviction campaign of 2005/06, code-named Operation Murambatsvina.[30] For hundreds of thousands of urban dwellers in the high-density areas across the country, years if not decades of determined savings and investment in their homes, in small businesses, in the education of their children – in the possibility of 'getting ahead' in a believable and viable future – were destroyed overnight.

Given the evolution of decline preceding 2000, Zimbabwe's poorer citizens in particular had long been confronted with chronic hardships. Under such conditions, many had begun to develop skills, practices and networks that were no longer reliant, or at least not substantially reliant, on the formal economy, or on the structures and support of an increasingly unreliable and unsympathetic state. Some of this would be important for dealing with the much harder years to come, and may go some way towards explaining the unexpected levels of resilience observed in the post-2000 crisis period. And yet, as emerging empirically based research has begun to demonstrate, a whole new range of skills, defences and adjustments had to be adopted.[31] The latter have included a widespread turn to irregular, informal or illicit practices of survival for a substantial proportion of the population.[32] While necessary, this has made people more vulnerable to the political and economic whims of state authorities. While increasingly 'absent' in the sense of failing to provide for or protect ordinary citizens, such authorities have nonetheless become ominously present in people's everyday lives, not least through intensified (yet often disguised) surveillance. Additionally, they routinely draw on the notion of 'legal infractions' to apply to an ever-widening range of ordinary arenas of life, to punish and/or extract rent from these same citizens for actual or perceived political disloyalties.[33]

For a small minority, this same turn to the informal and illegal – sometimes accompanied by violence or the threat of violence – has led to forms of profiteering that have generated the accumulation of lesser and larger fortunes. Some examples of these are discussed below.

Evolving realms of repositioning

The most overt cases of mostly mass physical dislocation in post-2000 Zimbabwe, precipitated largely by the party-state, include: the extensive evictions of large-scale commercial farmers and farm workers as part of the Fast Track Land Reform Programme (FTLRP), which began in 2000; the mass urban evictions and destruction of informal businesses during Operation Murambatsvina (Vambe 2010) in 2005; the sustained dislocations due to ongoing political threats and violence against mostly MDC opposition supporters in both urban and rural areas; and the wide-scale and multilayered displacement effects, including displacement-in-place, of chronic structural violence in the face of severe economic decline. These key manifestations of displacement since 2000 are connected to one another as well as to much older displacement histories (Hammar 2008a). Collectively they have interrupted, reversed or redirected former patterns of labour, production, exchange and accumulation, and hence also altered class positions. The selected empirical examples below are intended to make more concrete the sense of Zimbabwe's evolving displacement economy.

Agrarian restructuring: new dispensations and relations in commercial farming As already noted, the post-2000 farm occupations and subsequent evictions resulted in the systematic displacement of thousands of white commercial farming families and hundreds of thousands of black farm-working families. While this started off somewhat spontaneously as highly politicized land invasions following the rejection of ZANU-PF's position in a constitutional referendum in February 2000, the subsequent wide-scale evictions were soon dominated, legitimized and directed through the official FTLRP. In the process over 4,500 commercial farms were allocated to approximately 170,000 new farmers, representing a 'massive agrarian restructuring' (Scoones et al. 2012: 503). This dramatic alteration of the spatial, racial, class and gendered landscape produced new kinds of political, economic, social and institutional forms within all land tenure categories (including commercial, former resettlement and communal areas). With regard to land and land use specifically, structures of ownership, the nature of on-farm investment, labour arrangements, scales of production, and the dynamics of marketing all changed. At the same time, social infrastructure and public services in rural areas more generally were severely depleted. Consequently, both the position of public servants and the emergence of parallel modes of authority became more complex and contentious. Social relationships were disrupted equally by politics and poverty, with some old alliances breaking down and new ones surfacing. Families were split up and strained by loss and dislocation, and forced to reconfigure former patterns of provision and responsibility.

In terms of production, although some of the trends have begun to be reversed in recent years, in the first part of the decade there was a significant drop in output of most major crops, a massive loss in domestic as well as foreign currency earnings, and a dramatic rise in food insecurity.[34] Yet Scoones (2008) has argued that even if the statistical production indicators were down for the majority of agricultural commodities, what this reflected was 'the collapse of the old, formal, commercial agricultural economy *but not the whole agricultural economy*, particularly in the smallholder sector' (emphasis added). Now, some thirteen years after the FTLRP was initiated, the picture on the ground is far more mixed than the more common global figures or generalizations would imply (Scoones et al. 2010; Moyo 2011; Matondi 2012). In Masvingo Province in south-west Zimbabwe, for example, after a decade's worth of research in the area, Scoones et al. (2010) have observed a wide range of new relations and dynamics emerging: 'There are now new people on the land, engaged in new forms of economic activity, connected to new markets and carving out a variety of livelihoods' (ibid.: 233). Yet they also recognized that these new socio-economic processes are 'creating new patterns of class, gender and generational differentiation' (ibid.). This is occurring 'within households, between households in a particular place and between sites' (Scoones et al. 2012: 504).

One particularly striking example of changes in Masvingo's agrarian landscape was the fairly radical restructuring of the livestock sector (or 'beef value chain'). The farm evictions in the province and consequent disappearance of most large-scale commercial ranching resulted in a decline in the quality of beef and the collapse of the export beef sector. Instead there has been

> a major transition from a highly concentrated and regulated commodity chain dominated by a few players to a huge diversity of actors at all levels of the commodity chain. This has been accompanied by a decline in state control and management of the market system to a growth in independent, increasingly informal economic activity and entrepreneurialism. (Mavedzenge et al. 2008: 6)

For some observers this more complex and diversified production and marketing system is considered 'haphazard', 'disorganized' and 'chaotic'; a real retreat from order and the neat, safe and narrow routes to 'progress'. For others, even if the market has become less predictable and efficient, it has allowed space for a much wider range of actors at various levels, including intermediaries in the buying and transport arenas.[35] In addition, following on from the liberalization of meat markets in the 1990s, there has been a further mushrooming of private abattoirs as well as local butchery slaughter. This has encouraged local trade in meat that often contravenes veterinary regulations.

One interesting element in this changing market is that several of the evicted white commercial ranchers have managed to maintain significant cattle holdings, albeit under very different conditions. This is done, for example, through lease-grazing on the low-stocked and low-financed new resettlement farms, or through barter arrangements whereby former ranchers provide services to the under-resourced new farmers. These latter include water pumps, veterinary drugs, transport or fuel in return for access to paddocks on their former or others' ranches. Nonetheless, as Mavedzenge et al. (ibid.: 13) note, the old 'social networks on which the markets of the beef industry operate have changed beyond recognition', and entirely new networks and relations have had to be formed. They summarize this particular dimension of change as follows (it is worth quoting at length):

> The pattern prior to 2000 was based on a tight, often racially-defined, integration of a limited number of players who had strong connections, often based on many years of interaction. The white rancher-speculator-abattoir owner/operator chain was one that had developed over the past fifty years, with strong business, friendship and kin relations being the basis of the network, reinforced in turn by a tight, rather insular social milieu centred on the sports and social clubs of regional towns such as Masvingo. Recent events have shattered this social and economic world, often with traumatic consequences for those involved. While in the past white business interacted with African producers and labourers largely on their own terms, this is no longer possible. Both the political and economic conditions have changed so radically that the functioning of the cosy, inward-looking social basis of business and trade is no longer feasible. (Ibid.)

Across the country in Mashonaland West Province, Conrade Zawe (2006) observed unexpected relationships of complementarity and cooperation between former white commercial farmers and new settlers in cooperative irrigation schemes. At Elmly Park Farm, for example, the former white farm owner provided advice on operation and maintenance of the irrigation infrastructure. In addition he supplied the bulk of the farming inputs and services as well as transporting all inputs to the farm and produce to the market (ibid.: 284). Initially the arrangement involved the farmer retrieving a 90 per cent share of the profits in order to repay the investment costs. But the settlers were gradually able to take over many of the activities themselves, and were steadily able to shift the terms of the contract from retaining only 10 per cent, to 60 per cent, and then eventually 100 per cent of yields. At that stage, they were able to make impromptu cash payments to the former farm owner turned service provider for each service rendered.

A slightly different dynamic unfolded on nearby Chifundi Farm, where an Irrigation Cooperative Association had been established by the new settlers, with assistance from the government's agricultural extension service, AREX. Some of the AREX officials themselves became plot holders and association members. The sophisticated irrigation equipment available on the scheme had been bought (unusually so) from the former farmer, but could not be operated by the new settlers since it required specialized expertise. The Department of Agricultural Engineering was significantly understaffed and could not assist. At this point, the Provincial Irrigation Specialist (PIS) negotiated with the former farm owner to contract him for a year to train the new settlers in the use of the equipment, which he was more than willing to do. However, when the PIS presented this solution to his boss, the Chief Irrigation Officer, the latter's response was: 'You must be crazy! Who do you think will listen to you? Also are you openly admitting to government that our department has no capacity to assist the farmers? Then we will all be fired' (ibid.: 264).

But even if this first plan 'went up in smoke', the former owner proposed a creative alternative that turned out to be acceptable. Instead of being contracted himself, notes Zawe, 'he suggested that ... the same result could be achieved by re-engaging some of his farm workers, who were key in the operation of his irrigation system' (ibid.). In the end, five of the farm's former workers were incorporated as members of the irrigation scheme and made up part of the scheme's first production unit.

Zawe's encounters with these and other cases led him to comment on the irony of those considered 'enemies of the state' – namely white commercial farmers – proving to be 'the most reliable partners available to the invader settlers in their endeavours to make the fast track resettlement programme a farming success' (ibid.: 291). Yet mostly these more productive relationships between former farm owners and new settlers have been hidden below the official radar screen. This is due to the campaign by ZANU-PF hardliners to ensure absolute exclusion of whites from the agricultural sector.[36] And in fact, for the majority of evicted commercial farmers, these examples do not apply. All but a few hundred out of over 4,500 large-scale commercial farmers lost their farms, and many hundreds of thousands of farm workers lost livelihoods, homes and both short- and long-term security.[37] Thus there has to be some caution to counter Scoones's (2008) overoptimistic interpretation of the new dynamism in the restructured rural economy, including new enterprises and new opportunities for employment. While there are certainly promising signs in some areas, there is sufficient anecdotal evidence and some research pointing to desperation and suffering from other parts of the country to temper if not contradict this picture (Magaramombe 2010; Matondi 2012).

With respect to commercial farmers, very few were able to retain a foothold in or close to their land in the ways described by Zawe and Mavedzenge et al. Many were left both economically and psychologically battered, yet still commanding a certain degree of bravado. Much like Jones's (2010) young men in urban Chitungwiza, hustling their way through the unknowable present, these white farming men and women were constantly 'making a plan'. Many had to become 'townies' and reinvent themselves in a range of new enterprises, not only having lost the bulk of their capital, but also having to survive at a time of severe economic crisis overall. Not surprisingly, many of these businesses lasted for only short periods, while new ones kept surfacing often in response to opportunities that the crisis itself, with its various shortages and gaps and shadows, threw up.[38]

Urban dealings: shady trading in Bulawayo's 'World Bank' In the early 2000s, the nature of Zimbabwe's crisis was defined mostly in terms of what was happening on 'the land'. The primary focus of attention politically and economically among most commentators was on the farm invasions, extensive displacement of both farmers and farm workers, and the loss of production, in turn prompting loss of foreign currency earnings, fuel shortages and overall economic decline. At the same time, concerns were focused on the persistently high levels of political violence, especially around elections, the increasing authoritarianism through repressive legislation, and a range of security concerns and human rights abuses.

However, by the mid-2000s a different dimension of crisis had kicked in. Formal unemployment skyrocketed when urban informal livelihoods were destroyed during the mass urban evictions and destruction of property and livelihoods under Operation Murambatsvina. Added to this was the collapse in the value of the Zimbabwe dollar, the printing of money by the Reserve Bank, and the introduction of price controls that made manufacturing pointless and ironically made scarce goods unaffordable. Literal cash shortages began to affect every aspect of life: not just businesses or the payment of private and public sector wages, but the ability of ordinary citizens, both poorer and wealthier, simply to take money out of the bank to pay for basic commodities for their families' daily survival. This exacerbated the already profound forms of insecurity experienced by the majority of Zimbabweans, adding new dimensions to what Jane Guyer has called 'the actualities of a desperately disturbed everyday life' (Guyer 2007: 410).

It was in this context, at the height of Zimbabwe's historic hyperinflation in 2008, that Alois Matongo undertook fieldwork on the emergence of 'roadside' foreign currency dealers in Bulawayo's street trading market, ironically titled 'the World Bank' (the basis for Mawowa and Matongo 2010). Dealing in 'forex' mushroomed in most major towns across the country, but especially in areas closer to international borders. Clearly, in the worst period of hyperinflation and cash shortages (2007/08), when there were vast discrepancies between the official and unofficial or 'parallel market' rates, there was a great deal of profit to be made. Such opportunities were not just taken up by 'illegal' small-scale dealers. Local police used their positions to cut their own deals through bribery and protection rackets – an accumulation practice that allegedly allowed many to invest in (and partly control) such sectors as urban transport in cities like Bulawayo.[39] More significantly, what largely fuelled the illicit forex market were the various 'chefs' positioned in or close to the appropriate state institutions, who could easily access US dollars at the ridiculously deflated official rate and then sell them at the parallel rate. Similarly, gains were to be made through access to Zimbabwe dollars in cash, which would then be 'sold' at a premium under conditions of extreme shortage.

One of the important contributions that Mawowa and Matongo make – despite the research challenges inherent in the secretive nature of the illicit activities under investigation – is in revealing the relationship between macro-level monetary policies, corrupt state and elite practices, and the micro-level entrepreneurial strategies and practices of mainly small-scale forex dealers.[40] Among other things, their study provides insights into some of the ways in which the extreme shrinking of the economy simultaneously opened up new opportunities for accumulation among a group of enterprising 'informal' traders, previously employed in the formal sector. Fieldwork conducted in May 2008 among the dealers in the 'World Bank' in Bulawayo identified several different kinds of currency dealers. The majority were a mix of poorer and wealthier 'social dealers', 'lone dealers' and 'nomadic dealers', each seeming to emanate from and/or occupy different social class positions that partly defined their possibilities and practices.

The poor social dealers, for example, were

> mainly young, unemployed men of low educational qualification. They doubled-up as commuter omnibus touts when not dealing in foreign currency.

Because of limited working capital and education, such social dealers had no long-term investment project and tended to be survivalist. They spent almost all the cash they generated on food. (Ibid.: 327)

Those identified as 'the moderately richer' dealers were mostly well educated, some holding high academic and professional qualifications, and formerly in professional jobs. They included teachers, police officers, prison guards and artisans and a number of electricians from the parastatal electricity utility enterprise, ZESA. Many were women who preferred to 'never return' to formal employment 'even if things normalised'. Within this category, many appeared to own 'at least one motor vehicle of reasonable age and reliability', unlike 'their former colleagues still in employment [who] could no longer afford' this luxury (ibid.: 328). Others also now owned or were renting 'a residential house or flat in the western suburbs as well as an undeveloped residential stand' (ibid.: 328).

The 'lone dealers' often operated from within expensive vehicles from which they also traded other high-end items such as phones or even cars. Usually they traded in large sums, which gained some of them the title 'cash barons'. However, they were viewed by informants as fronting for others, acting as 'agents of powerful politicians and members of Mugabe's feared spy network', the CIO (Central Intelligence Organization) (ibid.). They were said to possess firearms and were allegedly ignored by the police despite being conspicuously situated while undertaking their illicit trade.

Finally, and least common, the 'nomadic dealer' appeared only occasionally 'on the World Bank stage', 'especially just before the introduction of a new banknote' (ibid.: 329). According to one of the part-time dealers – a university student who dealt in forex during her vacations – usually these 'nomadic' dealers would arrive in teams of three at one of the busy cross-sections in Bulawayo where such deals were known to take place, 'each driving a posh sedan car' (ibid.):

The boot of one of these cars, usually the Mercedes Benz, would be filled with brand new banknotes in sealed plastic packets of the Reserve Bank of Zimbabwe (RBZ). Brisk trading in a targeted currency would begin with an instant and dramatic fall in the exchange rate of the local currency against the targeted currency on the 'World Bank'. At one time, it is alleged, the rate tumbled by over 200 per cent within minutes of the arrival of this trio. (Ibid.)

This same informant recounted that on one such occasion 'she recognised a former schoolmate among the trio who then invited her to pick a few bundles of banknotes from the boot without even checking how much she had taken' (ibid.). Such practices led other dealers in the 'World Bank' to suspect that these 'nomads' were proxies for those with contacts in the Reserve Bank. As

Mawowa and Matongo noted, 'this suspicion was heightened by the observation that the occasional dealer never *sold* foreign currency but only ever bought it' (ibid.). Stories such as these, while seemingly far fetched, became perfectly plausible as things spiralled out of control, especially in the period of hyperinflation and extreme cash and forex shortages.

This brief window into just one site of foreign currency dealing in Zimbabwe reveals a number of things. First, in the face of the severe economic meltdown and political violence which displaced people from formal jobs and homes as well as previous informal yet 'legal' livelihood practices, the very same conditions that undermined livelihoods opened up new market spaces for illicit and complicit trading. Secondly, while this facilitated a range of opportunities, and clearly created substantial upward mobility for some, the illicit nature of the market itself meant that many of the players were highly dependent on various vertical and horizontal networks, not all of which could be considered stable. Thirdly, the trade in itself relied on the continuity of crisis which sustained the shortages, as well as on the disintegration of the rule of law that allowed not just ordinary citizens, but the police, politicians and other officials protected by their party affiliation, to act illegally with impunity.

Following the signing of the Global Political Agreement between the contesting political parties in early 2009, the then newly sworn-in MDC-T minister of finance, Tendai Biti, formally dollarized the economy, indefinitely shelving the Zimbabwe dollar. Among other things, this removed the Reserve Bank's (and hence ZANU-PF's) 'advantage' of being able to print money. Besides controlling inflation almost immediately and stabilizing the economy in general (although not reversing wide-scale impoverishment), it also meant that illegal dealing in foreign currency and the selling of Zimbabwe dollars was no longer lucrative. What remains unclear is what has happened to all those who altered their fortunes – and class positions – through this shady trade.[41]

Conclusion

One of the main concerns of this chapter has been to consider shifts in patterns of wealth and trajectories of accumulation in a post-2000 Zimbabwe marked by persistent crisis, but to a large extent generated by overlapping forms and dynamics of displacement, and *re*placement. Such shifts necessarily have implications, present and future, for different social, economic and political domains. In combination, the new conditions have deepened the advantages and extended the opportunities for a small yet significant minority – mostly but not all associated with ZANU-PF – while confronting the majority of Zimbabweans with a range of difficult and often debilitating challenges. These include respatialized and exacerbated vulnerabilities, restructured access to key resources and security, altered and extensively curtailed spaces and practices of production and exchange, and reversals in the terms and directions of social status and mobility. In other words, the conditions of chronic crisis, displacement and uncertainty have redefined the parameters of the possible with respect to the intersecting dimensions of livelihoods, property, identities, citizenship and everyday living. To a large extent they have generated irreversible material and symbolic losses, often entailing the permanent disruption or destruction of former homes, social networks and the means – and meanings – of earning an income.

Millions of Zimbabweans have thus far had the previous certainties of everyday life and their anticipated trajectories of accumulation and social mobility dramatically undermined or even reversed. At the same time, para-doxically, these same destructive dynamics have created new opportunities for accumulation and upward mobility, not only for politically well-connected and loyal elites, but even for many 'ordinary' Zimbabweans. Yet in contemporary Zimbabwe, as elsewhere, such repositioning is not a linear or even process, and new positions are unlikely to be fixed for long. This could not really be otherwise in a situation in which the security of access to or control over property and assets remains in doubt; where the value of such assets is unpre-dictable; where certain resources and assets and former possibilities for wealth creation and accumulation have been permanently destroyed; and/or where displacement has generated permanent relocation yet uncertain grounding in the new spaces of re/settlement.

There is a further paradox in that while there has been (and continues to be) a profound loss of certainty in Zimbabwe – a loss of the ability to plan for either the near or far future – at the same time there has been an intensified focus, even obsession in some quarters, on accumulation. Under 'normal' circumstances this would imply a form of planning for something. However, in such a seemingly 'abnormal' environment, we need to keep asking: who is accumulating what, for what ends, and with what effects?

Notes

1 Many thanks to Brian Raftopoulos for insightful comments on an earlier draft of this chapter, as well as to Finn Stepputat and Bjørn Møller, who were discussants on a version presented at a conference in Copenhagen in November 2011.

2 A leading economist in Zimbabwe, John Robertson, provided these figures. See *Bulawayo24*, 22 April 2013, bulawayo24.com/index-id-business-sc-economy-byo-29277.html, accessed 29 September 2013. Unemployment figures are predict-ably open to (politicized) interpretation.

The then finance minister, in June 2013, dismissed the high estimates, claiming that 'only 9%' of Zimbabweans were economically 'inactive'. But within this he included those working as farmers, street vendors and in various other informal sector activities. The Poverty Income Consumption and Expenditure Survey 2011/12 Report compiled by the Zimbabwe National Statistics Agency (Zimstat) has indicated that only 22 per cent are em-ployed formally.

3 See Sutcliffe (2012) for some interest-ing reflections on changes in the politics

of unions during the 2000s. Yet he pays surprisingly little attention to the actual drop in union membership due to mass unemployment. Zimbabwe Congress of Trade Union figures indicate a decline in unionization from 200,000 in 1990, to 197,000 in 1997, and 162,000 in 2013 (cited in Solidarity Peace Trust 2013).

4 This is based on personal observations and those of others over the past several years.

5 The debates concerning these changes and their effects are intense and extensive and are not covered here for lack of space, but among varying positions are those espoused and/or critiqued by Moyo and Yeros (2005); Hammar (2008b); Scoones et al. (2010); Magaramombe (2010).

6 For a sophisticated analysis of the mining sector overall through the 2000s – providing insights into at least one key sphere of Zimbabwe's displacement economy – see Saunders (2008). See also Mawowa (2013) on the links between the growing mining sector and new patterns of accumulation.

7 See news.bbc.co.uk/2/hi/programmes /newsnight/8509149.stm, accessed 14 April 2010.

8 See, for example, 'Mugabe blames sanctions for Zimbabwe food shortage', *cbcnews online*, 17 November 2009, www. cbc.ca/news/world/story/2009/11/17/ mugabe-zimbabwe-food-summit.html; and 'Robert Mugabe blames sanctions for Zimbabwe's woes', *Daily Telegraph*, 21 September 2010, www.telegraph.co.uk/ news/newsvideo/8016668/Robert-Mugabe-blames-sanctions-for-Zimbabwes-woes. html.

9 The only sustained period since independence during which ZANU-PF has not been the dominant party was during the just-ended Government of National Unity (GNU) from 2009 to 2013, when it was forced into partnership with the two main opposition parties, MDC-T (led by Morgan Tsvangirai) and MDC-M (led at the time by Arthur Mutambara and subsequently by Welshman Ncube). See analysis by Raftopoulos (2010). ZANU-PF's election victory in July 2013 has re-established it as the sole ruling party.

10 Moore (2012) asks a related if differently framed question concerning 'progress' in Zimbabwe.

11 See Moore's (2012) discussion of the relationship between accumulation and violence in Zimbabwe. See also Sachikonye (2011) on 'coercive accumulation' in Zimbabwe, historically and in the present.

12 The extremes of impoverishment linked to displacement and dispossession have been closely and consistently documented by Solidarity Peace Trust, including attention to these dynamics both within Zimbabwe and across the borders, especially in South Africa. See reports, for example 'Gone to Egoli' (2009) and 'Desperate lives, twilight worlds' (2010a), 'Operation Murambatsvina: five years on' (2010b) and 'Matabeleland: urban deindustrialization – and rural hunger' (2011), www.solidaritypeacetrust.org/.

13 Many of these challenges are addressed in contributions to a special issue of the *Journal of Southern African Studies* (36(2), June 2010) that focuses on post-2000 Zimbabwe and the southern Africa region through the lens of displacement. Specifically on the complex strains on or avoidance of previous social relationships, especially among those in or trying to enter the diaspora, see Worby (2010), McGregor (2008), Pasura (2010).

14 See Stepputat (2008) in a Latin American context.

15 This differs from more classic, particularly Marxist, definitions and categories which remain prevalent in some of the scholarship on agrarian change in southern Africa, including post-2000 Zimbabwe. See, for example, Cousins (2010), Moyo and Yeros (2005), Scoones et al. (2012).

16 See, for example, the collection by Hunt (1977).

17 See Hanlon and Mosse (2010) for an interesting comparison with the changing orientations and practices of

Mozambique's post-independence political-business elite in relation to national development.

18 Some of these conditions in fact changed after the signing of the Global Political Agreement in early 2009, but not others.

19 See, for example, 'Zanu PF splits over white farmer's eviction', Radio VOP, www.radiovop.com/, accessed 7 November 2009.

20 On labour history and politics in Zimbabwe, see, for example, Raftopoulos and Sachikonye (2001).

21 See Saunders (2008) with respect to the mining sector.

22 On the historical development of the black middle class, including its role in nationalist politics, see, for example, West (2002) and Ranger (1995). For a discussion of class and factionalism in the liberation movements (whose ripples are still being felt in the present conjuncture), see Sithole (1984).

23 I would disagree with Chagonda's (2012) definition of teachers – and banking staff – as part of the 'working class'. Of interest, though, is the fact that salary conditions and perks for those in the banking sector were substantially better than for similar levels of professionals elsewhere, until dollarization in 2009. At that point thousands were retrenched from the banking sector, whereas many teachers initially returned to their professions when they were offered upgraded standard salaries for all civil servants of US$100/month.

24 This is not to underestimate quite different scales and degrees of suffering among the most radically dispossessed, destitute and violated Zimbabweans in and outside Zimbabwe over the past decade. See, for example, Solidarity Peace Trust (2009, 2010a), Parsons (2010), Alexander (2010), Orner and Holmes (2010). See also McGregor (2008) on abjection among Zimbabweans in the UK.

25 There had been de facto dollarization (meaning use of the US dollar and other convertible currencies) in many formal and informal economic arenas well before this, given the ever-decreasing value of the Zimbabwe dollar.

26 See Vigh's (2008) perspective on crisis as endemic and chronic – that is, crisis *as* context rather than merely *in* context – countering more common conceptualizations of crisis as episodic.

27 The evolution and effects of the multilayered crisis have been extensively documented and debated in both scholarly work and creative literature and popular media. For one useful bibliographical listing of key literature over the past decade, see concernedafricascholars. org/further-reading-on-zimbabwe/. See also various journal special issues in more recent years, such as the *Journal of Southern African Studies*, the *Journal of Contemporary African Studies*, the *Journal of Peasant Studies*, and so on.

28 Mugabe subsequently used this 'denial' of funds (denied on grounds of non-servicing) to fuel his generalized claim that 'Western-imposed sanctions' against Zimbabwe were in large part responsible for the ongoing crisis.

29 Personal observations, while working in the central state during the 1980s and into the early 1990s. In evidence was a combination of highly formalized proceduralism on the one hand, and increasing politicization on the other, which undermined professionalism and bureaucratic principles and fuelled increased forms of patronage and 'informal' resource allocation.

30 On Murambatsvina and its effects see, for example, work by Potts (2008), Kamete (2004, 2012), Musoni (2010) and Vambe (2010).

31 In the special issue of *Journal of Southern African Studies*, 36(2), see articles by Bolt, Hammar, Jones, Magaramombe, and Mawowa and Matongo.

32 For interesting comparisons of internal or local 'regulation' of seemingly unregulated economies under crisis conditions, see Chingono (1996), on the 'grassroots economy' of wartime Mozambique (1975–92), and Venkatesh (2006), on

'the underground economy' of an urban ghetto on the Southside of Chicago.

33 There is a wealth of literature produced by local, regional and human rights organizations that has closely documented these practices and their effects. See, for example, reports produced by Zimbabwe Lawyers for Human Rights, Solidarity Peace Trust, Human Rights Watch, Amnesty International, etc.

34 See Robertson Economic Information Services, accessed through Sokwanale at www.slideshare.net/Sokwanale/zimbabwe-economy-october-2009?from=email, accessed 3 November 2009.

35 Regarding ownership of cattle, however, there is generally a very skewed distribution of animals ranging from one to thirty-eight across all communal and A1 sites researched.

36 On the prevalence of leasing of A2 farms to white farmers, and the backlash from within ZANU-PF, see 'Chombo, Shamu leasing farms – Mliswa', *Zimbabwe Independent*, 14 February 2010, www.zwnews.com/print.cfm?ArticleID=22089, accessed 14 February 2010.

37 For a report on the situation of farm workers, see GAPWUZ (2009). I do not address the shifts in the positions of farm workers here. Rather, see Magaramombe (2010). On Zimbabwean farm workers on farms in northern South Africa, see, for example, Bolt (2010) and Rutherford (2008, 2010).

38 A trawl through the business ads during the period 2006–08 in the JAG (Justice for Agriculture) newsletter – servicing mostly the evicted white commercial farming community – gives an indication of this fluid environment of uncertainty and opportunity.

39 Anecdotal evidence from fieldwork in Bulawayo, September 2013.

40 See Bracking (this volume) on some of the challenges of researching contexts related to financial secrecy.

41 However, see Chagonda (2012) with respect to retrenchment of bank workers following dollarization.

References

Alexander, J. (2006) *The Unsettled Land. State-making and the Politics of Land in Zimbabwe 1983–2003*, Oxford/Harare/Athens: James Currey/Weaver Press/Ohio University Press.

— (2010) 'The political imaginaries and social lives of political prisoners in post-2000 Zimbabwe', *Journal of Southern African Studies*, 36(2): 483–503.

Bolt, M. (2010) 'Camaraderie and its discontents: class consciousness, ethnicity and divergent masculinities among Zimbabwean migrant farm workers', *Journal of Southern African Studies*, 36(2): 377–93.

Bracking, S. and L. M. Sachikonye (2007) 'Remittances, poverty reduction and the informalisation of household well-being in Zimbabwe', Conference paper, Stellenbosch, 27/28 March.

Bratton, M. and E. Masunungure (2007) 'Popular reactions to state repression: Operation Murambatsvina in Zimbabwe', *African Affairs*, 106(422): 21–45.

Chagonda, T. (2012) 'Teachers' and bank workers' responses to Zimbabwe's crisis: uneven effects, different strategies', *Journal of Contemporary African Studies*, 30(1): 83–97.

Chingono, M. F. (1996) *The State, Violence and Development. The Political Economy of War in Mozambique, 1975–1992*, Aldershot: Avebury.

Cousins, B. (2010) 'What is a "smallholder"? Class analytical perspectives on small-scale farming and agrarian reform in South Africa', Working Paper 16, PLAAS, University of the Western Cape.

Cramer, C. (2006) *Civil War is Not a Stupid Thing. Accounting for Violence in Developing Countries*, London: Hurst & Co.

Cross, E. (2009) 'The cost of Zimbabwe's continuing farm invasions', *Cato Institute Economic Development Bulletin*, 12, 18 May, www.cato.org/pub_display.php?pub_id=10206, accessed 12 February 2010.

Davies, R. (2004) 'Memories of underdevelopment: a personal interpretation of Zimbabwe's economic decline', in B. Raftopoulos and T. Savage (eds), *Zimbabwe. Injustice and Political Reconciliation*, Cape Town: Institute for Justice and Reconciliation, pp. 19–42.

Dawson, M. and T. Kelsall (2011) 'Anti-developmental patrimonialism in Zimbabwe', Working Paper 19, Africa Power and Politics Programme (APPP), London: Overseas Development Institute.

Derman, B. and R. Kaarhus (eds) (2013) *In the Shadow of a Conflict: Crisis in Zimbabwe and Its Effects on Mozambique*, Harare: Weaver Press.

GAPWUZ (2009) 'If something is wrong ... the invisible suffering of commercial farm workers and their families due to "land reform"', Harare: GAPWUZ.

Gibbon, P. (ed.) (1995) *Structural Adjustment and the Working Poor in Zimbabwe*, Uppsala: Nordiska Afrikainstitutet.

Guyer, J. I. (ed.) (1995) *Money Matters: Instability, Values, and Social Payments in the Modern History of West African Communities*, Portsmouth, NH: Heinemann.

— (2007) 'Prophecy and the near future: thoughts on macroeconomic, evangelical, and punctuated time', *American Ethnologist*, 34(3): 409–21.

Hammar, A. (2001) '"The Day of Burning": Eviction and reinvention in the margins of northwest Zimbabwe', *Journal of Agrarian Change*, 1(4): 550–74.

— (2003) 'The making and unma(s)king of local government in Zimbabwe', in A. Hammar, B. Raftopoulos and S. Jensen (eds), *Zimbabwe's Unfinished Business: Rethinking Land, State and Nation in the Context of Crisis*, Harare: Weaver Press, pp. 119–54.

— (2008a) 'Reflections on displacement in Zimbabwe', *Concerned Africa Scholars (ACAS) Bulletin*, 80, Autumn, pp. 28–35.

— (2008b) 'In the name of sovereignty: displacement and state-making in post-independence Zimbabwe', *Journal of Contemporary African Studies*, 26(4): 417–34.

— (2010) 'Ambivalent mobilities: Zimbabwean commercial farmers in Mozambique', *Journal of Southern African Studies*, 36(2): 395–416.

— (2013) 'Settling for less? Zimbabwean farmers and commercial farming in Mozambique', in B. Derman and R. Kaarhus (eds), *In the Shadow of a Conflict: Crisis in Zimbabwe and Its Effects on Mozambique, South Africa and Zambia*, Harare: Weaver Press, pp. 92–120.

Hammar, A., J. McGregor and L. Landau (2010) 'Introduction: Displacing Zimbabwe: crisis and construction in Southern Africa', *Journal of Southern African Studies*, 36(2): 263–83.

Hanlon, J. and M. Mosse (2010) 'Mozambique's elite – finding its way in a globalized world and returning to old development models', UNU-WIDER Working Paper no. 2010/105, Helsinki: UNU-WIDER.

Harris, A. (2008) 'Discourses of dirt and disease in Operation Murambatsvina', in M. Vambe (ed.), *The Hidden Dimensions of Operation Murambatsvina*, Harare: Weaver Press.

Hunt, A. (ed.) (1977) *Class and Class Structure*, London: Lawrence and Wishart.

Jones, J. (2010) '"Nothing is straight in Zimbabwe": the rise of the Kukiya-kiya economy 2000–2008', *Journal of Southern African Studies*, 36(2): 285–99.

Kamete, A. Y. (2004) 'Home industries and the formal city in Harare, Zimbabwe', in K. T. Hansen (ed.), *Reconsidering Informality: Perspectives from Urban Africa*, Oslo: Nordiska Afrikainstitutet, pp. 120–38.

— (2012) 'Not exactly like the phoenix – but rising all the same: reconstructing displaced livelihoods in post-cleanup Harare', *Environment and Planning D: Society and Space*, 30(2): 243–61.

Lubkemann, S. C. (2008) 'Involuntary immobility: on a theoretical invisibility in forced migration studies', *Journal of Refugee Studies*, 21(4): 454–75.

Magaramombe, G. (2010) 'Agrarian displacements, replacements and resettlement: "displaced in place" farm workers in Mazowe District', *Journal of Southern African Studies*, 36(2): 361–75.

Matondi, P. B. (2012) *Zimbabwe's Fast-track Land Reform*, London/Uppsala: Zed Books/Nordiska Afrikainstitutet.

Mavedzenge, B. Z., J. Mahenehene, F. Murimbarimba, I. Scoones and W. Wolmer (2008) 'The dynamics of real markets: cattle in southern Zimbabwe following land reform', *Development and Change*, 39(4): 613–39.

Mawowa, S. (2013) 'The political economy of crisis, mining and accumulation in Zimbabwe', Unpublished PhD thesis, University of KwaZulu-Natal, South Africa.

Mawowa, S. and A. Matongo (2010) 'Inside Zimbabwe's roadside currency trade: the "World Bank" of Bulawayo', *Journal of Southern African Studies*, 36(2): 319–37.

McGregor, J. (2008) 'Abject spaces, transnational calculations: Zimbabweans in Britain navigating work, class and the law', *Transactions of the Institute of British Geographers*, 33(4): 466–82.

— (2010) 'Introduction: The making of Zimbabwe's new diaspora', in J. McGregor and R. Primorac (eds) (2010) *Zimbabwe's New Diaspora. Displacement and the Cultural Politics of Survival*, New York and Oxford: Berghahn, pp. 1–33.

McGregor, J. and R. Primorac (eds) (2010) *Zimbabwe's New Diaspora. Displacement and the Cultural Politics of Survival*, New York and Oxford: Berghahn.

Moore, D. (2012) 'Progress, power, and violent accumulation in Zimbabwe', *Journal of Contemporary African Studies*, 30(1): 1–9.

Moyo, S. (2011) 'Three decades of agrarian reform in Zimbabwe', *Journal of Peasant Studies*, 38(3): 493–531.

Moyo, S. and P. Yeros (2005) 'Land occupations and land reform in Zimbabwe: towards the National Democratic Revolution', in S. Moyo and P. Yeros (eds), *Reclaiming the Land: The Resurgence of Rural Movements in Africa, Asia and Latin America*, London: Zed Books.

Musoni, F. (2010) 'Operation Murambats-vina and the politics of street vendors in Zimbabwe', *Journal of Southern African Studies*, 36(2): 301–18.

Mustapha, A. R. (2011) 'Zimbabwean farmers in Nigeria: exceptional farmers or spectacular support?', *African Affairs*, 110(441): 535–61.

Orner, P. and A. Holmes (eds) (2010) *Hope Deferred. Narratives of Zimbabwe Lives*, San Francisco, CA: Voice of Witness/McSweeney's Books.

Parsons, R. (2010) 'Eating in mouthfuls while facing the door: some notes on childhoods and their displacements in eastern Zimbabwe', *Journal of Southern African Studies*, 36(2): 449–63.

Pasura, D. (2010) 'Zimbabwean transnational diaspora politics in Britain', in J. McGregor and R. Primorac (eds), *Zimbabwe's New Diaspora. Displacement and the Cultural Politics of Survival*, New York and Oxford: Berghahn, pp. 103–21.

Potts, D. (2008) 'Displacement and livelihoods: the longer term impacts of Operation Murambatsvina', in M. Vambe (ed.), *The Hidden Dimensions of Operation Murambatsvina in Zimbabwe*, Harare/Pretoria: Weaver Press/Institute of South Africa, pp. 53–64.

Raftopoulos, B. (2010) 'The Global Political Agreement as a "passive revolution": notes on contemporary politics in Zimbabwe', *The Round Table: The Commonwealth Journal of International Affairs*, 99(411): 705–18.

Raftopoulos, B. and L. M. Sachikonye (eds) (2001) *Striking Back: The Labour Movement and the Post-colonial State in Zimbabwe, 1980–2000*, Harare: Weaver Press.

Ranger, T. (1995) *Are We Not Also Men? The Samkange Family and African Politics in Zimbabwe 1920–1964*, Oxford/Harare: James Currey/Baobab.

Rutherford, B. (2008) 'An unsettled belonging: Zimbabwean farm workers in Limpopo Province, South Africa', *Journal of Contemporary African Studies*, 26(4): 401–15.

— (2010) 'Zimbabwe's farmworkers in

Limpopo Province, South Africa', in J. McGregor and R. Primorac (eds), *Zimbabwe's New Diaspora. Displacement and the Cultural Politics of Survival*, New York and Oxford: Berghahn, pp. 59–76.

Sachikonye, L. M. (2003) 'The situation of commercial farm workers after land reform in Zimbabwe', Report prepared for the Farm Community Trust of Zimbabwe, Harare.

— (2011) *When a State Turns on Its Citizens: 60 Years of Institutionalised Violence in Zimbabwe*, Harare/Johannesburg: Weaver Press/Jacana.

Saunders, R. (2008) 'Crisis, capital, compromise: mining and empowerment in Zimbabwe', *African Sociological Review*, 12(1): 67–87.

Scoones, I. (2008) 'A new start for Zimbabwe?', Livelihoods After Land Reform (LALR), www.lalr.org.za/news/a-new-start-for-zimbabwe-by-ian-scoones.

Scoones, I., N. Marongwe, B. Mavedzenge, J. Mahenehene, F. Murimbarimba and C. Sikume (2010) *Zimbabwe's Land Reform. Myths and Realities*, Woodbridge/Harare/Auckland Park: James Currey/Weaver/Jacana Media.

Scoones, I., N. Marongwe, B. Mavedzenge, F. Murimbarimba, J. Mahenehene and C. Sikume (2012) 'Livelihoods after land reform in Zimbabwe: understanding processes of rural differentiation', *Journal of Agrarian Change*, 12(4): 503–27.

Sithole, M. (1984) 'Class and factionalism in the Zimbabwe liberation movement', *African Studies Review*, 27(1): 117–25.

Sjaastad, E., T. Kalinda and F. Maimbo (2013) 'Home away from home: land, identity and community on Mkushi Land Block', in B. Derman and R. Kaarhus (eds), *In the Shadow of a Conflict: Crisis in Zimbabwe and Its Effects on Mozambique, South Africa and Zambia*, Harare: Weaver Press, pp. 285–308.

Solidarity Peace Trust (2009) *'Gone to Egoli': Economic Survival Strategies in Matebeleland: A Preliminary Study*, Johannesburg: Solidarity Peace Trust.

— (2010a) *Desperate Lives, Twilight Worlds: How a million Zimbabweans live without official sanction or sanctuary in South Africa*, Johannesburg: Solidarity Peace Trust.

— (2010b) *A Fractured Nation. Operation Murambatsvina: Five Years On*, Johannesburg: Solidarity Peace Trust.

— (2011) *'Hard Times' Matabeleland: Urban Deindustrialization – and Rural Hunger*, Johannesburg: Solidarity Peace Trust.

— (2013) *The End of a Road: The 2013 Elections in Zimbabwe*, Johannesburg: Solidarity Peace Trust.

Staunton, I. (ed.) (2009) *Damage. The Personal Costs of Political Change in Zimbabwe*, Oxford: African Books Collective.

Stepputat, F. (2008) 'Forced migration, land and sovereignty', *Government and Opposition*, 43(2): 337–57.

Sutcliffe, J. (2012) 'The labour movement in Zimbabwe 1980–2012', *e-International Relations*, www.e-ir.info/2013/03/07/the-labour-movement-in-zimbabwe-1980-2012/, accessed 29 September 2013.

Tevera, D., J. Crush and A. Chikanda (2010) 'Migrant remittances and household survival in Zimbabwe', *IDRC Bulletin* (online), 198.62.158.214/en/ev-158068-201-1-DO_TOPIC.html, accessed 2 October 2013.

Vambe, M. (ed.) (2010) *The Hidden Dimensions of Operation Murambatsvina*, Harare: Weaver Press.

Venkatesh, S. A. (2006) *Off the Books. The Underground Economy of the Urban Poor*, Cambridge, MA, and London: Harvard University Press.

Vigh, H. (2008) 'Crisis and chronicity: anthropological perspectives on continuous conflict and decline', *Ethnos*, 73(1): 5–24.

West, M. O. (2002) *The Rise of an African Middle Class. Colonial Zimbabwe, 1989–1965*, Bloomington: Indiana University Press.

Worby, E. (2010) 'Address unknown: the temporality of displacement and the ethics of disconnection among Zimbabwean migrants in Johannesburg', *Journal of Southern African Studies*, 36(2): 417–31.

Zawe, C. (2006) *Reforms in Turbulent Times. A Study in the Theory and Practice of Three Irrigation Management Policy Reform Models in Mashonaland, Zimbabwe*, Unpublished PhD thesis, Wageningen University, Wageningen.

PART II

Reshaping economic sectors, markets and investment

5 | Rapid adaptations to change and displacements in the Lundas (Angola)

Cristina Udelsmann Rodrigues

Introduction

One schematic way of analysing migration and displacement in the Angolan north-eastern diamond provinces, the Lundas – Lunda Norte and Lunda Sul provinces – in the last half-century is to look at the massive movements of the population that concentrated in the region's cities and towns. These were a result of both the colonial mining policy – more active in the 1960s – and of the post-independence (1975) war that lasted until 2002. Moreover, significant movement both through voluntary migration and forced displacement can be observed in terms of the large number of individuals and groups from other provinces and from abroad who arrived in these provinces during the war, attracted to the countryside's diamond fields.

Taking a definition of displacement as 'enforced changes in interweaving spatial, social and symbolic conditions and relations' that include both enforced movement and enforced confinement (see Hammar, Introduction, this volume), it is unquestionable that displacement has been one of the main characteristics of the Lundas since the late colonial period. In colonial times, it involved a large number of forced labourers coming from other provinces, but largely from within the Lundas provinces, to the newly created mining cities. Although right before independence the forced character of displacement to the mining sites was no longer present, the war following independence again pushed large numbers of people to move to the safety of cities, either in the Lundas or in other provinces.

The first type of dislocation related to war was that of military personnel, both government troops and Unita guerrillas, who stayed for long periods in provinces other than their places of origin, including the diamond-rich Lundas. The second type included those who were compelled to move to safer places to avoid the war. Among these, a large majority moved to Luanda or other coastal cities, while others remained in government-controlled Lundas cities. This second type was simultaneously a result of displacement from smaller countryside towns and villages to the larger cities at the beginning of the war, and created a situation that gradually transformed itself into a form of forced *confinement* in those cities. A third type of displacement during the war which also evolved into forced confinement involved those workers and families who were forced by the guerrilla military to work in the mines and/or at the mining sites to supply the guerrillas. Both displacements and confinements were highly conditioned by the war and the strict control of movement and circulation in the region. The fourth and last type of significant displacement during the Angolan war concerned those fleeing from the DRC (Democratic Republic of Congo). Especially from 1998 to 2003, at the height of the war in this neighbouring country, when economic opportunities were scarce (see, for instance, Wheeler and Pélissier 1971; Brinkman 2003), many managed to find a 'lesser evil' destination in Angola.

These four types of displacement, linked in turn to certain groups of actors, will be analysed in detail later in the chapter. However, it is worth recalling that, together with the forced displacement of military personnel, internally displaced Angolans moving to cities, and refugees from elsewhere, other kinds of physical movements have coincided with these at different times and in different contexts. Internal migrants (and immigrants from other countries), with other motivations for moving into and out of the Lundas besides forced labour or the war, have also crossed into and settled in the provinces in wartime. It is therefore necessary to emphasize that the focus of the analysis here is on displacement and not on those whose movements have involved various degrees of choice.

Still working schematically, we see that the various types of displaced people have normally engaged in certain kinds of survival-based economic activities that evolved from those initially 'available': colonial forced labourers often became wage workers in the company mines; those displaced by war in the cities resorted to and augmented the urban informal economy; and diamond 'workers' and the military increasingly profited from their skills and opportunities to engage in the diamond business and in the *garimpo* (manual diamond digging, often illegal).

However, strategies mobilized by these different types of actors in different contexts and periods, to cope with the evolution of the economic and political situation, are far less schematic in practice, as the changes in the available economic opportunities have occurred quite fast. The transformation of forced labour into sought-after jobs in the colonial mining companies, for example, took place in no more than a decade[1] (between the 1950s and the 1960s). A few years of post-independence 'freedom' to engage in *garimpo* were then followed by heavy military control of the region, both of population circulation, and of the mining activities themselves, beginning in the first years of the 1980s. The few years of preparation for the 1992 elections in Angola motivated some to return to the Lundas while demobilization of the military and plans to recover formal mining were under way. But the situation was rapidly reversed with the post-electoral resumption of the war. By the end of the 1990s, war in the neighbouring DRC again changed the labour and economic environment in the region with the massive arrival of refugees and other migrants, while the ongoing Angolan civil war was subject to a series of advances and setbacks. Both government (colonial and post-colonial) and guerrilla modifications of the 'rules' governing access to resources (diamonds and others) accompanied all these changes and consequently required the displaced populations to adapt.

Among all those involved in migration and displacement, there are particular individual itineraries that show how complex and varied the trajectories of people have been. Simultaneously, they show that since the beginning of diamond exploration in Angola in colonial times, rapid adaptive strategies were needed to cope with recurring social and economic transformations. Major changes in the social, political and economic context of the Lundas provinces have required significant adjustments and resilience on the part of the actors involved in the diamond industry – both its formal and informal sectors – and of those performing related activities, such as trade, services, lodging and security, among others. Displacement was one of the most important features of transformation, and it imprinted particular characteristics on to the region, as well as on to the country overall. Both colonial corporate rule (until 1975) and the civil war (from 1975 to 2002), as well as peacetime, shaped the way settlement and economic activities – and particularly those linked to diamonds – were conducted. This affected the placement and displacement of the economic agents and triggered their adaptive, flexible and at times ambiguous coping strategies. Considering the relatively short period of time that has elapsed since the diamond economy was initiated in the region at the beginning of the last century, the changes that have occurred in the structure and composition of the population in the region – mostly due to the war but also to other factors – and in the economic dynamics are considerable.

This chapter is based on data collected in 2011 that include accounts from Lunda key informants regarding the last decades. The contextualized analysis of changes and related displacements focuses on the strategies mobilized by the different displaced actors – namely forced labourers, the military, immigrants and the local population in general – often spanning life courses across extended periods of time and multiple locations. These show not only the rapidity of changes and the various actors' malleability, but also the importance of these at times overlapping, combined or successive changes in moulding life courses and in shaping adaptive strategies in relation to the society and the economy as a whole. The analysis accepts that displaced individuals 'have much wider, longer histories to tell ... one person may combine memories of Angola, Zambia, Botswana, South Africa, Namibia and other countries. These complex sets of personal experiences include memories of different periods ...' (Brinkman 2005: 36).

One important notion to retain in the analysis of how displacement has produced a rapid reinvention and re-creation of survival and economic strategies is that despite the fact that mobility in general deeply marks much of society and culture in Africa (De Bruijn et al. 2001) – and not least in Angola – the changes that took place in the Lundas were particularly significant owing to the impacts of war and the conflict over mineral resources. As noted by De Bruijn et al. (ibid.: 1), 'Mobility in its ubiquity is fundamental to any understanding of African social life.' However, the specific conditions that triggered the movements in the Lundas call for a distinction between displacement and migration, and at the same time attention to how these processes combined throughout the last century. Moreover, and in individual terms, migration and displacement are often parts of the same life stories. Even within families, experiences of mobility include several members with different motivations and 'enforcing' conditions.

The Lundas also display an additional characteristic of mine migrancy. This is a well-documented field of research in southern Africa (Crush and James 1995; Davies and Head 1995), again mostly highlighting voluntary migratory motivations. However, in the later decolonized Angola, mobility and a particular context of mine migrancy overlaid the long-term displacement effects of the colonial mining economy. The colonial mining companies' system of forced labour in Angola initially caused workers to move to the Lundas, and in some cases also forced people out of mining concession areas.

The post-independence war simultaneously impeded the majority of the population freely choosing where to live (Brinkman 2005) and forcefully immobilized many (Lubkemann 2008). These conditions dictated the forms and possibilities of survival and economic activity. While both mandatory and sought-after work in the colonial mining companies constituted the principal way of accessing monetary resources, the later disruption to the system imposed by war altered the sources of income for families. 'Both enforced displacement and emplacement were seen as the major factors in destroying people's livelihood during the war ... and likewise, both the freedom to move and the freedom to live and stay in the place of one's own choosing are given as examples of freedom' (and non-freedom) (Brinkman 2005: 205). As many Angolans were forced to move to safer cities and remain there during the war, this constrained their economic possibilities: often 'involuntary immobility can be more disruptive and disempowering than wartime displacement and migration' (Lubkemann 2008).

The exact numbers of the population subject to displacement both in relation to the colonial mining cities and throughout the war are not definitive. By the end of the 1940s, Diamang[2] had an estimated total of 7,000 African workers, of which 6,000 were contracted and 1,000 volunteers (Cleveland 2008). Given the shifting nature of the work and the prevalence of limited engagements with the company (usually twelve months), the total figures for the workforce mobilized to the mines from the 1920s to independence in 1975 are estimated to be very high. Many families relied on this source of income, counting on successive generations of men who had assured access to this type of employment.

Wartime figures are likewise uncertain. 'Angola's internally displaced are strongly heterogeneous, having been displaced at different times during Angola's civil war, resulting in cyclical waves of displacement' (Porto and Parsons 2003: 9). In the Lundas, in 2002, the number of internally displaced people was over 600,000[3] (around 438,000 in Lunda Norte and 185,000 in Lunda Sul). Given these two main sets of conditions for settlement and displacement – namely the colonial economic system and the long-lasting Angolan civilian war – the strategies of these hundreds of thousands of families to cope with rapid changes had to be concomitantly rapid and flexible. In this chapter the focus is on the above-mentioned categories of displaced populations in the Lundas, as active agents in building their destinies, 'negotiating their way through the maze' (Shanmugaratnam et al. 2003). The responses to change include urban migration, integration and avoidance of formal mining labour, negotiation with wartime forces controlling the mining activities, the extremely important *garimpo* and, more recently, the search for business and employment opportunities within the reconstruction of economic networks in the Lundas provinces.

Mobile Lundas

As already noted, migration and displacement in the Lundas provinces have been a result of particular political and economic conditions since colonial times. The first important one was the establishment of mining companies in the region in the 1920s. This implied massive labour recruitment, not only within the two provinces but also from other regions of the country. According to Cleveland (2008), forced labourers accounted for 25,000 annually by the 1960s and were primarily from among those native to the Lundas. The second major change affecting the various populations and the nature of settlement was the civil war. It forced many people to take refuge in major cities (including some already established mining cities) both in the Lundas and in other parts of the country. It also prompted the arrival of other types of actors in the countryside mining areas, namely the military and the immigrants. At the same time, varied populations – mainly from the smaller villages and the countryside who could not escape to the cities – were forcibly 'immobilized' in the diamond areas. The most recent major change came with peace in 2002 when informal illegal diamond mining became more controlled and caused the exit of a significant portion of the population: the already 'established' *garimpeiros* and the diamond business networks created during the war; the illegal immigrants; and consequently the military. This was combined with the reactivation of other economic and labour opportunities, namely in the administration, in trade and services, and in the mining companies. This not only began to attract people from other provinces but also contributed to the return of formerly displaced Lundas populations. These various trends will be discussed below.

All these recent changes are key elements in understanding the present-day options available for the local population and for those who came from other places to the Lundas. Optimistically, it may contribute to predicting future trends based on the extremely adaptive capacities of the population in general.

Mining companies and settlement in the Lundas Before the establishment of mining companies in the Lundas in the early twentieth century, the area was known to be sparsely populated, far from the sea and communication routes. Colonial settlement in the region followed a logic of penetration to the interior, military occupation and agricultural exploitation. However, the number of settlers was not significant as compared to coastal provinces, but similar to other hinterland areas (Dias 1989). In the meantime, the colonial government did not abandon the hope of finding gold and copper in the area. The first discoveries of diamonds were in 1912 in the Mussalala river, an eastern margin tributary of the Chiumbe river, both tributaries of the Cassai river (Pereira et al. 2003: 190). PEMA (Companhia de Pesquisas Mineiras de Angola – Angolan Mining Research Company) was founded that same year and Diamang, a state-owned Portuguese company with capital from De Beers and other European firms, was set up in 1917 after recognition of the viability and economic importance of diamond exploitation. Diamond prospecting began the following year, and the first open-cast mines were opened in 1919 in Cavuco, Camimanga, Cassanguidi and Luaco (ibid.: 190).

The expansion of mining in the Lundas required bringing in a significant labour force that was not available in the newly created mining sites. Initially, forced labour suited the purposes of this enterprise, and through this mechanism Diamang was able not only to proceed with the diamond explorations but also to enhance its ability to organize and manage the settlement of the population. It created towns based on the compound system, controlling the number and location of the population/workers by establishing a very peculiar form of 'open' compound urbanization, of which Dundo, the administrative centre, is a good example (Cleveland 2008). The mining companies provided medical and educational facilities for their employees and their dependants, thereby attracting even greater numbers who saw in the company a way of improving their lives (ibid.: 7). These features contributed later in colonial times to the 'conversion' of displaced mineworkers into formal contract workers.

While Diamang was in charge of the mining towns, the colonial authorities became more concerned, especially in the late 1960s and early 1970s, with the expansion of the provision of services and infrastructure to the population in an environment of growing rebellion against the colonial system. One of the mechanisms to support this expansion was the fusion and reorganization of existing *bairros* or villages. The colonial administration created the indigenous *bairros* of Saurimo – the most important non-mining city – strategically placed to administer the territory, then called *camuzanguissa* (meaning 'obligation'), merging the inhabitants of several scattered houses and small villages. The first unified village in Saurimo was Sacombe and the second Santo António (in 1965). The rationale behind this unification was better management and provision of such infrastructure as health services, churches, water supply and schools, while at the same time controlling the population. This type of forced displacement through the imposition of relocation, though significant, did not affect as much of the population as forced labour did. However, it stimulated an increased urban migration from scattered small sites to major Lundas towns, such as Saurimo, Lucapa and Dundo. On the other hand, urbanization trends based on migration were already significant in these provinces, attracting growing numbers of people to the urban centres in search of economic opportunities. Saurimo, for instance, grew from 3,100 inhabitants in 1960 to 12,900 in 1970, reaching over 20,000 in 1980 (E-Polis n.d.).

During the colonial period, there was 'forced' labour in the mines of Dundo and other concession areas of the Diamang, but also some clandestine mining activities. These involved a varied set of local operators – businessmen, traders, civil servants, the local population – but also, increasingly, the dismissed forced labourers who had acquired some experience while working in the mines and reoriented their life strategies based on this available opportunity. As one informant recalled: 'In the beginning [until the end of the 1960s] the population could not easily sell diamonds to anyone. But then clandestine networks of diamond trade began to appear and *caixeiros-viajantes* [travelling salesmen] came to buy diamonds in the prospection settlements' (F.G., Tchizaínga II, 24 July 2011).[4] Moving to the Lundas at this period, then, was simultaneously motivated by the search for formal employment in the mines and by the opportunity of engaging in the *garimpo*. Another noted: 'In 1965 there was already voluntary mine work, of those who finished their contracts, because there were "winds of the revolution" coming from the Congo and so the government authorized these workers to continue working for the mines' (M., Itengo, 30 July 2011). On the 'informal' side, in the late 1960s/early 1970s, 'local traders and shop/canteen owners had already enticed some workers to search for diamonds. They would get rich but invested the money in Malange or in Luanda not to attract the attention of the Diamang. The same happened right after independence with the military. They invested in Luanda, bought houses from the Portuguese that were leaving the country' (A.M., Cacolo, 28 July 2011).

While the formal and informal networks linked to diamond resources set the conditions for population mobility and settlement in the Lundas, they offered a range of possibilities for accessing income to a heterogeneous mass of population. Among the large numbers of formerly displaced mineworkers, a significant portion were absorbed in the local mining economy. In this period too, as individual life stories reflect, the common reality of many people was generating income from both formal and informal activities, from forced labour, wage work and *garimpo*.

We either move to the city or go to the *garimpo* The migratory and displacement trends of the colonial period were entirely reversed when Angola became independent in 1975. There was a massive exit of the population from the mining areas – both Portuguese and contracted workers – caused by the civil war and the cessation of mining production. As the Angolan civil war was mainly played out in the rural areas, as previously noted, it forced substantial numbers of people to take refuge in the main cities that were controlled by the government. The majority of the population preferred to move to Luanda, though many others opted for other safer cities. However, a significant number of families were unable to leave Saurimo or Dundo in the Lundas, which remained under siege for many years. For these latter, mobility was highly restrained as the military controlled circulation within the region. Many of those who managed to move to other provinces did so right at the beginning of the 1980s, and the smaller numbers that managed to leave during the more intense periods of war had to resort to complex strategies and networks. These included, for example, drawing upon relations with the networks supplying the cities (including the government and the World Food Programme, WFP) and/or relations with the guerrillas themselves.

Unita increasingly controlled the countryside mining areas and diamonds became more and more crucial in financing the war. While the UN's well-known 'blood diamonds' resolution[5] was not initiated until 2000, the guerrillas' dependency on diamonds to finance military action was enormous. Again, labour resources needed for this enterprise stimulated the arrival of thousands of job seekers as well as 'fortune seekers' (Calvão 2011: 369). They included increasingly higher numbers of those involved in related businesses (buyers, commodity suppliers, traders). But a significant proportion of the human resources needed for the diamond industry were recruited locally, as many of those who remained in the countryside were forced to work for the guerrillas. Together with this 'enforced immobility', a new wave of displaced workers came from the neighbouring villages of the DRC and even from other countries. 'Tens of thousands of Congolese entered – and still continue to enter – Angola [in the early 1990s]' (De Boeck 2001: 554). These new actors joined the thousands of military controlling the mining activities – they, too, being displaced – and together reshaped and altered the composition of the population in the region. Displaced (and forcibly immobilized) workers, military and a vast range of related actors constituted a single, interrelated economic dynamic in the mining areas, creating new agglomerations and towns as well as new displacement economies. Consequently, this generated new adaptive strategies, as described in the following personal account of someone who had been directly affected by the changing environment, showing the constantly changing social and economic status, directly determined by war and displacement.

I was born in 1938 in Xassengue and became a teacher in Cacolo in 1961. In 1986, I became deputy Municipal Administrator of Cacolo. After independence, many people from Xassengue, Cucumbi and Alto Chicapa came to Cacolo because of the war, especially in 1983. During the war in those years, the town would be alternatively occupied by the government and the Unita for two to three months. During the occupations, the population would escape to Saurimo. In August 1995, we walked to Saurimo to escape the war. Thirteen died on the way. Some remained in Cacolo, in captivity [cativeiro] because they could not go to Saurimo. They stayed in Cacolo doing small gardening, especially women because the men had to work for the Unita in the garimpo. Those who remained had a hard life. Whoever could get some more money with the garimpo escaped to Saurimo or to the Congo. There were traders from Zaire based here that exchanged directly products for diamonds with the population; no money was even used. These traders brought cloth, guns, other commodities. Those who went to Saurimo at least had the help of WFP. (M.S., Cacolo, 27 July 2011)

The alteration of the conditions to secure income and access to economic resources had direct implications for people's mobility and called for creativity within the new displacement economies. For some, it meant multiple displacements, each time requiring adaptation to new and difficult circumstances, as the trajectories noted below indicate.

I came back to Angola in 1994 when my father [since colonial times a business-man in the region, in Cacolo] needed me. My father died in 1996 with a landmine and I had to catch his body remains. Between 2000 and 2002 I went to live in Brazil because one could not cope with the war. I left Cacolo in 1998 inside an army tank because I was not well seen by the Unita because I supplied the government troops. (S., Luanda, 15 August 2011)

I was born in Lubalo in 1962; I escaped to Saurimo in 1978 because of the war. I worked for the Ministry of Construction and then went to the army [FAA] in 1984, to serve in Uíge. I left in 1989 and as I had no job, I came to Luó. I spent the war here, doing agriculture. I chose this place because it was safer and I worked in the *garimpo*. I raised a family here; my children are in Saurimo. (S., Luó, 31 July 2011)

Such accounts of war-related displacement, involving long-distance international and in-country dislocations, are abundant in Angola and in the Lundas. Often, these forced displacements integrate distant locations into personal life stories and imply long periods of settlement in other provinces or even foreign countries.

Post-war resilience As in many other Angolan cases – and examples abound also in other African countries (Bryceson and Jamal 1997) – large-scale return to the rural areas did not take place after the war in Angola. On the contrary, increased government control of the illegal *garimpo* and the cessation of Unita activities in the Lundas area, together with the reopening of formal mining companies, caused the removal of significant numbers of people from the mining provinces. This included thousands of foreigners who had settled in Angola during the war. Among these, the displaced Congolese from the DRC were a large majority and 'evictions' back to the DRC, organized by the Angolan government,[6] took place in the mid-2000s. Also, there was a significant mass of population with the status of internally displaced persons (IDPs) who had to start finding ways to cope with the new social and economic conditions created by peace. For example, in 2005 there were an estimated 7,500 internally displaced people in a refugee camp in the region of Catoca (Saurimo) who were not absorbed by the Catoca mining company and had to find their means of living elsewhere.

There are many examples of informal mines and mining towns that grew without state control and which by the end of the war concentrated significantly large numbers of people together: Samupafo (Luachimo), Chivumbe Mazanza, Sanjungo (Lucari), Sassuaha or Samuhondo, Muxinda, Xa-Muquelengue, Cafunfo or Luremo. The same phenomenon also took place on the other side of the border, in the DRC, in places like Tembo and Kahemba, where the diamond business flourished and 'booming diamond settlements' arose (De Boeck 2001: 550) that hosted a substantial number of displaced people and also migrants who developed a particular type of economic network. But when the existing diamond economy networks were 'dismantled' and government control tightened, these places also witnessed a reduction in their population. A proportion of this population still lives in the formerly booming wartime *garimpo* towns. However, as the *garimpeiros* were evicted and even activities such as hunting or coal production became highly controlled by the government, there tended to be a decrease both in terms of population size and in the scale and scope of economic dynamism in these areas, as the brief personal narratives below illustrate.

Muxinda and Xa-Muquelengue had many population, many diamond stores with heavy security. Today they are empty cities, with less movement; only the houses by the road remain, profiting from some of the traffic to do business. (T., Luó, 10 August 2011)

For instance, Lucapa was between 1992 and 1994 sized for 10,000 people and 100,000 were living there because the government 'closed the eyes' to the *garimpo*. *Garimpeiros* lived in houses rented in Lucapa. The city was never occupied by the Unita but Capaia, right next to it, was and functioned as an active city by that time. (M., Luanda, 18 August 2011)

The *garimpo* brought many people but today the population is getting into bankruptcy because of the control; they have to dig furtively. (Soba P., Luó, 31 July 2011)

Luó was much bigger in the 1990s. Now it is decreasing and there are empty houses. People move to the city. Luó is now growing more in terms of agriculture. (M., Luó, 9 August 2011)

Ironically, there is a correlation between increased concentrations of artisanal mining and the reduction in opportunities for getting richer: 'overexploitation leads to excessive employment. Finding a diamond is a matter of chance. As more and more miners search for diamonds, every new miner reduces other miners' chances of finding a diamond' (Davies 2009: 2). This, along with the need of the post-war government to seize control of the informal mining areas, has again caused a significant relocation and displacement of the population from the once booming areas in the Lundas. Currently, the boom phenomenon is beginning to be seen in Bié, Nharea and Bailundo, to the south, where *garimpo* has started only recently and therefore where control is not as organized as in the Lundas. Many former *garimpeiros* of the Lundas, those who were not able or willing to alter their economic activity, and new *garimpeiros* in Angola, are starting to move to these locations, where formal control is looser.

Reorganization of formal mining and the appearance of new concessions in the Lundas area have contributed, however, to the settlement of a significant number of people in major towns associated with the formal mining activity. In relation to large mines like the Catoca, approximately 6,000 people lived in the vicinity in 2005 and it employed 2,000 Angolans and about 200 expatriates. SDM (Sociedade de Desenvolvimento Mineiro), in the same year, employed 1,293 people, of whom 119 were expatriates, the rest Angolan nationals from other provinces and about 600 local residents. About one third of the employees were brought in from Luanda and elsewhere and housed at the mine itself; the rest were local residents. There is also a significant important number of local families associated with the large mines, employed in the provision of services and in trade.

At the same time, towns in the Lundas have once again become attractive owing to the increased employment opportunities beyond the mining sector, namely in the administration, education or health sectors, or in trading or the provision of services. Urban migration not only constitutes an alternative for those involved in the *garimpo* during the war but also continues to attract rural inhabitants and others from various provinces to the main cities and towns. Where commercial activities have grown quickly because of the reopening of roads – as in border cities like Ondjiva in the south or Malanje connecting to the Lundas and to the DRC, or in cities and towns where important industrial/ commercial infrastructures were established or reinstituted, including the mining activities in the Lundas – a significant movement of people has taken place in the last decade. This time, the changes have not been led solely by the diamond-related activities. These newer changes constitute the base from which formerly displaced populations as well as regular migrants strategize to rebuild their lives and livelihoods.

Changing adaptive economic strategies over time

Various periods of displacement, migration and change in Angola as a whole, and in the diamond-rich Lundas in particular, have posed major challenges of economic survival and adaptation for the diversely affected populations. Earlier discussions have already hinted at some of the strategies developed in relation to these challenges. The following sections provide further insights into the creative agency of such mixed populations at different times in relation to the opening and closing of wider social, political and economic rifts. This reveals the interplay between the particular strategies of different groups and transformations of the local economy. The first section below revisits the colonial period, the second section addresses the era of the civil war, and the third explores the period of peace and reconstruction.

Colonial displacement: forced labour and urban migration The establishment of an adequate workforce for the mines in such sparsely populated areas as the Lundas was a hard undertaking that required significant efforts by the mining companies in order to 'import' labour to the region. As already mentioned, this type of resource was initially obtained forcibly (and subsequently voluntarily) through mechanisms such as coercive recruitment (Cleveland 2008; Clarence-Smith 1979). 'Recruited' workers had to carry out a one-year assignment and in theory would return to their home towns after that. Despite this, the mining jobs usually represented an important source of income for the mineworkers' families as they would get paid after that period.

Notwithstanding the rigid control of companies over urbanization and settlement in mining towns, other groups of people chose to move there in search of jobs and businesses. This contributed to the development of the non-mining local economy and made these places more attractive in terms of opportunities, even for the dismissed forced labourers. Among the first to arrive were the colonial settlers, usually in search of permission to undertake trade and establish commercial houses in such an appealing milieu. Another significant category of people that moved to the Lundas during this period were Congolese from the neighbouring areas to work in the mines. This migration, associated with increased economic opportunities and urbanization, contributed to a more regular rural migration to the peripheries of the Lundas towns by people who envisaged ways of improving their living conditions there. Mineworkers as well as traders and businessmen, while relying on formal wage work and on profits from their activities, did not ignore the possibility of making money in diamonds. An unaccounted number of these and others used *garimpo* as an extra, sometimes a fortune-making, way of generating an income. The first networks of illegal mining for diamonds were built precisely to circumvent the highly controlled operations of the Diamang mines.

As these formal and informal possibilities of generating income developed and forced labour was replaced by contract work, the displaced mineworkers considered ways of integrating themselves into the economy of the flourishing mining towns. Despite the differing individual life courses, the main possibilities found there were the mine jobs and the available urban activities that were being developed at that time.

Refuge and the search for diamonds during civil war When civil war started after independence, the strategy of the majority of the population in the Lundas was primarily to escape to the capital city, or other major cities, and there initiate new jobs and activities. Massive displacement to Luanda and other Angolan cities and towns because of the war involved a significant number of people from the Lundas, not counting the massive numbers of displaced Portuguese who left the country. The following are examples of the multilayered displacement effects during this period:

I was born in Cacolo, grew up in Saurimo and in 1975 went back to Cacolo. But then, with the war, I had to escape to Luanda, in 1983, and stayed there as a refugee until 2003; I had a [cooking] gas agency. I came back to Cacolo in 1992 but had to leave again because of the war. (A.M., Cacolo, 28 July 2011)

I lived in Saurimo since I was born [1943] and in the late 1960s/early 1970s lived in Lobito. In 1975 I came back to Saurimo to work and in 1978 went to Portugal because of the war. I ran a livestock firm there until 1992, when I came back to manage the CATEPA [cattle raising]. In that year we lost everything with the war. (B., Saurimo, 3 August 2011)

Scholarship about the strategies put into practice by the displaced population in Luanda has been more abundant than that concerning those who remained in secondary cities (Udelsmann Rodrigues 2006, 2007; Costa and Udelsmann Rodrigues 2008). From independence onwards, the capital city hosted an increasing number of people from the rest of the country, growing from roughly 600,000 inhabitants to an estimated four million in the 2000s. This growth is above all due to displacement caused by the war, and by migration. The second-most common 'option' was to stay in the Lundas towns. This represents a case of extensive forced immobility of the urban population, who remained for many years isolated from the surrounding rural areas, from other parts of the country, and from economic opportunities and possibilities. They lived essentially on external aid from the World Food Programme (WFP).

However, those who could not escape to the cities and remained in areas where diamond digging was controlled by the Unita forces were also compelled to stay in captivity. In those areas, they were later joined by foreigners working within the *garimpo*, all living under the control of the guerrilla army. A multitude of actors was then involved in the complex and diverse diamond-trading economy: '*garimpeiro* diggers working alone or under the control of armed patrons ... a multitude of buyers, both licensed and illicit ... unlicensed dealers operating in the diamond fields or in Luanda' (Dietrich 2000: 317). Among these were the enforced local populations, as well as another type of displaced population that came from the DRC. From the mid to late 1990s, conditions of insecurity and war-related violence saw a major shift from immigration to emigration in DRC (Jonsson 2009), with significant movements of people especially to Angola in search of diamonds (Sumata 2002). These displaced foreigners were rapidly integrated into the diamond economy as they were potentially 'easy to control; they have no long-term commitment to the region, and if they misbehave, they can be thrown out as the authorities choose' (Pearce 2004). *Artivistes*, employed by Unita to supervise the digging activities, were, for instance, Congolese (De Boeck 2001: 554).

During this long period, a complex network of exchange of commodities for diamonds was built, involving not only the activities in Angola but also connections with bordering countries and transnational buyers (ibid.: 553). The economic and social situation in the border regions of the DRC and the importance of diamond mining in Angola – together constituting a broader regional displacement economy – contributed to intense migration from one country to the other (Marques and Campos 2005: 9).

The connections between Angolans and Congolese is close not only because the border is porous but because there is an ethnic/historical link. The difference between the Angolan and Congolese *garimpeiros* is that the Angolans work for eating and the Congolese, like emigrants, have the idea of saving. They are hired to work and when they invest in Angola it is because they form a family here and because the DRC is difficult and troubled. *Garimpeiros* and traders from other West African countries do invest all profit in their countries. (S., 15 August 2011)

The contact and extensive relationships established during the war period account not only for a more permanent settlement in diamond-digging sites that became towns, but also for deep social, cultural and economic relations between those who lived together in a 'displacement' situation.

Until 2005 there were more foreigners in the Lundas than nationals. People who lived here all the time even learned to speak English, French or Arabic because they lived together for many years. (M., Saurimo, 25 July 2011)

'Yet besides "greed-driven" warlords using forced labour, hundreds of thousands of men, women, and children also engaged in diamond mining, hoping, in a context of chronic poverty and widespread abuses, that "luck be stronger than death"' (Le Billon 2008: 346). Despite the control by Unita of this network and the mining areas in Lunda, 'informal' digging also continued to attract an increasing number of people. This was not only the rural population outside the control of the guerrillas but also urban 'refugees' from all cities in Angola that could find mining spots uncontrolled either by government forces or by Unita. Simultaneously, many 'tacit' arrangements were established during the long-lasting period of the war, opening and shutting down opportunities for all sorts of different actors.

UNITA gave freedom of movement to the population to dig diamonds in the non-government mining areas. There were buyers that would come by helicopter, mercenaries. The youth would get money from the *camanga* [illegal diamond trade] and bought things in Saurimo, that was supplied by air [including WFP goods]. (F.G., Tchizaínga II, 24 July 2011)

Some of these opportunities were not even necessarily created by the *garimpo* itself but by a combination of war, *garimpo*, trafficking and trade or food provision activities related to the diamond digging.

You did not even need to be digging diamonds or in the business; food and drink business has always been more profitable. (M., Luanda, 18 August 2011)

Goods of all sorts were particularly needed – and paid for – by the *garimpeiros*. This not only fuelled the war efforts through the well-documented chain of supply to Unita (Le Billon 2008; Malaquias 2001a, 2001b; Pearce 2004; Marques and Campos 2005) but also revolved around the everyday life of *garimpeiros* who were not necessarily working for the guerrillas. So, for example, finding a good diamond, a *lubóia*, usually meant celebrating with a big party where food and beverages were of particular importance. In addition, there was the buying of all sorts of expensive commodities that suddenly appeared in the middle of war-torn, non-urbanized settlements: expensive cars, luxury watches, clothes:

> By then, there were no banks and so the *garimpeiro* would spend his money right away, paying higher prices for the commodities; they could buy crates of beer to wash the cars they bought. (D.T., Itengo, 24 July 2011)

In this complex but simultaneously economically attractive context of the mining sites, opportunities became increasingly more available, even for those who were forced to work for the guerrillas. The displaced Congolese escaping the war in their country may have found ways of integrating into these complex economic networks more quickly, but the 'immobilized' Lundas – and to some extent the displaced military – eventually also found ways of mobilizing the capital they acquired during the war: on the one hand, skills for digging diamonds and, on the other, the power to put a production chain in place. The strategies to do so were found outside the guerrilla-controlled economy, opening new 'informal within the informal' *garimpos* and trading networks.

Coping with more change: peace and reconstruction By the end of the war, massive evictions and deportations of foreigners were taking place. For instance, in 2004 in a government action called *Operação Brilhante*, over 100,000 foreign citizens were forcefully expelled and repatriated. Ninety per cent of these were from the DRC, according to the Angolan National Police (Marques and Campos: 2005: 9). With regained control of the region and with the need to assure that newly created mining investments could be attractive and secure, the government allegedly proceeded with mass evictions not only of foreigners but also of illegal miners from the targeted mining areas.

Artisanal informal mining became highly valued and simultaneously hidden. In other words, though dangerous, it continued to be undertaken by many people. A 2009 annual report on mining in Angola concluded that 'for the vast majority of informal artisanal producers in Angola, the new code does nothing. Large scale commercial *garimpo* – of the type that produces some 30% of Angola's diamonds by value each year – was illegal under the old regulations, and remains so under the new code' (Smillie 2009: 3). However, the new law passed in June 2011[7] foresees the legalization of artisanal mining dependent on compliance with certain rules, which might again introduce some changes to the social and economic environment.

In the formal sector, with the reactivation of mining companies from 2002 onwards, and new actors becoming active in the field, displacement (actual and potential) became again a source of tension between the population living in diamond-rich areas – including the illegal miners still living at mining sites – and the companies. There are several studies revealing how mining-induced displacement and resettlement have significant impacts locally (Downing 2002). In Angola, for the mining companies this is a sensitive area, as can be observed in most of their reports. Employment of (unskilled) wage labour, however, is less widespread than in the colonial times owing to improved technology, which does not make the new mining jobs a plausible economic alternative. At the same time, qualified workers are not recruited locally as there is a shortage of this type of human resource in the Lundas.

In general, it is in major Angolan cities that new opportunities have started to emerge. Population growth and economic dynamism are more evident here, and the main cause for this is the re-established peace. On the one hand, it has allowed for more investment in private tertiary activities (such as transportation, wholesale trade and retail or accommodation) that rely on more attractive urban markets. On the other hand it has generated more formal jobs in the administration services and in the health and education sectors. Some return to the Lundas from Angola's major cities and from neighbouring countries has taken place since the war finally ended, although this is no longer directed to the rural home town areas. Many of the formerly displaced in Luanda or in other cities had already developed other forms of survival that no longer accord with the rural way of living.

But a certain visible tendency to revert to an 'urban' economy does not imply a full abandonment of *garimpo*. Increased company and state control of mining together with growing opportunities in the public sector and business have not reduced completely the importance of informal mining within the range of possible income-generating activities. Those with no urban economic background – that is, with no qualifications or capital to get into formal mining, the state and administration services, or to engage in urban businesses – have to rely on their key qualifications acquired during the war. That is one of the main reasons, as mentioned before, why new areas, farther to the south in neighbouring provinces, are now attracting informal miners, most of them with Lundas wartime experience. The *garimpo* activities still under way in the Lundas are carried out by a complex network of hidden *garimpeiros* who have done this all their working lives, and by those who were able to get richer during the war and became buyers or sponsors.

Conclusion

One key focus in this discussion has been an examination of the continuities between the informal diamond digging that accompanied the establishment of colonial mining companies and the civil war, and the ongoing importance of such activities in the current strategies of Lunda people, particularly the displaced categories initially identified: coerced colonial workers, displaced military, enforced immobilized urban and mining site dwellers, and displaced immigrants.

Being the centre of the economy in the region since colonial times, the weight of diamonds in the economy is still significant, both nationally and at the level of families' incomes. Diamond digging is a deeply rooted activity for the population of the Lundas and has been a way of absorbing the displaced population into the local economy. Undoubtedly there were and might still be many informal miners motivated by the idea of a 'diamond rush' and others depending totally on this activity. However, there are others who see diamond digging as a common complementary economic activity. Miners' motivations are above all linked to their background, skills and competencies rather than to a fever to get rich (Hilson 2010). In fact, farming is frequently combined with diamond mining in diamond-rich African countries (Maconachie and Binns 2007). This has become increasingly the way of living in the Lundas.

With the transformation of colonial mining organization and the many implications of war (and peace) for the economy and for displacement of the population, particularly rapid and deep in the last decades, new forms and combinations of economic activity and opportunities emerged during different periods. The recurringly 'displaced' in the Lundas have adapted to these changes and creatively combined, merged or moved from one to another economic possibility, shaping the local economic tissue and the chances for integration into the new dynamics of society and economy.

More general stability and less attraction to mining, as seems to be the trend in the Lundas, may foster more standard forms of development in mineral-rich areas. There are examples of how Namibia and Botswana, by restricting diamond mining, promoted the development of other sectors, such as agriculture, whereas Sierra Leone and Angola did not (Davies 2009). Should there be indications of this more developmental tendency, there could be positive prospects for the consolidation of peace in the country and for local development in general. Associated with this, the actions and perspectives of the youth, that see more of a future in state and trade than in *garimpo*, may also be the key. One of the main ingredients for coping with these new shifts in the economy and political situation in the Lundas is the capacity shown historically by the population to deal with change, particularly the displaced, and to develop integrative strategies. This was demonstrated first in colonial times, by the transformation of forced labourers into contracted urban workers. Subsequently, the displaced immigrants entered the wartime diamond economy, and this was followed by the participation of the military in this economy. Finally, the confined urban and rural populations were capable of resorting to the informal urban or *garimpo* economy under conditions of war.

Notes

1 Following the independence of African states, beginning in the 1950s, and Portugal's ratification of the International Labour Office's treaties regarding fair labour practices (Cleveland 2008).

2 Diamang (Companhia de Diamantes de Angola) was established in Angola in 1917, and by the 1970s – with a country-wide concession to mine diamonds – had grown into the largest commercial enterprise in Portugal's African empire. Source: www.embangola-can.org/diamonds.html.

3 Figures provided both by the government and international agencies. Of these, fewer than 100,000 were confirmed after the Peace Memorandum of 2002 (Porto and Parsons 2003: 11).

4 Interview references indicate the interviewee's initials, the place where it was conducted and the date.

5 As the UN recognized the role that diamonds played in funding the Unita rebels, in 1998 it passed United Nations Security Council Resolution 1173, followed by United Nations Security Council Resolution 1176, banning the purchase of what came to be called 'blood diamonds' from Angola.

6 According to Marques and Campos (2005), in 2005 this expatriation operation, called *Operação Brilhante*, had already targeted 100,000 foreigners, 90 per cent of them from the DRC.

7 Law no. 31/11, *Diário da República*, 184, I Série, 23 September 2011.

References

Brinkman, I. (2003) 'War and identity in Angola: two case-studies', *Lusotopie*, pp. 195–22.

— (2005) *A War for People: Civilians, mobility and legitimacy in South-east Angola during the MPLA's war for independence*, Cologne: Rüdiger Köppe Verlag.

Bryceson, D. F. and V. Jamal (1997) *Farewell to Farms: De-agrarianisation and employment in Africa*, London: Ashgate.

Calvão, F. (2011) 'When boom goes bust: ruins, crisis and security in megaengineering diamond mining in Angola', in S. D. Brunn (ed.), *Engineering Earth*, Dordrecht: Springer Netherlands, pp. 367–82.

Clarence-Smith, W. G. (1979) *Slaves, Peasants and Capitalists in Southern Angola (1840–1926)*, Cambridge: Cambridge University Press.

Cleveland, T. (2008) 'Rock solid: African laborers on the diamond mines of the Companhia de Diamantes de Angola (Diamang), 1917–1975', Unpublished PhD thesis, University of Minnesota.

Costa, A. and C. Udelsmann Rodrigues (2008) 'Famílias e estratégias de sobrevivência e reprodução social em Luanda e Maputo', in I. Raposo and J. Oppenheimer (eds), *Subúrbios de Luanda e Maputo*, Lisbon: Colibri, pp. 139–61.

Crush, J. and W. James (1995) *Crossing Boundaries: Mine migrancy in a democratic South Africa*, Cape Town: IDASA/IDRC.

Davies, R. and J. Head (1995) 'The future of mine migrancy in the context of broader trends in migration in southern Africa', *Journal of Southern African Studies*, 21(3): 439–50.

Davies, V. A. B. (2009) 'Alluvial diamonds: a new resource curse theory', Unpublished PhD thesis, University of Oxford.

De Boeck, P. (2001) 'Garimpeiro worlds: digging, dying and "hunting" for diamonds in Angola', *Review of African Political Economy*, 28(90): 549–62.

De Bruijn, M., R. van Dijk and D. Foeken (eds) (2001) *Mobile Africa: Changing patterns of movement in Africa and beyond*, Leiden: Brill.

Dias, J. R. (1989) 'Relações económicas e de poder no interior de Luanda ca. 1850–1875', in *1ª Reunião Internacional de História de África: Relações Europa-África no 3º Quartel do século XIX*, Lisbon: Instituto de Investigação Científica Tropical, CEHCA, pp. 241–58.

Dietrich, C. (2000) 'Porous borders and diamonds', in J. Cilliers and C. Dietrich (eds), *Angola's War Economy*,

Pretoria: Institute for Security Studies, pp. 317–45.

Downing, T. E. (2002) *Avoiding New Poverty: Mining-induced displacement and resettlement*, Mining, Minerals and Sustainable Development project, International Institute for Environment and Development (IIED).

E-Polis (n.d.) *Urban Populations 1880–2020*, e-geopolis.eu/spip.php?article193&id_article=193.

Hilson, G. (2010) '"Once a miner, always a miner": poverty and livelihood diversification in Akwatia, Ghana', *Journal of Rural Studies*, 26: 296–307.

Jonsson, G. (2009) *Comparative Report: African migration trends*, African Perspectives on Human Mobility Programme, International Migration Institute, University of Oxford.

Le Billon, P. (2008) 'Diamond wars? Conflict diamonds and geographies of resource wars', *Annals of the Association of American Geographers*, 98(2): 345–72.

Lubkemann, S. C. (2008) 'Involuntary immobility: on a theoretical invisibility in forced migration studies', *Journal of Refugee Studies*, 21(4): 454–75.

Maconachie, R. and T. Binns (2007) '"Farming miners" or "mining farmers"?: diamond mining and rural development in post-conflict Sierra Leone', *Journal of Rural Studies*, 23: 367–80.

Malaquias, A. (2001a) 'Making war and lots of money: the political economy of protracted conflict in Angola', *Review of African Political Economy*, 28(90): 521–36.

— (2001b) 'Diamonds are a guerrilla's best friend: the impact of illicit wealth on insurgency strategy', *Third World Quarterly*, 22(3): 311–25.

— (2007) *Rebels and Robbers: Violence in post-colonial Angola*, Uppsala: Nordiska Afrikainstitutet.

Marques, R. and R. F. de Campos (2005) *Lundas: as pedras da morte*, Lisbon: Relatório sobre os Direitos Humanos, Grafispaço.

Pearce, J. (2004) 'War, peace and diamonds in Angola: popular perceptions of the diamond industry in the Lundas', *African Security Review*, 13(2): 51–64.

Pereira, E., J. Rodrigues and B. Reis (2003) 'Synopsis of Lunda geology, NE Angola: implications for diamond exploration', *Comun. Inst. Geol. e Mineiro*, 1(90): 189–212.

Porto, J. G. and I. Parsons (2003) 'Sustaining the peace in Angola: an overview of current demobilisation, disarmament and reintegration', Paper 27, Bonn International Centre for Conversion.

Shanmugaratnam, N., R. Lund and K. A. Stølen (eds) (2003) *In the Maze of Displacement: Conflict, migration and change*, Norway, Høyskoleforlaget.

Smillie, I. (ed.) (2009) 'Diamonds and human security', *Annual Review 2009*, Partnership Africa Canada, www.pacweb.org/Documents/annual-reviews-diamonds/AR_diamonds_2009_eng.pdf.

Sumata, C. (2002) 'Migradollars and poverty alleviation strategy issues in Congo (DRC)', *Review of African Political Economy*, 29(93/94): 619–28.

Udelsmann Rodrigues, C. (2006) *O Trabalho Dignifica o Homem: Estratégias de sobrevivência em Luanda*, Lisbon: Colibri.

— (2007) 'Survival and social reproduction strategies in Angolan cities', *Africa Today*, 54(1): 91–105.

Wheeler, D. L. and R. Pélissier (1971) *Angola*, Westport, CT: Greenwood Press.

6 | Somali displacements and shifting markets: camel milk in Nairobi's Eastleigh Estate

Hannah Elliott

Introduction

It is 11 a.m. in Eastleigh, and 7th Street is a hive of activity. The *Waso Raha* bus has just drawn into the Isiolo stage, laden with yellow plastic jerrycans of camel milk, inscribed with women's names: Habiba, Rahma, Zeinab ... Somali women crowd around the bus to collect their jerrycans; others wait at their selling spots on 7th Street for *hamali* (porters) to carry the milk to them for a meagre ten shillings. In the Mashallah camel milk bar, Somali men await the fresh *caano geel* (camel milk) for which the small restaurant is locally famed, some impatiently barking to the bartender, '*Maziwa wapi waryaa?*' (Hey, where's the milk?).[1]

Camel milk has become ubiquitous on the streets of Nairobi's Eastleigh estate, which has acquired the nickname *Mogadishu Ndogo* (Little Mogadishu).[2] Somali women sit in clusters on 7th and 13th Streets selling milk from jerrycans by the litre, while on Jam Street it is found in small quantities by makeshift stalls, sold alongside other goods such as dates, biscuits and ghee. The majority of Eastleigh's restaurants also serve camel milk, as well as *shaah caano geel* (camel milk tea). Though more expensive than cow milk tea, *shaah caano geel* is far more popular, often selling out around afternoon *casiriya* (teatime). Dotted around the estate are informal outdoor tea shops where women cook and sell *shaah* to Somali men sitting on plastic chairs in the shade of large umbrellas. The Mashallah milk bar is the only formal venue in Eastleigh specifically for the sale and consumption of camel milk, sold by the litre in polythene bags for home consumption, or by the 500ml tankard-style plastic cup.[3] The milk bar is frequented by Somali men of all ages, and is fertile ground for lively debates. A number of regulars to the milk bar are visitors to Nairobi from the Somali diaspora, on long holidays from America, Canada and Britain, and claim to travel across the city from more affluent estates to drink milk at this particular spot, where the milk is renowned for being *fresh kabisa* (totally fresh).

But camel milk has not always been sold in Eastleigh, and certainly not in the quantities we see today, having reached urban markets only in recent years. Traditionally among Somali pastoralists, camel milk production and consumption was restricted to a subsistence basis, and exchanged between family and clan members (Anderson et al. 2012). Selling camel milk was taboo; to resort to sale indicated desperation, a curse on the camel and hard times ahead (ibid.). With the collapse of Somalia's Barre administration in 1991 and the subsequent flood of Somali refugees into Kenya, camel milk has broken free of its domestic, rural domain, entering urban markets to meet new demand. Markets in Eastleigh and the Dadaab refugee camp complex in the north-east of the country – now said to be the third-largest city in Kenya (Guardian 2011) – are full of fresh (*day*) and soured (*susaac*) camel milk. This chapter examines the relations surrounding camel milk in Eastleigh as a product which has acquired particular socio-economic value in the midst of a crisis that has, among other things, generated large-scale dislocations. Through the lens of the camel milk market, it thus explores the effects of parallel and interlacing processes of displacement among diverse Somali populations from across the Somali regions and the global Somali diaspora.

In recent years there has been a proliferation of scholarship on the Somali community in Eastleigh (see, for example, Carrier and Lochery 2013; Abdulsamad 2011; Lindley 2007, 2010; Chebichi 2009; Mwiandi 2007; Campbell 2005, 2006). These studies have explored Eastleigh's booming economy, the role of refugee capital in this transformation, and refugees' possibilities for social, economic and legal integration in the estate. These works have tended to take refugees as their focus, though acknowledge the important role that Kenyan Somalis have played. The latter provided not only a 'pull factor' for refugees to the estate but also have enabled refugees to circumvent legal restrictions on their livelihoods, for example through partnering with Kenyan Somalis and licensing businesses in their names. These authors find that Somalis in Nairobi, and historically in Kenya more generally,[4] nevertheless face discrimination, harassment and suspicion.[5] What remains less explored in the existing scholarship are the interactions between the refugee crisis in Somalia and parallel processes of displacement among Somali pastoralist populations in Kenya, and the social, political and economic effects that these interactions are generating.[6] From a displacement economies perspective, Eastleigh's milk markets are fertile ground for exploring the creative processes taking place within and in response to these interlacing displacement contexts, which draw in Somali actors from diverse backgrounds across the Somali regions and national borders. This includes the Somali diaspora from Western countries visiting or doing business in the estate, refugees from Somalia and the Ogaden (the Somali region of Ethiopia), 'ex-pastoralists' from northern Kenya, and nomadic camel herders.

A number of scholars have investigated the development of camel milk marketing in Somalia itself (Herren 1990 for Mogadishu; Talle 1992 for Belet Weyne in central Somalia; Little 1994 for southern Somalia; Nori 2009 for Puntland). Research has recently also been undertaken on camel milk marketing trends in the Ogaden (Hussein 2010). There is also some NGO literature on the camel milk trade in north-eastern Kenya and opportunities for developing and formalizing the sector (SNV 2006 for Isiolo; CARE Kenya 2009 for Garissa). An article co-authored with David Anderson, Hassan Kochore and Emma Lochery (Anderson et al. 2012) explores the commodification of camel milk in Kenya, tracing the transformation of camel milk from a subsistence good to a valuable commodity. The focus of these analyses has mainly been on the supply side of the trade, touching only superficially on the demand from the migrant consumer base that drives it. Demand for camel milk in urban centres in Somalia, Ethiopia and Kenya has generally been viewed as an inevitable consequence of urbanization in a pastoralist setting, whereby settled people, familiar with drinking camel milk in their rural homes, are unable to access the means of production in town and are thus forced to buy it. The value of camel milk for urban consumers remains unquestioned in most scholarship. Furthermore, the pivotal role of forced displacement in shaping camel milk markets in Kenya has not been explored. The 'greater logic' (Friedman 2004) connecting camel milk's supply and demand is key to understanding the processes behind Eastleigh's booming camel milk markets. This 'greater logic', as we shall see, can tell us something about socio-economic transformation and community- and identity-making among Somalis in Eastleigh in response to the changes wrought by parallel and interlacing displacement processes.

Following Appadurai's (1986) premise that 'things' have 'social lives', I attempt to elucidate the transformative effects of displacement on camel milk markets by examining camel milk's 'life history' (Kopytoff 1986) and tracing its trajectories to the Eastleigh market. In response to demands for 'home' and 'our culture' from Somali refugees and visitors from the global Somali diaspora in Eastleigh, the commodification of camel milk has triggered shifts in the social relations which traditionally surrounded milk production, exchange and consumption. Commodification has not meant a total departure from these social relations, however. Trade in camel milk continues to bond Somalis across rural and urban spheres into an integrated system of interdependence, reminiscent of its earlier gift exchange. The broadening of the Somali community in Eastleigh following mass displacement from Somalia has meant that these connections have been extended beyond clan or kin affiliations on the broader basis of a shared identity as 'Somali'.

Historical context: who are the 'Somalis' in Eastleigh?

Eastleigh is home to many thousands of refugees from Somalia, and has become strongly associated with the ethnic Somali community in Kenya. Yet the 'Little Mogadishu' label glosses over its diverse population and the heterogeneity of the Somali community itself, as well as a long-established

Kenyan Somali presence in the estate which provided a 'pull factor' for the more recently arrived refugee population. 'Somali' describes one ethnic group consisting of a number of clans and sub-clans that span four nations in the Horn of Africa – Kenya, Somalia,[7] Ethiopia and Djibouti – collectively known as the Somali regions.[8] Since the collapse of the state of Somalia in the early 1990s, Somalis from the former Somali Republic have been dispersed across the world, constituting a global diaspora. However, the majority of these displaced Somalis have remained within the eastern Africa region, either in Somalia as internally displaced people or as refugees in neighbouring Ethiopia and Kenya. At the same time, some segments of Eastleigh's Somali population have migrated to the estate from other parts of the Somali regions, particularly from within Kenya, and have their own turbulent histories also characterized by displacement. Manifest in Eastleigh is the overlaying of intersecting histories and patterns of Somali migration and displacement, linked by a common Somali ethnic identity and language.

Eastleigh estate was established under the colonial administration be-tween 1910 and 1914. In its early stages, the estate was sold to an Indian businessman and quickly developed as an Asian residential quarter, with a few Asian-owned shops and businesses (Campbell 2005). There was also a significant Isaaq presence in Eastleigh at this time, known by the Brit-ish as the 'alien Somali' to distinguish them from their Somali pastoralist cousins from northern Kenya, who were Kenyan nationals. Isaaq Somalis are urbanites who may have arrived in Nairobi as early as 1900 (Mwiandi 2007), having migrated from British Somaliland as traders, soldiers in the British army and employees of Europeans (Goldsmith 1997). Isaaq in Eastleigh were connected to kinsmen in towns across Kenya, and particularly in the north, linking the estate to a wider Kenyan Somali population. The Somali presence in Eastleigh also attracted Somalis from other clans to visit and settle there, as well as other Muslim and pastoralist communities from northern Kenya (Carrier and Lochery 2013).

Independence and the Africanization of Kenya saw the emigration of many Kenyan Asians to Britain. Many of those who remained in Nairobi moved out of Eastleigh to more affluent parts of the city (Campbell 2005), though some stayed to oversee their businesses (Goldsmith 2008). By the 1970s, Eastleigh was largely occupied by urbanized Africans, including the aforementioned small but well-established Somali community (Campbell 2005). A significant proportion of formerly Asian-owned properties were bought by Kikuyu, Kenya's largest ethnic group, in line with their economic ascendancy during the post-independence era (Goldsmith 2008). During this period, it is probable that the Kenyan Somali community in Eastleigh continued to expand owing to rural–urban migration of Somali pastoralists from northern Kenya, drawn to the opportunities represented by the existing Somali presence in the city. The

Somali population exploded, however, with the influx of refugees from Somalia during and following Somalia's collapse in the early 1990s. Besides the existing Somali presence in Eastleigh, Somali-operated lodgings and transport links between northern Kenya and the estate were a major attraction for refugees (Carrier and Lochery 2013; Campbell 2005). Kikuyu landlords quickly began selling their properties to refugees (ibid.) as the value of housing soared, and the estate's existing residents moved into other parts of Nairobi, finding rental accommodation unaffordable (Lindley 2007). Today, the majority of landlords and tenants in Eastleigh are Somali (Campbell 2005).

Transnational Somali linkages have also played an important role in Eastleigh's transformation. Extensive Somali trade networks, traceable to long-established links between Somalia and Gulf markets which pre-date Somalia's civil war, today span the globe. They connect the Somali diaspora business community, bringing goods to the Eastleigh market from nodes such as Dubai, China and Thailand (Carrier and Lochery 2013). Shiny new malls line Eastleigh's streets, with names referencing these international connections, such as 'Bangkok' and 'Hong Kong', alongside older enterprises bearing names of towns in north-eastern Kenya, such as 'Garissa Lodge' and 'Mandera Lodge', reminiscent of Eastleigh's Kenyan Somali roots. The currency of business in Eastleigh is the US dollar, and many foreign exchange bureaus have set up shop in the estate (Wairimu 2011). Eastleigh also hosts numerous money transfer agencies which facilitate the sending and receiving of remittances between Somalis in the global diaspora, Eastleigh and Kenya's refugee camps (Lindley 2010). The estate is frequented by Somalis from across the diaspora visiting relatives, searching for spouses and learning 'their culture'.

Growing trade and market opportunities in Eastleigh have also catalysed rural–urban migration trends from northern Kenya. While intersecting with the displacement trends that have brought Somali refugees to the estate, this migration trend must also be examined in its own right in relation to broader historical, political and environmental changes in northern Kenya which have disrupted pastoralist economies and forced Kenyan Somalis and other pastoralist communities to diversify out of pastoralism. Northern Kenya has historically been marginalized, the region's predominantly pastoralist livelihoods undermined by colonial and independent government policies, war, conflict and climate change. This has resulted in high fallout rates from pastoralism and rapid sedentarization and urbanization as pastoralists drift to northern towns seeking economic opportunities. Migration trends are also oriented towards major urban centres, and particularly to Eastleigh; the International Organization for Migration (IOM) identifies the estate as both a destination and a transit point for Somali 'ex-pastoralists' from Garissa District (IOM 2010). There is growing recognition that pastoralist sedentarization should be viewed as displacement as opposed to economic migration. One recent report calls for pastoralist 'drop-outs' to be granted the status and legal protection of internally displaced persons (IDPs) (Sheekh et al. 2012).

Nevertheless, urbanization and sedentarization should not be read as a complete departure from pastoralism: many town dwellers diversify between town-based livelihoods and livestock in the bush. Pastoralists are also adapting their livestock investments to cope with climatic shifts, and are increasingly investing in camels because of their durability through drought (Anderson et al. 2012). These investments are also a response to demand in urban markets, and the growing interest in keeping camels for milk trade is a clear example.

Conceptualizing consumption and commodification of camel milk

In order to explicate how displacement has reshaped a market and system of production, we need to understand the processes behind the shift in camel milk's sociocultural and economic value. This can be done first through de-lineating consumption, exchange and commodification, and then by looking at these apparently distinct phenomena as part of one overall system of value.

'Things' function as mediating materials in processes of identity-making (Douglas and Isherwood 1978). Consuming things is a means through which people can reify, reassert or reinvent their identities in situations where they have been destabilized. Some things lend themselves to these roles more than others, and food has been shown to be particularly important in processes of identity construction at times of rapid socio-economic change, upheaval and displacement (Searles 2002; Holtzman 2009; Abbots 2011). Food's synaesthetic qualities and capacity to evoke memory enable people to retrieve the past and connect with a sense of something lost (Sutton 2001). This can be a crucial resource for forcibly displaced people, and consequently foods can become embedded in narratives of 'home', the nation or a region, or of 'us' and 'our culture'. These narratives may also serve as vehicles through which people can comment on the processes of socio-economic change that characterize experiences of displacement (Holtzman 2009). For Somalis in Eastleigh, as we shall see, drinking camel milk has become a way of alleviating and making sense of exile.

But the power of 'things' in facilitating identity construction lies not only in their consumption but also in their exchange. While there is a rich literature on the significance of eating, commensality and exchange of food for the production of social relations and identities (Carsten 1995; Sutton 2001), it is often assumed that when food is commodified, these relations are somehow lost (Sutton 2001; Counihan 1984). Yet romanticizing a moral, uncommercial past in sharp contrast to an amoral, commercial present may be misleading (Willis 1999) in that it obscures the possibility that processes characteristic of gift exchange may also be found in the marketplace (Van Binsbergen 2005; Friedman 2004). Appadurai's seminal volume *The Social Life of Things* (1986) was crucial in bringing anthropologists' attention to commodities and commodification processes because it critiqued and collapsed this gift/commodity dichotomy. According to Appadurai, commodification is a situational process; a 'thing' becomes a commodity only in particular situations which are socially and culturally defined. Furthermore, 'things' have varying degrees of commodity potential.

If the commodity phase of a thing is just one phase in its whole 'life history' (Kopytoff 1986), in order to understand the true value of a commodity – what makes a thing commodifiable in certain moments – we need to investigate its full 'social life', its '*total* trajectory from production through exchange/distribution to consumption' (ibid.). Appadurai uses the metaphor of 'paths and diversions' to elucidate the historical social and political processes which draw a thing in and out of its various phases. This processual view suggests that commodification is unlikely to involve a complete and sudden departure from the social relations surrounding that thing as it was formerly produced, exchanged and consumed, although these relations are likely to change. As we will see, in the Eastleigh context the social relations surrounding commodified camel milk on the one hand may be seen as a continuation of gift exchange of milk. Camel milk exchange continues to build social relations and interdependence across rural and urban spheres. At the same time, the political and environmental forces which have differentially displaced diverse Somali populations and induced camel milk's commodification have also prompted an extension of social relations. Social ties have thus not been lost, but they have changed in response and adaptation to these upheavals.

In spite of his important contribution to studies of commodities and commodification, Appadurai has come under criticism for focusing his analysis rather exclusively on exchange and the commodity phase of a thing's social life. Friedman argues that by defining the commodity phase as one in a larger social process there is the risk of losing 'the logic of the larger system' (Friedman 2004; Carrier 2007). Indeed, by focusing on the commodity phase we neglect other important aspects of a thing's social life where its exchangeability is not to the fore, including situations of consumption (Carrier 2007). Although consumption as 'the origin of a specific structure of demand' (Friedman 2004) drives commodification, Appadurai's approach leaves us with a sense of disjunction between exchange of commodities and their consumption, as if they were distinct phenomena (ibid.). According to Friedman, what is lacking here is a sense of the 'greater logic' which connects the different phases of a thing's social life. This greater logic, he suggests, is where we should expect to find the key to understanding the dynamics of demand (ibid). Following Friedman, I investigate the full social life of the camel milk which reaches the Eastleigh market in order to elucidate the shifting dynamics surrounding its production, trade and consumption.

'Drinking culture' in Eastleigh: 'we [Somalis] like rice, spaghetti, but we drink also our culture'[9]

The camel and camel milk have become symbols of Somali identity in Eastleigh and elsewhere in the Somali diaspora, and most informants referred to drinking camel milk as 'Somali culture'. According to one informant, a historian from Mogadishu, this was not always the case – camel milk used to have negative associations among townspeople in Somalia as it connoted a rural and 'backward' way of life. In the Eastleigh context, he noted, the value of camel milk has changed. This is because camels and camel milk are synonymous with 'home' and the lost nation;[10] drinking camel milk 'is tantamount to nostalgia'. Although in Somalia (as well as the other Somali regions), not all Somalis are 'camel people' (Ahmed 1995), in Eastleigh camel milk was portrayed as a symbol of 'Somaliness' and 'home' common to all Somalis, regardless of background. This was often conveyed through the association of camel milk with rural life in the *badia* (countryside), in spite of the fact that most informants hailed from urban areas across the Somali regions. It was common for informants to refer to the benefits of drinking camel milk in the desert, for example, or the possibility of living entirely on camel milk in a pastoralist context. The *badia* was conveyed by informants as 'home' for all Somalis.

Camel milk was a vehicle for romanticizing this 'home' and commenting on the ills of urban life, often through the idiom of health. A number of informants noted that grandparents in the *badia* often live to over a hundred, one adding that his grandfather of 104 years had a seven-year-old son. Elders' health was attributed to their traditional pastoralist diets of mostly meat and milk, while the younger 'spaghetti generation'[11] was weaker with a shorter lifespan because of their poor diets of 'modern' foods and sedentary lifestyles. It was generally agreed that Somalis these days often suffer from poor health and 'modern' diseases such as high blood pressure, hypertension, obesity and diabetes – illnesses which do not affect those with traditional lifestyles. While this may be read as an articulation of ambivalence around the changes brought by rural–urban migration, the discourse has been employed particularly in the context of forced migration, and people noted that these illnesses have worsened with war and exile. Camel milk was widely spoken of in interviews as *dawa* (medicine) for such diseases.[12] Three stories were recounted to me by different informants which were variations on the same theme: a man from the Somali diaspora (in Britain/America/Tanzania) fell ill with hypertension/diabetes/cancer and went to live in the *badia* in Somalia/northern Kenya for three months, drinking only camel milk. On his return, the doctor found him cured. A similar story featured a Somali girl who fell ill and, on visiting the doctor, was found to be HIV positive. After living in the *badia* and drinking only camel milk for a number of months, she tested negative. Such stories speak of concerns about particular aspects of social change which come with life in Eastleigh, which may be remedied with 'traditional' values and practices. Implicit in the story about the HIV-positive Somali girl, for example, is anxiety around women's sexual morality in the city.

The surge in demand for 'culture', 'home' and 'medicine' accompanying the growth of Eastleigh lies behind the booming milk trade in the estate and demonstrates how certain 'things' can become imbued with a new or particular significance in a context of displacement. In order to explore the shift in economic and social relations that the heightened value of camel milk induced and the 'greater logic' connecting its demand dynamics with its supply, we now turn to camel milk's 'life history' and trajectories in relation to the Eastleigh market.

Paths and diversions: the 'life history' of camel milk

Camel-herding communities across the Horn of Africa have long celebrated the camel for its durability in arid lands and provision of meat and milk in an ecologically challenging environment (Farah et al. 2004). As compared to other livestock, camels excel when it comes to dairy products. They have a longer lactating period than cows and are able to produce as much as 20 litres of milk per day under dry conditions (SNV 2006). In addition, camel milk is often considered special among camel pastoralists and valued above milk from other livestock, owing to its attributed healthful properties.[13]

Camels also play a key role in facilitating social relations, functioning as bridewealth as well as *diya* (blood compensation) following feuds between clans (Lewis 1961; Farah et al. 2004). Their centrality to the Somali pastoralist economy is celebrated in Somali poetry (Abokor 1987), and manifest in the great respect and rituals surrounding their treatment.[14] Under this ritualized system, camel milk was not sold but consumed by the calves and household or exchanged as a gift between relatives to strengthen ties and spread risk (Anderson et al. 2012; Hussein 2010; Nori 2009). Selling milk was considered shameful and implied desperation (Anderson et al. 2012; Nori 2009).

As we have seen in Eastleigh, camel milk has moved away from its domestic, gift status and is now sold and acquired on the market. As scholars have found for other Somali regions, rapid urbanization around administrative and trading centres in northern Kenya, in part a response to political and environmental shifts which undermined pastoralist livelihoods, diverted camel milk from its traditional trajectories towards the market (Anderson et al. 2012). This demonstrates, in the words of Appadurai, 'creativity in a crisis' (1986: 26) on the part of pastoralist communities in the region. Selling milk is a way for poor pastoralists to remain pastoralists, rather than being forced to sell the few camels they still have.

The growth of urban centres in northern Kenya and elsewhere in pastoralist areas of the Horn during the colonial era saw the onset of early rural-to-urban exchange of milk. Pastoralists would visit relatives and friends in urban centres carrying fresh or soured milk as a gift, or send the milk with a camp member making the trip to town. This may be seen as a continuation of traditional customs of gift exchange as a means of strengthening existing social relations and safety nets (Nori 2009). The integration of the arid lands of the Horn into national and international markets[15] meant that pastoralists were increasingly able to access commodities such as tea and sugar,[16] and even more so with the development of urban centres around colonial administration posts. Poorer pastoralist households also increasingly relied on grains in diversifying their traditional diets (Herren 1990). Sending milk to urban relatives was a way of accessing these commodities. My research assistant recalled how in pre-mobile phone Kenya, illiterate relatives in the *badia* around Garissa town would send jerrycans of milk to their urban cousins with 'messages' attached in the form of a small bag of sugar, for example, or a piece of cloth, to indicate the commodities they required in return.[17] As well as consuming the milk themselves, urban relatives might sell some of the milk in order to purchase these goods. Nomadic women would also sporadically come to town themselves with milk, hawking it from plot to plot, using the proceeds to buy the goods they needed in the market.[18]

This early rural-to-urban exchange and small-scale sale of camel milk developed into a more comprehensive and disaggregated trade with the emergence of urban-based traders who acted as 'middlewomen' (Anderson et al. 2012), connecting camel herders in rural and peri-urban areas with town markets. Urban traders were women originally from pastoralist families who settled in towns following drought, insecurity or other hardships, or in search of petty trade opportunities. Studies of milk marketing have found that many urban women traders have been socially displaced following divorce or being widowed, and sought opportunities in town to improve their economic status and support their families (Little 1994; Nori 2009). Urban traders nevertheless maintained their nomadic links, often going into milk trading in partnership with a relative in the bush with access to camel herds (Nori 2009; Little 1994).

Urbanization and displacement processes in northern Kenya thus diverted camel milk out of its domestic domain and on to the market. Yet it was the dramatic growth of Eastleigh from the early 1990s with the influx of Somali refugees following the collapse of the Barre state which saw the diversion of camel milk on an unprecedented scale, this time from small urban centres in northern Kenya to meet new demand in the capital. This new demand has had important ramifications for how camel milk is produced and traded. Anderson et al. (2012) recount the activities of the Anolei Women Group, who were the vanguard of an organized, coordinated camel milk trade to Eastleigh from Isiolo. These women, and other 'middlewomen' from other source markets, go into partnership with Somali women in Eastleigh, typically relatives of Kenyan nationality who have moved to the estate in search of economic opportunities. Middlewomen send milk to these business partners, splitting the profits between them.

'Camel milk is all we know': the camel milk business and socio-economic change

Requiring little start-up capital, milk trading is one of the most accessible of petty trades for poor women. Most women milk traders of both Kenyan and Somali nationality interviewed in Eastleigh commented that milk trading was 'all we know' and the only means through which they could meet their families' day-to-day needs. In relation to ex-pastoralist women, Oba (1989) notes that increased poverty and displacement from traditional pastoralist livelihoods can draw women into new roles as income generators, increasing their negotiating power at the household level. Indeed, studies of pastoral dairying have shown that it is usually poorer households which sell milk all year round, while wealthier households are able to prioritize calf and household consumption during the dry season and sell milk only during the rainy season when there is a surplus (Herren 1990; Little 1994; Buhl and Homewood 2000).

Nori (2009) emphasizes that extensive milk marketing in Somalia has been possible precisely because milk trading is women's work. In Puntland, he found that men initially participated in the milk business but have since been sidelined, having run into problems accessing the milk from different clans' camels, and thus struggling to accumulate enough milk to make the business profitable (ibid.). Since use rights over camel products such as milk and meat pertain to members of a *diya* (blood compensation)-paying group (Samatar 1994, cited in ibid.), it is not easily acceptable for milk from camels of one clan to be used to generate profit for another (ibid.). Women's ambiguous clan identities and 'neutrality' vis-à-vis the clan organizational structure enable them to purchase milk from camels owned by different clansmen and to network with other actors outside of their husbands' or fathers' clans.

Beyond the *badia*, in Eastleigh the flexibility of women traders' identities and affiliations in the camel milk market is quite apparent. While middlewomen in source markets have traditionally sent milk to trading partners in Eastleigh who are relatives or clan members and typically Kenyan nationals, as their networks become more extensive they appear to be drawing in other actors from beyond their immediate families, garnering trust through more commercial relationships.[19] Women sitting and selling milk together have diverse backgrounds: women from both Kenya and Somalia, of different clans and who arrived in the estate in different waves, sit side by side. Most traders said they had met each other only 'in business'. Milk sellers commented that the number of people going into milk trading was increasing, and that newcomers are often recently arrived refugee women from Somalia.

Refugee women from Somalia now engaging in milk trading were said to be often initially employed as domestic workers for wealthier Somali families on arriving in Eastleigh, and to have come into contact with milk traders when buying milk for the household. On becoming more established in the estate and seeking independence and more profitable work, these women approach the veteran milk traders. Key players – typically Kenyan Somali women who are better connected to source markets – who manage larger quantities of milk will give these aspiring traders small quantities of milk (usually a 20-litre jerrycan) which they then sell from the roadside or hawk from household to household. Once the new trader has sold the milk, she returns with the empty jerrycan and pays the larger trader for the milk, keeping a small profit for herself. Giving aspiring traders milk was said to be based solely on trust. Saida, a milk trader on 7th Street, commented that established traders usually do not know who these women are or which clan they belong to, but trust them on the basis of their shared Muslim faith and Somali identity. Unconnected newcomers, then, by virtue of their Somaliness alone, are able to join the business and access milk through the trade networks that were carved out by Kenyan Somali women in response to the growth of Eastleigh.

The camel milk trade thus functions as a vehicle for economic integration for refugee women in the estate, as well as facilitating social integration between new and more established migrants. However, while mutual respect and trust within the milk business was emphasized, this discourse may be deployed primarily as a strategy for increasing sales and may not necessarily be practised in other spheres of social life.[20] I witnessed a physical fight between two milk traders on one occasion, said by observers to be over jerrycans of milk which they had both claimed an entitlement to. Where refugee women are caught up in such disputes, they may be vulnerable to being pushed out by the Kenyan Somali women upon whom they depend to access the market.

The reshaping of the camel milk economy following the Somalia refugee crisis – and the concurrent expansion of demand generated both by refugees in Nairobi and visiting Somalis from the wider diaspora – has induced major shifts in the pastoral economy. As a result, a new kind of pastoralism is emerging in Kenya in response to the new camel milk markets.[21] This is a pastoralism no longer centred in the bush, but increasingly oriented towards commodification through urban milk markets. 'Town pastoralists'[22] continue to move according to where there is pasture but also to places close to markets where there is a ready demand for milk. This trend is not only happening around Nairobi, but also around other urban centres with significant and growing Somali populations from both Somalia and Kenya, such as Mombasa and Nakuru. Mass displacement from Somalia into Kenya has steered this reorientation through its intersection with pastoralist sedentarization and adaptation processes. Poor Kenyan Somali women, displaced from their traditional roles in the pastoral economy, have been crucial in facilitating this shift, creatively carving out new roles for themselves amid interlocking crises. Economic and social relations among diverse Somali actors are thus being reworked in the upheaval of displacement, producing a new 'order' through which the parameters in which people can act are redefined.[23]

Conclusion

Tracing camel milk's 'life history' and trajectories to the Eastleigh market enables us to delineate the shifts in relations of production, trade and consumption of camel milk that have been induced by the mass dislocation of Somalis from Somalia into Kenya. It also illuminates the paradoxical creativity that has occurred at the intersection of this sustained crisis with economic displacement processes among Kenyan Somali pastoralists. Central to these shifts is the forging of a common 'Somali' identity through which to cope with the effects of these crises. This common 'Somaliness' appears to circumvent clan, occupational, national and regional identities, and emerges as the 'greater logic' governing the camel milk market in Eastleigh, connecting the different actors who participate in its production, sale and consumption (Friedman 2004).

As Appadurai's processual and situational approach to commodities suggests, the commodification of camel milk has not curtailed its traditional functions and value; camel milk embodies its 'life history'. While milk exchanged as a gift between rural and urban relatives serves to strengthen social relations and spread risk, trade in commodified milk in Eastleigh continues to span rural and urban spheres, drawing both realms into an integrated system of interdependence, with these relationships becoming increasingly market-based and relying less heavily on familial connections as more actors are drawn into the business. These processes should not be seen as detrimental to the social relations around camel milk exchange, however. Contrary to early anthropological assumptions about commodity exchange, the market does not exist outside of social life as a 'thing apart'. The camel milk market in Eastleigh functions in the reproduction of a 'Somali' social order, in a way that resonates with Mauss's *The Gift* (1970 [1923]).

'Being Somali' through producing, selling and consuming camel milk emerges in this study as a mechanism for coping with the change and upheaval that have characterized parallel experiences of displacement among the diverse Somali communities in Kenya. Camel milk trade is a vehicle for social and economic integration both among poor 'ex-pastoralist' Kenyan Somalis and refugee women from Somalia. At the same time, commercial production of milk is a means through which pastoralists can diversify their livelihoods and remain pastoralists in the face of threats to subsistence pastoralism. For consumers, drinking camel milk brings 'home' in the *badia* to town. Drinking milk in Eastleigh helps refugees from Somalia to manage the symptoms of exile and precarious urban life and reconcile the ambivalence of being both Somali and urban.

More broadly, studying how Somali displacements have altered systems of production, trade and consumption of camel milk offers insights into an evolving Somali identity in Kenya since the arrival of hundreds of thousands of Somali refugees. The emergence of Eastleigh as a Somali displacement hub has rendered it a base from which a heterogeneous Somali population can cultivate, celebrate and cash in on a common 'Somaliness'. Goldsmith (1997) notes that clan identities, often cited as the root cause of the failure of the Somali nation-state, appear less important in the Kenyan context. In Eastleigh, Somalis from across the Somali regions and the diaspora rub along together, reconstituting 'the original unitary and borderless nature of Somali society, but within a more cosmopolitan and international context mitigating the primordial loyalties of clan and lineage' (ibid.: 473). While clan has not disappeared in Kenya, its meaning and application as a social and political guiding structure have changed (Mwiandi 2007: 64). The dispersal of Somalis prompted the formation of new, more inclusive identities in Eastleigh, which equip Somalis to make sense of and adapt to dislocation, change and upheaval. Reading Eastleigh's camel milk markets closely through a displacement economies perspective has elucidated some of the processes behind this transformation.

Notes

1 The fieldwork on which this chapter is based was conducted in Nairobi's Eastleigh estate, Mombasa, Kajiado town and Bissil between June and August 2011. Over fifty interviews were carried out, along with participant observation in restaurants and milk bars and informal discussions with traders and consumers. I am grateful to the British Institute in Eastern Africa (BIEA) for funding the project and to my research assistant, Abdi Dagane, whose inputs and language skills were invaluable. The analysis in this chapter also draws upon research in Isiolo, Kenya, between May and September 2010 with Hassan Kochore, Emma Lochery and Badr Shariff for a BIEA-funded project under the guidance of David M. Anderson. This chapter is an adaptation of my MA thesis, submitted in September 2011 to the School of Oriental and African Studies, University of London. Amanda Hammar read the thesis manuscript, provided insightful comments and suggested it be adapted for this volume.

2 The label is not used so much by ordinary people living in or visiting the estate, but more by the national and international media.

3 According to one informant, 'This [camel milk] is our beer.'

4 See Lochery (2012).

5 In recent years, Somalis and other Muslims in Kenya have become popularly associated with 'Islamic radicals'. This has intensified since the Kenya Defence Force's military incursion into Somalia to oust the militant group Al Shabaab which began in October 2011. The incursion prompted a string of low-level attacks in Nairobi as well as in the Dadaab refugee camps, other urban centres across north-eastern Kenya and at the coast. Towards the end of 2012, following several grenade

attacks in Eastleigh, the Kenyan govern-ment declared that all urban refugees would be sent to the camps, in spite of there being no evidence the attacks were linked to refugees or indeed to Somalis. This was followed by heightened police violence towards refugees and Somalis in Eastleigh (Human Rights Watch 2013). According to recent research by the Herit-age Institute for Policy Studies, significant numbers of Somali refugees have left Eastleigh and retuned to Somalia, citing insecurity in Kenya, rather than improv-ing security in Somalia, as a push factor (Nur 2013).

6 An exception is Goldsmith (1997).

7 Including the self-declared-independent states of Somaliland and Puntland.

8 The national borders dividing the Somali territories are porous, and cross-border social, economic and politi-cal linkages are strong. While different displacement contexts across the Somali regions should be delineated, it should also be emphasized that these processes are occurring in close proximity and interaction.

9 Stated by Mohamed (not his real name), a Somali refugee from Ethiopia's Ogaden region who drinks in the Mashal-lah camel milk bar in Eastleigh.

10 Mansur (1995) writes that with the birth of Somali nationalism towards the end of the colonial era, the camel became central to the idea of the Somali nation. Poets produced patriotic verses in which the camel was a symbol of the country and independence. At independence, the new nation was compared to a she-camel called Maandeeq, which gave abundant milk to the people, or to a herd of camels looted by thieves but later retrieved by their owner.

11 My research assistant Abdi's term.

12 It should be noted that research has proved camel milk's high nutritional value over and above milk from other livestock and its effective use in treatment of diabetes, peptic ulcers, skin cancers and TB and HIV/AIDS-related problems (Agrawal et al. 2006; Nori et al. 2006).

13 Celebrating camel over cow milk in Somalia, according to Talle (1992), is also a way of reifying the superiority of pastoralism over sedentarism, as seden-tary peoples usually keep cattle. This is expressed again in terms of health – one who drinks camel milk will be lean – ideal for a nomadic life – whereas cow milk is more fattening.

14 See Schlee (1989) on the 'camel complex' among camel pastoralists in northern Kenya.

15 Perhaps since as early as before the mid-nineteenth century – see Abir (1968).

16 Indeed, commodities such as sugar and tea have long been ubiquitous in pastoralist households (Holtzman 2003).

17 Nori (2009) notes similar arrange-ments characterizing early rural–urban exchange of milk in Puntland.

18 Talle (1992) finds similar trends in Belet Weyne in central Somalia.

19 Also found by Nori (2009) in the Puntland context.

20 This point is also made by Carrier and Lochery (2013) in relation to a broader discourse around trade and trust in Eastleigh.

21 Hussein (2010) describes a similar phenomenon in the Ogaden, albeit likely to be on a smaller scale.

22 From Hussein (2010).

23 It remains to be seen whether women will remain in control of these networks, however, or whether actors with better access to capital will seize the market (Anderson et al. 2012). One informant spoke of today's camel owners as 'business people' purchasing camels solely for milk business. Camel owners in such cases are likely to have the capital to organize their own transport and supply milk directly to customers, relying less heavily upon middlewomen. Ahmed, a manager at a Somali restaurant near Nairobi's Jamia mosque, told us that his father owns 500 camels in Voi and sup-plies milk to a number of Somali restau-rants in the city centre and Eastleigh. The milk is brought to the restaurants directly by the family's own vehicle.

References

Abbots, E. (2011) '"It doesn't taste as good from the pet shop": guinea-pig consumption and the performance of transnational kin and class relations in highland Ecuador and New York City', *Food, Culture and Society*, 14(2): 205–23.

Abdulsamad, F. (2011) 'Somali investment in Kenya', Chatham House Briefing Paper (online), www.chathamhouse. org/sites/default/files/public/Research/Africa/bp0311_abdulsamed.pdf, accessed August 2013.

Abir, M. (1968) 'Caravan trade and history in northern parts of East Africa', *Paiduma*, 14: 103–20.

Abokor, A. C. (1987) *The Camel in Somali Oral Traditions*, Sweden: Motala Grafiska.

Agrawal, R. P., S. Budania, P. Sharma, R. Gupta, D. K. Kochar, R. B. Panwar and M. S. Sahani (2006) 'Zero prevalence of diabetes in the camel milk consuming Raica community of north-west Rajistan, India', *Diabetes Research and Clinical Practice*, 76: 290–96 (online), ipac.kacst.edu.sa/eDoc/camel/166841_1.pdf, accessed August 2013.

Ahmed, A. J. (ed.) (1995) *The Invention of Somalia*, Lawrenceville, NJ: Red Sea Press.

Anderson, D. M., H. Elliott, H. H. Kochore and E. Lochery (2012) 'Camel herders, "middlewomen" and urban milk bars: the commodification of camel milk in Kenya', *Journal of Eastern African Studies*, 6(3): 383–404.

Appadurai, A. (1986) 'Introduction', in A. Appadurai (ed.), *The Social Life of Things*, Cambridge: Cambridge University Press, pp. 3–63.

Buhl, S. and K. Homewood (2000) 'Milk selling among Fulani women in northern Burkina Faso', in D. L. Hodgeson (ed.), *Rethinking Pastoralism in Africa*, Oxford: James Currey, pp. 207–26.

Campbell, E. H. (2005) 'Formalizing the informal economy: Somali refugee and migrant trade networks', *Global Migration Perspectives*, 47: 1–35 (online), www. unhcr.org/refworld/country,,GCIM,,SOM,456d621e2,435f87254,0.html, accessed August 2013.

— (2006) 'Urban refugees in Nairobi: problems of protection, mechanisms of survival, and possibilities for integration', *Journal of Refugee Studies*, 19(3): 396–413.

CARE Kenya (2009) 'A report on the camel milk marketing clusters in Garissa', Nairobi, CARE Report (online), www. elmt-relpa.org/FCKeditor/UserFiles/File/elmt/201003/Report%20on%20Camel%20Milk%20Hygiene%20and%20Business%20Skills%20Training_CARE%20Kenya.pdf, accessed August 2013.

Carrier, N. (2007) *Kenyan Khat: The Social Life of a Stimulant*, Leiden and Boston, MA: Brill.

Carrier, N. and E. Lochery (2013) 'Missing states? Somali trade networks and the Eastleigh transformation', *Journal of Eastern African Studies*, 7(2): 334–52.

Carsten, J. (1995) 'The substance of kinship and the heat of the hearth: feeding, personhood, and relatedness among Malays in Pulau Langkwai', *American Ethnologist*, 22(2): 223–41.

Chebichi, J. (2009) *The 'legality' of illegal Somali migrants in Eastleigh Estate in Nairobi*, MA thesis, University of the Witwatersrand, Johannesburg (online), wiredspace.wits.ac.za/bitstream/handle/10539/8194/Chebichi%20J.pdf?sequence=1accessed, accessed August 2013.

Counihan, C. (1984) 'Bread as world: food habits and social relations in modernizing Sardinia', *Anthropological Quarterly*, 57(2): 47–59.

Douglas, M. and B. Isherwood (1978) *The World of Goods: Towards an Anthropology of Consumption*, London: Routledge.

Farah, K. O., D. M. Nyariki, R. K. Ngugi, I. M. Noor and A. Y. Guliye (2004) 'The Somali and the camel: ecology, management, and economics', *Anthropologist*, 6(1): 45–55.

Friedman, J. (2004) 'Introduction', in J. Friedman (ed.), *Consumption and Identity*, London: Routledge, pp. 1–16.

Goldsmith, P. (1997) 'The Somali impact on Kenya 1990–1993: the view from outside the camps', in H. M. Adam and R. Ford (eds), *Mending Rips in the Sky: Options for Somali Communities in the Twenty-first Century*, Lawrenceville, NJ: Red Sea Press, pp. 461–83.

— (2008) 'Eastleigh goes global', *East African Magazine* (online), www.theeastafrican.co.ke/magazine/-/434746/457396/-/view/printVersion/-/1susaz/-/index.html, accessed August 2013.

Guardian (2011) 'Somali refugee settlement in Kenya swells as row grows over empty refugee camp', 11 August, www.guardian.co.uk/world/2011/aug/11/somali-refugees-kenya-camp-empty, accessed October 2013.

Herren, U. J. (1990) 'The commercial sale of camel milk from pastoral herds in the Mogadishu hinterland, Somalia', Working paper, Overseas Development Institute (online), www.odi.org.uk/work/projects/pdn/papers/30a.pdf, accessed August 2013.

Holtzman, J. (2003) 'In a cup of tea: commodities and history among Samburu pastoralists in northern Kenya', *American Ethnologist*, 30(1): 136–55.

— (2009) *Uncertain Tastes: Memory, ambivalence and the politics of eating in Samburu, Northern Kenya*, Berkeley: University of California Press.

Human Rights Watch (2013) *You are All Terrorists: Kenyan Police Abuse of Refugees in Nairobi*, Human Rights Watch (online), www.hrw.org/sites/default/files/reports/kenya0513_ForUpload_0_0.pdf, accessed August 2013.

Hussein, A. A. (2010) 'Town camels and milk villages: the growth of camel milk marketing in the Somali region of Ethiopia', *FAC Research Update* (online), www.future-agricultures.org/index.php?option=com_content&view=article&id=577:pastoralism-theme-overview&catid=126&Itemid=523, accessed August 2013.

IOM (2010) 'Rapid baseline assessment with exclusive focus on pastoralist drop-outs (Garissa Municipality)', IOM Report, Nairobi (online), reliefweb.int/sites/reliefweb.int/files/resources/47D74D4B4B2979A949257758000BAB52-Full_Report.pdf, accessed August 2013.

Kopytoff, I. (1986) 'The cultural biography of things: commoditization as process', in A. Appadurai (ed.), *The Social Life of Things*, Cambridge: Cambridge University Press, pp. 64–94.

Lewis, I. M. (1961) *A Pastoral Democracy: A study of pastoralism and politics among the northern Somali of the Horn of Africa*, London, New York and Toronto: Oxford University Press.

Lindley, A. (2007) 'Protracted displacement and remittances: the view from Eastleigh', New Issues in Refugee Research Research Paper no. 143 (online), www.unhcr.org/46ea519d2.html, accessed August 2013.

— (2010) *The Early Morning Phonecall: Somali Refugees' Remittances*, New York: Berghahn.

Little, P. D. (1994) 'Maidens and milk markets: the sociology of dairy marketing in southern Somalia', in E. K. Fratkin, A. Galvin and E. A. Roth (eds), *African Pastoralist Systems: An integrated approach*, Boulder, CO: Lynne Rienner, pp. 165–84.

Lochery, E. (2012) 'Rendering difference visible: the Kenyan state and its Somali citizens', *African Affairs*, 111(445): 615–39.

Mansur, A. O. (1995) 'Contrary to a nation: the cancer of the Somali state', in A. J. Ahmed (ed.), *The Invention of Somalia*, Lawrenceville, NJ: Red Sea Press, pp. 107–16.

Mauss, M. (1970 [1923]) *The Gift: Forms and functions of exchange in archaic societies*, London: Cohen and West.

Mwiandi, S. G. (2007) *Exploration into the reinvention of Somali identity and social structure in Kenya*, BA dissertation, Miami University (online), etd.ohiolink.edu/ap:0:0:APPLICATION_PROCESS=DOWNLOAD_ETD_SUB_DOC_ACCNUM:::F1501_ID:muhonors

1176954033,attachment, accessed August 2013.

Nori, M. (2009) *Milking Drylands: Gender networks, pastoral markets and food security in stateless Somalia*, Wageningen: Wageningen University.

Nori, M., M. B. Kenyanjui, M. A. Yusuf and F. H. Mohamed (2006) 'Milking drylands: the marketing of camel milk in north-east Somalia', *Nomadic Peoples*, 10(1): 9–28.

Nur, A. (2013) *Hasty Repatriation: Kenya's attempt to send Somali refugees home*, Mogadishu: Heritage Institute for Policy Studies (online), www.heritage institute.org/images/Hasty%20 Repatriation%20Report.pdf, accessed August 2013.

Oba, G. (1989) 'Changing property rights among settling pastoralists: an adaptive strategy to declining pastoral resources', in P. Baxter and R. Hogg (eds), *Property, Poverty and People: Changing rights in property and problems of pastoral development*, Manchester: University of Manchester Press, pp. 38–44.

Schlee, G. (1989) *Identities on the Move: Clanship and Pastoralism in Northern Kenya*, Nairobi: Gideon S. Were Press.

Searles, E. (2002) 'Food and the making of modern Inuit identities', *Food and Foodways*, 10(1/2): 58–78.

Sheekh, N. M., A. Atta-Asamoah and R. D. Sharamo (2012) *Kenya's Neglected IDPs: Internal displacement and vulnerability of pastoralist communities in northern Kenya*, Nairobi: Institute for Security Studies, http://www.issafrica.org/ uploads/SitRep2012_8Oct.pdf, accessed August 2013.

SNV (2006) *The Camel Milk Industry in Kenya*, SNV Report, Nairobi (online), www.ebpdn.org/download/download. php?table=resources&id=2337, accessed August 2013.

Sutton, D. E. (2001) *Remembrance of Repasts: An Anthropology of Food and Memory*, London: Berg.

Talle, A. (1992) 'Trading camel milk: coping with survival in a Somali pastoral context', in A. Hjort (ed.), *Security in African Drylands: Research, development and policy*, Uppsala: Research Programme on Environment and International Security, Departments of Human and Physical Geography, Uppsala University, pp. 139–57.

Van Binsbergen, W. (2005) 'Commodification: things, agency, and identities: introduction', in W. van Binsebergen and P. Geschiere (eds), *Commodification: Things, Agency and Identities (The Social Life of Things Revisited)*, Munster: Lit, pp. 9–51.

Wairimu, M. (2011) 'Somali immigrants drive business, controversy in Nairobi', Global Press Institute (online), www. dailykos.com/story/2011/04/28/971075/- Somali-Immigrants-Drive-Business- Controversy-in-Nairobi-Suburb, accessed August 2013.

Willis, J. (1999) 'Enkurma Sikitoi: commoditization, drink and power among the Maasai', *International Journal of African Historical Studies*, 32(2/3): 339–57.

7 | Diaspora returnees in Somaliland's displacement economy

Peter Hansen

Introduction

This chapter explores how and why members of the western Somaliland diaspora with particular histories of displacement engage economically in Somaliland. Members of the Somaliland diaspora often perceive the Somaliland homeland as under-explored, as a place of opportunity where fortunes can be made and individual dreams fulfilled (see Hansen 2008). Many come to establish themselves as private business owners, hoping not only to make money, but also to redefine individual identities and their place and status in society.

Engaging with Somaliland is intricately tied to histories and experiences of displacement. In other words, experiences from and links to Western countries are often crucial in understanding how and why members of the diaspora engage with the homeland. The chapter understands displacement as 'enforced changes in interweaving spatial, social and symbolic conditions and relations' (see Hammar, Introduction to this volume). Focusing on diaspora returnees, the chapter not only examines histories of displacement and its effects, but also the process of self-emplacement taking place when diaspora dwellers engage with their homeland. Diaspora returnees often engage in a discourse on return and share a wish to settle in Somaliland permanently (Hansen 2007). However, in practice most diaspora returnees continue to move back and forth between Somaliland and their Western host countries, taking advantage of opportunities existing in both places. Reflecting the definition of displacement, emplacement is understood in this chapter as a spatial process that is tied to social and symbolic processes. What will be clear in the chapter is that the processes of emplacement, understood in its combined physical, social and symbolic senses, are tied to past experiences and strategies of coping with displacement. In other words, displacement and emplacement go hand in hand.

Individual histories of displacement reflect the most recent political history of Somalia. Before the creation of the Somali Republic in 1960, outmigration from Somalia did not take place on a grand scale. Before 1960, diaspora communities had been established, particularly in Great Britain, but it was not until the 1960s and 1970s when thousands of Somalis went to the Gulf states and the Middle East to work in the booming oil industry that outmigration from

Somalia increased substantially (Gundel 2002: 263; Kleist 2004: 5). Outmigration was often caused by lack of employment possibilities and decreasing business opportunities for those not directly linked to the Somali regime (for example, members of the Isaq clan from present-day Somaliland). In the 1970s many also went to the USSR, Somalia's Cold War ally, for education.[1]

The political violence that erupted in Somalia at the beginning of the 1980s forcibly displaced thousands of Somalis from present-day Somaliland, some of whom were later given political asylum in Western countries. At the same time, throughout the 1980s thousands from all areas and clans of Somalia migrated to Western countries for employment and education. The bombing in 1988 of Hargeisa and Burao in present-day Somaliland signalled the outbreak of the civil war in Somalia and caused hundreds of thousands to flee across the border to Ethiopia and Djibouti, and farther afield to Europe and North America.

The declaration of the independence of Somaliland in 1991 enabled the return of thousands of refugees from the refugee camps in Ethiopia (Ambroso 2002). However, as peace settled in Somaliland in the early 1990s, the civil war broke out in southern and central Somalia, again displacing hundreds of thousands of people.[2] Thousands of Isaqs living in Mogadishu fled to Somaliland, where the extended family provided shelter, food and security. Hundreds of thousands fled to Kenya and found refuge in the growing refugee camps or went to the capital, Nairobi, with hopes of further onward migration to Europe or North America (Horst 2003; Hyndman 2000. See also Elliott, this volume). The civil war that erupted in Somaliland in the middle of the 1990s again caused thousands to flee across the border to Ethiopia and Djibouti.

Since the declaration of independence in 1991, Somaliland has reconciled former warring clans and set up a viable political system integrating Western-style democracy and local political structures (Bradbury et al. 2003; Gundel 2006; Hoehne 2006; Renders 2007).[3] Somalilanders based in Western countries started engaging with Somaliland in larger numbers around 1997 with peace and stability being established more permanently. Some have come to Somaliland out of nostalgia or curiosity, to look for a first or second spouse, to chew fresh Ethiopian khat (Hansen 2009, 2010) or to work for one of the numerous international NGOs and UN organizations engaged within the development field in Somaliland (Hansen 2007). Some have also come out of disappointment with the West, because of the difficulty of finding employment matching their formal qualifications and aspirations, and because of racist and xenophobic discourses and practices (Kusow 2006; McGown 1999). Whereas motives for coming to Somaliland vary, most come with economic and sociocultural resources that have been accumulated in the West. In other words, it is often the most successful part of the diaspora that engages with Somaliland.

In this chapter, I will explore some of the most typical ways in which members of the diaspora invest in Somaliland. Moreover, the chapter will examine the motives, conflicts, challenges and perceptions of immense possibility that are often associated with such diasporic engagements in Somaliland. It will further highlight how diaspora investors use their links to and experiences from Western countries when setting up and marketing businesses locally in Somaliland. In this sense, the chapter highlights an economy of displacement that reflects traditional Somali nomadic practices and values. The chapter is based on thirteen months of fieldwork in Somaliland in a period from 1998 to 2006 and two months of fieldwork among Somalilanders in London in 2003. Additionally, the chapter draws on my continuous engagement with Somalis living in Copenhagen.

Land rush in Hargeisa

The most common way in which members of the diaspora invest in Somaliland is to buy plots and build houses. The construction of houses gives birth to new neighbourhoods in Hargeisa that are given names like Half London, Norway Corner, New York and Berlin. The brightly painted and rather futuristic villas, often two or even three storeys high, are symbols of the status and wealth of the owner and his or her family. To underline their links to a global outside, members of the diaspora have started decorating their compound walls and rooftops with small and symbolic miniature satellite dishes, thereby trying to distinguish themselves from the local population. Moreover, besides stone, which is readily available in Somaliland, all other building materials used for the construction of these new houses are imported. This underlines the status associated with being well connected to a consumption-oriented global outside, and which again contrasts with the traditional nomadic dwellings that are entirely made out of locally produced materials. Besides showing the wealth, success and global ties of the individual diaspora house owner, owning a house in Hargeisa also makes visiting easier for those from the diaspora, as they will not have to worry about staying in a hotel or with relatives. Building a house also demonstrates identification with a particular place, and can be seen as a way for members of the diaspora to forge continuing and meaningful ties with their homeland and establish stable points of identification (Thomas 1998).

Buying land and constructing houses can also be seen as investments, as they can either be rented out or sold at a later stage. Numerous diaspora Somalilanders bought plots on the outskirts of Hargeisa in the middle of the 1990s for a few hundred dollars, and are now selling these plots for several thousand dollars, as the price of land has doubled several times in just ten years. One of the consequences of this property trend in Somaliland is the creation of an investment rush. Many feel that they have to invest now, or they will never be able to afford to build their own house in Somaliland, given the escalating prices already mentioned. Another consequence of this land and property rush is an escalation of conflicts over land, which have become one of the most common causes of violence in Somaliland.

One Somalilander from Norway, Amina, had come to Somaliland partly to secure a plot in Hargeisa that she had bought in 1984. She always knew that she wanted to return to Hargeisa, and also wanted to secure a place for her daughter, who lives in Norway. The plot was in the area of town where her sub-clan are traditional landowners, and which is usually seen as one of the most expensive neighbourhoods. Back in 1984, the plot was part of the city plan for Hargeisa, and she had bought it for only US$1,000, whereas today it is worth around US$5,000. During a visit of three months in Hargeisa in 2003, she had many difficulties with the plot. She had a title deed from 1984 issued by the old Somali authorities, and a new title deed from 2003 issued by the Somaliland authorities. However, she had made the mistake of not building a house or a wall demarcating the plot. Neither had she piled any stones on the plot to indicate ownership and the intent of building, and therefore faced difficulties with some of the locals, who applied their own strategy of also claiming ownership of the plot.

I spent a few days with Amina trying to secure her plot, and one day we visited the plot together with her uncle, who worked as a public notary and kept the title deeds. The uncle had brought the city plan for Hargeisa from 1998, the two title deeds and a tape measure to help demarcate the exact location of the plot. As we were putting down corner stones, a young man came up to us, started abusing Amina and claimed that it was his father's plot, explaining that his family had 'used it for generations'. Locals know that claiming a plot that is owned by someone from the diaspora can be a way of making a living. Holding a title deed is not a guarantee that a plot is not claimed by someone else, which inevitably complicates matters. Many diaspora Somalilanders are reluctant to get into a conflict they only partly understand and are afraid of escalating, and therefore often end up paying the local claimant in order to end the conflict. Amina and the other claimant were both members of the same clan, but from different sub-clans, and theoretically their clan elders representing both sub-clans should have been able to mediate and come up with a settlement. After having visited the plot, we spent a few hours looking for both elders. We found the elder representing Amina's sub-clan in a roadside teahouse, but the other elder lived in the rural areas far from Hargeisa, and the settlement meeting had to take place another day.

Amina explained that she didn't want to involve the authorities in Somaliland, and that she felt more comfortable settling the dispute through the clan system. Her title deeds, which had been issued by shifting Somali(land) governments, were not particularly helpful in a situation where she just wanted to end the dispute as fast as possible. Moreover, Amina feared that involving the authorities would only escalate the dispute into a violent conflict between the two opposing sub-clans, each having the backing of different sections of the police.

Private sector pioneers

Besides buying plots and building houses, and facing the problems associated with this, many diaspora Somalilanders also open small-scale businesses, something that is very difficult and expensive to do in a Western country. One such diaspora investor, Zainab, used to live in Toronto but returned to Somaliland, where she now owns a restaurant, a café and a beauty salon. She went to Canada to study in the middle of the 1980s. Her father was quite wealthy, and he sent all his children to Canada and the USA to study. She had returned to Somaliland not because she was a victim of racism or because she didn't like living in Canada, but because of her dream of opening her own business, and being her own boss:

> ... I wanted to do a business on my own ... and I always wanted to be my own boss ... so I was thinking if I make a business in Toronto maybe I might face many difficulties, because that was not my country ... and it has too many business ... if I open a salon in Toronto ... there are too many salons ...

Zainab came to Hargeisa in 1995, and in 1998 she opened her first salon. The many salons in Hargeisa are reflections of the dispersal of Somalis, and the interaction of ideas, goods and people between Hargeisa, Europe and North America. The salons, or *coffers* as they are also known, are special shops that thrive on the increasing number of weddings being held in Hargeisa.[4] The naming and the history of these shops indicate not only the flow of people, but also how Western names are considered good for business – especially when it comes to dressing up women. The coffers have names like Washington, New York, Paris, London and Copenhagen, pointing to the fact that they are often owned by women who have been living in the West, and to the fact that images of the West are often used for marketing purposes. The salons provide the bride with the proper wedding dress bought in Dubai, hair extensions bought in India, make-up, henna decoration and a wedding cake. Today, marriages across great distances are quite common, and the colour of the bride's wedding dress testifies to these practices. If the bride wears a pink, brown or black wedding dress, as opposed to the more usual white dress, this is an indication that a stand-in and not the real groom is present for the wedding ritual. Travelling to Somaliland for the groom may be difficult or risky, as he may live illegally in the West, have ongoing applications for residency or citizenship, or it may simply be too expensive.

Zainab knew that she wanted to come back, and when she finally did so in 1995, having finished her education and having worked and saved some money, she found Hargeisa half empty and a family that begged her not to settle permanently as they thought it would be too risky. Zainab, however, believed that things were improving, and was confident that investing in Somaliland was the right thing to do. At that time she was not married, and therefore freer to make her own decisions. With children she would most likely have remained in Canada, as they would need good medical care and schooling that, in the eyes of many, are still not found in Somaliland. Zainab married a Somali man from the USA in Hargeisa in 1997, and they now have two children.

Many returnees like Zainab invest in Somaliland because it is less difficult than opening a shop in the West. Unlike in the West, there are practically no rules and regulations on how to set up a business in Somaliland. As of now the taxation on private businesses is minimal, and always negotiable by the individual business owner. There are no minimum wages, no trade unions and no fixed opening hours. Somaliland looks much like an economic Wild West where nothing is regulated or restricted, and where everything is possible for an industrious investor. The destruction caused by the civil war and the newness of Somaliland make investments particularly attractive. Zainab explained that:

> Because this is a new country, after the civil war it became a new place ... there was nothing and they came back from Ethiopia and the other places ... they came to the city and there was nothing ... and I was thinking that if I came back at that time there were many things that I could do ... many spaces ... like everybody that was here had never been outside, and they had never seen any- thing else ... like everybody that was living here was Somali people, they have never been to anywhere else in the world, and they have never seen anything else, so I saw many, many places and I said that if I come back ... so I knew that if I came back I could do something before everybody else ... so I can do it before them ... like this salon I knew that there were no salons in Hargeisa ... so I opened the first ...

The experience of having been to Canada puts Zainab in a privileged posi- tion vis-à-vis locals who had 'never been outside', and 'never seen anything', as she puts it. The strategy of opening a salon was indeed a good business idea. There clearly was a market for her salon, which is doing well and generating good profits. Zainab has now employed a number of local girls to do the actual work in the salon. She has also invested in a restaurant that is suc- cessful in attracting young people who meet there to play pool, listen to pop music and have soft drinks and fruit juices. Zainab deliberately caters to the Somaliland youth by playing on her links to and experiences from the West, and her market strategy is to provide an opportunity for the locals to engage in activities associated with youth in the West. The restaurant is a meeting place not only for the local youth but also for youngsters from the diaspora who are on holiday in Hargeisa.

Zainab's story illustrates how continued practices of travel, as well as cultural images and experiences from Western countries, are used when investing in Somaliland. However, not everything about the West and diaspora investments is unproblematic. During my stay in Somaliland, Zainab ran into some problems with the police, who harassed her and accused her of selling alcohol in her restaurant, which is strictly forbidden in Somaliland. Moreover, she was also arrested on charges of having a pool of bleach in the backyard of her salon used to whiten the skin of young Somaliland girls. Both accusations were false but quite telling of local forms of resistance, especially towards the changes and success brought to Somaliland by female members of the diaspora. Nonetheless, Zainab often travels to North America and Europe. During my stay in Hargeisa in 2003 and 2006, she went several times to Canada and Holland for holidays and to visit friends and family. When she compared her life with that of her relatives in Europe and North America she felt privileged and free. Whereas she is free to travel around the world, they are tied down by mortgages and loans. Zainab has her own house in Hargeisa, and doesn't need to worry about mortgages, bills, loans and insurances. Still, as she says, you never know what will happen. Right now her only security is her Canadian passport, which will ensure her ability to travel out of Somaliland and entry into Canada if things don't work out, or if the war breaks out again.

Among most diaspora investors there is a belief that owing to the destruction caused by the civil war, everything is possible in Somaliland. Like Zainab, Hodan was a very active and successful businesswoman who had returned from the West. Originally born in Zambia, and therefore referred to by locals as *sijui*, she had spent two years in England, where she did not feel at home.[5] She had invested in a number of plots, houses and shops, and also worked as a programme officer for the European Union. Like many others, she had come because of the opportunities in Somaliland. She explained that:

Somaliland is a country that is coming up ... it is a place that nobody knows ... it is an undiscovered place ... go back to history and look at it ... no one has a lot of information about it ... second it is a country that is starting from scratch trying to develop on its own ... so there are opportunities that you could get here that you can't get anywhere else, because those opportunities have been discovered by other people who are already in the businesses ... here if you have the idea, if you have the money to start business ... a bit of education ... you can start something ...

As seen in the discussion on houses and land previously, there is a rush among returnees to get to Somaliland to invest as soon as possible, and before all the others. Sometimes, however, people bring ideas that are not based on common sense and on a good analysis of what is possible or not, but on sheer overoptimism and perhaps nostalgia, and therefore they end up broke and with the only option of going back to the West to look for more money or a new and better business idea. Still, the rush to Somaliland is telling of a very strong identification with Somaliland as a place of hope and opportunity and prospects for advancement (Hage 2003: 15). As such, people identify with Somaliland not only for patriotic, historical or sociocultural reasons, but also for very pragmatic reasons. For many, Somaliland represents an opportunity for self-realization and socio-economic mobility.

Becoming somebody

Many diaspora investors feel that they are able to live a life in Hargeisa that is less stressful and more comfortable than in the West, where they have to do all household chores themselves, constantly worry over bills and mortgages and even have to spend time in traffic jams. Life in Somaliland is often described as freer, more social and less complicated and hectic than life in a Western urban environment. Describing life in Somaliland as freer and less stressful is related to being free of the stigma of living in the West as a black refugee. Many diaspora investors used to hold prestigious jobs and positions in the former Republic of Somalia. When they fled to the West they were not seen as former ministers, professors or heads of private companies, but merely as black refugees, and they have had to stand in line with other welfare clients waiting for their social benefits.[6] When returnees open private businesses, buy plots and build houses they reclaim individualities and avoid the stigmatizing categories of the West. Returning to Zainab with her salon and restaurant in Hargeisa, we see the significance of owning a private business in Somaliland. In 2003 I asked her what the best thing was about being in Hargeisa. She explained that:

> I like that everybody knows me and they all know my family ... but in Toronto if I go there, and set up a business and become rich ... and a well-known person ... I will still be the black woman ... then you are a black person who opened a business in that place ... and you are a nobody ... nobody will know Zainab Ali Muse ... her grandmother, her grandfather and all those things ... nobody knows that ... so this is the place where everybody knows me ... my grandfather, grandmother and my mother and everything, and that means that everybody respects me ... but if I go back to Canada, even though I did many good things, I'm still the black person ... I'm still the Somali refugee ... they don't know anything about Somalia ... they don't know the personality, and how they live ... they only see that you are a refugee, and don't understand that they have also good people ...

To Zainab, Somaliland provides an opportunity to reclaim her individuality as opposed to living in a country where, irrespective of what she does or achieves, she will forever remain subjected to stigmatized and stereotyped identities. Moreover, her success as a businesswoman needs to be seen in relation to her membership of a particular family, whereas in Canada she will always remain an anonymous refugee or black person with a shop.

The situation of another informant, Ibrahim, also illustrates how investments and engagements in Somaliland are linked to issues of individuality and recognition. Ibrahim lives in both London and Hargeisa. In Hargeisa, he has invested in a restaurant that serves burgers, French fries, fried chicken and other kinds of Western food, and in an internet café. He also owns a big house and a big four-wheel-drive vehicle. He lived close to where I lived, and we therefore often met in his restaurant. He always said that he had opened his restaurant and come to Somaliland to serve and help his country. He employed a number of locals, and thereby played his part in the development of Somaliland, he argued. I'm sure that the well-being of Somaliland was close to his heart, but I'm also confident that he enjoyed the attention, and sometimes even admiration, he got from the locals.

His life in Hargeisa contrasts with his life in London, where I also met him several times. In London he did not own a car, and we had to get around by public transport. He explained that the old and impressive buildings of London made him feel small. One experience always reminds me of him, as it illustrates the importance of being recognized as a particular individual with a particular story. We walked by a Mercedes cabriolet parked in the area of North London where he lived. I said that it was a very nice car, and he agreed. Then he shrugged his shoulders and explained that the car was nice, but that there was no point in owing such a nice car in London, as '... no one knows you here ... so what is the point of buying a Porsche or a Mercedes ... in Hargeisa people know you'. Similarly, a returnee from the USA explained that he appreciated how people in Hargeisa knew who he was. He illustrated his point by telling of an experience he once had in France:

> I was walking in France with a friend and after two hours we realized that we had met no one that knew us ... this can be nice, but when you come here everybody knows you ... when you arrive in the airport even the porter knows who you are ... this gives you status, and it makes you feel part of society ... status is important for older people ... for people to know you ... status is not difficult to get ... it is always there if you are a man with a certain history ...

Naturally, there is a flipside of being somebody with particular stories and networks. In Hargeisa, a lot of time is spent on gossiping about each other, which for men mostly takes place during khat-chewing sessions. In this context, being somebody often entails the fabrication of rumours and increased social control.

During my fieldwork I was also subjected to rumours about myself that I had little control over. For example, I was arrested by the police on the basis of rumours that I was working as a spy for neighbouring Puntland, since I was living outside the usual expatriate environment. Moreover, there was a rumour that I had married my local Somali housekeeper, simply because she lived in the house with me. Often it seemed that people knew where I had been and with whom I had talked the previous day. Later I found out that this was because I drove a particular kind of car, of which there was only one in Somaliland. Later, a car similar to mine appeared in Hargeisa, which was quite a relief as it gave me some degree of anonymity, being able to say that 'it must have been the other guy'. Having taken an interest in this phenomenon of cars, individuality and anonymity, I spoke to a young Somalilander from Manchester, who explained that the reason why he and the majority of people in Hargeisa drove the exact same car, a white Toyota Mark II, was precisely because it gave them anonymity in a city that was known for its big ears and big eyes. This should remind us that some choose not to come to Somaliland, as they appreciate the anonymity provided by a Western metropolis and would have difficulty adjusting to a life in what they sometimes refer to as 'village Hargeisa'. Women in particular often experience urban anonymity and the lack of social control as a blessing.

An economy of return

Few investors settle in Somaliland for good, but instead continue to move back and forth between Somaliland and their adopted Western country, where they often hold citizenship. Rather than settling in Somaliland permanently, it is simply a better livelihood strategy to remain mobile, as this gives both access to the Somaliland markets and the opportunities and securities of the West. Moreover, being in the West rather than returning to Somaliland is often what is expected of this diaspora. People in Somaliland are highly dependent on remittances (Ahmed 2000; Gundel 2002; Hansen 2004; Lindley 2006; Warsame 2002), and therefore expect family members to remain in the West and thereby to honour the obligation of providing for poorer members of the family back home.

The government of Somaliland also expects the diaspora to remain abroad and officially opposes the permanent return of its Western diaspora. By remaining in the West, the diaspora is viewed as being able to lobby Western governments regarding the issue of the recognition of Somaliland. If members of the diaspora are interested in engaging with Somaliland, they should do so on a flexible basis, moving back and forth between Somaliland and the West. In this way, they are viewed as bringing investments, knowledge and networks from the West to Somaliland. In many ways, sustained displacement, rather than permanent emplacement back in Somaliland, seems to define identities and livelihoods among most diaspora Somalilanders.

Not all of the diaspora investors are successful. Others, whom I term here opportunistic diaspora investors, stay in Somaliland only for a limited time. They come with high hopes but often end up broke and disappointed. In other words, Somaliland is not the land of opportunity for everyone. Therefore, it is important to ask who among the large Somali diaspora are able to take advantage of the opportunities for business in Somaliland, and what resources are required? Most diaspora investors represent an elite. Even if they experience racism, xenophobia and Islamophobia and find it difficult to access Western job markets, they have been able to accumulate capital, knowledge and networks that are necessary for their engagements in Somaliland. The life trajectories of the diaspora investors that we have met so far illustrate how relative success or incorporation into Western societies is often a precondition for taking advantage of socio-economic opportunities found in Somaliland. As such, diaspora investors in Somaliland have been able to take advantage of opportunities found in the West. This also means that those diaspora Somalilanders who have not accumulated human and financial resources while in the West are unlikely to invest in or engage with Somaliland. Reflecting on the question of who among the large diaspora actually invest and engage with Somaliland, a diaspora Somalilander from Sweden explained:

> I think that those who are successful in Sweden will also be successful here, and mostly when they get their Swedish or Danish passport or whatever pass ... then they are secure enough, and then they can come back, they can go back ... they can experiment, but until they get this naturalization they don't come back ... all those who are successful in Sweden ... become employed in Sweden ... collect some money, send some money, build a house while he is away ... those are the people who are coming here ... the losers will never think about coming back ... because they are not anything there in Sweden, they are not involved there, and they cannot be involved here also ... but even some people are not educated and still very involved ... some people are born clever ...

A first clear indication of how a degree of incorporation into Western societies is a precondition for some form of success in Somaliland is that virtually all investors hold Western citizenships (Portes 1999). Passports give access to mobility. They enable people to do business both in the West and in Somaliland. They make it easier to obtain import-export licences in Western and neighbouring countries, and provide access to accounts and loans in Western banks. In addition, they provide access to lucrative international, as opposed to local, contracts with the UN, the World Bank and international NGOs.

One of my key informants, Mohammed, was a rather successful businessman from Sweden. I first met him in 2003 when he was overseeing the construction of his seventeen-bedroom house, and working hard setting up his transport company. Most of the year he works as a taxi driver in Stockholm and usually spends around three months in Somaliland taking care of his house and his business activities. He was born and grew up in Mogadishu, a city he is unable to invest in owing to his being a member of the Isaq clan, which dominates in Somaliland but is largely restricted from doing business in south-central Somalia. In 2003 the EU imported food aid to Ethiopia through Somaliland, creating a lucrative transport sector and opening up new opportunities for Somalis like Mohammed. The evolution of this sector expresses one of the paradoxes of displacement. People displaced by violence and natural disasters often find themselves in a situation of crisis and vulnerability. However, these same situations generated by displacement simultaneously also open up new domains of economic activity and opportunity for particular people.

Mohammed lived with his grandfather, father, mother, sisters, brothers and cousins in a house that has been in the family for many years. Belonging to a well-known family, he found that everybody seemed to know who he was. Mohammed was well placed to take advantage of the new demand for local transport, owning two trucks that he had bought in Sweden and shipped back to Somaliland via Holland and Djibouti. Since 2003, he has expanded his engagements in Somaliland. Today, he exports fish from Somaliland to Ethiopia; imports potatoes, onions and other vegetables from Ethiopia to Somaliland; and imports rice from India and pasta from Italy that he resells in Ethiopia. He also buys second-hand clothes and second-hand cars in Scandinavia that he, or someone from his family, sells in Somaliland or Ethiopia. Owing to heavy taxation in Ethiopia, cars are very expensive and profits comparatively higher than in Somaliland.

What enables him to be a successful businessman relates to his simultaneous ties to Sweden, Somaliland and Ethiopia. His access to the Swedish labour market enables him to accumulate the capital necessary for investing in Somaliland. His well-developed understanding of the Swedish language, society and norms also enables him to buy second-hand cars, trucks and clothes to be exported to Somaliland. His success also relates to skills and resources in relation to Somaliland itself, to Hargeisa and the larger Horn of Africa. He speaks Somali as it is spoken in Hargeisa and knows how to find and approach the right people to do business with. He also knows how to cross the border to Ethiopia avoiding customs and state officials and how to handle the traffic police in Somaliland. Moreover, he has extensive knowledge of existing and upcoming markets, and of competing business people.

Most importantly, he is a member of a respected family which provides him with financial and physical security, and makes him a trusted business partner. If, for example, he gets into a traffic accident, members of his extended family will step in and work as an insurance company, paying or compensating for material or physical damages. Also, if for some reason he is arrested by the police, or gets into some other kind of trouble, his extended family will secure his release or help him in whatever way they can. His Swedish citizenship also provides him with some form of security and help from the Swedish state should he get into trouble in Somaliland, but what really matters is his family. The fact that people trust him because they know his family is very important. Without a well-known and trusted family it would be very difficult for him to do business in Somaliland. In this sense, '*being somebody*' in Hargeisa enables him to take advantage of the opportunities found in Somaliland. At the same time he takes advantage of opportunities offered to him in Sweden, where he has access to a low-status but relatively well-paid job as a taxi driver.

As illustrated in the example above, diaspora investors use skills, networks and money accumulated in, and relating to, Western countries when investing in Somaliland, while simultaneously relying on specific personal backgrounds and clan-based networks linking them to Somaliland. In this sense, diaspora investors need to be both local and non-local at the same time. In order to get by in Hargeisa, especially as a business person, you need to be well connected to local contexts, and to know your way around the social fabric of society. Most things in Somaliland work through personalized networks, and rarely through bureaucratic structures, or formalized systems. In this sense, Hargeisa presents a big challenge for people without friends, family and sociocultural skills. As already noted, people use their connections, friendship ties and family relations whenever they want to achieve or obtain something, and a lot of time is spent on socializing simply because you want to expand your network for potential future use (Simons 1995). If a returnee is not well connected in Somaliland, he or she will not be able to establish him- or herself as a successful business owner. You may have the opportunity to invest hundreds of thousands of dollars but without the right local connections to key business partners, the government, clan elders and other important persons and institutions, this investment will most likely give poor returns.

As I have shown so far, the private business sector is booming and attracts several diasporic investors. However, even though it looks promising at the moment, salaries and profits are still not high enough to encourage people to stay permanently in Somaliland. Many come to Somaliland with the plan of investing in some form of a private business. They open kiosks, restaurants, internet cafés and many other small-scale businesses that they hope will provide for them and their families in Somaliland. However, many investors copy what other investors are doing, opening the same kinds of shops, selling the same kinds of things. Therefore, many are unsuccessful and return to the West.

Conclusion

As shown in this chapter, spatial practices are integral to the ways in which members of the diaspora engage with Somaliland. This economy of return, which is one way of characterizing Somaliland's displacement economy, is deeply informed by past and sometimes sustained conditions of displacement. This is not unique but reflects a much wider pattern of mobility typifying Somali histories. As such, it comes as no surprise that mobility is important in defining livelihood strategies and identities among diaspora Somalis engaging with Somaliland. One of the defining sociocultural aspects of Somalis, namely clan identities and networks, is itself a clear reflection of the importance of mobility or nomadism as it is typically referred to in a Somali context. As such, the history of Somalia and the Somali people is a history of both voluntary and involuntary forms of mobility that interweave over time.

The chapter has also shown how the process of engaging with Somaliland is ridden with problems and challenges, as diaspora Somalilanders are sometimes unsuccessful in making their investments, or met with resentment and taken advantage of by the local population. As such, the physical process of return does not necessarily reflect an easy process of reintegration or re-emplacement. The identity of representing a diasporic outside not only enables the diaspora to invest in Somaliland, but also causes local tension and conflicts. Therefore members of the diaspora have to strike a delicate balance between being both locals and diasporic outsiders.

Despite Somaliland being characterized by peace and stability, it remains unrecognized as an independent nation-state and as such continues to be displaced within the national order of things (Malkki 1992). The chapter has shown how the lack of recognition creates particular opportunities for the Somalilanders themselves, as foreign investors are very reluctant to invest in Somaliland. Moreover, the existence of weak government institutions means that investments can be made quite freely, without having to meet any official requirements, and without being subjected to heavy government taxation. For these reasons, since the unilateral declaration of independence in 1991, the diaspora has been the primary private investor in Somaliland, with interests ranging from small shops to the larger import-export companies and the international telecommunications, transport and remittance companies. This can be explained by the fact that the displacement economy of Somaliland is itself highly globalized. For example, virtually all consumer goods and food items are imported via Dubai, and the most important income locally in Somaliland is remittances sent from Western countries. As such, members of the diaspora, having links to a global outside, have an advantage when it comes to investing in and setting up businesses locally in Somaliland.

Typically, diaspora investors share an experience of having accumulated sociocultural and economic resources in the West. Moreover, ties to and experiences from the West also define sociocultural processes of reintegration in Somaliland. As such the chapter has highlighted how access to and experiences from Western countries not only define individual identities in Somaliland, but are also used when engaging economically in Somaliland. At the same time, what motivates many diaspora investors is an experience of sociocultural displacement and exclusion living in the West. As such, histories and experiences of displacement are important when understanding diasporic engagements or processes of emplacement in Somaliland.

Notes

1 With the end of the Cold War educational migration turned more towards Western countries (Kleist 2004: 7). More recently, Somalis have turned to India, Pakistan and Malaysia for education.

2 It is estimated that the violence at the beginning of the 1990s caused between 800,000 and 1.5 million to flee Somalia and created another 2 million internally displaced persons (Kleist 2004: 7). The largest war-related displacements from the south took place from 1991 and 1993 (Gundel 2002: 264). The war in the south was especially hard on the racial minorities, who lacked the support of clan networks (Besteman 1999).

3 Somaliland's case for separate statehood is based on its history of having been a British protectorate, and on the existence of a functioning political system which sets it apart from other parts of Somalia (ICG 2005; Menkhaus 2000, 2007a, 2007b; Møller 2009).

4 The word *coffer* most likely stems from the word 'coiffure', which also means beauty salon or hairdresser.

5 *Sijui* is Swahili and means *I don't know*, and is used by local Somalis to refer to a Somali who has been born and raised in the Swahili-speaking part of East Africa. In the eyes of local Somalis the *sijui* are unable to speak proper Somali, and are not as Somali as they are. When asked about something in Somali they will often say *sijui*, simply because they cannot understand Somali.

6 Contrary to how other migrants and refugees have turned racial identities on their heads and used them to construct alternative, positive self-identities (Miles 1993: 28), Somalis have largely rejected the category of being black. Especially in the UK, many Somalis point out that they are not like other immigrant and refugee groups. The rejection of being black is tied to racial discourse in Britain. Neither in Denmark, nor in Somaliland, have I experienced the same reluctance among Somalis in relation to being black or African.

References

Ahmed, I. I. (2000) 'Remittances and their economic impact in post-war Somaliland', *Disaster*, 24(4): 380–89.

Ambroso, G. (2002) 'Pastoral society and transnational refugees: population movements in Somaliland and eastern Ethiopia 1988–2000', *New Issues in Refugee Research*, 65, Brussels: UNHCR.

Besteman, C. (1999) *Unraveling Somalia: Race, Violence, and the Legacy of Slavery*, Philadelphia: University of Pennsylvania Press.

Bradbury, M., A. Y. Abokor and H. A. Yusuf (2003) 'Somaliland: choosing politics over violence', *Review of African Political Economy*, 30(97): 455–78.

Gundel, J. (2002) 'The migration–development nexus: Somalia case study', *International Migration*, 40(5): 255–79.

— (2006) 'The predicament of the "Oday". The role of traditional structures in security, rights, law and development in Somalia', Nairobi: Danish Refugee Council and Novib-Oxfam.

Hage, G. (2003) *Against Paranoid Nationalism. Searching for hope in a shrinking society*, London: Merlin Press.

Hansen, P. (2004) 'Migrant transfers as a development tool. The case of Somaliland', Migration Policy Research Working Papers Series no. 3, June, Geneva: International Organization for Migration.

— (2007) 'Revolving returnees in Somaliland', in N. Nyberg Sørensen (ed.), *Living across Worlds: Diaspora,*

Development and Transnational Engagement, Geneva: International Organization for Migration, pp. 129–50.

— (2008) 'Circumcising migration. Gendering return migration among Somalilanders', *Journal of Ethnic and Migration Studies*, 34(7): 1109–25.

— (2009) 'Governing khat. Drugs and democracy in Somaliland', DIIS Working Paper no. 24, Copenhagen: Danish Institute for International Studies.

— (2010) 'The ambiguity of khat in Somaliland', *Journal of Ethnopharmacology*, 132(3): 590–9.

Hoehne, M. (2006) 'Political identity, emerging state structures and conflict in northern Somalia', *Journal of Modern African Studies*, 44(3): 397–414.

Horst, C. (2003) *Transnational Nomads. How Somalis cope with refugee life in the Dadaab camps of Kenya*, PhD thesis, University of Amsterdam.

— (2006) *Transnational Nomads. How Somalis Cope with Refugee Life in the Dadaab Camps of Kenya*, New York and London: Berghahn.

Hyndman, C. (2000) *Managing Displacement. Refugees and the Politics of Humanitarianism*, Minneapolis: University of Minnesota Press.

ICG (2005) 'Somalia's Islamists', Africa Report no. 100, International Crisis Group.

Kleist, N. (2004) 'Nomads, sailors and refugees', Sussex Migration Working Paper no. 23, University of Sussex.

Kusow, A. M. (2006) 'Migration and racial formations among Somali immigrants in North America', *Journal of Ethnic and Migration Studies*, 32(3): 533–51.

Lindley, A. (2006) 'The influence of migration, remittances and diaspora donations on education in Somali society', *Social Development Papers, Conflict Prevention and Reconstruction*, 38.

Malkki, L. (1992) 'National geographic: the rooting of peoples and the territorialization of national identity among scholars and refugees', *Cultural Anthropology*, 7(1): 24–44.

McGown, R. B. (1999) *Muslims in the Diaspora: The Somali Communities of London and Toronto*, Toronto, Buffalo and London: University of Toronto Press.

Menkhaus, K. (2000) 'Somalia: a situation analysis', Geneva: Centre for Documentation and Research, UNHCR.

— (2007a) 'The crisis in Somalia: tragedy in five acts', *African Affairs*, 106(424): 357–90.

— (2007b) 'Governance without government in Somalia. Spoilers, state building, and the politics of coping', *International Security*, 31(3): 74–106.

Miles, R. (1993) *Race After 'Race Relations'*, London: Routledge.

Møller, B. (2009) 'The Somali conflict. The role of external actors', DIIS Report no. 3, Copenhagen: Danish Institute for International Studies.

Portes, A. (1999) 'Conclusion: towards a new world – the origins and effects of transnational activities', *Ethnic and Racial Studies*, 22(2): 463–77.

Renders, M. (2007) 'Appropriate "governance-technology"? – Somali clan elders and institutions in the making of the "Republic of Somaliland"', *Africa Spectrum*, 42(3): 439–59.

Simons, A. (1995) *Networks of Dissolution. Somalia Undone*, Boulder, CO: Westview Press.

Thomas, P. (1998) 'Conspicuous construction: houses, consumption and "relocalization" in Manambondro, southeast Madagascar', *Journal of the Royal Anthropological Institute*, 4(3): 425–46.

Warsame, A. M. (2002) *Queens without Crowns. Somaliland women's changing roles and peace building*, Uppsala: Life and Peace Institute.

8 | Financial flows and secrecy jurisdictions in times of crisis: relocating assets in Zimbabwe's displacement economy

Sarah Bracking

Introduction

The displacement economy of Zimbabwe which developed from 2000 onwards has had multiple effects on economic relationships and institutions at all scales, including the family, and local, district, national and international spaces. People in Zimbabwe have relocated and externalized their goods and money, particularly up to 2008, moving them into international institutions, public and private, formal and informal, as a consequence of displacement processes taking place within Zimbabwe. This chapter explores the processes of relocation and externalization of people, money and non-pecuniary assets which resulted from political violence, dispossession and displacement in Zimbabwe from the first violent election of 2000, up to the installation of the Government of National Unity in 2008. While these processes of relocation were initially reactive to crisis, over time we can see how they then contribute to a continuation of Zimbabwe's displacement economy and the particular form it takes.

While much has been said in the general case, about externalization practices and the role of secrecy jurisdictions in undermining the political economy of southern African development (Bracking 2012), this chapter looks specifically at how, first, relocation of money and assets occurred as a consequence of crisis in Zimbabwe; and secondly, what effects and ramifications this has for the political economy of Zimbabwe characterized as a 'displacement economy'. These externalization processes link back to the contexts and conditions that have generated and intensified them. These have consequent and recurring effects on the local and national scales, and impact on the institutional structures of the displacement economy. They also affect the (additional) opportunities for participants within it to externalize their assets in survivalist and/or extractive activities.

The displacement economy of contemporary Zimbabwe, generated through coercion, expulsion and dispossession, has institutional nodes such as the parent companies of large firms in the banking, agricultural, manufacturing, minerals and service sectors, which are absent in the sense that they have been relocated elsewhere, many to South Africa, the UK or to secrecy jurisdictions. Thus, paradoxically – since this is rare for low-performing economies – Zimbabwe exhibits a high degree of internationalization and connectedness with the regional and international economy. This feature may prove to be of some expedient use to a government committed to managing the economy in the interests of the public good.

A note on terminology In this volume displacement refers to 'enforced changes in interweaving spatial, social and symbolic conditions and relations' (Hammar, Introduction to this volume). There is, importantly, a connection between the particular context of violence and enforced change in Zimbabwe, and the way in which its 'displacement economy' has come into being as a result of multiple practices and sites of enforced removal, dispossession and abjection (Hammar et al. 2010; Hammar and Rodgers 2008; Hammar and Raftopoulos 2003; Sachikonye 2011). In this chapter those persons moving money and goods outside Zimbabwe as a consequence of economic and political crisis, particularly those relatively more wealthy, can be viewed as retaining some element of choice in the purposive and avowed intent of their behaviour. There is a certain rationality about moving one's assets away from punitive taxation or predatory theft by a malignant government administration and ruling party with a well-developed political militia armed for the purposes of violence (Sachikonye 2011: 28–52).

What this underscores is that there are always elements of choice alongside enforcement in displacement contexts. At the same time the parameters of such choices are defined by a range of factors – not least class – that differentiate groups and individuals, as well as the nature of things themselves. In the Zimbabwe case, both people who have been displaced, and others who remain *in situ*, are relocating and in some cases externalizing things of value within the framework of (and contributing to) the current displacement economy. Here, the *voluntary* externalization of funds and the use of secrecy jurisdictions does not in itself constitute 'displacement' of funds, at least not in the way displacement is broadly understood and used in this volume in terms of enforcement. However, what it does do is *emerge* out of – and *simultaneously help construct* – a specific displacement economy context, in this case Zimbabwe during the present era of crisis.

This chapter examines the relocation of both the lower and upper echelons of an economy which has accompanied the political crisis from 2000. The chapter attempts to draw on work on the displacement of the poor and vulnerable, and see how far it can provide insights into the simultaneous displacement of the rich and wealthy, and how these processes interact with and contradict one another. The chapter argues that an examination of the interweaving processes of displacement and relocation of people, things and money shows how the 'normal' structures of international economy, and the salience of its offshore nodes, proved remarkably amenable to assisting the newly emergent, ruling-party-affiliated elites of Zimbabwe in their spoils politics (Bracking 2009). Were a democratic government of the future to choose to expose these practices, it might point to the warlike basis of the national space during the post-2000 crisis, the endemic political violence inflicted on the population, and the displacement economy all this engendered. On this basis it might ask its neighbours for full financial disclosure of accounts and assets removed by Zimbabwean nationals from 2000 onward, in order to repatriate that which was stolen.

Displacement and relocation

Wealthy people are generally more mobile than their poorer counterparts, and historically less prone to forced migration or displacement through violence. However, globally there are pockets of wealthy persons who are subject to directly predatory behaviour by governments wishing to divest them of their assets, and/or evict them from their states. For example, Mitchell (2006), making a 'moral case for tax havens', sees them as providing wealth protection services to 'high net worth individuals' (HNWIs) facing persecution for religious or political beliefs, ethnic origin, sexual preference or from predatory government. He uses the example of a Zimbabwean family using a tax haven to protect its wealth from political persecution and an economic meltdown under hyperinflation (ibid.). He similarly identifies ethnic Chinese persecuted in Indonesia and the Philippines who place their assets in Singapore, or Saudi Arabian homosexuals who require tax haven services (ibid.; McLaren and Passant 2010: 11–12). McLaren and Passant further argue that banking secrecy is an important protector of rights, reminding us that Swiss banking law was constructed to protect German nationals from the Nazi government. These authors build this into their (ultimately unconvincing) positive case for secrecy jurisdiction operations (ibid: 20–1).

In Africa, examples of the forced displacement of relatively wealthy people include the early post-colonial eviction of Asians from Kenya and Uganda in the 1970s, or in our case, members of the Zimbabwean white commercial farming community during the Land Reform process of 2000–08 (Hammar 2010). Less well known, but comparably violent, was the 'Industrial Chimurenga' in Zimbabwe, referring to occupation of businesses, and linked to a discourse of indigenization. This also forced the egress and displacement of industrialists from around 2004 onwards as a separate moment of strategic political violence by ZANU-PF and its youth militia (Sachikonye 2011). The violence of mass urban displacements across the country in the punitive Operation Murambatsvina following the 2005 national elections, and the Operation Makavhotera Papi (Operation Whom Did You Vote For?), which followed the March 2008 elections

163

until the presidential run-off in July, were used to punish and destroy the urban MDC vote. They were also used simultaneously to seize or destroy businesses and property, as well as to torture and take lives (Masunungure 2009; Sachikonye 2011: 49–61; CCJPZ 2009; HRW 2008a, 2008b). Thus the context in which economic relationships have been conducted since 2000 has been far from the classical economics of textbooks where buyer and seller, both free to make rational choices, can optimize their profits and incomes. In Zimbabwe, owners and managers of firms, particularly large ones, have had to keep cognizant of the demands of the ruling party ZANU-PF. They have had to pay into party funds to stop their premises being vandalized or sequestrated, and have had to allow political appointments to be made within their companies in order to access bank loans from the Reserve Bank (Bracking 2009).

The premise here is that the earlier theoretical work on displacement economies – defined formerly in terms of the notion of 'political economies of displacement' (Hammar and Rodgers 2008; Hammar et al. 2010) – has focused more on the weak and vulnerable. Yet this approach, now reframed within the concept of displacement economies, can be usefully applied to elites who, also in circumstances of crisis, relocate their wealth, economic and financial relationships, and assets outside the country, often using secrecy jurisdictions. Hammar and Rodgers (2008) and Hammar et al. (2010) describe the paradoxes that link losses and gains and poverty and wealth creation in the overall social articulation of multiple dimensions of displacement. In their work, displacement is essentially paradoxical in that it both produces and sustains wealth at the same time as generating loss, destruction and impoverishment. My own evidence here of both the financial processes of survivalist remittances (Besado and Moyo 2008; Bracking and Sachikonye 2010a; Mukwedeya 2012) and wealth relocation by the wealthy (Bracking 2009, 2012), either voluntarily (to avoid tax) or forced (to avoid seizure), concurs within this overall theoretical approach, particularly in terms of its insistence on complexity and paradox.

In the case of the wealthy, in comparison to the poor, there is less likelihood of high degrees of coercion, although in the Zimbabwean setting there was also a degree of violence which catalysed these processes in many instances. There were definite accumulation opportunities inherent in the crisis situations generated through political violence and spoils politics (Bracking 2009), as there are in other generic cases of crisis, through the potential rents from hoarding, bartering and smuggling – see David Keen's seminal *The Benefits of Famine* (1994). Illicit financial flows from such activities naturally seek private, opaque storage facilities available in secrecy jurisdictions, joining flight capital to decimate the national capital supply. These forms of extraversion allow elites to 'hook up' with development finance institutions, European venture capital funds, private equity funds, pension funds and other 'high net worth individuals', in order to remanifest their own selves back in the domestic economy as (wealthy) foreign investors, with all the privileges that accompany this classification (termed 'round-tripping') (see Bracking et al. 2010). In other words, by a 'round trip' offshore and back again, criminally acquired funds are cleansed and turned back into the generic classification of foreign direct investment (FDI).

Indeed, there are complex interactions of displaced people and things. People often attempt to carry their most valuable assets with them, as the Solidarity Peace Trust's report *'Gone to Egoli'* so memorably recorded (2009). Some persons who anticipate dispossession or eviction attempt to move assets beforehand, such as the way in which white commercial farmers attempted to move vehicles and farm equipment over the border into Mozambique, or the smaller acts of victims of Operation Murambatsvina who removed their own corrugated roofs before the army came to destroy their homes (Bracking 2005). In practice it is hard to think of processes of displacement consisting solely or wholly of just people or just things, or which do not connect the poor and the wealthy together in complex networks and dependencies (see also Jones, this volume). The French tradition, following Latour's (2005) actor network theory, and Callon's (1998, 2007) work on how markets are made or performed in a deliberative way, is of use here, in theorizing how networks of economic processes, consisting of persons, things and institutions, are displaced in combination.

Building from this literature on the performativity of economics (MacKenzie 2005, 2006; Nik-Khah 2006; Fourcade 2007; Callon 2007; Lee et al. 2008), we can see how the multiple acts of so many variously displaced people in Zimbabwe were enacted within prior existing economic logics and institutions. These allowed them to take advantage of the utility found in the offshore economy, normally reserved for transnational corporations. There had been an increasing amount of capital redomiciling offshore since structural adjustment programmes across Africa in the 1980s (and from 1990 in Zimbabwe), which had begun the process of opening up economies and removing capital controls. By the 2000s, a well-used and relatively well-known infrastructure for the movement of money was in place, ready for an exodus of people with a new incentive to use it who, prior to the onset of crisis, would not have thought to move assets and money away from 'home'.

But it is more complex than this. While finding these structures of use, there were also acts of bricolage by those in situations of forced displacement, whereby whole new banking arrangements emerged, including multiple forms of informal exchange and transit. We do not know, and cannot find out accurately, how many people moved where, or what value or scale of assets were moved and to where, although we have some idea of scale extrapolated from case studies (cf. Solidarity Peace Trust 2009; Bracking and Sachikonye 2010a). Instead, we can describe the contours and calculative logics of displacement economies at a more general level. We can, among other things, describe how the crisis period in Zimbabwe, especially since 2000, has hollowed out the domestic economy, generating portals of exception to regulation, such as the Chiadzwa diamond mine. Taking this approach, this chapter is organized into three parts which explore, in turn: financial relations in displacement economies that are made and used by the poor; those that are made and used by the wealthy; and then how the two are connected through transnational financial networks, with tax havens as the core node for draining southern Africa and Zimbabwe of its resource rents and otherwise payable taxes.

Displacement of the vulnerable

The *Journal of Southern African Studies* special issue on displacement in Zimbabwe published in 2010 made conceptual advances in the study of displacement economies within contexts of social displacement, crisis and distress (see Hammar et al. 2010). Earlier studies tended to focus on the discovery of certain 'rationalities' in the context of chaos (Keen 1994; Chabal and Daloz 1999) in places such as Somalia (Little 2003), or the Congo (Trefon 2004). These contexts sometimes prompt horizontal solidarity and new social behaviours of survival and 'getting by', expressed in Shona as *kukiya-kiya* (Jones 2010b). Informalized businesses turn to clever but shadier practices to seize opportunistic chances to make money (ibid.). In Hammar et al. (2010), these reflections are developed into a conceptual map of displacement economies, where displacement is widely viewed as intimately related to concepts of statecraft, the nation, citizenship and belonging in evolving political economies that are 'reshaping patterns of production, accumulation and exchange' (ibid.: 266). The special issue includes an article detailing the informalized parallel economy for foreign currency, prior to the withdrawal in 2009 of the Zimbabwe dollar as the national currency and US-'dollarization' of the economy. In this era, money-changing became a central livelihood option, especially for women in Bulawayo's street-level 'World Bank' (Mawowa and Matongo 2010, and see discussion in Hammar's chapter, this volume). The collection establishes that displacement in Zimbabwe has a long history of colonial forms of governance and restricted citizenship, while also being a contemporary moment and response to both political and economic crisis. Among other things, it illustrates the unevenness of such contexts for different actors, as many who could not perform the back-street barter trading and other informal practices necessary to survive, especially in 2005–08 (Jones, this volume), fell into desperate poverty or succumbed to disease and early death. At the same time, others accumulated immense wealth precisely derived from the chaos and crisis (Hammar et al. 2010).

Displacement has principally been forced on the marginalized by the state elite, who have used eviction, displacement and strategic violence to maintain state power (Bracking 2005; Hammar 2008; Sachikonye 2011). As Hammar summarizes, 'state induced displacements and the multi-layered violence accompanying such practices ... are not an aberration. Rather they appear to be an ever-present possibility if not actuality, integral to contemporary as well as past modes of rule and state making' (Hammar 2008: 417). In particular the security services (*sic*), led by the Joint Operations Command, are a de facto junta working behind and through the shell of a liberal democratic state, using their power to terrorize the population when the former ruling party, ZANU-PF, has been threatened by electoral defeat (Sachikonye 2002; Chan 2003; Bracking 2005; Masunungure 2009; Sachikonye 2011: 34–44). This authoritarian core in the Zimbabwean state remains intact, despite regular terror campaigns, as mediation by the Southern African Development Community to date has been unwilling to address its fundamental powers (Raftopoulos 2011). The security services led the political violence between the March and June elections in 2008, in which 500 were murdered (CCJPZ 2009; CSVR 2009; HRW 2008a, 2008b). In the same period the country's currency completely imploded with inflation running into the millions of per cent. At the same time, the rate of diasporization increased one-hundred-fold in Matabeleland between 2008 and 2009, with one person per family migrating annually (Solidarity Peace Trust 2010: 8) as egress became the single survival option.

The urban displacement wrought by Operation Murambatsvina – both in terms of physical dislocations and various forms of displacement-in-place – caused the 'deconstruction of urban society', and 'escalated by the ruralisation and diasporisation of 2008–9 in the wake of political violence and economic collapse, has undermined the social movement and the MDC's ability to organise' (ibid.: 8). The scale of physical dislocation in itself has had an effect on the overall political economy of the country and on the political situation. Solidarity Peace Trust writes that 'the social fabric of Zimbabwe has been ripped apart' (ibid.: 11), as people dislodged by Operation Murambatsvina were joined by a further wave of people on the move as a result of the economic and political collapse of 2008/09. The United Nations Development Programme (UNDP) notes that Zimbabwe has reversed the normal development trend of gradually formalizing informal sector employment. The Economic Structural Adjustment Programme of 1991–94 began a process of contraction in formal sector jobs, and Operation Murambatsvina accelerated this dramatically, reaching a nadir in 2008 (UNDP 2010, cited in ibid.: 23). As UNDP noted, informalization occurred as the economic environment deteriorated:

> With an increasingly worthless currency, coupled with bank withdrawal limits,
> a growing scarcity of commodities, and frequent price control offensives
> which often left producers in a situation in which they were forced to sell at
> a fraction of the cost of their inputs, survivalist strategies kicked in and there

was growing recourse by remaining formal-sector operators to informal trans-actions, often on the basis of barter exchanges. (Ibid.)

However, Operation Murambatsvina is paradoxical in this respect. It cat-alysed further informal economic and survivalist activities at the same time as destroying informal businesses *partly* because they had grown so profitable as to represent a challenge to the power base – and related economic control – of ZANU-PF in the formal yet depleted neo-patrimonial economy (Bracking 2005). As Musoni (2010) captures so well, the displaced street vendors of Makomva Business Centre in Harare's Glen View Township practised adaptive resistance to the forces of violence, showing a critical level of political thinking in finding means to revive their economic activity in subtle ways.

Financial patterns generated by displacement of the vulnerable

The channels by which money moved around and out of Zimbabwe during the 2000s and the period of hyperinflation brought on by economic crisis opened up new informal and formal financial institutions and infrastruc-ture (Bracking and Sachikonye 2006; Solidarity Peace Trust 2009; Magunha et al. 2009). Even some medium- and small-scale entrepreneurs and traders arranged 'offshore' bank accounts to externalize their money and assets to neighbouring territories. The actions of migrant remitters, including those who had physically relocated elsewhere primarily as a result of crisis, opened new vertical avenues for financial transactions which avoided national accounting systems and the formal sector banking institutions (Bracking and Sachikonye 2006; Magunha et al. 2009). New distal, transnational and electronic banking structures emerged, often in association with mobile phones, internet and email accounts and subsequently retail banks (Chiumbu and Nyamanhindi 2012). In this process, an odd synergy emerged between institutions built up to meet the needs of elites – to move funds offshore – and those built up by survivalist family networks.

However, the traditional literature on the informal sector does not adequately explain informalization in the context of displacement economies rendered in crisis and violence. This is because, first, it tends to view informality as largely a preserve of the poor, displaced and ill-connected people at the 'bottom' of a society who cannot, for want of birth or income or social exclusion, access a formal economic position in the economy, rather than a logical system of connections that endure and signify inclusion. Secondly, the informal sector is widely associated with crime and illegality, a pathology borrowed by the Zimbabwean state to legitimize its various campaigns to control and police dissent (Solidarity Peace Trust 2010). But this 'social exclusion' emphasis, and the criminalization of informality, hides the larger story in the Zimbabwean case of a mass population forced to survive by any means possible, via practices of *kukiya-kiya* or making do (Jones 2010b), where traditional norms of morality and reciprocity were by necessity suspended in some contexts. Marx famously wrote that 'capitalism sinks its roots' into the economy of everyday life which provides the opportunities of survival, if they are received at all, to the most displaced and destitute. The means and mechanisms of this economy are only dimly in view, but are more complex than is captured within a pathologized view of informality, or indeed by the more anodyne, but still inflexible, livelihoods framework that is often used to analyse such contexts (see Moyo 2009 on Bulawayo).

When persons are displaced from (or within) their society through conflict and poverty, they inhabit the informal sector in a range of quasi-accepted professions and occupations, with a range of legal statuses, and with different relationships with law and authority (Little 2003 on Somalia; Trefon 2004 on Congo; Mate 2005 on Beit Bridge at Zimbabwe's southern border). This kind of survivalist moment has been well documented, wherein an informal sector arises, often using a different currency to the one in general circulation, which might be suffering from inflation or hyperinflation. Additionally, it may exhibit a pattern of cross-border or internal migratory movement, perhaps with a link to an internationalized family structure for periodic or sporadic remittance income (Bracking and Sachikonye 2010b). These patterns have distinct urban, semi-urban and rural dimensions, with rural coping and informality having a long provenance (see Mararike 2009 on rural Zimbabwe).

Jones (2010a) describes the nadir of the hyperinflationary period in Zimbabwe from 2007 up to dollarization in February 2009, as one popularly referred to as 'mad'. In this environment, 'Daily life became a time trial: getting money from the bank, buying goods before the price went up, storing and carrying stacks of cash – all had to be done quickly' (ibid.: 338–9). At the same time, 'staid middle- and working-class lifestyles' were also being 'liquidated', and the 'truth' of a 'fair price' disappeared (ibid.: 339). Jones analyses how the government used a ritual effort to cure the madness by imposing prices across the whole system, with 'enforcement' in the hands of the youth militia and police, who forced shopowners to reduce prices. Shops emptied and the parallel (unofficial) market reigned, with at one point the government using the printing of money to buy up foreign exchange from the 'illegal' parallel market. Of course, those in the government and former ruling party who had access to Zimbabwe dollars, petrol and some other scarce commodities became central to the supply of goods into the 'illegal' markets and saw rates of return that made them rich within a surprisingly short time span. Jones uses the example of the official price of petrol per litre being ZWD450 on 20 June 2007, against a parallel market price of ZWD200,000; namely a 40,000 per cent profit rate. Given the Reserve Bank's own shortage of foreign exchange pre-2009, and periodic freezing or raiding of foreign currency from account holders, the natural place to put such profits was outside the country (see Sharife 2010).

Bracking and Sachikonye (2010a) reported that over 50 per cent of urban households in Harare were in receipt of migrant remittances in 2005, with poorer households relying on contributions from regional migration to pay essential bills and to buy food, and those in wealthier neighbourhoods tending to rely on an international migrant. A Solidarity Peace Trust report subsequently questioned whether the figures could be generalized to other parts of Zimbabwe, as their own evidence from the Matabeleland diaspora to South Africa indicated a much lower level of successful remittances (Solidarity Peace Trust 2009). But work done by Besado and Moyo (2008), and Mukwedeya (2012) in a case study of Glen Nora in 2008, at the height of the crisis, confirms the central importance of remittances for both household incomes and the economy. Mukwedeya cites figures from the *Herald* (a state-run newspaper) that remittances in 2006 represented 7.2 per cent of the country's GDP, and also uses Besado and Moyo's (2008) figure of US$490 million annually during this period (Mukwedeya 2012: 44). In Mukwedeya's sample of households in Glen Nora the average monthly remittances to households was about US$400 in 2008 (ibid.: 48), and in addition, 87 per cent of households were receiving in-kind remittances in 2008 (ibid.: 44). This figure had risen since Pendleton et al.'s earlier estimate of 68 per cent of households in 2006 (cited in ibid.: 44). Mukwedeya notes how both types of transfer were essential for households' survival in the context of hyperinflation and the chronic shortage of basic commodities at that time, with the in-kind remittances sponsoring barter trade among households in the context of empty shelves in the shops (ibid.: 44).

The move to dollarization by early 2009 largely removed the benefit of externalization of hard currency given that the rent associated with its re-importation in the context of an overvalued official exchange rate could no longer be earned by receiving families. The volume and value of remittances shrank accordingly, but remained critical to many local households' survival needs. In 2011, Solidarity Peace Trust still reported that 17 per cent of rural households in Matabeleland were dependent on monthly migrant remittances for food, in the context of South Africa beginning deportations of migrants back home, adding to pressures on families (Solidarity Peace Trust 2011: 34). In October 2011, 47 per cent of households in Matabeleland reported having family members in South Africa, although of these, 44 per cent had never remitted money or goods, 17 per cent remitted monthly, while the remaining 38 per cent had sent one-off support during the previous year (ibid.). The report concludes that 83 per cent of the rural population were 'benefiting only very occasionally or not at all' from having family abroad (ibid.). While 'holding death from starvation at bay', the generally small amounts reported to the research team of between US$25 and US$50 could do little more than that (ibid.).

Newland (2003) has suggested that in badly governed countries, productive absorption of remittances as formal sector investments – should there be any funds left after survival needs have been met – will be lower than in better-governed ones. In Zimbabwe's case, incoming remittances during the 2000s were largely directed to households by informal means, and little absorption appears to have occurred. Remittances also produced other adverse effects such as increases in economic *inequality* between households. Local price inflation for basic goods left non-receiving households in an even more precarious position in terms of their food security (Bracking and Sachikonye 2010a, 2010b). The situation is made more complex when the politicization and command structures of the (former) ruling party and government are considered. For example, the management of key parallel market commodities was conducted in Zimbabwe's hyperinflationary period by politically well-placed persons. In this structure, incoming foreign exchange from remittances contributed to shoring up the position of ZANU-PF, as informalized traders at various levels collected up foreign exchange and returned it to commodity traders. Also, patronage goods were used in successive elections, purchased with the foreign currency acquired from street traders and theft from informal vendors (Mawowa and Matongo 2010; Solidarity Peace Trust 2010) as well as from other sources.

Economic informalization of the formal sector

The problematic use of the terms 'informal' and 'formal' (which has been discussed critically in specialist literature, reviewed by Gërxhani 2004) continues when we consider how economic space is conceptualized in order to underpin the dyad. In mainstream economics the firm takes a particular institutional form in a commercial, public space, while the family is seen as a private space beyond economics. But the money transfer networks in Zimbabwe's emerging displacement economy were critically family centred. Data showed a greater reliance on known persons and relatives rather than on commercial companies in goods and money transit. This suggests that 'informalization' takes distinct forms, including a paradoxical de facto commercialization of familial networks (Bracking and Sachikonye 2006: 24–7). This occurs as persons who begin by assisting a relative or two to transfer money attract friends of friends to the point where they are managing a regulated business with characteristics similar to those of a commercial firm, even though this may remain in the informal sector. The ambiguous nature of informality, both in theory and practice, can also be seen in movements between the formal and informal spaces which travel in the other direction. For example, previously formal firms may fall out of favour with political patrons, or with banks, or are chased by competitors or creditors, and move 'underground' to the informal sector (although commercial operations with clients may remain largely as before). The growth in backyard businesses, within family space, at least until Operation Murambatsvina, is a case in point.

But informalization of productive businesses is not the whole story, as in Zimbabwe this also occurred in the financial sector, which indeed contributed to the 2003 banking crisis. Managers were paid excessive fees for various services rendered to their own employers, demonstrating that informality can also be a feature of the 'commanding heights' of a distressed economy. Mangena et al. (2011) have examined the relationship between board and ownership structures and firm performance in two periods in Zimbabwe since 2000: the pre-presidential-election period of 2000–02, which was relatively stable, and the post-presidential-election period of 2003–05, which exhibited a hostile political and economic environment. They found that 'board size, ownership concentration and executive directors' share ownership increased, while the proportion of non-executive directors fell' in the second period (ibid.: 1). Meanwhile, firm performance also dropped in the second period as executive directors' share ownership rose (a reversal of the relationship in the former period) (ibid.).

Mangena et al. (ibid.) suggest that these changes occurred because the agency costs of the firm – the amount disposed of by executive directors in an unproductive way – rose in the crisis, as the means and incentives to expropriate wealth grew in a poorly regulated environment (ibid.: 2). Also, executive directors' share ownership rose from 1.6 per cent in the pre-presidential period to 4.6 per cent in the post-presidential election period (ibid.: 10). This had a negative effect on performance, but shows that 'agency costs' – a polite way of referring to backhanders and rents – rose for shareholders. However, the evidence used by Mangena et al. is somewhat ambiguous in that there were also indications of shareholders incorporating new persons to ward off risk and monitor executive directors. This type of increased share ownership concentration suggests the 'buying in' of politically connected persons, and indeed performance did rise as board size grew in the more turbulent 2003–05 period (ibid.: 3). Politically connected firms could get better access to scarce but critical resources such as fuel and foreign currency, while warding off threats of extortion (see Roe 2003, cited in ibid.). This evidence shows the 'revolving door' importance of the 'politically exposed person' or PEP (terminology used in anti-corruption literature, referring to persons active in the private sector who simultaneously hold public office). This is someone who moves between the public and private spheres gaining both personal enrichment and political risk reduction for the firm.

The broader context here was of a breakdown in the rule of law following the Zimbabwe presidential elections in 2002. The elite practices of the revolving door, which can be understood as risk reduction and/or extortion of previously independent firms, were mirrored locally and on a wider scale in factories and farms by some politicized war veterans, and ZANU-PF deployees, who extorted money from a number of firms (*Independent*, 26 April 2002). These persons demanded, sometimes violently, ownership shares and assets of the businesses affected, with no effective response from the law enforcement authorities or courts (Goredema 2003; Kriger 2003; Mangena et al. 2011: 4). The discourse of economic restitution, in ZANU-PF hands, simultaneously became one of theft and extortion. In this context, inflation soared and the official exchange rate became seriously overvalued. Firms resorted to the parallel market for foreign exchange, as the centralized allocation system failed to provide enough.

In 2004, this situation became further politicized as the central bank accused a number of mostly independent (non-ZANU-PF) entrepreneurs of externalizing foreign exchange (see also Bracking 2009; Mangena et al. 2011). Some lost all their shareholdings to the government, such as the telecommunications company, Econet Wireless, whose directors were arrested for allegedly externalizing US$1.3 million. Meanwhile, in a much publicized case, Mutumwa Mawere, both a director and a major shareholder of SMM Holdings, lost all his firms to the government (Mangena et al. 2011: 5). These types of predatory practices increased the likelihood that executive directors would externalize funds, or hide assets, either with the full knowledge of shareholders or in a purposive relocation of their own wealth, anticipating a threat from the ruling party which they could not counter by legal means.

Thus localized political violence, physical dislocation and relocation encouraged a range of people to externalize their assets and money, facilitated by generic processes of contemporary globalization. This process took place within the informal economy but also fed from it, translating into a parallel relocation of formal institutions and the assets previously stored within them. The higher echelons of the commercial, retail, banking and productive sectors diminished in value as liquid and non-fixed assets were externalized. This happened through company redomicile and the illicit movement of private wealth, as well as through mispricing in share and investment transactions. The periodic banking crises in Zimbabwe, starting from 2003, also proved a powerful catalyst for owners to relocate financial service firms and commercial banking operations. The Government of National Unity (GNU), through dollarization, has made some progress since 2009 in generating liquid reserves in banks. However, up until 2012 the banks remained exceptionally short of credit for customers and small businesses. Capital markets have not recovered. The former Zimbabwe minister of finance, Tendai Biti, and the now late chair of the Mines and Mining Development Committee, Edward Chindori-Chininga, often spoke of the difficulty of taxing minerals incomes, or even identifying the beneficial owners of key firms, including owners of the controversial diamond mines at Chiadzwa (Mail and Guardian 2013).

Externalization of the assets of the wealthy

Indeed, studies of capital flight from Zimbabwe undertaken during the post-2000 period have recorded a massive outflow from Zimbabwe. Makochekanwa (2007), for example, estimated this as being in the region of US$10.1 billion over the whole period from 1980 to 2005 (ibid.: 2), caused by 'large public sector deficits, exchange rate misalignment, financial repression, accelerating inflation, slowing economic growth, capital availability (revolving door), political instability, overvalued exchange rate, and rising taxes' (ibid.: 4). Makochekanwa dates the largest outflows from the 1997 watershed, the advent of a resilient opposition from 1999, and the land reform and indigenization programmes of 2000 onward (ibid.: 5). The expulsion of white farmers, the expropriation of their property, and their progressive denial of full citizenship within reconstructed views of the 'nation' (Hammar and Raftopoulos 2003) provided the main catalyst for the first salient period of externalization and capital flight during the 2000s. This was then followed by the expulsion from the country of business people of all ethnicities who would not bend to ideas of patriotic history and nationalism (Ranger 2004), of patrimonialism under the ruling party (Bracking 2009) and an increasingly virulent discourse of indigenization (Hammar and Raftopoulos 2003). Trade mis-invoicing appears to have been a central means of facilitating capital flight (Hermes et al. 2002), as residents under-invoiced exports and over-invoiced imports (ibid.: 16). In Makochekanwa's study, capital flight is also positively correlated to changes in external debt and FDI inflows, indicating some recycling of borrowed funds (Makochekanwa 2007: 30). This is a pattern which conforms to the general case of 'odious debt', whereby external borrowing is manipulated by residents into private assets abroad (Jayachandran and Kremer 2006: 82–92).

Considering continent-wide trends for forty sub-Saharan African countries, Ndikumana and Boyce (2008a) have estimated capital flight at 420 billion in real US dollars for the period 1970–2004, rising to 607 billion if interest earnings on past capital flight are included (ibid., cited in Ashman et al. 2011: 15). Just 25 per cent of this flight capital is more than twice the volume of debt relief for the countries concerned, while inflows of FDI are much smaller (ibid.). In other words, Zimbabwe's economy is sufficiently commensurate with others in the wider region to be characterized as a net exporter of capital, while Africa as a whole has the highest proportion of assets held abroad of any region (Collier et al. 2001). There is an 'irony here', noted by Ndikumana and Boyce, that not only is sub-Saharan Africa a net creditor to the world but 'a substantial fraction of the money that flowed out of the continent as capital flight appears to have come to the subcontinent via external borrowing' (2008b, cited in Sharife 2010). Heggstad and Fjeldstad (2010) also report this relationship between debt and capital flight, whereby a 'revolving door' relationship means that public loans leave the country as private assets, with sometimes up to 80 per cent of the initial value turning into flight capital (ibid.: 2, citing Ajayi and Khan 2000. See also Boyce and Ndikumana 2001; Cerra et al. 2005; Ndikumana and Boyce 2008b).

These general trends were augmented in size and scope within Zimbabwe by the logics of crisis and displacement. Informalized relationships and opaque institutions and transactions certainly grew in the upper echelons of Zimbabwean society, economy and state. Key banking and manufacturing firms developed an 'offshore' moment, in order to hide illicit wealth and the proceeds of state subsidies to supporters (Bracking 2009). MacLean (2002: 522–5) provided early evidence of these informal networks in relation to the military intervention in the Congo. Established tax avoidance practices, including transfer pricing, multiple accounts, offshore accounts, offshore record-keeping and redomicile in a booking centre or tax haven (Heggstad and Fjeldstad 2010), also proved to have a high utility for a relocating commercial elite.

But critically, informalization deepened in the state itself, as even the Reserve Bank developed a system of separate accounting for 'off balance items' and liabilities, printing money to buy foreign currency and sending the economy at large into hyperinflation (Muñoz 2007). According to Muñoz, in an IMF research paper, the Reserve Bank created new money and issued RBZ securities to meet quasi-fiscal losses of an estimated 75 per cent in 2006, leading to four-digit inflation (ibid.: 1). In addition, purportedly large expenditures from the Treasury to the Office of the President (also including the two vice-presidents, the Ministry of State Security, the Central Intelligence Organization and the presidential household) were not subject to parliamentary oversight during this period (Doig 2006: 75), which added to the sense of informality in high office. Indeed, even the ombudsman was disempowered from investigating complaints of maladministration against the president, the Ministry of State Security and any other member of that office (ibid.: 73). Thus the official budget and expenditure accounts covered only a small part of the actual flows from the Treasury and Reserve Bank to the Office of the Presidency, and those assigned to ministries for onward distribution to supporters. A particularly large contribution to the quasi-fiscal deficits of the Reserve Bank was the supply of cheap foreign exchange to government personnel, when the official exchange rate bore little resemblance to the real value of the Zimbabwean dollar (Muñoz 2007).

While there are no present estimates of what part of the Zimbabwean economy is currently offshore, we can deduce from the capital flight data that it must be substantial. The wider literature on the offshore economy, as above, can be invoked here to support this view. There is also, however, the contributing factor that banking regulation in Zimbabwe is porous and does little to prevent tax avoidance or evasion, or externalization of currency dealing, such that illicit flows are easily facilitated and thus probably also large.

Thus reflecting on the aftermath of the 2003 banking crisis in Zimbabwe, Mambondiani (2011a) notes that the attempted prosecutions of bankers by the state – beginning with the allegations against the ENG executives Nyasha Watyoka and Gilbert Muponda for 'economic sabotage', and then including William Nyemba, Mthuli Ncube, Julius Makoni and Jeff Mzwimbi, and most latterly Nicholas Vingirayi – have all been futile owing to failures in banking regulation. In total, the 2003 banking crisis led to the collapse of thirteen indigenous banks, where '[b]etween December 2003 and June 2004, five banks were placed under curatorship, two were liquidated and four were on a financial drip through the Troubled Bank Fund' (ibid.). These businesses were neatly parcelled up and redistributed by the Reserve Bank, however, with no recompense to owners. On the other hand, there was a virtual amnesty declared in 2009 which saw the return of many of the accused to CEO positions (ibid.). Mambondiani argues that insider ownership concentration is the main problem which caused the 2003 crisis, and which remains insufficiently regulated to date. This 'resulted in corporate governance weaknesses in private indigenous banks such as insider lending, abuse of depositors' funds and speculative activities ... [but] this financial dexterity may have been immoral but not illegal' (ibid.). It is, however, the context in which large sums of money have been externalized from Zimbabwe.

Global tax havens, or secrecy jurisdictions, are well placed to help 'externalizers', as they become 'high net worth individuals' (HNWIs) and 'permanent tourists' (PTs), in the language of the offshore economy, leaving their nation-states and joining a privatized international space. In the Zimbabwean case, the diamond industry is particularly opaque, and the opposition participants in the initial period of the GNU in 2009 had a very early spat with their ZANU-PF 'partners' over the location of diamonds and diamond-related earnings for a number of mines connected to the political elite. This dispute has remained ongoing (Guma 2011a). These income streams were not properly accounted for in the Reserve Bank's official records, but had been privatized. The diamond empire is also internationally connected with equity funds managed from Hong Kong. As Sharife (2011a) documents for the Angolan context, Manuel Vicente has risen to vice-president in José Eduardo dos Santos's government. But he is also head of Angola's state oil company, Sonangol, which is 'interlocked, through no less than nine different subsidiaries, with private Hong Kong-based entity China International Fund (CIF). The CIF is Zimbabwe's largest foreign investor (US$8 billion), active in various sectors, including infrastructure but also diamonds, via the entity Sino-Zim' (ibid.).

In Hong Kong, a tax haven, companies are not required to disclose trusts, company ownership or beneficial ownership, and can use nominees to hide the identity of people involved. The China International Fund Limited (CIFL) provides US$2.9 billion in funding for Angolan construction projects, administered by Angola's Gabinete de Reconstrução Nacional, while China Sonangol and CIF documented further investments of US\$7 billion in Guinea and US\$8 billion in Zimbabwe in 2009. In Zimbabwe, 'the company, Sino-Zimbabwe, incorporated as Sino-Zim Diamond Limited – a Hong Kong entity – evidences the close ties between international diamond magnate Lev Leviev, the Angolan government and the CIF' (ibid.). These lines of credit from offshore tax havens liquidate companies by involving members of the political elite. For example, another Chinese company mining for diamonds, Anhui Foreign Economic Construction Co. Ltd, invests in Anjin, a joint venture with the Zimbabwean government. This is led and managed on a daily basis by 'Emmerson Mnangagwa, General Constantine Chiwenga of the Zimbabwe National Army (ZNA) and key architect of the opaque Joint Operations Command (JOC), and Colonel Sedze – a senior member of the ZNA' (Sharife 2011b). These are all key figures in a security sector that openly pledges its support for Robert Mugabe and ZANU-PF.

The wealthy and the poor 'meet' offshore

While some externalization occurs in the context of normal capitalist growth, in the Zimbabwean case this was augmented by the multidimensional economic and political crisis. In the case of the multilayered economic displacement in Zimbabwe which accompanied the political crisis from 2005 (Hammar et al. 2010; Sachikonye 2011; Jones, and Hammar, this volume), politically exposed persons were active in externalizing networks for money and goods on which the poor relied. This included parallel markets for food staples and petrol. In the foreign exchange market, vertical chains of informality linked state personnel from the Reserve Bank to roadside money changers in cross-border and foreign currency trading networks (Mawowa and Matongo 2010). At the same time, spoils politics drained the Zimbabwean state and its institutions of wealth and assets. In turn, many independent business people reacted to the increasing spoils moment and chose to disguise their wealth and economic transactions in order to flatten their balance sheets and escape predatory state attention. There were thus months in 2007 where next to no formal receipts of foreign exchange or of tax revenue were received by the Reserve Bank of Zimbabwe or the Zimbabwean Revenue Authority. And yet the authoritarian moment of the state remained and it did not 'collapse', 'fail' or reach 'terminal spoils' (Bracking 2009). The legacy of this period is a disarticulated and displaced commercial sector whose ownership is opaque.

The movement of Zimbabwe's emerging rich elite into an informal financial sector during the 2000s in turn reshaped productive practices in manufacturing and agriculture, with the latter increasingly relying on the former for critical foreign exchange, as official exchange auctions ran dry. But these informalized financial circuits also had an intimate connection with the survivalist circuits of the poor. For example, the use of electronic transfer media, such as telephony and the internet, spawned an informal remittance transfer system among the Zimbabwean diaspora that was especially robust between around 2003 and 2008. The informal remittance system was allegedly headed by well-connected members of the elite, with links to the commercial banking sector, and 'hubs' in the UK, Canada and America, where some subsidiaries of Zimbabwean commercial banks were registered, albeit disguised by shell and holding companies. Through diaspora payments into bank accounts in the UK and elsewhere, they could collect quite large volumes of foreign exchange. Using a gradually elongating time frame between receiving the money from the expatriate family and paying out the domiciled family in Zimbabwe with local currency, this could then be used for all sorts of trading and investment ventures, provided of course that the investment dividend could be realized in Zimbabwe and/or the external country such as the UK. It is alleged, but notoriously difficult to prove, that key PEPs such as Gideon Gono, the Reserve Bank governor of Zimbabwe, have in this way been able to externalize their assets and build up property portfolios and commercial assets in, for example, the Manchester area in the UK.

In other ventures, money collected in the UK from diaspora remitters would be transferred to a bank account in South Africa, or even offshore through Mauritius, where it was used to fund a tanker of petrol to travel across the border into Zimbabwe. The petrol was then sold on the parallel market, receiving an above-market-level rent and profits on the original investment. From these profits, the recipient relatives in Zimbabwe could be paid the value of their UK-based relatives' contribution (minus a fee). The excess Zimbabwe dollars (when this was still the national currency) could then be locally realized and consumed by the expatriate business person's family. Or more likely, the foreign exchange collected in the UK would be used to fund the petrol imports in this 'triangular trade', but some could be left externalized as the investor would not need it all in order to make enough money on the commodity to pay all the relatives. Excess profits left in the UK could then fund a migration, or university fees or some such activity abroad, or they could be stored as externalized wealth.

Thus networks sponsored by PEPs became key movers of money and goods on which, paradoxically, some of the poor also relied, at least those with access to remittance funds. However, other uses of the informal sector were made by PEPs with no tangential benefit to the poor, but rather with the principal effect of further impoverishing the economy and in the process those who were most vulnerable within it. The grand thefts of spoils politics during the crisis period drained the state and its institutions of wealth and assets, concentrating these in the hands of a small elite class, who additionally then did not invest in job-creating productive sectors. Under such conditions, especially during the extremes of hyperinflation in 2007/08, the government of Zimbabwe, or more accurately the ZANU-PF junta, was forced into a game of 'find the forex', competing with the mass of the population in order to fuel their own accumulation strategies. When those in the industrial and manufacturing sectors learned the tactic of declaring themselves formally bankrupt as a practice of resistance, state agents had to turn elsewhere to elicit rents. They could then only harass street money-changers and other vendors and the urban households made vulnerable by the mass displacements of Operation Murambatsvina, in order to meet their accumulation requirements.

Conclusion

This chapter has shown how transnational financial structures became channels for the relocation of finances generated under conditions of crisis and displacement in Zimbabwe. A small ruling-party-affiliated elite were involved in extrajudicial killing and in organizing the violence surrounding the stolen elections of the 2000s and the terror and torture meted out to the political opposition (Sachikonye 2011). This same elite, and sometimes the same people, simultaneously organized criminal financial networks to channel the spoils that they secured from the crisis they precipitated and sustained, which included spoils from the war in the eastern Congo in which Zimbabwe was involved in the late 1990s (Guma 2011b). In the Zimbabwean case there was also an alleged uncomfortable closeness between some of these criminal networks and the informal remittance transfer systems used for the survivalist needs of the majority in times of crisis and displacement, as key ruling party members allegedly grew to control major remittance hubs.

There is always a methodological challenge when researching the absence of something – in this case invisible or displaced capital flows, people and wealth, mostly to secrecy jurisdictions. In terms of Zimbabwe, the externalization of illegal, illicit, parallel economy profits, rents and spoils to secrecy jurisdictions can be deduced from capital flight statistics, and from individual case studies which sporadically appear, normally when a key entrepreneur has a public disagreement with the political elite. Secrecy jurisdictions provide extra profitability, while for some they are additionally part of a process of egress in the face of crisis and predatory government. The remittance economy and the banking systems that it has generated since 2000 also contributed to the externalization of private wealth, as well as sometimes funding outmigration, and the national economy was reshaped accordingly. Centrally, however, externalization and relocation processes have emerged out of crisis in Zimbabwe, and simultaneously contributed to perpetuating the marginalization and impoverishment of those physically and economically displaced by the broader political crisis.

In conclusion, a number of insights emerge from this analysis. First,

Zimbabwe's displacement economy is characterized by new forms of informality which are arguably at the centre of financial markets in Zimbabwe itself and beyond. This links it to a transnational and globalized economy of opaque business and private transactions, many of which are conducted offshore. These markets are characterized by a lack of transparency that has far-reaching negative effects for the economy as a whole and for most ordinary Zimbabweans. Other member states of the Southern African Development Community (SADC) in particular, and farther afield, could contribute to reversing such conditions by taking out bilateral tax information exchange agreements in order to properly track and account for externalized assets – and then to have the political will to return them. Some volume of this pecuniary and non-pecuniary wealth may have been moved by vulnerable or persecuted citizens to avoid a predatory state, and could be encouraged into voluntary return, but the rest has its origin in the theft of sovereign-owned assets and deserves to be returned to a democratic dispensation, once that is actualized. In short, displacement and economic informality in Zimbabwe pervade the whole society, and have their roots in political and economic crisis and strategic political violence. While this violence continues, and various forms of displacement result, it compromises the well-being, incomes and security of the mass of Zimbabweans, while supporting a small and morally bankrupt state class of ZANU-PF stalwarts.

References

Ajayi, S. I. and M. S. Khan (eds) (2000) *External Debt and Capital Flight in sub-Saharan Africa*, Washington, DC: International Monetary Fund.

Ashman S., B. Fine and S. Newman (2011) 'Amnesty international? The nature, scale and impact of capital flight from South Africa', *Journal of Southern African Studies*, 37(1): 7–25.

Besada, H. and N. Moyo (2008) 'Zimbabwe in crisis: Mugabe's policies and failures', Working Paper no. 38, Centre for International Governance Innovation (CIGI).

Boyce, J. K. and L. Ndikumana (2001) 'Is Africa a net creditor? New estimates of capital flight from severely indebted sub-Saharan African countries, 1970–96', *Journal of Development Studies*, 38: 27–56.

Bracking, S. (2005) 'Development denied: autocratic militarism in post-election Zimbabwe', *Review of African Political Economy*, 32(104/5): 341–57.

— (2009) 'Political economies of corruption beyond liberalism: an interpretative view of Zimbabwe', *Singapore Journal of Tropical Geography*, 30(1): 35–51.

— (2012) 'Secrecy jurisdictions and economic development in Africa: the role of sovereign spaces of exception in producing private wealth and public poverty', *Economy and Society*, 41(4): 615–37.

Bracking, S. and L. Sachikonye (2006) 'Remittances, poverty reduction and the informalisation of household well-being in Zimbabwe', Global Poverty Research Group Working Paper no. 44, www.gprg.org/pubs/workingpapers/pdfs/gprg-wps-044.pdf, accessed 13 April 2013.

— (2010a) 'Migrant remittances and household wellbeing in urban Zimbabwe', *International Migration*, 48(5): 203–27.

— (2010b) 'Remittances, informalisation

and dispossession in urban Zimbabwe', in J. Crush and D. Tevera (eds), *Zimbabwe's Exodus*, Ottawa/Cape Town: IDRC/Unity Press, pp. 324–45.

Bracking, S., D. Hulme, D. Lawson, K. Sen and D. Wickramasinghe (2010) *The Future of Norwegian Development Finance*, official document no. 0902364-55 (The Report), Oslo: Government of Norway.

Callon, M. (ed.) (1998) *The Laws of the Markets*, Oxford: Blackwell.

— (2007) 'What does it mean to say that economics is performative?', in D. Mackenzie, F. Muniesa and L. Siu (eds), *Do Economists Make Markets? On the Performativity of Economics*, Princeton, NJ: Princeton University Press, pp. 311–57.

CCJPZ (Catholic Commission for Justice and Peace in Zimbabwe) (2009) *Graveyard Governance*, Harare: CCJPZ.

Cerra, V., M. Rishi and S. C. Saxena (2005) 'Robbing the riches: capital flight, institutions, and instability', IMF Working Paper WP/05/199.

Chabal, P. and J.-P. Daloz (1999) *Africa Works: Disorder as Political Instrument*, London/Bloomington: James Currey/Indiana University Press, in association with the International African Institute.

Chan, S. (2003) *Robert Mugabe: A Life of Power and Violence*, London: I. B. Tauris.

Chiumbu, S. and R. Nyamanhindi (2012) 'Negotiating the crisis: mobile phones and the informal economy in Zimbabwe', in S. Chiumbu and R. Nyamanhindi (eds), *Crisis! What Crisis? The Multiple Dimensions of the Zimbabwean Crisis*, Johannesburg: Human Sciences Research Council, pp. 62–80.

Collier, P., A. Hoeffler and C. Pattillo (2001) 'Flight capital as a portfolio choice', *World Bank Economic Review*, 15(1): 55–80.

CSVR (Centre for the Study of Violence and Reconciliation) (2009) *Subliminal Terror? Human rights violations and torture in Zimbabwe during 2008*, Johannesburg: CSVR.

Doig, A. (2006) 'Dirty hands and the donors: dealing with corruption in a post-Mugabe Zimbabwe', *Political Quarterly*, 77(1): 71–8.

Fourcade, M. (2007) 'Theories of markets and theories of society', *American Behavioral Scientist*, 50(8): 1015–34.

Gërxhani, K. (2004) 'The informal sector in developed and less developed countries: a literature survey', *Public Choice*, 120(3/4): 267–300.

Goredema, C. (2003) 'Zimbabwe', in P. Gastrow (ed.), *Penetrating State and Business Organised Crime in Southern Africa*, vol. 2, Monograph no. 89, www.iss.co.za/Publs/Monographs/No89/Chap1.htm, accessed 23 November 2012.

Guma, L. (2011a) 'Biti says diamond exports and revenues not tallying', *SW Radio Africa*, 27 July, allafrica.com/stories/201107280003.html, accessed 11 April 2013.

— (2011b) 'General Solomon Mujuru legacy divides opinion', *SW Radio Africa News*, 16 August, www.swradioafrica.com/news160811/legacy160811.htm, accessed 17 April 2013.

Hammar, A. (2008) 'In the name of sovereignty: displacement and state making in post-independence Zimbabwe', *Journal of Contemporary African Studies*, 26(4): 417–34.

— (2010) 'Ambivalent mobilities: Zimbabwean commercial farmers in Mozambique', *Journal of Southern African Studies*, 36(2): 395–416.

Hammar, A. and B. Raftopoulos (2003) 'Zimbabwe's unfinished business: rethinking land, state and nation in the context of crisis', in A. Hammar, B. Raftopoulos and S. Jensen (eds), *Zimbabwe's Unfinished Business: Rethinking Land, State and Nation in the Context of Crisis*, Harare: Weaver Press.

Hammar, A. and G. Rodgers (2008) 'Introduction: Notes on political economies of displacement in southern Africa', *Journal of Contemporary African Studies*, 26(4): 355–70.

Hammar, A., J. McGregor and L. Landau

(2010) 'Introduction: Displacing Zimbabwe: crisis and construction in southern Africa', *Journal of Southern African Studies*, 36(2): 263–83.

Heggstad, K. and O.-H. Fjeldstad (2010) 'How banks assist capital flight from Africa: a literature review', Chr. Michelsen Institute, commissioned by Norad, 8 March.

Hermes, N., R. Lensink and V. Murinde (2002) 'Flight capital and its reversal for development financing', WIDER Discussion Paper no. 2002/99.

HRW (Human Rights Watch) (2008a) *All Over Again: Human Rights Abuses and Flawed Electoral Conditions in Zimbabwe's Elections*, New York: Human Rights Watch.

— (2008b) *'Bullets for each of you': State-sponsored violence since Zimbabwe's March 29 elections*, New York: Human Rights Watch.

Independent (2002) 'Firm pays $7m after war vets' threats', 26 April.

Jayachandran, S. and M. Kremer (2006) 'Odious debt', *American Economic Review*, 96(1): 82–92.

Jones, J. (2010a) 'Freeze! Movement, narrative and the disciplining of price in hyperinflationary Zimbabwe', *Social Dynamics*, 36(2): 338–51.

— (2010b) 'Nothing is straight in Zimbabwe: the rise of the Kukiya-kiya economy 2000–2008', *Journal of Southern African Studies*, 36(2): 285–99.

Keen, D. (1994) *The Benefits of Famine: A Political Economy of Famine and Relief in Southwestern Sudan, 1983–1989*, Princeton, NJ: Princeton University Press.

Kriger, N. (2003) 'War veterans: continuities between the past and the present', *African Studies Quarterly*, 7, web.africa.ufl.edu/asq/v7/v7i2a7.htm.

Latour, B. (2005) *Reassembling the Social: An introduction to actor-network theory*, Oxford: Oxford University Press.

Lee, R., A. Leyshon and A. Smith (2008) 'Rethinking economies/economic geographies', *Geoforum*, 39: 1111–15.

Little, P. D. (2003) *Somalia: Economy without State*, London: James Currey, in association with the International African Institute.

MacKenzie, D. (2005) 'Is economics performative? Option theory and the construction of derivatives markets', Paper presented at the History of Economics Society, Tacoma, WA, 25 June, mimeo.

— (2006) *An Engine, Not a Camera: How Financial Models Shape Markets*, Cambridge, MA: MIT Press.

MacLean, S. J. (2002) 'Mugabe at war: the political economy of conflict in Zimbabwe', *Third World Quarterly*, 23(3): 513–28.

Magunha, F., A. Bailey and L. Cliffe (2009) 'Remittance strategies of Zimbabweans in northern England', University of Leeds, zimbabweinstitute.org/wp/wp-content/uploads/2012/10/Remittance-Strategies-of-Zimbabweans-in-Northern-England.pdf, accessed 17 April 2013.

Mail and Guardian (2013) 'Zim: trouble in diamond fields', by Wongai Zhangazha, 21 June, mg.co.za/article/2013-06-21-00-trouble-in-diamond-fields, accessed 5 September 2013.

Makochekanwa, A. (2007) 'An empirical investigation of capital flight from Zimbabwe', Working Paper 2007-11, University of Pretoria, July, web.up.ac.za/UserFiles/WP_2007_11.pdf, accessed 29 December 2011.

Mambondiani, L. (2011a) 'The futility of bankers' prosecution', *New Zimbabwe*, 26 November, www.newzimbabwe.com/blog/index.php/2011/11/lmambondiani/the-futility-of-bankers-prosecution/, accessed 9 April 2013.

— (2011b) 'RBM collapse: a failure of regulation', *New Zimbabwe*, 17 June, www.newzimbabwe.com/blog/index.php/2011/06/lmambondiani/rbm-collapse-a-failure-of-regulation/, accessed 9 April 2013.

Mangena, M., V. Tauringana and E. Chamisa (2011) 'Corporate boards, ownership structure and firm performance in an environment of severe political and economic crisis', *British Journal of Management*, 23(S1): 23–41.

Mararike, C. G. (2009) *Survival Strategies in Rural Zimbabwe: The Role of Assets, Indigenous Knowledge and Organisations*, Harare: Mond Books.

Masunungure, E. (2009) 'A militarised election', in E. Masunungure (ed.), *Defying the Winds of Change*, Harare: Konrad Adenauer Foundation and Weaver Press.

Mate, R. (2005) *Making Ends Meet at the Margins?: Grappling with Economic Crisis and Belonging in Beitbridge Town, Zimbabwe*, Dakar: CODESRIA.

Mawowa, S. and A. Matongo (2010) 'Inside Zimbabwe's roadside currency trade: the "World Bank" of Bulawayo', *Journal of Southern African Studies*, 36(2): 319–37.

McLaren, J. and J. Passant (2010) 'Tax havens: do they have a future providing banking and financial services?', *Canberra Law Review*, 1, www.canberra.edu.au/faculties/law/attachments/pdf/the-canberra-law-review-articles/McLaren-and-Passant-Tax-Havens-Do-they-have-a-future-providing-banking-and-financial-services2.pdf, accessed 23 July 2012.

Mitchell, D. (2006) 'The moral case for tax havens', Occasional Paper 24, Potsdam: Liberal Institute of the Friedrich Naumann Foundation.

Moyo, P. (2009) *Urban Food Insecurity, Coping Strategies and Resistance in Bulawayo, Zimbabwe*, PhD dissertation, University of Leeds, mimeo.

Mukwedeya, T. (2012) 'Enduring the crisis: remittances and household livelihood strategies in Glen Norah, Harare', in S. Chiumbu and M. Musemwa (eds), *Crisis! What Crisis? The Multiple Dimensions of the Zimbabwean Crisis*, Johannesburg: Human Sciences Research Council, pp. 42–61.

Muñoz, S. (2007) 'Central Bank quasi-fiscal losses and high inflation in Zimbabwe: a note', Working Paper no. 07/98, 1 April, www.imf.org/external/pubs/ft/wp/2007/wp0798.pdf, accessed 10 April 2013.

Musoni, F. (2010) 'Operation Murambats-

vina and the politics of street vendors in Zimbabwe', *Journal of Southern African Studies*, 36(2): 301–17.

Ndikumana, L. and J. K. Boyce (2008a) 'New estimates of capital flight from sub-Saharan African countries: linkages with external borrowing and policy options', Working Paper no. 166, Political Economy Research Institute, University of Massachusetts, Amherst.

— (2008b) 'Capital flight from sub-Saharan Africa', *Tax Justice Focus*, 4(1): 5.

Newland, K. (2003) *Migration as a Factor in Development and Poverty Reduction*, Migration Information Source, www.migrationinformation.org/Feature/displace.cfm?ID=136, accessed 3 April 2011.

Nik-Khah, E. (2006) 'What the FFC auctions can tell us about the Performativity Thesis', *Economic Sociology*, 7(2): 15–21.

Pendleton, W., J. Crush, E. Campbell, T. Green, H. Simelane et al. (2006) 'Migration, remittances and development in southern Africa', Migration Policy Series no. 44, Cape Town: SAMP.

Raftopoulos, B. (2011) 'The spell of indecision in Zimbabwean politics', Johannesburg: Solidarity Peace Trust, www.solidaritypeacetrust.org/1135/the-spell-of-indecision-in-zimbabwean-politics/, accessed 27 July 2012.

Ranger, T. (2004) 'Nationalist historiography, patriotic history and the history of the nation: the struggle over the past in Zimbabwe', *Journal of Southern African Studies*, 30(2): 215–34.

Roe, M. J. (2003) *Political Determinants of Corporate Governance: Political Context, Corporate Impact*, New York: Oxford University Press.

Sachikonye, L. (2002) 'The situation of commercial farm workers after Land Reform in Zimbabwe', Report for the Farm Community of Zimbabwe (FCTZ), Harare.

— (2011) *When a State Turns on Its Citizens: Institutionalized Violence and Political Culture*, Johannesburg: Jacana Media.

Sharife, K. (2010) 'Treasure islands: mapping the geography of corruption', *Pambazuka News*, 492, www.pambazuka.org/en/category/features/66286, accessed 5 October 2012.

— (2011a) 'The ties that bind: China, Angola and Zimbabwe', *Pambazuka News*, 550, 29 September, www.pambazuka.org/en/category/features/76740, accessed 5 October 2012.

— (2011b) 'Zimbabwe: a tale of two Chinas', *Pambazuka News*, 550, 29 September, www.pambazuka.org/en/category/features/76739, accessed 21 October 2011.

Solidarity Peace Trust (2009) *'Gone to Egoli': Economic Survival Strategies in Matabeleland: A Preliminary Report*, Johannesburg: Solidarity Peace Trust, www.solidaritypeacetrust.org/download/report-files/gone_to_egoli.pdf, accessed 3 December 2012.

— (2010) *A Fractured Nation. Operation Murambatsvina: Five Years On*, Johannesburg: Solidarity Peace Trust, www.solidaritypeacetrust.org/download/report-files/fractured_nation.pdf, accessed 21 July 2012.

— (2011) *'Hard Times' Matabeleland: Urban Deindustrialization – and Rural Hunger*, Durban: Solidarity Peace Trust, www.solidaritypeacetrust.org/download/report-files/Hard%20Times%20Nov%202011.pdf, accessed 23 July 2012.

Trefon, T. (ed.) (2004) *Reinventing Order in the Congo: How People Respond to State Failure in Kinshasa*, London: Zed Books.

UNDP (2010) 'The informal economy, SMEs and the "missing middle" in Zimbabwe: some observations', Working Paper 9, Comprehensive Economic Recovery in Zimbabwe.

PART III

Confinement and economies of loss and hope

9 | The IDP economy in northern Uganda: a prisoners' economy?

Morten Bøås and Ingunn Bjørkhaug

Introduction

The IDP (internally displaced person) camps of northern Uganda are about to be closed, that is if the Lord's Resistance Army (LRA) does not return to its place of origin, but continues to be based in the borderland between the Democratic Republic of Congo (DRC), Sudan (North and South) and the Central African Republic (CAR). However, the extended experience of displacement in northern Uganda that started in 1996 was so unique that it is not only bound to have long-term consequences for the displaced, but also needs closer analysis, as there is no guarantee that this could not happen again both in northern Uganda and elsewhere in Africa. The first aspect of this particular displacement context which we must come to terms with is the sheer number of people displaced. As the war peaked in 2005, 1.3 million people were displaced; that is, almost the entire rural population of the districts of Gulu, Kitgum and Pader were physically relocated into IDP camps. Secondly, while these people were very effectively displaced, their displacement – and relocation – occurred at only a short geographical distance. In some cases, people could see their homes, but could not go there owing to the security regime under which they were placed by the Ugandan army (UPDF). Thirdly, the very tight regime under which they lived severely limited their mobility, failing to offer them security while leaving them in appalling living conditions from which any form of escape was very difficult. Fourthly, and consequently, they were constantly afraid and extremely poor. They had limited cash income opportunities, almost no credit available, and very few received remittances from relatives outside of the war zone. It is this combination of extreme and localized constraints over a sustained period which constituted the overall conditions for the IDPs of northern Uganda.

The consequence of these conditions was a violent life-world of inactivity, the kind of 'beggars cannot choose' prison-style economy whose very crude logic of governmentality forced people to carve out a living at the very margins of existence. In the IDP camps, life became 'life as biopolitics', where human beings were reduced to 'bare life' (Agamben 1998). Rather than living a qualified life, the IDPs were deprived of almost all rights and thereby the possibility of dignity. As such, the IDP camps bear a resemblance to the concentration camps studied by Agamben and what he called the 'conditio inhumana'. On the other hand, the IDP camps of northern Uganda were not governed by law or decree, but rather by vagueness and the unwillingness of the government to accept responsibility. Yet the effect on 'life' and 'body' was nonetheless almost the same, as what was supposed to be temporary – a brief exception – became the rule and the norm. In effect, life was reduced to the existence of 'bare life', as in Agamben's (1998, 2005) 'state of exception'. It was in this highly circumscribed state that the inhabitants of the camps were trading, bartering and begging, but mainly waiting for whatever little bits of material goods and money could come their way.

This represents a very extreme version of a displacement economy: of changes wrought in lives and livelihoods by a confluence of forced disloca- tion and sustained confinement; such conditions created tragic paradoxes, but little in the way of productivity in a positive sense. The IDPs were effectively locked up in camps by a combination of the security approach adopted by the UPDF, and the international community's understanding of the LRA war. The latter resulted in a largely unquestioned acceptance of the approaches of the Ugandan state and army to the war and to the civilian population. This meant that the camps and the parts of northern Uganda most severely affected by the conflict were isolated from the rest of Uganda. This clearly limited livelihood opportunities for the IDPs, who had very little room for the kind of creative manoeuvring and social navigation in relation to events, agents and structures observed in refugee and IDP camp situations elsewhere (Turner 2010). As the war-affected north was politically isolated, there were few avenues for seeking political influence, and apart from for economic actors connected to the UPDF, there were few if any opportunities for the IDPs to invest in clientelistic relationships with potential patrons or 'Big Men'.

The story we tell from northern Uganda is therefore an extreme case, but we still claim that the prison-like economy that it created and the paradoxes that this entailed offers a picture of the conditions of displacement that is of value to a perspective that seeks to illuminate the paradoxes of crisis and creativity inherent in displacement economies. Even in an extreme 'prison' like the camps in northern Uganda there is some degree of productive agency, but in such a context this often primarily reflects a tactical agency that is short in time horizon and with a transformative capacity that is likewise low.

This chapter analyses this kind of life-world in northern Uganda by utilizing data the authors gathered in 2005 (see Bøås and Hatløy 2005).[1] This was the first large IDP profiling exercise implemented in northern Uganda. In this exercise, UNDP (the United Nations Development Programme) was the lead agency of the international community in Kampala, acting in collaboration with the Ugandan Office of the Prime Minister. However, UNDP also sought co-financing from the European Union Acholi Programme, the Norwegian Ministry of Foreign Affairs and USAID Uganda. The aim of the 2005 study was to gather systematic data about the situation of the IDPs. These data were to become the basis for national and international humanitarian interventions in northern Uganda. In addition, the chapter also draws on material gathered from a series of follow-up studies conducted in the region from 2006 and onwards by the authors (see, for example, Bjørkhaug et al. 2007).

Origins of the camps Several armed groups have been fighting against the Museveni government in northern Uganda since the National Resistance Army (NRA) seized power in 1986. The most durable of these has been the LRA. The LRA, led by Jospeh Kony, was established in 1988, and from 1994 it operated from bases in southern Sudan. Since 2006, although no longer operating in northern Uganda, it has spread in and between the DRC, the CAR, Chad and Sudan (see Allen 1991; Behrend 1999; Doom and Vlassenroot 1999; Finnström 2003, 2005; Bøås 2004; Prunier 2004, 2009).

Kony and the LRA have never attempted to become a mass uprising. If we were to remove all the spiritual elements associated with it, it might be considered a brilliant but extremely brutal case of classic guerrilla warfare: operating in small, highly mobile units of often no more than four to five persons. In the beginning of the conflict, however, there was an unspoken agreement that the LRA's struggle was directed against the UPDF, and as long as the Acholi population did not actively support the government they would by and large be left in peace.[2] Thus, while the population lived in their original villages they could negotiate agreements with local LRA commanders. Some of these relationships were friendly and mutually supportive, others cordial, and some hostile. At the time, the behaviour of the UPDF was so violent – they plundered, raped and killed – that at least in some areas Kony's men could count on support from the local population. This relationship started to change, however, when the government initiated the 'bow and arrow' groups (local defence groups), and it deteriorated completely with the establishment of the IDP camps all over Acholiland in 1996. Both in Kitgum and Gulu districts the population was forced by the UPDF to form civil defence groups. These were not very efficient as a protection force, but Kony and his men interpreted their formation as a betrayal and treason against the cause they were fighting for. This marked the beginning of the relative isolation of the LRA from the civilian population they were supposedly fighting for. Driven further into isolation by the establishment of the camps, the LRA increasingly turned inwards, creating its own cosmology of violence nurtured by a sense of betrayal.

Some of these camps were established voluntarily, some by order and others by force. The stories people tell about the establishment of the camps and the degree to which they voluntarily moved into them differ not only from camp to camp but also from person to person. Some reported that they received orders from the Ugandan army to leave their home and go to a camp. However, it is also clear that others moved voluntarily because they were afraid of the LRA, and wanted to be protected. The people who refused to go were moved with the use of different degrees of force by the UPDF (see also CSOPNU 2004a).

In Coo-pe camp in Gulu, the story commonly told was that people had moved to what had been started as a 'protected village' in 1999. Prior to the war, this was such a little village that it did not even have a name. More people arrived in Coo-pe owing to increased insecurity in 2002, and eventually so many had come that it was recognized as a camp in February 2003. As the camps were never officially declared as either being made or established by the Ugandan government, this meant that a camp like Coo-pe was recognized as a camp only when its inhabitants started to receive regular supplies from humanitarian agencies. In Karo Lapainat (also called Tee Tugi), another camp in Gulu, the common story told was a different one. The majority of the IDPs in this camp originate from Koro sub-county, and they were told by local UPDF commanders that they had forty-eight hours to leave their homes. As no directions had been given about where they should go, they first went to Gulu Town. However, Gulu was already overcrowded with IDPs, and there was very little space for them there. They were therefore relocated to Karo Lapainat by the government. The camp there was finally established on 18 November 2003. These and several other stories suggest that the establishment of the camps was undertaken in a haphazard and uncoordinated manner. In between ad hoc government approaches to the IDP crisis and an underfunded and understaffed international response, there was very little coordination among the different actors. The main reason was that the camps were meant as a short-term solution to an emergency situation, but they ended up as an almost permanent disruption and reorientation of traditional Acholi life.

The establishment of the camps was supposed to contribute to bringing a swift conclusion to the war: by clearing out the countryside the government believed it would cut off rebel resources and give free rein to UPDF units. The entire operation of moving people into camps was meant to be brief and decisive. Ten years later, however, people were still in the camps and their number had grown immensely (Bøås and Hatløy 2005).[3] After the start of UPDF's Operation Iron Fist against the LRA in September 2001, up to 95 per cent of the rural population of Gulu, Kitgum and Pader had been displaced into IDP camps (ibid.; Human Rights Watch 2003) as the war continued apace.

Confinement and the production of fear

As noted above, the camps were supposedly established in order to defeat the LRA and to facilitate the army's ability to protect the civilian population. People were to be offered protection, and in order for their security to be increased they had to give up some of their freedom of movement. This entailed the establishment of security zones around each IDP camp, limiting the distance that camp inhabitants could walk from the camp in which they lived. Thus, one way of understanding the situation is that people either voluntarily or through force made a trade-off, very much like 'man' in Hobbes's *Leviathan*, between individual freedom and security (Hobbes 1958). However, with hindsight it is clear that these IDPs did not get what they may have believed that they bargained for. Having little choice, they moved to the camps, but this did not substantially increase their feeling or the reality of being secure. On the contrary, people were generally afraid both within and outside the camps. As Figure 9.1 shows, 90 per cent were afraid to leave the camp where they lived in order to fetch firewood; a large percentage feared cultivating their land or visiting neighbouring towns and villages; and as many as 60 per cent expressed fear inside the camp as well.

The size of the security zones around each camp varied substantially, from 300 metres to several kilometres, but generally movement was allowed only between nine in the morning and five in the afternoon. Beyond these hours a curfew was imposed, and those who ventured outside of the security zone at the wrong times ran the double risk of either being attacked by the LRA or accused of being a rebel or a rebel collaborator by the UPDF.[4] The UPDF experienced casualties regularly, and when it encountered people where no

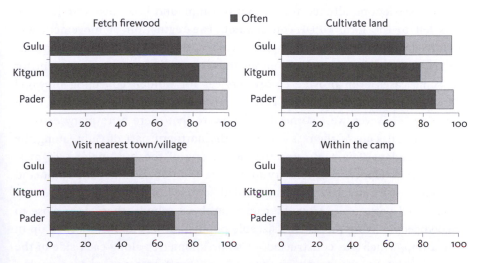

9.1 Fear of being mugged, attacked, raped, shot or harassed by LRA, by district in per cent by adult population

civilians were supposed to be, it was easy to act under the assumption that they must be LRA, or in collaboration with the LRA.

Movement in the bush around the camps was even more strictly regulated. As Table 9.1 shows, not many IDPs were able to move outside of the camp more than three kilometres. Some were not even allowed to move as much as one kilometre. Only 6 per cent could move more than five kilometres from the camp. The restrictions were the harshest in Pader, followed by Kitgum and Gulu. However, in all the three districts, such regulations limited the movement of people. Among the many implications of these conditions was that people were denied access to their land, which became a strong marker of the prison economy we discuss later in the chapter. Another of the increasingly severe effects was decreased access to firewood, needed for daily life inside the camps. The longer the camps endured the less firewood there was to be found near by – that is, inside the security zone. This made it especially difficult and dangerous for women to obtain firewood.

TABLE 9.1 How many kilometres people could move outside the camps, by percentage of the adult population

District	< 1	1	2	3	4	5	> 5	No restrictions
Gulu	2	9	37	26	10	8	8	1
Pader	1	27	36	25	5	2	3	0
Kitgum	1	19	46	17	5	3	8	0
TOTAL	2	16	39	24	7	6	6	1

The restrictions differed from camp to camp, and how they were handled was left to the local UPDF commander. The regulation of movement was enforced more pragmatically in some camps, where local leaders or groups of IDPs were able to negotiate either reduced restrictions on movement, or in some cases even provide escort services for women collecting firewood through the establishment of cordial relationships with local UPDF commanders. However, we also need to be aware that there were many extreme cases as well. One of them is Attiak, in the northern part of Gulu, along the road to Sudan. This camp was the site of one of the first major LRA massacres. This happened in January 1995 when LRA rebels under the command of Vincent Otti attacked the camp, killed several hundred people and burnt substantial parts of it. After the camp had been rebuilt, there were close to 29,000 people living there. This sizeable population was de facto locked up in this camp, which was constructed for some kilometres along each side of the road. Inhabitants could walk on the road only between 9 a.m. and 4 p.m., but to where? The nearest city was far away, and the security zone was no more than 300 metres wide at its narrowest point. One can only guess at the kind of long-term psychological effects this had on the population. Formally, the camps may have had some of the features of protected IDP camps elsewhere in the world, but in essence they became prisons. Yet at the same time they were without adequate protection. This turned them into a system of spaces that mainly produced fear.

Safety in numbers or a 'fear factory'? An important feature of camp life was the extreme population density. As Table 9.2 shows, one third of the households were situated on squares with eight households or more.

TABLE 9.2 Number of households in each Selection Area (SA = 625 m2) as percentage of Selection Areas

	Gulu	Pader	Kitgum	TOTAL
0–3 households	22	17	18	19
4–7 households	43	52	45	47
8 + households	34	31	37	34

There were of course variations between the camps in this regard. Some were better organized, some worse, some extremely densely populated and others somewhat less. One of the most densely populated camps was Labuje camp, just outside of Kitgum Town in Layamo sub-county. Here 17,000 people lived on just 17 hectares of land. This camp was established in August 2003 by the inhabitants themselves after they were directly threatened by Vincent Otti, the then second-in-command in the LRA. One of Otti's many 'wives' originated from Layamo, but during the summer of 2003 she managed to escape. Otti made it clear to the population of her sub-county that he not only wanted her back, but also wanted compensation in the form of food, money and more wives and children, for the humiliation her escape had caused him. First the inhabitants of Layamo tried to ignore Otti's threats, but when LRA units started to attack their villages, and told survivors that Otti had ordered them to kill all who lived in the area until his wife had been returned and he had been compensated, they saw no other protection than that to be found in density and numbers. People desperately afraid of Otti and his men established Labuje camp on a small plot of land. Initially they were not that many, but the camp rapidly grew in size as Otti's men roamed the countryside searching for those who remained. Three years later 17,000 people lived there, still in constant fear, waiting for Otti's revenge. None of them believed he had forgotten his promise to kill every single one of them. To the majority of the population, the camp became a 'fear factory', their lives characterized by constant fear.

Fear of the LRA and of particular commanders was one thing. There were, however, also many other factors of fear related to camp life. As many as 75 per cent of the female-headed households in Pader had more than three persons living in each hut. Such a dense living and livelihood context can clearly be defined as congested. About 60 per cent of the rest of the population were also living like this. This carried a number of obvious risks. For example, in such a situation of overcrowding both within and between huts, a small fire could easily set the whole camp ablaze. Similarly, the sanitary conditions were also a problem, as the limited space available for each household had to be shared by animals, children and adults, and was used for cooking, sleeping and storage (Bøås and Hatløy 2005).

It is against the background of the totality of the camp situation that one might understand the worries about the future that the IDPs expressed. Usually people think that tomorrow will be better than today, even under the harshest circumstances. This was not the case in Acholiland. When people expressed their perception about the future, as many as 55 per cent predicted it would be worse than the present, and 24 per cent predicted it would be the same. The people in Pader were even more pessimistic than their 'brothers' and 'sisters' in Gulu and Kitgum, where as many as 65 per cent anticipated life would be worse than it was now. This pattern was general across Acholiland. Overall, the living conditions were 'bad' in Gulu, even 'worse' in Kitgum and the 'worst' in Pader (ibid.).

A reversing of space-time compression By any standards, this was a deeply constrained and abject life. The IDPs were poor and hungry, and had insufficient supplies (of water and food) and services (health). The majority lived this way for a long time: some were displaced as far back as the early 1990s, but the majority between 1995 and 2002 (ibid.). Their misery was further increased by the fact that, unlike many other camp populations elsewhere (that is, both for IDPs and refugees), the IDPs in northern Uganda had not moved very far from their original dwellings and from the land that had previously allowed them an independent livelihood.

As shown in the report from 2005 (ibid.) only 5 per cent of the camp population were displaced to a district other than where they were born. One of four people lived in camps in the same place as they were born, and an additional 40 per cent lived in the same sub-county. This means that two out of three people were encamped in the same sub-county as where they were born and had been living prior to their displacement. Some of the IDPs, however, were forced away from their place of origin for a long time: 6 per cent had had to move for the first time even prior to 1991. Yet we should also note that the temporal pattern of displacement was not the same in the three districts that this chapter is concerned with. More than 50 per cent of the displacements in Gulu took place in the period between 1995 and 2001, whereas the overall majority of the displacements in Kitgum and Pader first started after Operation Iron Fist was initiated in September 2001 (ibid.).[5]

In other parts of the world we are currently witnessing what is called 'space-time compressions' (Harvey 1989). The world is increasingly being made 'smaller' owing to modern communications and fast travel, meaning large distances are crossed in shorter time. In Gulu, Kitgum and Pader, the opposite was happening. The total size of Acholiland is roughly the same as Belgium,[6] yet most of this territory was completely emptied of people, apart from the occasional UPDF patrols and roaming bands of LRA, whose whereabouts nobody seemed to know with much precision. The IDPs, on the other hand, were by and large confined to their crowded camps on the edges of this vast, empty space, with restricted room to move. In many cases, the IDPs being interviewed could easily point out the direction of their place of origin and often it was even visible from the camp. The actual distance was not far at all, but they were effectively removed from it and unable to return. They could not cultivate their land and most had not even been able to visit it for many years. One can imagine the frustration of literally being able to see your land, your home, your place of origin, and not being able to visit it, to bury your dead there, or take care of your fields. Instead, your movement and everyday life are confined to the camp, the small security zone around it, and the roads, between nine in the morning and five in the evening. For the people of northern Uganda, war and displacement reversed the compression of space and time experienced elsewhere, by creating a vast gulf separating them from their homes, livelihoods and cultural heritage.

A prison economy

The combined conditions of dislocation, confinement, isolation and continued insecurity and violence ensured that the IDPs in northern Uganda remained poor and marginalized. They had little or nothing in terms of basic household equipment and tools, had little money, and were almost exclusively without access to both formal and informal credit arrangements. One therefore needs to ask what sustained those who survived under such debilitating conditions.

Dependence on aid Given the extreme forms of securitized enclosure and lack of opportunities for production or exchange, the majority of those living in the camps were almost entirely dependent on humanitarian assistance (Bøås and Hatløy 2005). As Table 9.3 shows, 85 per cent of the households interviewed had received food aid. Approximately half of the households also reported receiving non-food items such as jerrycans, blankets, cultivation tools and seeds. However, this assistance was not equally distributed across camps.

People in Kitgum reported having received most assistance in terms of such items. There might be a number of reasons for this, but the most likely one is that these are items distributed less frequently than food and other daily essentials. There was more of this type of distribution in Kitgum as the camps were established there much later than in Gulu. In Pader, on the other hand, this kind of assistance had not yet started properly at the time of the study in 2005.

TABLE 9.3 Humanitarian assistance received by percentage of households

	Gulu	Kitgum	Pader	ALL
Food aid	83	93	85	85
Jerrycans	36	72	47	46
Blankets	38	76	36	45
Cultivation tools	41	67	34	45
Seeds	39	67	32	43
Kitchen utensils	29	73	26	37
Medicines	31	29	23	29
Clothes	9	12	5	9
School fees	5	6	5	5
School supplies	6	2	3	5
Shelter material	5	4	1	4

There may be several reasons why some households reported not having received food aid,[7] but one is the relative isolation of some camps. There were certain camps that were not serviced directly by the World Food Programme (WFP) owing to security considerations. In a camp called Omee Lower in Gulu (currently Amuru District), the inhabitants reported that WFP did not come to their camp for such reasons. This camp was very isolated with a distance of over twenty kilometres to the next camp, and the road was extremely narrow and the bush surrounding it dense. The escort service from the UPDF did not feel comfortable driving on this road when we visited the place in 2005. In theory food was delivered to this camp, as supplies were dropped at the nearest camp 20 kilometres away. The only option the inhabitants therefore had was to walk to collect it along a long and dangerous road. Another challenge involved in this process was that, for security reasons, the scheduling of WFP supplies was kept secret (in theory). It could therefore take quite some time before the inhabitants of Omee Lower were informed that supplies were waiting for them in the other camp. They reported that often, when they finally arrived to collect their supplies, there was not much left for them as other IDPs had helped themselves to their supplies. This kind of 'opportunity' to benefit from others' vulnerabilities reflected a context of desperation that compelled one marginalized group to steal from another.

The question about whether or not people had ever received assistance was important. However, given the extreme levels of dependence on such aid, it was even more crucial to know when they had last received food and non-food items. Among the 85 per cent who reportedly received food aid, as many as 15 per cent had not received assistance in the previous two months (Bøås and Hatløy 2005). This is a high figure given the fact that the rations were intended to cover 70 per cent of household needs for one month.[8] This shows that even though most people did receive some food aid, there were still nearly 30 per cent of the households which either did not get any food aid at all or received it irregularly. However, it should also be noted that the supply of food that did take place saved a number of lives, as the alternative would have been a situation of mass starvation.

Coping through food aid and petty trade As shown above, the IDPs mainly survived on humanitarian aid, including food and non-food items distributed by WFP and other humanitarian agencies. Yet, even if the economic opportunities in the camps were few, people still tried to negotiate their everyday existence by brokering the few deals that could be made. The typical IDP in northern Uganda was therefore a figure existing betwixt and between the 'beggar' and the 'broker'.

Some IDPs were involved in petty trading, and all the camps had some sort of market. Some of these markets were well established; this was particularly the case for the larger camps that were situated along major roads and/or close to frequently travelled crossroads. The rest tended to be much smaller and more informal.

TABLE 9.4 Use of food aid by district and by percentage of those who received food aid

	Gulu	Kitgum	Pader	ALL
Used by household members	92	94	98	94
Sold food ration	19	10	7	14
Shared with others	18	10	6	13
Saved	5	1	1	3

Note: Households might use the food aid for multiple purposes; the percentage adds up to more than 100

Table 9.4 shows that the majority of the households used the food distributed to them for their own consumption. However, it was also common to sell some of the food aid. Here there is a difference between the districts – it was much more common in Gulu to sell part of the food rations than in Kitgum and Pader. This was not because people were poorer in Gulu, but because there were more opportunities for this type of trade in Gulu than in Pader especially, but also in Kitgum. Gulu is more centrally located than the two other districts and the roads passing it were also more frequented by people with some purchasing power than in the two other districts. Gulu is the political and economic centre of Acholiland, and therefore there was generally more economic activity and more money in circulation there during the war.

Access to land and cultivation strategies As already indicated, the IDPs in northern Uganda – despite continued close proximity to former homesteads – were almost completely dislocated from their land. However, some were still able to supplement their household income with limited small-scale agricultural activities. This was usually conducted in the form of small garden plots in the security zone surrounding the camps, along the roads, or on small plots around their huts. A few people also continued to commute back and forth to their home of origin to cultivate their land, despite the huge personal risk this involved. But as shown in Table 9.5, only one out of five households had access to land outside the camp.

TABLE 9.5 Access to land for cultivation adjacent to the camp, percentage of households

	Gulu	Kitgum	Pader	ALL
Access to land	26	18	16	22
No access to land	74	82	84	78

Yet not all those with access to land cultivated it. As Table 9.6 shows, 13 per cent did not cultivate the available land. The reasons for this were mainly linked to security concerns (see also Figure 9.1).

TABLE 9.6 The use of cultivation land – percentage of households with cultivation land adjacent

	Gulu	Kitgum	Pader	ALL
Not cultivating on accessible land	13	9	18	13
Cultivating on accessible land	87	91	82	87

The volatile security situation, alongside the extreme spatialized constraints of the IDPs, also led to some changes in agricultural practices. LRA units by and large sustained themselves on what they could loot, and those that were most vulnerable to looting were mainly the civilian population (that is, the IDPs). This led some people to start cultivating crops that were not as easy to loot or which demanded careful preparation before they could be consumed. Crops such as rice and cowpeas were less attractive as loot for the rebels, who most of the time relied on hit-and-run tactics and high mobility. Another new coping strategy for those who were able to cultivate was to sell their products as soon as possible after harvesting, in order to avoid the looting and destruction of their granaries (see also Finnström 2003). This provides one example of how people adapted strategically to the events happening in their midst and the conditions of existence over which they otherwise had little if any control.

Alternative coping strategies The hardships in the camps led to a life where it was difficult to make money and living was mainly a matter of barely surviving. This is further illustrated by looking at people's income in the month preceding our interview. This is captured in Table 9.7. Few were engaged in economic activities as a result of limited economic resources and the lack of external trade networks. In all districts more than half of the population reported zero income the previous month.

TABLE 9.7 Preceding month's income by those who had engaged in economic activities in the previous year, by percentage of adult population

	Gulu		Kitgum		Pader	
	No activities	Activities	No activities	Activities	No activities	Activities
0 UGX	63	53	71	61	78	67
< = 5,000 UGX	17	17	12	22	14	15
5,000–10,000 UGX	6	10	5	5	4	7
10,000–30,000 UGX	9	10	7	6	3	7
Above 30,000 UGX	5	9	5	6	2	3

Note: one dollar = 1,715 Ugandan shillings, reference year 2005

As in all war zones, one possible and also obvious coping strategy, in particular for young men, is to join an armed faction or an army. War-making can without doubt be seen as (violent) labour, and in the case of northern Uganda, the most likely option was the government-established Local Defence Units (LDUs). LDU recruits were normally employed on short-term contracts, but should have, in theory, received a month's training, a uniform, a weapon and ammunition, as well as a monthly salary of 40,000 Ugandan shillings. Most of the recruits did receive some payment but it was highly irregular,[9] leaving the LDUs without much motivation. For those who did receive their pay cheque at relatively regular intervals, this was invaluable as it was one of the few ways of making some money. Nevertheless, it appears that the IDPs did not trust the LDUs very much as they were generally perceived as badly trained and little match for a battle-hardened crew of senior LRA fighters. However, the cash income they injected into the community was certainly appreciated, given how few other sources of cash were available in the camps.

An economy of fear and uncertainty

On the other side of the coin, the LRA itself had to find its own ways of surviving. In strictly military terms, it was not particularly strong. It was not an armed movement that could overthrow the government. Nevertheless, it should not be underestimated either. The LRA has been able to keep its struggle going for a remarkably long time by strategically using fear to maximize perceptions of threat. Its violence in northern Uganda was random, unpredictable and highly visible and symbolic. Its killings, mutilations and abductions were a method implemented to institute control over the population, and the randomness of its violence compensated for its inferiority in numbers. The situation in Pader was a good example of this. Dominic Ongwen, the LRA commander in this district, did not have that many men at his disposal. The numbers reported by different UPDF commanders varied from eight to twenty.[10] But owing to the ability of these men to move great distances at high speed in a random pattern, they were very hard for the UPDF to catch, and the extreme violence they unleashed when they attacked instilled immense fear in the civilian population.[11]

An economy of abduction and violence Abductions, killings and shootings were all too frequent. As Table 9.8 shows, as many as 14 per cent of the households interviewed in 2005 had been the victim of a crime or a violent encounter in the previous month. The most frequent encounter was abduction; up to 7 per cent of all households had experienced this. The issue of abduction, and in particular the number of children who were abducted, is one of the key features of the war in Acholiland, but also remains a highly contested issue with regard to scale. The actual number of abductions remains unknown, but it is obvious that the figures described in most reports about this subject do not correlate with the number of active LRA soldiers. This means that the number of abductions reported must also have included attempted abductions and temporary abductions, as well as more long-term abductee situations. In-depth interviews suggested that a significant number of the abductions lasted only for a short time, from some hours to a few days. People were captured by LRA units and used as porters to carry looted goods to certain destinations, and thereafter released.

TABLE 9.8 Households with victims of crime or violent encounter during the month prior to interview, by percentage of households

	Gulu	Kitgum	Pader	ALL
No victim	85	87	86	86
Abduction	8	7	6	7
Assault/beatings	2	1	3	2
Armed robbery/theft	1	1	2	1
Murder	1	2	1	1
Harassment for money or goods	1	1	1	1
Shooting	1	1	1	1
Mutilation	–	0	0	0
Verbal threats	1	–	0	0
Other	0	1	1	1

While in the battlefield, the LRA's strength was its mobility and ability to separate into very small units, often just two or three fighters moving together. When this was the case, taking abductees to be kept for a long period was not an option. It was neither physically nor economically viable. This only took place when units were moving back to more permanent bases outside of the war zone. In addition, in the same category, we also have cases where people were abducted but either set free by the UPDF or they were able to escape themselves because the LRA unit that had captured them was engaged by the UPDF.

On the other hand, levels of violence were consistently high. Table 9.8 shows that 1 per cent of the households interviewed in 2005 experienced the killing of a household member in the previous month. Even though the exact number is difficult to estimate with any great degree of precision, it does suggest that a high number of people were violently killed every month in 2005.[12] What all this adds up to is that the IDPs felt helpless and forgotten, unable to change or influence the circumstances under which they lived. It had a great impact on both their feeling of insecurity and on the economic situation they faced every day. From their point of view, each attack by the LRA undermined the government's authority and legitimacy because it was seen as a demonstration of the latter's inability or unwillingness to protect them (see also Doom and Vlassenroot 1999). In this interpretation, Joseph Kony was beginning to be viewed as omnipotent, his forces being able to strike the IDPs apparently at will. Of course, this was not the case in reality. The LRA also experienced heavy casualties and its room for manoeuvre in the area decreased after the signing of the peace agreement in southern Sudan. And yet this was not necessarily how the situation was perceived in the camps. There, the IDPs were still effectively locked up in a regime of control combined with an environment of immense fear and insecurity.

The stories told by people living in camps close to a place called Omoro Hill in Gulu illustrate this. This is the area from which Kony originates, and according to local beliefs he is supposed to receive his powers from Omoro Hill, a small hill with a rather particular stone formation on the top of it. In order to preserve his power he must return to Omoro Hill once a year in order to perform certain rituals. Nobody could or wanted to specify what these rituals consisted of, but several people related that they had seen fire with many colours coming from the mountain followed by explosions during the night. This was believed to be Kony performing his rituals. Whether this was true or not is of little relevance. What is much more important is how this was interpreted. As one informant bitterly complained, 'why doesn't the government blow up this mountain', whereas another bystander argued that 'the UPDF should deploy around the whole mountain to catch Kony'.

When asked why they thought the army was not doing this, two explanations were offered: first, that the UPDF 'does not care about us'; secondly, that its soldiers are afraid. Of the group we talked to when we stopped on the road to look at this hill, the majority supported the second explanation. The soldiers, they believed, were afraid of venturing near the mountain; they were scared of Kony's spirits. The real strength of the LRA was (and most likely still is) not its numbers of men at arms or the violence it used in itself, but rather its symbolic connotations and the perceptions of strength, power and threat that it instilled in the population living in the LRA area of operation.

Conclusion

As this chapter has demonstrated, the IDP situation in northern Uganda is among the most extreme cases of displacement. The conditions people faced, as discussed in this chapter, had a profound impact on their life choices and livelihood opportunities. Very few of the more common social navigation opportunities available to refugees and IDPs were within reach in northern Uganda. Here, the IDPs were constantly afraid and extremely poor, physically confined, and highly dependent on humanitarian aid. In effect they were locked into a camp situation that was meant to be temporary but turned out to be almost permanent exile from their homes and fields. The fact that they were so close to their former homes – many could even see their fields from the camps in which they lived, but could not go there – added a particularly painful dimension to their displacement.

This situation of such complete dislocation and confinement over so many years affected people's aspirations for the future. They did not think that the situation would improve; they rather thought it would deteriorate further. Time after time the government had told the inhabitants of Acholiland that the LRA would soon be defeated: it was 'the last kick of a dying horse', as the UPDF commanders preferred to call it. However, in the IDPs' experience, the sitation was getting worse year by year, month by month, even day by day. They found themselves living in what can best be described as a 'fear factory': they were afraid both of the LRA and the UPDF. But this was not the only source of insecurity that the IDPs were concerned about. Just as much as they feared for immediate violent threats to their lives, they were also faced with profound and persistent food insecurities. This produced a sense of constant waiting: waiting for the handouts of food from the international community; waiting for the few customers that might show up at their market; waiting for the LRA or the UPDF; but more than anything else, just simply waiting as there was so little left to do and so few places to go.[13] This could be said to reflect a condition of 'bare life': an existence that could be said to be the very essence of Agamben's state of exception. It suggests a place where not much happens and the days pass silently and uneventfully for those confined, with few to bear witness.

And yet, through a displacement economies lens, one is pushed to explore the interweaving historical, spatial, structural and social layers that constitute a displacement context, and to uncover some of the less visible dynamics that coexist alongside a condition of seeming inactivity. Adopting such an approach, the discussion here has underscored the fact that even in, and in fact because of, such a severely circumscribed displacement context as the IDP camps in northern Uganda, some kinds of productive – if primarily survivalist – activities are at play.

Notes

1 A combination of quantitative and qualitative data was collected for this study. The quantitative data came from a household survey of 3,000 households. In addition, one randomly selected individual was interviewed in each household, and a number of qualitative interviews were conducted during the fieldwork.

2 This was also confirmed in the many interviews we conducted with IDPs for the northern Uganda Internally Displaced Persons Profiling Study (see Boås and Hatløy 2005), but the findings from this part of the interviews were not published in that report.

3 One should note that this was not the first time such camps were established in Uganda. They also existed during the war in the Luwero Triangle (1981–86). Each time Milton Obote's forces reclaimed an area from Museveni's National Resistance Army, they forced the civilian population into camps, under the presumption of improving their security but actually to control them (see Kasozi 1999).

4 The risk of falling prey to the LRA was higher than the risk of ill treatment by the UPDF. However, several IDPs interviewed also worried about being discovered by the UPDF outside of the security zone (see also Human Rights Watch 2005).

5 These figures correspond well with the numbers provided by WHO/Ministry of Health (2005).

6 The combined size of Gulu, Kitgum and Pader is 29,787 square kilometres, whereas the size of Belgium is 30,513 square kilometres.

7 Cases of under-reporting cannot be ruled out as it may make sense for people living under conditions such as this to under-report on assets and assistance, and over-report on household members, as this could mean that they would receive more assistance if the data collected were used to plan future humanitarian interventions.

8 Interview with Norwegian Refugee Council (NRC) representative, Gulu, 8 June 2005.

9 It was claimed that it was not uncommon for LDU members to go almost six months without any pay at all. The main explanation for this is corruption within the ranks of the UPDF. See also Prunier (2004).

10 Most likely another case of underreporting, as the LRA 'brigade' Ongwen led out of Pader to South Sudan in 2006 was clearly a larger force than this. IDPs we have talked to who met them talked about 'hundreds' and 'many', 'many'. The only one who may know the exact figure is Ongwen himself.

11 Ongwen has been indicted by the International Criminal Court for crimes against humanity together with four other LRA commanders; these four others are Joseph Kony, Vincent Otti (confirmed dead), Okot Odhiambo and Raska Lukwiya (reported dead). Ongwen has a reputation as a brutal commander and he is much feared, but his case also highlights the human tragedy of the war as he is reportedly a former abductee himself who has grown up in the movement. As the older generation of commanders either dies or surrenders, his generation has moved up in the LRA hierarchy under the supreme leadership of Joseph Kony.

12 In the Health and Mortality Survey, there is an estimate of 3,971 people killed from January to mid-July 2005. See WHO/Ministry of Health (2005).

13 One might compare this with the kind of 'active' waiting Jones (this volume) discusses.

References

Agamben, G. (1998) *Homo Sacer: Sovereign Power and Bare Life*, Stanford, CA: Stanford University Press.

— (2005) *State of Exception*, Chicago, IL: University of Chicago Press.

Allen, T. (1991) 'Understanding Alice: Uganda's Holy Spirit Movement in context', *Africa*, 61(3): 370–99.

Behrend, H. (1999) *Alice Lakwena and the Holy Spirits: War in Northern Uganda 1986–97*, Oxford: James Currey.

Bjørkhaug, I., M. Bøås, A. Hatløy and K. M. Jennings (2007) *Returning to Uncertainty*, Kampala: Office of the Prime Minister/UNDP.

Bøås, M. (2004) 'Uganda in the regional war zone: meta-narratives, pasts and presents', *Journal of Contemporary African Studies*, 22(3): 283–303.

Bøås, M. and A. Hatløy (2005) *Northern Uganda Internally Displaced Persons Profiling Study*, vol. 1, Kampala: Office of the Prime Minister/UNDP.

Branch, A. (2005) 'Neither peace, nor justice: political violence and the peasantry in northern Uganda, 1986–1998', *African Studies Quarterly*, 8(2), webafrica.ufl.edu/asq/v8/v8i2a1:htm.

CSOPNU (2004a) *Land Matters in Displacement: The Importance of Land Rights in Acholiland and What Threatens Them*, Kampala: CSOPNU.

— (2004b) *Nowhere to Hide: Humanitarian Protection Threats in Northern Uganda*, Kampala: CSOPNU.

Doom, R. and K. Vlassenroot (1999) 'Kony's message: a new *Koine*? The Lord's Resistance Army in northern Uganda', *African Affairs*, 98(390): 5–36.

Ehrenreich, R. (1998) 'The stories we must tell: Ugandan children and the atrocities of the Lord's Resistance Army', *Africa Today*, 45(1): 79–102.

Finnström, S. (2003) *Living with Bad*

Surroundings: War and Existential Uncertainty in Acholiland, Northern Uganda, PhD thesis, Uppsala Studies in Cultural Anthropology no. 35, Uppsala.

— (2005) 'For God and my life: war and cosmology in northern Uganda', in P. Richards (ed.), *No Peace, No War: An Anthropology of Contemporary Armed Conflicts*, Oxford: James Currey, pp. 98–116.

Harvey, D. (1989) *The Conditions of Post-modernity: An Enquiry into the Origins of Cultural Change*, Oxford: Blackwell.

Hobbes, T. (1958) *Leviathan*, Indianapolis: Bobbs-Merrill.

Human Rights Focus (2002) *Between Two Fires: The Plight of the IDPs in Northern Uganda*, Gulu: HURIFO.

Human Rights Watch (2003) *Abducted and Abused: Renewed War in Northern Uganda*, New York: Human Rights Watch.

— (2005) *Uprooted and Forgotten: Impunity and Human Rights Abuses in Northern Uganda*, New York: Human Rights Watch.

Kasozi, A. B. K. (1999) *The Social Origins of Violence in Uganda*, Kampala: Fountain Publishers.

Prunier, G. (2004) 'Rebel movements and proxy warfare: Uganda, Sudan and the Congo (1986–99)', *African Affairs*, 103(412): 359–83.

— (2009) *From Genocide to Continental War: The Congolese Conflict and the Crisis of Contemporary Africa*, London: Hurst & Co.

Turner, S. (2010) *Politics of Innocence: Hutu Identity, Conflict, and Camp Life*, New York: Berghahn.

WHO/Ministry of Health (2005) *Health and Mortality Survey among Internally Displaced Persons in Gulu, Kitgum and Pader Districts, Northern Uganda*, Kampala: WHO/Ministry of Health.

10 | 'No move to make': the Zimbabwe crisis, displacement-in-place and the erosion of 'proper places'[1]

Jeremy Jones

Introduction

In November, 2008, the annual rate of inflation in Zimbabwe reached a staggering 89 *sextillion* per cent, marking the nadir of almost a decade of continuous economic decline, and nearly beating the world record for highest inflation figures ever recorded (Hanke and Kwok 2009). As prices increased and business closures and shortages spread, government provision of education, healthcare and utilities grew increasingly erratic. By 2008 many of those services were on the verge of collapse, cholera was spreading in major cities, Zimbabweans were flooding across the border to neighbouring countries, and formal economic transactions had been almost entirely replaced by black market trading, smuggling and other illicit moneymaking ventures.

In the international press, this crisis is often traced to a controversial land reform exercise, which the Zimbabwean government initiated in 2000, and the economic fallout that ensued, both locally and internationally. The 'Fast-Track Land Reform Programme' entailed the seizure of commercial farms owned by the white minority, and their redistribution to 'indigenous' (i.e. 'black') Zimbabweans (Moyo and Chambati 2013). Ostensibly, it was an attempt to redress profound racial imbalances in the country's landholding, which could be traced directly to colonial expropriations and evictions. But critics charge that it was actually intended to bolster the flagging political fortunes of the long-time ruling party, ZANU-PF, and that it opened the door to massive corruption and graft (Compagnon 2011). ZANU-PF, in turn, has consistently pinned the economic crisis on an 'illegal regime change agenda' and 'illegal economic sanctions' initiated and driven by the 'kith and kin' of the white farmers in 'imperialist' countries, as well as their 'puppets' in Zimbabwe's main opposition party, the MDC. The truth of the matter, as I will suggest, is more complicated than either of these narratives allows. One fact is beyond dispute, though: namely, that social, political and economic life in Zimbabwe has been significantly reordered during the past ten to fifteen years. Together with the other chapters in this volume dealing with Zimbabwe (Hammar, Bracking), I want to argue here that the idea of a 'displacement economy' helps illuminate the nature of that shift.

As Hammar notes in the introductory chapter, 'displacement' conventionally calls to mind the physical movement of people from one place (their 'home') to another. This association, she adds, has roots in ever-evolving efforts to deal with refugees and others forced to migrate by wars, famines, development projects and the like. Zimbabwe's long crisis certainly produced 'displacements' of this sort. Significant numbers of people were forced from their homes by political violence and government-led evictions, and large swathes of the population were pushed into migrating in search of economic opportunity. One notable result was the growth of a vibrant diaspora of Zimbabweans outside the country (McGregor and Primorac 2010), particularly in South Africa, Botswana and the United Kingdom. As Hammar et al. (2010) point out in an earlier discussion of Zimbabwe's 'displacement economy', though, the notion of 'displacement' suggests much more than just physical movement and dislocation. Rather, it offers a 'revealing prism' through which we can view a whole range of 'personal, political, economic and cultural transformations brought about by crisis conditions' (ibid.: 266). In fact, displacement need not imply any physical dislocation at all.

With that in mind, I will be discussing a group of young men who weathered the bulk of the Zimbabwean crisis in the familiar setting of what they called the 'ghetto'. Far from being dislocated from their homes, they often spoke of being 'stuck' there (see Hansen 2005). Nonetheless, I argue that they *were* displaced. Specifically, they experienced a profound '*in situ* displacement' (Feldman et al. 2003: 9) or 'displacement-in-place' (Magaramombe 2010), wherein it was their very livelihood that was 'dislodged' (Guyer 2008). In a context of relentless price hikes, mass unemployment and extreme material shortage, the economic strategies that they had once viewed as feasible, if not totally dependable, became entirely ineffective. This shift in the economic structure not only reduced them to a scramble to meet the basic demands of everyday reproduction, it also threatened their ability to follow expected life courses and enjoy what they understood as 'progress'. Following Stephen Lubkemann, I argue that this experience may be best understood as 'involuntary immobility' (2008a).

In making this argument, I also want to interrogate the underlying suggestion that an economy is made up of a collection of 'places'. What would it have actually meant for young men to be economically '*in*' place? Does being in place (as opposed to displaced) require a formal job, or do regular and/or predictable sources of income suffice? Can an *illicit* livelihood (Roitman 2005) – or one dependent on illicit components – ever be economically in place?

Specifying the nature of 'place' – and its relation to 'space' and 'time' – is never simple, as long-standing debates in philosophy, geography and political economy will attest (Casey 1998; Gieryn 2000; Harvey 2006). The analytic difficulties are compounded when 'place' is used metaphorically, as it is in this case. The key danger, I believe, lies in repeating the error of earlier work on refugees: namely, naturalizing the economic 'place' from which the displaced come, and reading it as a 'location' where they are 'rooted' and 'belong' (Malkki 1992). This functionalist notion of being economically 'in place' is particularly fraught in countries like Zimbabwe, where even before the post-2000 crisis, few people enjoyed secure, long-term formal employment.

In order to think through this problem, I will start by reading 'displacement-in-place' against Michel de Certeau's classic discussion of 'strategies' and 'tactics' (De Certeau 1984). As I point out, De Certeau views this division in terms of differential access to what he calls 'proper place' (*lieu propre*), where 'proper' refers to 'propriety' or 'ownership', not just moral correctness. By returning to this aspect of his analysis, I believe we can better account for the relational and power-laden character of different 'places' in the economy. Then, I work through the case of one young Zimbabwean, 'Mookie',[2] emphasizing his struggles to establish some kind of regular flow amid economic turmoil. His predicament, I argue, demonstrates that the economic 'ground' on which strategic and tactical actions are enacted cannot be taken for granted. In the past in Zimbabwe, that 'ground' entailed a complex configuration of spatial and temporal links associated with so-called 'real work'. With the coming of the political and economic crises of the 2000s, though, the foundations of the 'real work' economy began to 'fragment' (Vigh 2008), reducing nearly all economic activity to tactical feints and dodges, and creating a state of what I term *generalized* displacement-in-place. In effect, the 'displacement economy' became the *only* economy. Besides having profound consequences for Zimbabwean social life, this fact points to the complex and ever-evolving nature of displacement economies more generally.

Zimbabwe's political and economic crisis

I want to start by saying a bit more about the 'Zimbabwean crisis' (Raftopolous 2009). Scholars and activists have hotly debated its nature and causes, and a large literature has developed around the subject.[3] Rather than recapitulating this work, I will give a brief synopsis, which will cover key points in the history of political conflict, the land reform programme and the precipitous decline of the economy.

On the surface, the country's political crisis was a two-way contest between ZANU-PF, which had ruled the country since the attainment of majority rule in 1980, and the upstart MDC, which was formed in 1999. Political discontent and challenges to the ruling party were not new, though. ZANU-PF was forged in the country's long and violent war against white settler rule, and on several occasions it had been racked by internal battles and conflicts with nationalists from other parties, notably ZAPU.[4] Sometimes the arguments were ideological, as in debates about socialist orthodoxy, but they were also inflected by ethnic tensions, realpolitik and personal power struggles. After a brief period of unity in the run-up to independence, ZANU-PF dissolved its short-lived partnership with ZAPU, then proceeded to crush it, amid a violent (and, some would argue, genocidal) security crackdown (Sisulu 2007) that lasted throughout the mid-eighties. By 1987, Zimbabwe was a *de facto*, if not *de jure*, one-party state (Shaw 1986; Compagnon 2011).

In 1991, though, the government set aside its socialist platform and introduced an IMF-sponsored structural adjustment programme and accompanying neoliberal reforms (Mlambo 1997). The move helped shore up state finances, and was initially welcomed by the business community, but the new mix of austerity, privatization and open markets created mass immiseration. The urban poor, waged employees and civil servants were particularly hard hit (Mhone 1993), though a series of severe droughts over the coming years put further pressure on the already struggling population in rural areas as well. Ironically, even local industry suffered (Carmody 1998). ZANU-PF tried to promote the reforms as part of a programme of 'indigenization', which would see whites ceding their control of the economy to blacks. Indigenization in the 1990s ultimately benefited very few people outside a small clique of ruling party rentiers, though (Davies 2005). The stage was thus set for growing dissent from nearly all quarters of society.

In 1997, the government stemmed a possible revolt by veterans of the liberation war by offering them lump-sum payouts and granting them pensions. Politically, it was a critical move, as the same war veterans would soon become one of the party's most important and militant constituencies. It was financially disastrous, though. The payouts were not budgeted for, and the move contributed to a sharp drop in the value of the Zimdollar – the first of many to come. Making matters worse, the country soon became embroiled in the civil war in the Democratic Republic of Congo, leading to further unbudgeted expenditures, more charges of high-level corruption and misrule, and eventually a cessation of IMF financial assistance (Compagnan 2011).

All the while, an often uneasy mix of trade unions, business interests and civil society groups was aiming to effect changes in the country's political and economic system. The Zimbabwe Congress of Trade Unions (ZCTU) had vocally opposed structural adjustment from the start, and organized a series of successful work stoppages in the late nineties to protest against rising prices, unemployment and service fees. It also worked together with a variety of church groups, student organizations and NGOs to form the National Constitutional Assembly (NCA) in the hope of producing a new, 'people-friendly' constitution. Parallel to these developments, the wider business community – much of which was white-owned – was looking for ways to protect its interests in the face of increasingly vehement anti-white rhetoric from the ZANU-PF, and growing talk of farm and business expropriations.

Eventually, these different streams of dissent came together in the MDC. Most of the party's leaders were left-leaning trade unionists and former student activists, but it drew critical support from the business community as well, including white farmers. It enjoyed immediate popularity in urban areas and among the working class and ethnic minorities, and it also seemed to be the favourite of Western donors and governments. The MDC's first victory involved the constitution. In 1998, the government had sidelined the NCA in favour of its own constitutional commission, and a referendum on the resulting draft was held just months after the MDC was formed. The MDC and NCA alike charged that the draft was a ZANU-PF creation, and that it would solidify the ruling party's grip on power. ZANU-PF contended that the opposition to the document hinged on the inclusion of clauses allowing for the expropriation of white-owned agricultural land. In the end, voters rejected the draft, and many saw that as evidence that the MDC could win parliamentary and presidential elections as well. ZANU-PF initially conceded defeat, but just weeks later it began organizing the 'war for the land' (*hondo yeminda*), or Fast-Track Land Reform Programme (FTLRP), which would be at the centre of Zimbabwean politics throughout the decade to come.

The unequal distribution of land, and the policies that had created and maintained it, were long-standing points of contention in Zimbabwe. Indeed, the land was central to nationalist politics throughout the twentieth century, and colonial expropriations and interference in farming were key motivators for many of those who joined the war against settler rule (Mlambo 2009; Munochiveyi 2011). Efforts at resettlement after 1980 had mixed but broadly positive results (Deininger et al. 2004), but they were narrow in scope owing to funding constraints and a ten-year post-independence moratorium on uncompensated seizures. By promoting land reform, then, and by vocally supporting peasant-led land invasions, ZANU-PF was playing on both the desires and the simmering anger of many Zimbabweans. It claimed that the *hondo yeminda* would resolve the situation once and for all.

The timing made it clear that land reform was also being used to bolster the party's waning political fortunes, though. Indeed, the 'war for the land' was also a war against the MDC and its supporters. As noted above, ZANU-PF claimed that the MDC was a puppet of foreign interests, and it dedicated both the ruling party machinery and the state security forces to crushing it. That effort often involved outright violence and intimidation, but it also turned on a compendium of less conspicuous political manoeuvres, such as vote-rigging and gerrymandering, a relentless anti-MDC publicity campaign, a clampdown on opposition support among civil servants, the quashing of dissent from NGOs and the press, and the use of both the law and the security forces for partisan ends (Raftopoulos and Savage 2005).

All told, these political developments affected the economy in a number of ways. On one hand, white-owned commercial agriculture had been a key source of tax revenue and foreign currency inflows, and had played a critical role in the banking system and local industry. The drastic decrease in agricultural production – especially production for export – that resulted from the land invasion therefore reverberated throughout the economy. On the other hand, as the crisis deepened, foreign investment, credit and development aid to the Zimbabwean government plunged to near zero. Both the scope and the reasons for this isolation have been the subject of much controversy.[5] Some, including ZANU-PF, have insisted that it owed in whole or in part to 'imperialist' sanctions, introduced to punish the government for its decidedly illiberal land reform programme. Others argue that the plunge in external support was owing to the government's human rights abuses, combined with a pattern of government loan defaults and a generally unfriendly business climate.

Faced with this situation, the ZANU-PF government turned to an ever-changing array of economic policies, anchored by subsidies to 'new farmers' and 'indigenous' businesses on one hand, and price and exchange controls on the other. In many cases, its actions appeared ad hoc and politically driven. Policy pronouncements were accompanied by an endless stream of angry rhetoric, denouncing price-rising by the business community and linking it to the MDC and its 'illegal regime change agenda'.[6] The government's response arguably made matters worse, though, rewarding rent-seekers in government and the ruling party, and fanning the growth of a parallel (or 'black') market based on smuggling and speculation (Compagnon 2011; Jones 2010b). In time, the formal sector was progressively emptied of goods, and many industries and retailers closed or drastically reduced production.

In early 2009, the crisis reached a head. First, the Zimbabwe dollar collapsed entirely, and was replaced by legal trade in a variety of hard currencies. Secondly, the main political parties signed the so-called 'Global Political Agreement', which paved the way to a tenuously shared power. Both were critical developments, and well worth exploring, but the discussion that follows applies specifically to the pre-2009 situation in the country.

Interrogating the 'place' in 'displacement'

As I noted in the introduction, the Zimbabwe crisis witnessed a wide variety of 'displacements'. In fact, I will be arguing that displacement was the rule throughout the population, albeit displacements of different kinds and degrees. To start, though, I want to outline two kinds of physical dislocation as well as the paradoxical notion of '*in situ* displacement' (Feldman et al. 2003: 9) or 'displacement-in-place' (Magaramombe 2010). The latter, while extremely useful, poses some interesting analytic problems, and they will be my focus going forward.

With regard to physical dislocation, many Zimbabweans were forced to leave their homes by political conflict, intimidation, eviction or some combination thereof. MDC supporters were often targeted for eviction and intimidation by ZANU-PF activists, and certain areas of the country, particularly rural areas, were simply considered off limits to MDC members. To justify government's role in dislocations, ZANU-PF used the joint language of exclusion and sovereignty (Hammar 2008). In a word, those opposed to the ruling party and/or its policies were figured as a kind of 'matter out of place' (Douglas 1966; Harris 2008). 'True independence', the ruling party claimed, demanded that this 'dirt' be removed. Of course, white farmers and business owners were central to this calculus, simply because they were white. But anyone who could be associated with whites – or with practices and attitudes perceived to be 'white' – was subject to similar treatment. For instance, many farm workers had ancestry outside the country. This, when combined with their connection to white farmers, made them easy targets for abuse as 'foreigners' (Magaramombe 2010). ZANU-PF also portrayed anyone who supported the MDC as being brainwashed by white, 'foreign' ways. This argument was bolstered by the opposition's hold over urban areas, which had long been depicted as corrupted by the 'modern' ways of white people (*chirungu*). Like youth, who were also described as racially and culturally dissolute, urbanites were charged with being ignorant of the liberation war.

Perhaps the most infamous example of this rhetoric being put into practice occurred in 2005, when the government embarked on joint security operations entitled 'Operation Murambatsvina' and 'Operation Restore Order' (Vambe 2008; Solidarity Peace Trust 2005). The latter was ostensibly targeted at the 'black market' in foreign currency and basic commodities in urban areas, but police and ruling-party militias ended up destroying much of the physical infrastructure for the urban informal economy. The former entailed the mass demolition of 'informal' or illegal housing, particularly in 'high-density' townships/suburbs that surrounded every urban area.[7] In some cases, whole neighbourhoods were bulldozed. Notably, one translation of '*murambatsvina*' was 'reject filth' – with informal businesses and urbanites, many of them youth, figuring as the 'filth' (Harris 2008). Likewise, the government suggested that all true Zimbabweans had a 'real' home in the rural areas, and that they should return there, where they presumably 'belonged' (Solidarity Peace Trust 2005: 6).

If eradicating illicit economic activity and putting people back in their 'places' was the government's goal, then OM/RO was a profound failure. Actually, the operations had just the opposite effect, and contributed further to what was already a difficult economic environment. Even for those who were not directly affected by loss of a home or business, the economic impact was substantial. The pace of emigration, both documented and undocumented, which had been developing throughout the 2000s, quickened as Zimbabweans moved across borders in search of jobs. Likewise, stripped of their former modes of livelihood, many left their homes to engage in cross-border trade, smuggling, illicit mining and the black market.

While these physical dislocations had profound and lasting effects on Zimbabwean life, they do not tell the whole story. Many Zimbabweans spent the whole decade more or less 'at home'. Perhaps they would occasionally engage in cross-border trade, and perhaps they would be forced to shift their 'places' of work elsewhere in the vicinity, but generally they stayed put. It is this population which the idea of 'displacement-in-place' is meant to address: people whose experiences of displacement are based less on geographical dislocations than socio-economic ones (Feldman et al. 2003; Gellert and Lynch 2003). In a set of articles detailing Zimbabwean youth affected by Operation Murambatsvina, Amin Kamete succinctly defines it as the displacement of 'livelihoods' (Kamete 2008, 2010, 2012). Quoting literature on forced migration (Partridge 1989; Holtzman and Nezam 2004), he says it involves the 'destruction of productive assets and the dismantling of production systems', as well as 'separation' from 'ecosystems, workplaces ... and other foundations that anchor daily lives' (Kamete 2012: 244). He gives the example of young street vendors affected by Operation Murambatsvina. Government efforts to enforce 'proper planning' and purge the country's cities of 'spatial unruliness' (Kamete 2008) resulted in the vendors being chased from their physical 'places' of work – pavements, corners, car parks – and thus being disconnected from the income streams that sustained them.

A similar analysis could apply to many Zimbabweans, who witnessed the progressive 'dismantling' of their 'production systems', and who lost the 'foundations' for their economic lives in the process. Still, the equation of 'livelihood' and socio-economic 'place' or 'location' is a slippery one. Take vendors: exactly what socio-economic 'place' did they occupy before they were 'displaced' by the government? Many, including those responsible for their eviction, would argue that the vendors had no rightful 'place' to start with. The 'law' was largely on the side of government with respect to home demolitions as well. How, then, are we to locate 'illicit livelihoods' vis-à-vis 'licit' ones (Kamete 2010; Roitman 2005)? What does it mean to be economically 'in place'?

These are not just quibbles about semantics. The fact that an activity sustains individuals and/or groups does not mean that it has a straightforward 'place' in the wider economy. Note, first of all, that many economic activities are inherently difficult to 'locate', both as a matter of government policy, and as a matter of empirical observation. They are defined – if at all – by the fact that they *do not* occupy a clear 'place'. Sometimes ambiguity is even the key source of profits, as with criminality. Locating and bringing such activity to light would bring it to an end.[8] This is a classic political dilemma, and has been reflected in discussions of everything from nomads and 'floating populations' (Roitman

2005), to the so-called 'lumpenproletariat' (Stallybrass 1990). In Zimbabwean politics, the fight against vagrancy, begging, touting, unlicensed vending and other hard-to-place activities that 'contaminate' economic space dates all the way back to the early days of settler rule (Raftopoulos and Tsuneo 1999). While the colonial government was dead set against such activities 'taking place' at all, the post-independence ZANU-PF government alternated between looking the other way, violently repressing them, and attempting to corral them into places that it could control (and tax). That meant such forms of livelihood were recognized only in efforts to negate them or bend them towards the prerogatives of law and order.

We also need to account for the complex linkages between different 'places' in the economy. For example, some livelihoods have as their central aim the domination, displacement or outright elimination of others. The police beating up vendors and knocking down houses during Operation Murambatsvina claimed that they were 'just doing their job', on which their own livelihoods depended. More pointedly, capitalist economies may actually *depend* on displacement-in-place, in both historical and ongoing forms. Note the resemblance between 'destruction of productive assets', as Kamete puts it, and Marx's notion of 'alienation' from the means of production. This dynamic is especially evident in post-colonial (or 'neocolonial') contexts like Zimbabwe. The country's economy had its basis in a history of blatant (and 'properly planned') acts of racial exclusion, dispossession and evictions.

Clearly, then, it is a mistake to view economic 'place' through a functionalist lens of equality or equilibrium. The myth of a self-organizing division of labour, arranged by an 'invisible hand', remains just that: a myth. At the same time, the relation between different locations in the economy is not simply antagonistic. Historically, the main beneficiaries of 'proper planning' in Zimbabwe were those engaged in formal sector salaried and waged work (even when it was lowly paid). Abstract regularity, formal coordination, the propagation and enforcement of clear policies and laws – in short, the whole apparatus of 'law and order' – were all critical to their livelihoods. But, as has been repeatedly demonstrated elsewhere, 'informal' businesses were also linked, by degree, to the formal sector (Mbembe and Roitman 1995), as was peasant cash-cropping, which was bound up in a whole set of formal, abstract logistics (agricultural boards, purchase depots, road infrastructure, input provision). Interruptions or irregularities in 'proper planning' could therefore have profoundly detrimental effects for a large part of the population, including the very people exploited by those plans.

'Strategies', 'tactics' and upset economic 'ground'

In order to work through these complications, I suggest that we start by revisiting Michel de Certeau's famous discussion of 'tactical' and 'strategic'

action (De Certeau 1984). De Certeau's reasoning, recall, centres on an extended metaphor of place: more specifically, on differential access to what
he calls 'proper place' (*lieu propre*). He defines 'proper place' as 'a place that
can be delimited as its own' and which can 'serve as the base' for managing
'relations with an exteriority composed of targets or threats' (ibid.: 37). Those
with access to proper place can strategize. They can gain a synoptic view of
all the ground below and around them, and can use it to plot out actions
accordingly. Those without such access, on the other hand, must act 'tactically'
and 'opportunistically', 'poaching' from places that are not their own, and on
the basis of limited lines of sight (ibid.: xix). In contrast to English, where
'proper' most strongly suggests conformity with moral norms, *'propre'* in De
Certeau's original French phrasing points to clarity, order and ownership (or
'proprietorship'). To act strategically means to hold ground and to build it up
in accordance with one's goals; to act tactically means operating on someone
else's ground, however it is shaped.

This model illuminates a number of aspects of the Zimbabwean case. For the
government, strategic intervention meant creating places 'in conformity with
abstract models' (ibid.: 29). During Operation Murambatsvina, for instance,
ZANU-PF portrayed the country's cities as being overrun by youthful parasites
and 'rascals' (Kamete 2008: 1726), and declared the need to 'restore order',
first by reimposing abstract divides between public, private and commercial
space, then by clarifying the flow between them. This would ensure that economic action was carried out 'by the book', in reference to fixed principles,
rather than changing circumstances. It would also make economic relations
legible – and hence accessible – to state (and party) control. Those whom
government targeted, on the other hand, and who were 'displaced-in-place',
depended on tactics for their livelihood. They 'play[ed] on and with a terrain
imposed on [them] and organized by the law of a foreign power', operating
'in isolated actions, blow by blow', accepting 'the chance offerings of the
moment' (De Certeau 1984: 37). Because acting 'tactically' meant not having
a 'proper place', they were *structurally* vulnerable to being characterized as
a foreign substance ('dirt'). But some of them were also able to exploit and
manipulate the government's actions, 'poaching' profits from the very actions
designed to displace them.[9]

De Certeau's conceptualization fails to account for one critical detail in
Zimbabwe, though. As I have detailed elsewhere (Jones 2010a), 'tactical' economic activities that had long been seen as 'out of place' came to be seen
as 'necessary' amid the crisis of the 2000s. Virtually everyone was involved
in illicit economic activity of some kind, be it smuggling, fraud, forgeries or
black market trading. That included categories of people who had not only
occupied but had actively *symbolized* 'proper place', such as police, judges,
pastors and 'elders'. It also included both institutions of government and those

employed by them, which increasingly focused on opportunistic, 'tactical' acts. For instance, notwithstanding their rhetoric of propriety, many ZANU-PF figures were deeply involved in 'improper' black market dealings, and state resources were often blatantly directed towards private and partisan interests, rather than abstract, national ones. Likewise, a widespread rumour had it that the Reserve Bank, through its agents, was the biggest player on the illegal foreign currency market (Jones 2010b).

This, then, was not just a struggle to claim or poach from the 'high ground' in the economy; it was a crisis that reduced much of the old high ground to rubble. In a context of profound economic upheaval, abstract forms of clarity, order and ownership – that is, the ground of 'proper place' – were all called into question. The result was a state of *generalized* displacement-in-place, in which few socio-economic 'places' were secure. With all of this in mind, I want to take another step back and further explore the composition of economic 'ground'. How, exactly, does it anchor – or fail to anchor – different 'places' in the economy? An ethnographic case will help provide answers.

'Nothing is moving'

My subject, 'Mookie', was one of a group of thirty or so young men I met while carrying out research in Chitungwiza, a 'high-density' suburb located 30 kilometres outside the Zimbabwean capital, Harare. Like nearly all his friends, he was a member of the so-called 'born free' generation (so named since they were born after independence from white settler rule in 1980). He shared with them an involvement in illicit economic activities. As such, he was among those targeted as 'filth' in government rhetoric and interventions that intensified during the mid-2000s.

When we first met in late 2006, the economic crisis was getting worse by the day. At the time, Mookie was living with his older brother 'Stewart', Stewart's common-law wife, and a number of other family members, including several school-age children. They lived in a house built by his late parents. Thankfully, it had been largely spared during Operation Murambatsvina. Some shacks that they rented out in their yard were destroyed, though, and this meant they lost a vital and substantial stream of household income.

Mookie's mother, a government healthcare worker, had passed away two years earlier. His father, who did clerical work at a tobacco auction house, had died three years prior to that, just before Mookie had finished high school. Nevertheless, Mookie managed to continue with his education, passing his form four exams, and going on to acquire a diploma certification in computer repair. This accomplishment made him somewhat unusual among his friends, few of whom had even finished high school. Stewart, four years his senior, had followed a similar track, and using his diploma and connections at his father's former workplace, he enjoyed a brief stint in a salaried job at a tobacco auction house. However, disruptions in the agricultural sector led to his being laid off, and by the time Mookie had finished his schooling in 2002, the entire formal sector was in full-scale retreat.

As a result, Mookie turned to a variety of moneymaking ventures – 'anything and everything', as a neighbour put it. Computer work was out of the question: he lacked the connections to get a job or contracts in the formal sector, and given the mismatched state of wages and prices, he might spend everything he earned just travelling to and from work. Some days he did carpentry, despite having no qualifications and only the most basic tools. A permanent workshop, besides being expensive, might attract more in the way of unwanted police attention than customers, too, so he focused on piecework: building and repairing furniture, installing cabinets, or working on the new homes being built near by with diaspora money. Other days, Mookie joined a number of his friends who did 'wire-works', their name for the production of wire and bead sculptures sold as curios throughout southern Africa. Cross-border traders commissioned their production, and then sold them on in South Africa and Botswana at a substantial mark-up. Mookie could do three to five dollars' worth of work in a day, but the actual payment came only upon delivery of the entire consignment, so he could go several weeks without income.

In addition to these two recurring pursuits, he was always on the lookout for fleeting deals. Often that meant arbitraging the price differences opened up by shortage, inflation and government price controls. Other times, it meant engaging in activities that were clearly illegal, such as trade in stolen goods (small electronic goods were favourites) or in controlled minerals like alluvial gold and industrial-grade diamonds, both of which were common in Chitungwiza at the time. Still other times, he did odd jobs for wealthier neighbours, either for immediate pay or to cement a longer-term patronage relation.

Mookie and his friends often lumped all of these activities under one heading: '*kukiya-kiya*'. As I have argued previously (Jones 2010a), *kukiya-kiya* did not refer to a discrete activity. Rather, it named a logic of 'getting by', a 'tactical' approach to economic action. 'Whatever works' trumped efforts to do things the 'right way', even if that meant setting aside long-standing forms of moral and technical propriety. However, along with most of his peers, Mookie argued that it was circumstances in the country, and *not* some personal failing, which compelled people like him and his friends to engage in *kukiya-kiya*. They were 'forced by the situation', as a common saying went. As such, otherwise skilled forms of labour such as 'wire-works' and carpentry also counted as *kukiya-kiya*, insofar as they were characterized by irregular flows of money, short time horizons and a generally improvisational approach.

At one point in early 2007, Mookie and I were discussing a mutual friend, 'Tino', who had just come back from a border-jumping excursion to

Mozambique. Tino started by smuggling out several bottles of coveted Zimbabwean liquor and selling them for US dollars, which were plentiful across the border. Then he used the proceeds to buy cheap Chinese shoes and fake Colgate toothpaste, which he smuggled back into Zimbabwe.

Curious, I asked Mookie whether he would ever take a similar trip. No, he said, laughing: doing so required a certain inner drive (*shungu*) that he lacked. Tino had no compunctions about breaking the law, but like many Zimbabweans, Mookie insisted that he would go only if he could do it legally. 'What stops you from doing that?' I asked. He shook his head. A distant aunt living in the UK had sent him money to get a passport a few years earlier, he explained. He had used most of the money to cover household costs and lingering debts, though, then blew the remainder on what young men called '*joy*', which is to say beer, meat, cigarettes, women, etc.[10] Passports were incredibly expensive and hard to get – upwards of US$300, depending on one's connections, negotiating skill and patience. It was unlikely he would get his hands on that much money again, at least in the foreseeable future. He certainly could not ask his aunt for more.

MOOKIE: So now I'm just trying to figure out, you know, uh [*long pause*] ... See, the problem is that everything needs money. You need *cash*. That's what's frustrating.

JJ: So what are you going to do?

MOOKIE: Well, you know, work is frustrating here [in Zimbabwe]. I just wish I had gotten my passport, because *cross-border trading* is a better option. The carpentry we do ... it's getting hard, because there aren't many people buying, and plus, you need money and *machinery* and *samples*. Somebody will come and say that he wants a *three-piece divider* or *wall unit*. Let's say it costs 1.5 or 2 million Zimdollars to make [+/– US$100]. But he says it has to be a '*fix and supply*' deal [i.e. he will only pay upon receipt]. And you? You only have a hundred Zimdollars in your pocket. Not even enough for a cigarette [*laughs*]! So you lose the job unless you find somebody to loan you the *capital*.

JJ: Or maybe he'll tell you to do the work and then never pay ...

MOOKIE: Exactly. Then he'll come back in a year saying he wants something else [*more laughter*]. And with all the money you put into building that thing, you have no *back-up amount to keep the business alive*. Then you start looking around for a way to sell it, or maybe pay somebody to paint it, and eventually you end up selling it at a loss. So it's frustrating to *operate* like that ... That's why you find most guys like us will go to South Africa or Botswana to look for money. *When you come back* and the [exchange] rate [for Zimdollars] has gone up or down, *you won't be affected*, because you have *foreign currency*. It's got *power*.

The specificity of this account – or rather, this accounting – was typical of his peer group. They were all quite canny about what it took to run a small-scale enterprise, and constantly calculated potential profits and losses. The stakes of such calculation were not abstract; a few dollars could make a substantial difference in their quality of life. Still, it was less a matter of having no money at all, than of having the wrong kind of money. Mookie called it 'capital': money that could do something; money that would allow him to 'operate' not just today, but long-term; money that would 'keep the business going forward'; money with 'power'. The profits of *kukiya-kiya* did not count in that regard: they could only cover day-to-day reproduction, and sometimes not even that. Worse, the local currency lacked 'power' even if one managed to get some, so it was futile to base any long-term plans on it.

As the conversation proceeded, I asked Mookie to speculate on what he would be doing in five years. His response was both halting and revealing:

MOOKIE: Five years ago [2002] things were better ... that's when I started to think, you know ... that the way things were going [*shaking head*], and if they didn't get fixed ... [*long pause*] Well, I don't really know what will happen. Two years from now? Seriously, Jeremy, I don't even know what things will be like at the end of this year. I only know that there's no source of income, and prices are going up every day ...

JJ: No idea?

MOOKIE: Look at it this way: today the electricity people came and threatened to turn off the electricity. I knew the guy, so when he came I was like, 'just give me time and I'll look for the money'. He gave me till end of day. So you sit there ... your head is just spinning [*musoro uchingotenderera*]. Imagine. They only want a small amount, but to find that money [*shaking head*] ... Before, you could expect a customer to come with an order, but now there's nothing ... That's what's frustrating. Nothing is working [*hapana chiri kufamba*, lit. 'Nothing's moving']. There's 'no deal' here [*nyika haina dhiri*].[11] Nothing ... You just sit and bang your head [*kugaya,* lit. 'grind'].

To be clear, being cut off from the grid would not have saved him money, since electricity was much cheaper than alternative sources of fuel, such as firewood. The wider point was this: not only did Mookie struggle to conjure an image of his life in two years, he could barely think past the horizon of today. In fact, his immediate response to the question suggested that he found it hard to grasp the shape of things that had *already* happened. Writing of middle-class Mexicans, Claudio Lomnitz calls a similar state of 'present saturation': 'a reluctance to socialize viable and desirable images of the future' (Lomnitz 2003: 132). Mookie and his friends were not reluctant; they actually had any number of ideas and plans about the future. But they were in no position

219

to realize those plans, or even to plot out steps to get there. After all, just coming to terms with the demands of the here and now was hard enough, and demanded a painful, almost physical act of cogitation. Where 'before, you could expect a customer ...', now all you could do was sit, head 'spinning', and try to 'grind' [*kugaya*, slang for 'planning', 'plotting' or 'scheming'] out some possibilities that would see you through until tomorrow.

Like many young men, Mookie often claimed that he was not working, but rather 'just sitting' [*kungogara*]. Obviously, that was not true. *Kukiya-kiya* was a round-the-clock job, demanding constant attention to changing circumstances, and a lot of physical movement as well (see Simone 2005). There was a difference between moving and actually 'going somewhere', though. The latter required 'cash', or better yet, 'capital'; something that would extend action out of the here and now. Not only did he not have any himself, the whole Zimbabwean monetary system was collapsing around him. Money that people had saved in bank accounts was literally turning into nothing.

This state, in which young men were both weighed down by immediate needs and unable to plot a way out, was reflected in the language they used to describe life amid the crisis. Things were 'hard' or 'unyielding' [*zvakaoma*], they said. The situation was 'oppressive' [*zvakadzanya*], 'pressing' [*zvakapressa*], 'tied up' or 'knotted' [*'shinyazi*], and simply 'tight'. Another favoured phrase was '*hapana yekutamba*', meaning 'there's no move to make'. As in a stalemate in a game of draughts, every move seemed to be a bad one. To be sure, this language of restriction and compression was not new, and had long been used to speak about present suffering and long-term forms of personal blockage, including those caused by occult affliction (Bourdillon 1993). It was the sheer scope of impossibility which was novel. Nothing was working properly *anywhere* in the country, hence Mookie's conclusion that the only action that would produce lasting dividends, a future, was to establish some connection to the outside.

Grounding economic life

As I pointed out in the introduction, one of the ever-present dangers in discussions of displacement is the reduction of 'place' to stasis and 'rootedness' (Malkki 1992). This becomes more evident when we shift from an analysis of the actual physical locations and territories people inhabit to the more metaphorical notion of economic 'place'. To young men like Mookie, displacement in place consisted precisely in being 'static' or 'stuck', not in being uprooted per se. Being 'in place', on the other hand, would have entailed some kind of directed movement, both in space and over time.

Stephen Lubkemann refers to this state as 'involuntary immobility' (2008a). In his discussion of the prolonged civil war in Mozambique (2008b), for instance, he argues that Mozambican men considered labour migration to and from South Africa and Zimbabwe to be a normal part of their lives. Migration was part of their 'lifescape', i.e. 'a context of material, social and symbolic resources available to social actors for the realization of the life-courses they have been socialized to pursue' (ibid.: 192). As with Mookie, being 'displaced' meant that they were unable to participate in that lifescape. 'People become displaced', Lubkemann writes, 'when changes in structural conditions (such as those produced by war) deprive them of the vital social, economic, ecological, and symbolic resources required for social reproduction – and in the extreme for mere survival' (ibid.: 212).

Individual and group lifescapes can therefore only be grasped by reference to the wider 'econoscape' on which they are enacted (see Appadurai 1986). Econoscape is another way of referring to what I have called the 'ground' for economic life, and following from my discussion of De Certeau above, I believe that it is best understood as an ever-evolving configuration of spatial and temporal linkages. One's economic 'place', in turn, is not a static 'location', but rather a particular way of relating to this configuration.[12] The more organized, regulated, durable and predictable the spatio-temporal linkages are, the more they allow for 'abstract' economic action, and the more one can speak of an economy characterized by 'proper places' and 'strategies'. Governing this configuration sometimes demands force, but it also involves the subtle, microscopic inculcation of 'discipline', which, as Foucault notes, is far more effective, lasting and 'economical' than violence (Foucault 1977). The linkages are not given, though, and certainly not in abstract form, as the Zimbabwe crisis amply demonstrates.

From the colonial era forward, the focal point of Zimbabwe's 'econoscape' was what Mookie and friends called 'real work' (*basa chairo*). Real work literally referred to wage or salaried labour, but any kind of secure, licit, regular income might be counted as 'real', including income derived from the so-called 'informal' or 'peasant' sectors. On one hand, the 'real work' econoscape was 'built into' the very landscape of the country. For instance, Chitungwiza was a major hub for rural–urban migration and trade between city and countryside. It housed workers who commuted to jobs in nearby Harare, and was laid out in a geometric grid that separated 'lines' of residential areas from public areas like schools, churches, central shopping areas and bus termini. All bespoke a *geography* of 'real work'. On the other hand, the spatio-temporal configuration associated with 'real work' was also dispersed into an enormous set of everyday institutions, laws, norms and practices. Some were directly economic, such as pensions, mortgages, insurance and credit relations, as well as contracts, the stock market, professional societies, transport and logistics. Some linked the government to the market, as with labour, property and corporate laws, import/export arrangements, budgets, tenders, subsidies, tariffs and taxes, and the many facets of financial and monetary policy. Others still were biopolitical

(Foucault 2010), such as the provision and staffing of health and educational facilities, extension services, utilities and public health measures. Then there was the ideological apparatus of schools and curriculum development, the press, churches, public campaigns, and so on, all of them encouraging puritan restraint, hard work and the like. Finally, and perhaps most importantly, there was money, which always plays a critical part in establishing the 'ground' for economic life. Savings, credit and even strictly 'cultural' matters like marital exchange were underwritten by a stable currency.

As I have already insisted, this econoscape was not without contradictions and fissures. Economic ground, such as it was, was not uniformly flat, stable and uncontested. It was based on hierarchical and often blatantly exploitative relations, and much of it had roots in racist efforts to fix, 'discipline' and segregate the black workforce (Foucault 1977; cf. Wolpe 1972). Moreover, relatively few people had ever had access to 'real work' in the formal sector, and of those who did, many earned so little that they were hardly in a position to act strategically. The configuration as a whole thus had the effect of empowering a narrow set of the population, namely those who were wealthy, white, foreign or all three. It was they, in turn, who could exercise control over the composition of 'proper place'.

Still, for individuals, having 'real work', or close access to it, meant being integrated with the wider flow of economic life. It meant one's livelihood had a 'place' in the economy, and on the whole developments could be foreseen with a relative degree of certainty. As a result, long-term, 'strategic' action was both possible and morally valorized. Mookie's parents were perfect examples: both of them were formally employed, they had a house and a mortgage, and they encouraged their children to work hard in school, thus laying the ground for future success. This kind of judicious, transparent, well-planned building was what Mookie had in mind when he spoke of 'movement' and money that had 'power'. The *kukiya*-kiya-style activities he was dependent on to get by, on the other hand, had a long and negative association with strong-arm tactics, trickery and pilfering, all carried out in desperation and devoid of order.[13]

Displacement: from trespassing to disintegration

When Mookie told me that one could no longer count on customers, he was making a well-reasoned calculation regarding his moneymaking prospects. But when he said that 'nothing is working' (or, literally, 'moving') in Zimbabwe, he was making a *historical* claim. Like most people his age, he imagined the 1980s and 1990s to have been a time when things *did* work, when customers *did* come, when 'real work' could be found, and when disciplined effort paid off. As is generally true of nostalgia, this representation of the economic past was selective and quite often inaccurate. Life had been difficult for much of the population for a long time, and many people of his parents' generation had made a living from the same *kukiya-kiya*-style activities he depended on. Nonetheless, Mookie was right in one crucial sense: the economic situation had changed, and in a very specific way. Those changes, in turn, had important ramifications for the nature of displacement-in-place.

As I suggested earlier, in an economy dominated by the configuration of 'real work', displacement-in-place was a chronic risk for anyone who did not fit neatly into the grid of propriety. This population was often deemed to be 'marginalized'.[14] I concede that there is a certain truth in that designation, especially if one considers the average Zimbabwean's position in the global economy, but the metaphor is still somewhat misleading. As De Certeau's argument suggests, such people did not inhabit a space *outside* the economic landscape (on 'the margins'). They had a particular relation to the linkages from which it was comprised, though. Rather than being 'in place', they operated amid the places of others, from whence they 'poached' their livelihoods. Poaching took a variety of forms, from outright dependence, at one end of the scale (e.g. kin or clients subsisting entirely on money garnered from a wage-earner or patron), to illicit seizures and diversions of economic flow, at the other (i.e. property crime). All were insecure, unpredictable and contingent on flows and linkages controlled (or 'owned') by others. Since these interstitial livelihoods were premised on 'trespassing', they were easily displaced whenever the logic and practice of proper place demanded it.

Few aspects of this configuration remained by the time Mookie and I had our conversation, though. The *language* of proper place had not changed at all. In fact, amid the worsening crisis, the ZANU-PF government actually strengthened its rhetoric of law and order (as Operations Restore Order and Murambatsvina amply demonstrated). But this rhetoric thinly masked economic realities of a radically different sort. The new econoscape was not organized around 'real work', but rather *kukiya-kiya*. Gone were the patterns, institutions and relatively transparent strategies of yesteryear. In their place were 'zigzag' tactics, clever ruses and forms of accumulation that seemed, to outside eyes, quite miraculous (Jones 2010a; cf. Mbembe and Roitman 1995). Far from fighting against these changes, government and its representatives were seen by Mookie and many others to be at their forefront. For example, it was widely held in Chitungwiza that goods seized from black market traders were subsequently sold by the police for personal profit. Farther up the chain, well-connected individuals drew rents from access to price-controlled goods, foreign currency, government tenders and a variety of subsidies to 'new farmers' (Jones 2010b; Compagnon 2011).

Ironically, these shifts can be traced to the era of structural adjustment. As elsewhere, Zimbabwe's adjustment programme was specifically designed to reconfigure the 'ground' for economic life in the country. In the future, 'market forces' would organize and determine the nature of the econoscape, and a particular regime of laws and policies were set to facilitate this new configuration. The actual results were different from what was planned, though. On one hand, the urban poor and middle classes were thrust back on their own resources. Many turned to 'home industry' – that is, small-scale production and entrepreneurial activity, often carried out in homes, yards and other open spaces. The name itself was telling, insofar as it suggested a collapse of spatio-temporal relations built around the work–home dichotomy. Not coincidentally, the government wavered between promoting home industry and enforcing bylaws that had originally been designed to ensure that industry remained in one place, home in another. At the same time, ZANU-PF began promoting 'indigenisation' (Compagnon 2011), which in this case meant the transfer of ownership over the economy from whites to blacks. Like structural adjustment itself, to which it was intimately tied, at least in the beginning (ibid.: 199–207), indigenisation was specifically devised to reconfigure 'proper place', only according to a logic of racial autochthony and partisan purity, rather than one of abstract liberal economic subjects and free markets. Most of the beneficiaries were directly linked to the ruling party, and their dealings often consisted of rent-seeking rather than actual building of new enterprises (Davies 2005). What these new economic forms shared was a tendency to be organized by personal connections, charisma and the selective use of 'proper' rules and procedures.

For a while, people could still count on the old edifice of proper place. There were still public supplies of water and electricity. The police still responded to thefts. Formal sector stores still had goods for those who could pay. People could still 'bank' on the Zimdollar (both literally and figuratively). By 2007, though, none of that was true. Private property and debt relations were both uncertain and subject to blatant manipulation. Uniform taxes had given way to negotiated bribes. Police systematically looted the black market. Where it was not simply impossible, budgeting became an empty charade. Wage and salaried employment paid a pittance, while illegal and shady deals could produce fortunes. Every effort to save or establish economic regularity became an exercise in speculation instead of strict calculation.

In this context, displacement-in-place was no longer a matter of being expelled from proper place. Instead, it was owing to the disintegration of the very 'ground' on which proper place could be established. The most important consequence – and what I consider one of the most notable characteristics of Zimbabwe's displacement economy – was the progressive collapse of the entire divide between proper and improper (in both the economic and normative sense of 'propriety'). Viewed one way, that collapse created a moral problem – how were people to judge right and wrong when mere survival demanded that they break the law? Viewed another way, it made it hard to see who or what was directing change in the country. At its heart, though, the collapse was essentially a spatio-temporal matter – how were people to make economic connections across time and space in the absence of the institutionalized, abstract linkages? The answer, of course, was that they did so in whatever ways they could, with little regard for doing things the 'right' way, and without any illusion that the linkages they made would necessarily last.

Conclusion

In his discussion of a group of young men much like Mookie in Guinea-Bissau, Henrik Vigh (2008) calls this predicament 'fragmentation': a situation in which a whole or a unity has been dismantled and particularized into its parts (ibid.: 7). Crises characterized by fragmentation, he argues, force people to pay attention to the ways in which the ground below them is shifting, and to engage in 'provisional praxis and navigation', instead of following clearly marked-out trajectories (ibid.: 17). That, I think, was what people meant when they said there was 'no move to make': not simply that they could not make or follow proper plans, but that the 'grid' that used to facilitate and lend some guarantees to such plans could no longer be counted upon. No economic place was really secure, no place offered the clear lines of sight into the future that De Certeau describes.

Mookie's educational career bore witness to the widespread belief that the path to success lay in hard work in school and the transparent 'building' of a life. The path was there; one only had to follow it. Yet the situation he described showed how hard it was to reconcile his *expectations* of spatio-temporal linkage with changing *material circumstances* that made them impossible to realize, even for people like him who tried to do everything 'properly'. There was no longer a set route to occupy a proper place in the economy, and as such, he was confined to precarious living in the here and now.

As I have argued, this generalization of blocked livelihoods forces us as analysts to reconsider the terms of displacement-in-place, and to account for historical contexts where the very nature of place is uncertain. Economic activity is never 'in place' simply by virtue of its taking place. However, if in the past economic displacement in Zimbabwe could be 'mapped' on to a grid in which certain livelihoods 'fitted' and others constituted 'trespassing', the state I have described here was one of generalized displacement. In it, all economic action was tactical, and the ability to create linkages across time and space depended less on one's position vis-à-vis abstract institutions and orders, and more on charisma, personal connections and proximity to fragile centres of power. The truly displaced, as such, were those who lacked those qualities and connections; often enough, they were the most 'law-abiding' and 'hard-working' people in the country.

Further shifts have occurred in the time since. Even in the absence of political certainty, the new policy legalizing trade in foreign currency at the start of

2009 allowed Zimbabweans to begin re-establishing a degree of predictability and routine in day-to-day economic life. While ZANU-PF continues to argue that the economy of the future will be driven by 'indigenous' entrepreneurs and self-employment, the shape of future economic 'places' (and displacements) hinges much more on whether the econoscape continues to be organized around partisan, personalized networks, or whether it is reconfigured into a more abstract and inclusive framework of economic citizenship.

Notes

1 Research for this chapter was supported by the Nordic Africa Institute and the Centre for Rural Development at University of Zimbabwe, as well as a Fulbright-Hays overseas research grant. I presented versions of it at conferences organized by the Nordic Africa Institute and the University of Chicago African Studies Workshop, and I want to thank the conference participants for their input. Special thanks go to Amanda Hammar for her help throughout the writing process. Ross Parsons, Rihan Yeh, Mats Utas, Tsitsi Masvawure and John Comaroff all provided helpful comments on early drafts, and both Munyaradzi Munochiveyi and an anonymous reviewer helped with comments on the final version.

2 All names are pseudonyms.

3 For a primer, see the various contributions in Hammar et al. (2010), Hammar et al. (2003), Raftopoulos and Savage (2005), Mundy and Jacobs (2009), as well as a widely cited article by Ranger (2004). Raftopoulos (2009) offers a good summary.

4 ZAPU – Zimbabwe African People's Union. This story has been told in numerous places. For a first-person account, see Nkomo (1984).

5 See the debates in Mundy and Jacobs (2009) and Moyo and Yeros (2007).

6 This populist stance reached a head in 2007, when government instituted across-the-board price controls and arrested thousands of business owners for violating them (Jones 2010b). See below for more on 'indigenisation'.

7 In practice, the divide between the two operations was often not clear, and later reporting tended to refer only to Murambatsvina.

8 Institutional efforts to engage with so-called 'informal' economic activity are marked by a similar dynamic. Informality is a residual category, defined by what it lacks ('form'). To introduce such 'form' is, by degree, to change the nature of the activities involved.

9 Kamete (2010) provides an intriguing analysis of these evolving economic tactics, which included various forms of collusion with government insiders (pp. 67–9). Of course, the black market as a whole was based on a similar logic: when the government eventually dropped price and exchange controls, livelihoods based on black market trading collapsed.

10 Both English and Shona were used in the original. I often had a voice recorder turned on during such conversations, a practice I had first cleared with Mookie and the others.

11 Something 'without a deal' was considered useless, pointless, fruitless, etc.

12 My argument regarding spatio-temporal 'configuration' draws on Foucault's later work (Foucault 2010; Collier 2009), and has also been influenced by David Harvey (Harvey 2006).

13 The slang term 'kukiya', from which kukiya-kiya is derived, has various meanings, including 'lock', 'grab' and 'hit'. I discuss the 'real work'/'kukiya-kiya' dichotomy further elsewhere (Jones 2010a).

14 See, for example, Kamete's concept of 'resistance at the margins' (Kamete 2010: 76).

References

Appadurai, A. (1986) *The Social Life of Things: Commodities in Cultural Perspective*, Cambridge: Cambridge University Press.

Bourdillon, M. F. C. (1993) *Where are the Ancestors? Changing Culture in Zimbabwe*, Harare: University of Zimbabwe Publications.

Bozzoli, B. (1983) 'Marxism, feminism and South African studies', *Journal of Southern African Studies*, 9(2): 139–71.

Carmody, P. (1998) 'Neoclassical practice and the collapse of industry in Zimbabwe: the cases of textiles, clothing, and footwear', *Economic Geography*, 74(4): 319–43.

Casey, E. (1998) *The Fate of Place: A Philosophical History*, Berkeley: University of California Press.

Collier, S. J. (2009) 'Topologies of power', *Theory, Culture and Society*, 26(6): 78–108.

Compagnon, D. (2011) *A Predictable Tragedy: Robert Mugabe and the Collapse of Zimbabwe*, Philadelphia: University of Pennsylvania Press.

Davies, R. (2005) 'Memories of underdevelopment: a personal interpretation of Zimbabwe's economic decline', in B. Raftopoulos and T. Savage (eds), *Zimbabwe: Injustice and Political Reconciliation*, Harare: Weaver Press, pp. 19–42.

De Certeau, M. (1984) *The Practice of Everyday Life*, Berkeley: University of California Press.

Deininger, K., H. Hoogeveen and B. H. Kinsey (2004) 'Economic benefits and costs of land redistribution in Zimbabwe in the early 1980s', *World Development*, 32(10): 1697–709.

Douglas, M. (1966) *Purity and Danger: An Analysis of Concepts of Pollution and Taboo*, London: Routledge and Kegan Paul.

Feldman, S., C. Geisler and L. Silberling (2003) 'Moving targets: displacement, impoverishment, and development', *International Social Science Journal*, 55(175): 7–13.

Foucault, M. (1977) *Discipline and Punish: The Birth of the Prison*, New York: Vintage Books.

— (2010) *The Birth of Biopolitics: Lectures at the Collège de France, 1978–1979*, New York: Picador.

Gellert, P. K. and B. D. Lynch (2003) 'Mega-projects as displacements', *International Social Science Journal*, 55(175): 15–25.

Gieryn, T. F. (2000) 'A space for place in sociology', *Annual Review of Sociology*, 26: 463–96.

Guyer, J. (2008) 'Displacements, conversions and the struggle for value', Keynote address, conference on 'Political economies of displacement in post 2000 Zimbabwe', Johannesburg, 9–11 June.

Hammar, A. (2008) 'In the name of sovereignty: displacement and state making in post-independence Zimbabwe', *Journal of Contemporary African Studies*, 26(4): 417–34.

Hammar, A., J. McGregor and L. Landau (eds) (2010) 'Introduction. Displacing Zimbabwe: crisis and construction in southern Africa', *Journal of Southern African Studies*, 36(2): 263–83.

Hammar, A., B. Raftopoulos and S. Jensen (2003) *Zimbabwe's Unfinished Business: Rethinking Land, State, and Nation in the Context of Crises*, Harare: Weaver Press.

Hanke, S. and A. Kwok (2009) 'On the measurement of Zimbabwe's hyperinflation', *Cato Journal*, 29(2): 353–64.

Hansen, K. T. (2005) 'Getting stuck in the compound', *Africa Today*, 51(4): 3–16.

Harris, A. (2008) 'Discourses of dirt and disease in Operation Murambatsvina', in M. T. Vambe (ed.), *The Hidden Dimensions of Operation Murambatsvina*, Harare: Weaver Press, pp. 40–50.

Harvey, D. (2006) *Spaces of Global Capitalism*, London: Verso.

Holtzman, S. B. and T. Nezam (2004) *Living in Limbo: Conflict-induced Displacement in Europe and Central Asia*, Washington, DC: World Bank.

IDMC (Internal Displacement Monitoring Centre) (2008) *The Many Faces of Displacement: IDPs in Zimbabwe*, Geneva: IDMC.

Jones, J. L. (2010a) '"Nothing is straight in Zimbabwe": the rise of the Kukiya-Kiya economy 2000–2008', *Journal of Southern African Studies*, 36(2): 285–99.

— (2010b) 'Freeze! Movement, narrative and the disciplining of price in hyperinflationary Zimbabwe', *Social Dynamics*, 36(2): 338–51.

Kamete, A. Y. (2004) 'Home industries and the formal city in Harare, Zimbabwe', in K. T. Hansen (ed.), *Reconsidering Informality: Perspectives from Urban Africa*, Oslo: Nordiska Afrikainstitutet, pp. 120–38.

— (2008) 'Planning versus youth: stamping out spatial unruliness in Harare', *Geoforum*, 39: 1721–33.

— (2010) 'Defending illicit livelihoods: youth resistance in Harare's contested spaces', *International Journal of Urban and Regional Research*, 34(1): 55–75.

— (2012) 'Not exactly like the phoenix – but rising all the same: reconstructing displaced livelihoods in post-cleanup Harare', *Environment and Planning D: Society and Space*, 30(2): 243–61.

Lomnitz, C. (2003) 'Times of crisis: historicity, sacrifice and the spectacle of debacle in Mexico City', *Public Culture*, 15(1): 126–47.

Lubkemann, S. C. (2008a) 'Involuntary immobility: on a theoretical invisibility in forced migration studies', *Journal of Refugee Studies*, 21(4): 454–75.

— (2008b) *Culture in Chaos: An Anthropology of the Social Condition in War*, Chicago, IL: University of Chicago Press.

Magaramombe, G. (2010) '"Displaced in place": agrarian displacements, replacements and resettlement among farm workers in Mazowe District', *Journal of Southern African Studies*, 36(2): 361–75.

Malkki, L. (1992) 'National geographic: the rooting of peoples and the territorialization of national identity among scholars and refugees', *Cultural Anthropology*, 7(1): 24–44.

Mamdani, M. (2008) 'Lessons of Zimbabwe', *London Review of Books*, 30(23): 17–21.

Mbembe, A. and J. L. Roitman (1995) 'Figures of the subject in times of crisis', *Public Culture*, 7(2): 323–52.

McGregor, J. and R. Primorac (2010) *Zimbabwe's New Diaspora: Displacement and the Cultural Politics of Survival*, New York: Berghahn.

Mhone, G. (1993) *The Impact of Structural Adjustment on the Urban Informal Sector in Zimbabwe*, Geneva: ILO.

Mlambo, A. S. (1997), *The Economic Structural Adjustment Programme: The Zimbabwean Case, 1990–1995*, Harare: University of Zimbabwe Publications.

— (2009) 'From the Second World War to UDI, 1940–1965', in B. Raftopoulos and A. Mlambo (eds), *Becoming Zimbabwe: A History from the Pre-Colonial Period to 2008*, Harare: Weaver Press, pp. 75–114.

Moyo, S. and W. Chambati (2013) *Land and Agrarian Reform in Zimbabwe: Beyond White-settler Capitalism*, Dakar: CODESRIA.

Moyo, S. and P. Yeros (2007) 'Intervention the Zimbabwe question and the two lefts', *Historical Materialism*, 15: 171–204.

Mundy, J. and S. Jacobs (2009) *Concerned African Scholars*, 82: 1–63.

Munochiveyi, M. (2011) 'Becoming Zimbabwe from below: multiple narratives of Zimbabwean nationalism', *Critical African Studies*, 6: 84–108.

Nkomo, J. (1984) *The Story of My Life*, London: Methuen.

Partridge, W. L. (1989) 'Involuntary resettlement in development projects', *Journal of Refugee Studies*, 2(3): 373–84.

Raftopolous, B. (2009) 'The crisis in Zimbabwe, 1998–2008', in B. Raftopoulos and A. Mlambo (eds), *Becoming Zimbabwe: A History from the Pre-Colonial Period to 2008*, Harare: Weaver Press, pp. 201–32.

Raftopoulos, B. and T. Savage (2005) *Zimbabwe: Injustice and Political Reconciliation*, Harare: Weaver Press.

Raftopoulos, B. and Y. Tsuneo (1999) *Sites of Struggle: Essays in Zimbabwe's Urban History*, Harare: Weaver Press.

Ranger, T. (2004) 'Historiography, patriotic history and the history of the nation: the struggle over the past in Zimbabwe', *Journal of Southern African Studies*, 30(2): 215–34.

Roitman, J. L. (2005) *Fiscal Disobedience: An Anthropology of Economic Regulation in Central Africa*, Princeton, NJ: Princeton University Press.

Shaw, W. (1986) 'Towards the one-party state in Zimbabwe: a study in African political thought', *Journal of Modern African Studies*, 24(3): 373–94.

Simone, A. (2005) 'Urban circulation and the everyday politics of African urban youth: the case of Douala, Cameroon', *International Journal of Urban and Regional Research*, 29(3): 516–32.

Sisulu, E. (ed.) (2007) *Gukurahundi in Zimbabwe: A Report on the Disturbances in Matebeleland and the Midlands, 1980–1988*, New York: Columbia University Press.

Solidarity Peace Trust (2005) 'Discarding the filth – Operation Murambatsvina: interim report on the Zimbabwean government's "urban cleansing" and forced eviction campaign May/June 2005', Harare, www.solidaritypeace trust.org/180/discarding-the-filth-operation-murambatsvina/.

Stallybrass, P. (1990) 'Marx and heterogeneity: thinking the lumpenproletariat', *Representations*, 31: 69–95.

Thompson, E. P. (1969) 'Time, work discipline and industrial capitalism', *Past and Present*, 38: 56–97.

Vambe, M. T. (ed.) (2008) *The Hidden Dimensions of Operation Murambatsvina*, Harare: Weaver Press.

Vigh, H. (2008) 'Crisis and chronicity: anthropological perspectives on continuous conflict and decline', *Ethnos*, 73(1): 5–24.

Wolpe, H. (1972) 'Capitalism and cheap labour power in South Africa: from segregation to apartheid', *Economy and Society*, 1(4): 425–56.

11 | Captured lives: the precarious space of youth displacement in eastern DRC[1]

Timothy Raeymaekers

Introduction

For many reasons, the Democratic Republic of Congo (DRC) continues to figure as a prominent case of humanitarian crisis and human displacement (Callaghy et al. 2001; Turner 2006; Stearns 2011). In the long period of regionalized warfare the Congo has known since the early 1990s, between one and over two million inhabitants of the Kivu Provinces and Ituri (respectively in the east and in the north-east of the country) have been physically dislocated at one point or another. This means that a quarter of the population there is constantly on the move.[2] This fact alone provides a radical difference with surrounding displacement environments in East Africa and the Horn, but also with the aid architecture directed towards displaced people in general, where life (ostensibly) occurs mostly in relation to camps (see, for example, Bøås and Bjørkhaug, this volume; Malkki 1995; Turner 2005). Contrary to such environments, eastern DRC has almost no such formal settlements. Of the 2.1 million people officially termed 'internally displaced persons' (IDPs) in eastern DRC in 2010, for example, only 116,000 lived in one of the UNHCR-run campsites in the region, thus representing a mere 5.5 per cent of the total amount of officially recognized IDPs (IRIN, 27 January 2010). This number even dropped to 112,000 in mid-2013, representing one ninth of the official IDP population (UNHCR website).[3]

People fleeing war in eastern Congo do not stop at country borders, but often find refuge in neighbouring countries: 450,000 Congolese refugees are currently hosted in UNHCR camps, primarily in Angola, Rwanda and Burundi (ibid.). These massive population dispersals are caused predominantly by recurrent armed violence. Particularly the North and South Kivu provinces have been in constant military turmoil since the early 1990s. Following the official ending of armed hostilities in 2003, the DRC entered a phase of democratic transition in 2006/07, but pockets of cross-border armed rebellion still remain. Particularly in the east, the rebellions of the FDLR (Democratic Liberation Forces of Rwanda) and Raia Mutomboki[4] in South Kivu, the ADF (Allied Democratic Forces), NALU (National Army for the Liberation of Uganda), the CNDP (Congrès National pour la Défense du Peuple) and later M23 in North Kivu, and the LRA

(Lord's Resistance Army) in Ituri, actively resist the territorial claims of the Congolese government in the region. These ongoing conflicts over territorial sovereignty and access to (partly mineral-rich) land in eastern Congo can be compared somewhat to a smouldering fire, whereby violent eruptions in one place automatically influence tensions in another (Vlassenroot 2002; Richards 2005). In general, massive population displacements in the eastern parts of DRC continue to remind us of the extreme volatility of the current peace-to-war transition in Africa's Great Lakes region, even as individual governments officially embrace the international agendas of democratization and post-war reconstruction.

Besides the recurrent nature of displacement in the DRC, a distinction should still be made between those physically dislocated people who find shelter in so-called spontaneous sites, such as dilapidated buildings and improvised forest dwellings, and others who are hosted by Congolese households. As a result of recurrent military battles, eastern Congo has become dotted with improvised villages and forest settlements which have come to represent 25 to 30 per cent of the total officially recognized IDP population in both Kivu provinces. However, even during repeated fighting, the largest proportion of internally displaced persons in eastern Congo continues to stay with host families. This obviously causes a series of pressures and anxieties both to these families and their guests. Research carried out by the UN and Save the Children rehearses the widely held claim that hosts provide shelter to IDPs primarily because of family and kinship relations (IDMC website, 14 September 2011),[5] although this is not always the case, as I will show later. Particularly in urban areas like Goma, Bukavu and Butembo, the excessive reliance of displaced people on host families also creates additional strains on poverty-stricken urban households. Apart from their own members, the latter now have to assist displaced relatives, including vulnerable people such as pregnant women and the elderly. It has not been uncommon to notice a certain level of discontent emerging against locally settled IDPs in some eastern Congolese localities, sometimes even leading to expulsions and aggressions against the displaced (UNICEF/CARE 2008).

Despite the sheer scale of numbers as well as rising problems of cohabitation between self-settled refugees and eastern Congo's 'host population' aid agencies stubbornly continue to concentrate their relief efforts on formalized camp settlements. This lack of flexible responses on the part of international agencies is indicative of a rising relief crisis in Africa's Great Lakes region, whereby growing numbers of people needing assistance remain without help and consequently feel forced to 'fend for themselves'. This chapter thinks beyond the narrow framework of site-based policy analysis and relief operations in regions affected by protracted warfare. It concentrates instead on the networked nature of human displacement as a result of protracted armed conflict, which, as this volume indicates, is by no means confined to Africa's Great Lakes region alone.

Following Amanda Hammar's suggestion in the Introduction to this volume, I question what new forms and dynamics of accumulation, distribution and exchange emerge under conditions of human displacement in environments of protracted armed conflict, and what effects these dynamics produce in terms of social and political 'orders'. On the one hand, this approach entails a close association between the emergence of economic markets and the reproduction of the social world, in the sense that the constant remaking of categories of displacement in such contexts remains visibly dependent upon mechanisms of territorialization, exclusion and control.[6] On the other hand, and concomitant with the literature on self-settled refugees, displaced people are also *active agents*, occupying and remaking space through the best use of available resources, networks and capacities (Bakewell 2008; Lindley 2009). In other words, displacement is reproduced through particular interactions between people, their resources and their structural contexts, which in turn shape the process of forced (im)mobility itself. It is this process of living a 'life in limbo' – or what usually gets described as such for lack of better terms – which constitutes the focus of the current chapter.

Youth and armed conflict

The main empirical focus of this chapter concerns the specific case of *unarmed* eastern Congolese youth, a category that has remained particularly disregarded when it concerns displacement interventions in Africa (Sommers 2006: 4–5). In relation to this, a number of key questions are explored here, including the following: What is it like to be young and displaced in a post-war environment like eastern DRC? How do young people who have been dislocated by armed violence try to construct a living space between dispersed livelihood opportunities and affective relations? How do they chart out routes of survival through war-torn environments? And how do they reconcile their daily needs to make a living with their aspirations for a better life?

Driven by fears of demographic youth bulges and violent eruptions of armed young men in so-called developing societies, most studies involving young people in post-conflict environments still tend to concentrate on the problematic integration of armed youth into post-war society (Collier 1999; Urdal 2004). The idea that unemployed youth – particularly young men – are inclined to join a rebel movement still sounds particularly attractive as a conflict indicator in African contexts, especially when attached to dominant notions of 'social madness' among unattached youngsters (Shoumatoff 1988). Key proponents of this perspective have been World Bank consultants Anke Hoeffler and Paul Collier (Collier 1999; Collier and Hoeffler 2001), who in their analysis of factors pertaining to civil war outbreaks in 1960–99 used male secondary-school endowment and income opportunities as a proxy of conflict risk (or rather, the opportunity for armed rebellion). In his paper 'Doing well out of war', Collier (1999: 3) concludes that 'if young men face only the option of poverty they might be more inclined to join a rebellion than if they have better opportunities'. Similarly, Paul Richards and Jean-Pierre Chauveau (2007) conclude that 'hyper-mobile impoverished rural youth are not a sufficient cause of armed conflict, but their availability for recruitment when other employment opportunities fail is a major factor in fuelling insurgency'. As a result, they conclude that '[c]utting off the supply of recruits to militia factions by providing more suitable employment opportunities attractive to these young people would contribute to peace and stability ...' (ibid.: 7; see also Sommers 2003).

Other ethnographic studies have tried to point out the many difficulties for contemporary youth in building a life for themselves between several social attachments – with a growing focus on the *agency* of war-affected youth in African (post-)war environments (Utas 2005; Vigh 2006). In their critique against social determinism, however, these studies still risk being dominated by a continued preoccupation with the tactics of *violent* youngsters, thus, perhaps unwittingly, disregarding the role of *un*armed youth. Although such a focus certainly has its merits, it simultaneously distracts attention from large groups of youngsters who remain unattached to militia life-worlds yet nonetheless face difficult daily decisions (see Jones, this volume). The terminology of 'social navigation' (Vigh 2006, 2009), often used with respect to marginalized youth in Africa, seems insufficient to cover the spectrum of highly gendered livelihood patterns of these war-affected youngsters. This is because it never really specifies the complex social geography in which such livelihood or life-path decisions occur – apart from their being 'wavering and unsettled' (Vigh 2009: 420).

As the different contributions to this volume suggest, 'space matters', yet not only in terms of attention to actual and symbolic locations or places from which people are forced to determine their lives. One also needs to consider what such interconnected places mean in terms of the distances and proximities between them, as well as the desires and promises they generate in relation to the control and redistribution of resources and abilities to literally 'make' a life (see Behrends, Elliott, Hansen, Jones, and Rodrigues, this volume).

In this chapter I zoom in on unarmed youth and their struggles over access to livelihoods in a complexity of interrelations (Massey 1992). Through this, I try to elucidate the multiple repertoires and abilities (or 'skills, defences and adjustments', as Hammar refers to them in her chapter on 'paradoxes of class' in this volume) employed by young people who have been displaced by prolonged military conflict and who are trying to anticipate the interrelated consequences of violent political and economic restructuring in contexts of war.

The social geography of armed conflict

Even within an environment of dislocation and despair, it is possible to discern certain patterns of mobility and life-making (Vigh 2008: 15). Assuming that 'war is never all terror all the time' (Lubkemann 2008: 13), or better said, that 'war is never all terror all the time *all over the place*' (Korf et al. 2010: 386, emphasis in original), this observation prompts attention to the spatial dimension of Congo's displacement economy. Being forcibly displaced by war simultaneously opens up certain trajectories while foreclosing others, a paradoxical dynamic that I will discuss in the present chapter. More specifically, in the aftermath of such a long conflict which continues to produce violent outcomes today, it seems indeed legitimate to ask 'what is becoming of these unarmed youngsters in terms of capacities, practices and structural conditions?'. Rather than taking for granted the presumably pervasive conditions that make conflict, violence and abject poverty indistinguishable from the social fabric (Vigh 2008: 10, 15), I emphasize the multiscalar spatial landscape in which such youths' life-worlds unfold. This occurs primarily between rural home regions they have forcibly left behind and urban environments that have not yet become their own. The approach here is based on the presumption that the ongoing projects and future visions of young people in African war environments are not only intimately connected to their chances to develop local opportunities and associations, but also depend on the extent to which they can successfully construct and maintain an autonomous social space among multiple constraints and opportunities.

The ambition of this ethnographic approach is to empirically connect these structural conditions to the personal skills, ambitions and capacities of young boys and girls who are able to employ them in a rapidly changing environment. The conditions include their particular social backgrounds and displacement 'push' factors such as military combat and insecurity, as well as access to labour markets. As I state in another context (Raeymaekers 2011), youth opportunities in (post-)war environments are not exclusively attached to their material conditions of making a *living* (by which I refer to labour markets, and coping and adaptation mechanisms). They are also linked to their ambitions of making a *life*, which entails a number of important cultural reflections on what constitutes a good life and how one can go about it socially (Åkesson 2004). As discussed in this chapter, war radically transforms both these dimensions of youth livelihoods in the context about and from which I am writing.

Empirically, this chapter builds on a study carried out in North Kivu in the autumn of 2008 with a team of researchers from the University of the Rwenzori (Butembo). In this period, we conducted a total of 348 interviews with 190 male and 158 female displaced youngsters, as well as some focus group discussions in the city of Butembo and its rural periphery of Bunyuka (located just 10 kilometres outside the city's perimeters). Life environments of young displaced people differed substantially between gender and urban–rural divides, divisions I have discussed elsewhere (Raeymaekers 2011). Here, I focus primarily on these youths' multiple social attachments. The interviewed youth, whom we contacted through a focused sampling method (through contacting associations of displaced people in Butembo), were between fifteen and thirty-six years old, with 85 per cent of them in the range between the ages of eighteen and twenty-six. The combination of targeted surveys and (focus group) interviews enabled me to concentrate on the often multiple spaces in which youths' life chances are being constructed and reproduced, namely between rural backgrounds, and opportunities in the city and border towns (on the latter, see Raeymaekers 2009). Through this method, I tried to bring out the underlying identity struggles of youth in post-conflict environments as they try to establish stable attachments in such multiple spaces.

Displaced youth in Butembo

In the definitions of aid organizations, youth are often categorized according to what they are not: neither children nor adults. As a result youngsters often get ignored as a separate target group. When addressing youth in conflict, one must nonetheless pay attention to the historical, social and cultural structures that determine who within a given community gets classified as youth, and who does not (Honwana and De Boeck 2005: 4). For this study, I shall consider as 'forcibly displaced youth' those male and female youngsters who have left their maternal homesteads, mostly because of recurrent violence since the beginning of the second Congo war (1998), and who were aged between twelve and thirty-six.[7] This age spectrum emerged from preliminary focus group discussions as the minimum and maximum ages at which adolescents get married in urban and rural settings. Locally, as is also true elsewhere, marriage acts as a major marker of adulthood for both genders (although subtle differences apply). The fact that most interlocutors (85 per cent) I encountered during my research in Butembo and its rural periphery varied between eighteen and twenty-six years already indicates a larger shift towards later marriage and urbanizing lifestyles, even in eastern Congo's rural environments.

In geographic terms, a first characteristic of youth displacement in Butembo and its rural surroundings is that young IDPs generally live scattered over the rural and urban landscape. Very few young people actually choose to stay in camps. (The few IDP camps in Butembo's surroundings have practically been abandoned, owing partly to their distance from urban centres, partly to their very poor infrastructure and living conditions). The general tendency of young people fleeing violence is to either go to family members or to try to sustain a life on their own. However, many youngsters found it extremely difficult to establish so-called 'stable attachments' (Richards and Chauveau 2007). This incapacity of dislocated youth to attach themselves locally shows itself very clearly at the time of their arrival: for close to half of the youth I encountered, Butembo constituted an alien place, where they had no direct acquaintances or attachments to rely on. If true, these data constitute a significant difference from the broader IDP population of North Kivu, of which a reported 80 per cent stays with family and friends (UNICEF/CARE 2008: 7). They also confirm the rather unsettled and vulnerable status of eastern Congo's displaced youngsters in this urban context, where immigrant youth remain squeezed between their original rural homesteads to which they cannot or do not want to return, and a new urban environment about which they share no prior material or social knowledge. In this context, an interesting question to consider is how such 'navigating' youth constitute spaces of their own, and how they try to bend destiny to their own advantage.

The uniqueness of Butembo as a site of displacement – and relocation – involves two dimensions. One of these involves its relative safety as compared with the neighbouring territories of Lubero and Ituri, where pockets of armed resistance persist. While the level of registered IDPs is relatively low in Butembo (15,215 there, as compared to 452,678 in Lubero and 26,925 in Beni at the time of my fieldwork in 2008), the town offers the opportunity to study human displacement outside camp life and in relation to the broader urban fabric. Notwithstanding this apparent urban sanctuary, insecurity in Butembo has been on the rise in recent years. Targeted assassinations and robberies, for example, are daily realities.

This once again points to the highly unstable political and security context that displaced people find themselves in despite official peace declarations. A local news website, for example, talks about 278 murders since 2006, of which 123 occurred in the year 2010 alone.[8] Despite the official end of hostilities between armed factions in 2003 and two rounds of multiparty elections in 2006/07, North Kivu – particularly Rutshuru, Masisi and the southern parts of Lubero – still witnesses regular instances of armed violence in areas occupied by armed movements. In 2012, for example, a rebel movement founded by a former army commander in the east of the country once again disrupted the livelihoods of Kivu citizens, which were already under huge strain because of a lack of access to basic medical services, poverty and problematic land access. This permanent insecurity in the countryside provides a key reason for rural youngsters to come to the city, where their dislocation owing to armed conflict intermingles with hopes and possibilities for a better life.

Yet once in the city, young immigrants immediately have to cope with a closed urban fabric and labour market. In the city of Butembo, they are confronted with a closed group of transnational traders who dominate almost every aspect of urban economic life. This group is locally referred to as the G8. This nickname immediately arouses a clear sense of the powerful position G8 traders occupy in local political and economic constellations, which they effectively manipulate through their simultaneous stake in transnational business (among others, in arms trading), local government bodies and militias. Throughout the entire post-war period, they have been able to maintain a close grip on the local city administration in the absence of a credible democratic state in this part of the DRC. Much of this influence is also due to a sustained monopoly over the regional 'informal' economy. Because the main activity these traders engage in is the import and export of cheap Chinese commodities, as well as cash crops and minerals over the Congo–Ugandan border, they also control a majority of urban shops and agricultural retail businesses to which young people can possibly apply for jobs. Owing to this monopolistic economic organization, socio-economic interaction in Butembo has elsewhere been described as being bounded by a 'semi-permeable veil' (Geenen 2012b). Not dissimilar to the situation in other post-war environments in Africa (Cramer 2006), access to work and rights to wealth in Butembo remain channelled through an almost 'invisible hand'. It privileges the growth and development of some particularly well-connected people in society – particularly those who are closely related to the G8 businessmen – while fiercely blocking the access to 'outsiders'.

Owing to such structural discrimination, most young immigrants in Butembo have no other option but to find employment in the many temporary jobs in the urban informal economy that directly or indirectly depend on the G8 business conglomerate, and which are locally referred to as *bikakala*. *Bikakala* can involve any kind of temporary work, from digging toilets to crushing stones and carrying sand (usually done by men), to preparing fritters ('*beignets*'), selling bananas and '*aracque*' (an alcoholic maize drink) on the side of the road (mostly a woman's job), or loading trucks as a '*bombeur*' and driving a '*chukudu*' through Butembo's dusty streets.[9]

A *chukudu* is an onomatopoeic word for the wooden, non-motorized scooters that are used in eastern Congo for the transport of various commodities (from charcoal, jerrycans, boxes to foodstuffs). Because transport infrastructure is so inadequate, *chukudus* and bicycles have practically become the only affordable transport from Congo's eastern border to the densely forested areas of Kivu, Maniema and Oriental province. Young drivers are prepared to travel several weeks through the forest carrying palm oil, coltan and other valuable goods for a few dollars' wage. In Butembo, a *chukudu* driver can earn up to $10 a day carrying goods across town, so the profession is consequently much aspired to by displaced youngsters looking to earn a living in the urban economy.

In Butembo, *bikakala* has gradually come to constitute the economy of the marginalized and destitute.[10] For young and dispersed populations, it often constitutes the survival option of last resort, which is typically taken up by 'outsiders' who do not have access to more stable jobs (which include shopkeeping or any other activity associated with the town's main import-export businesses). A determining feature of *bikakala* jobs, for example, is the absolute lack of choice on the part of workers to determine or even slightly influence the terms of agreement with their temporary employers. In fact *bikakala* literally means 'through offer and demand'. In a typical *bikakala* assignment, labourers are recruited haphazardly and temporarily by their usually male bosses (*patrons*), who wish a given task to be finished in the shortest possible time.

This means that labour conditions are often harsh and devoid of job security, as illustrated by the following examples of some of my young informants. As one boy who used to spend some time with the Mayi Mayi militias in the forest explained to me: 'Here one simply says: hey, little boy, come here, I have some work to do there, so you simply do the work ... for example, to bend things, or make some bricks' (Kweli, 22 September 2008). Another boy added: 'One day I woke up at home and a boss sent me to buy some nails ... He asked me if I had a job. I say no, I don't. Then he asked me if I could agree to stay with him, for example to cut some boards. So that's how I accepted' (Pascal, 22 September 2008).

While they are trying to secure an income through such temporary assignments, an often-heard complaint from these youngsters concerns the complete lack of consideration on the part of their bosses, up to the point where some questioned the value of *bikakala* as a livelihood altogether. One boy from Mangina (a village north of Beni) came close to dying while he was digging toilet pits for a *patron* in Butembo. Having left Mangina years before when fleeing military violence in his home town, he had no choice but to stay in Butembo because his parents had died along the way:

[While fleeing Mangina], I arrived in Butembo, where I stayed for a few months ... I ran away and was lost in the city, because I did not master the environment. I was afraid to go back, so I had to find another home ... Since I was a visitor, fortunately a good Samaritan offered me to stay for three weeks. After these three weeks I was again expelled. Here no one knows me, no one knows where I came from. So I really had a very difficult time. I found a small house for rent ... There at least they cannot chase me, there I can go to sleep every time. So I said how am I going to do each time to [pay the rent]? So I started searching, digging holes here, toilets ... It was a very hard work, but it helped me anyway to pay my rent ... I thought it was too tiring, it's like my body was on fire. I thought I could even die before my age. But since here in Butembo there is all this tribalism, I failed to find another job ... So with the fear of dying, I continued to dig these wells. (Mumbere, 21 September 2008)

The statement of this young man from Mangina reveals some of the more subtle geographic mechanisms that constrain young people's trajectories in Butembo, confining them to a sequence of material and symbolic displacements. On the one hand, as already explained earlier, the marginal position that people like Mumbere find themselves in in Butembo partly results from the process of physical dislocation itself, which usually takes place abruptly and without prior knowledge of the city environment. This abrupt confrontation with the city often causes a great deal of distress, which may be compensated for by adept religiosity and imageries of heavenly salvation (see also De Boeck and Plissart 2004). In Mumbere's case, his arrival in town immediately caused a feeling of disorientation, of not fully mastering the town's social landscape. Although he found some temporary relief from a willing stranger ('a good Samaritan'), for most of his quest he relied totally upon himself. Mumbere was constantly confronted with the fear of being expelled, of being chased even from his precariously conquered space. It was as if everything the town had to offer needed to be paid for harshly and with the price of one's own body. These conditions nearly brought Mumbere to death. With 'fire' spreading throughout his body, he had no choice but to continue working and making a living in this hostile urban environment.

On the other hand, Mumbere and other displaced youngsters like him also explicitly interpret their experiences in relation to the legacy of discriminatory urban job markets and differential access to resources, which they directly relate to 'tribalism' (*tribalisme*). Youth access to jobs is severely blocked by a local politics of clientelism, which highly discriminates against outsiders. While speaking to a group of displaced youngsters, a girl who also fled Mumbere's town said she experienced several difficulties owing to her local status in Butembo as a 'stranger' (Swahili: *mukujakuja*, plural: *wakujakuja*) (Masika, 21 September 2008). Because she was not able to pay her school fees (or *minerval*) any more, she was told by her teacher to stay at home. At the same time other pupils in a similar situation, who were from Butembo, continued to attend classes. So Masika felt that her being a stranger somehow obstructed her from having a proper education, which she considered necessary for moving on with life. During the same meeting, another boy said he found it difficult to connect to the city because of the 'language' (Petit, 21 September 2008). This was because Nande from outside Butembo speak a different Swahili dialect to city-borns (which the latter define as more 'pure'[11]).

These examples, taken from the daily life of displaced young people in Butembo, show very clearly how, despite it being a mono-ethnic region, political 'tribalism' occupies a significant place in people's lives as a marker to gain or obstruct access to urban opportunities and resources. As Bruce Berman (1998), following John Lonsdale (1994), explains, African ethnic invention emerges through internal struggles over moral economy and political legitimacy tied to the definition of ethnic communities, on the one hand, and external conflicts over differential access to the resources of modernity and economic accumulation on the other hand. The latter Berman calls moral ethnicity, the former political tribalism. Without their entirely indicating a closed system of access, it is interesting to note how such 'tribal' categories as dialect and networks of patronage become productive of a political economy of access to the city's informal job market. Intensifying under conditions of displacement and relocation, this serves to exclude potentially 'rival' citizens who are thought to compete for access to scarce economic resources (Berman 1988: 324). At the same time, such categories of difference also become part of the rhetoric of sovereignty (about the sovereign 'right' to rule and protect one's own territory). This automatically encapsulates 'persons or groups of persons that others, with impunity, can treat without regard for their psychological and physical wellbeing' (Hammar and Rodgers 2008: 419; see also Buur et al. 2006). Not surprisingly, displaced/relocated youngsters in Butembo associate their social branding of being marginalized and excluded with a local value system of differentiation. This is defined by a broader system of knowledge in this restricted urban space – 'le tribalisme, c'est la connaissance', Mumbere said at one point – which differentiates Butembo's inhabitants from those who are categorically placed outside the city's closed social network. The fact that 'indigenous' Bubolais define immigrants as less pure, less part of and more 'stranger' to the town's social fabric confines these perceived outsiders to an invisible life in the margins, detached from stable opportunities and life chances. At the same time, however, displaced youth also adopt a discourse of self-exclusion. Through this they depict their host community as reactionary and inward-bound. Put off by this aggressive territorialization of ethnicity, they fashion a form of hybrid cosmopolitanism that 'resists both the reactionary xenophobia of the citizenry and the conventional state-centred notion of belonging' (Landau and Monson 2008: 326). This latter is determined by both the national bureaucratic and humanitarian assistance regimes, but by this very lack of territorial confinement becomes an impossible ideal to realize in this closed social geography.

In the end, I would argue that the condition of being a stranger in Butembo involves an even stronger discriminatory category than that of the armed militia member. This became apparent to me during a group interview with a number of ex-Mayi Mayi soldiers, some of whom had spent years in the forest fighting and digging mineral resources. During this interview, some ex-recruits explained to me their difficulties in revealing their identities, because 'if you do that, that will be the end' (Jeff, 22 September 2008). In particular, they emphasized the often exploitative labour conditions their forced invisibility placed them in, whereby their bosses continued to discriminate against them as outsiders while taking advantage of their vulnerability. The problem is that Butembo's patrons think everyone is just 'fending for themselves', one ex-Mayi Mayi explained to me (Pascal, 22 September 2008).

The expression to 'fend for oneself', regularly used in the context of Congo's urban informal economy, historically builds on the years of dictatorship in Congo-Zaire under the leadership of Désiré Mobutu. During this period of harsh economic downturn and political repression, people were forced to develop the 'art' of manoeuvring through haphazard opportunities (see also

Trefon 2004; Vigh 2009; Jones 2010). In Congolese French, this art is referred to as *débrouillardisme*: to get by, fix, organize, muddle through. Contrary to the aura of resistance that such informal survival mechanisms often acquire in academic writing (Azarya and Chazan 1987; MacGaffey 1987), it should not be forgotten that in the absence of credible state administration, informal accumulation and economic regulation have become important governmental technologies in many of Congo's war-torn cities. This has important consequences for the rights to work and wealth as well as the distribution of much-disputed resources. In Butembo's contemporary job market, the dire need on the part of great segments of the urban population to secure their daily bread has pushed some employers even so far as to demand 'a little something' (Pascal, 22 September 2008) for the opportunity to work with them and secure a livelihood.

To some extent, one could argue that state dictatorship in this region has been taken over by the sovereignty of the market and the pervasiveness of economic debt. The same 'invisible hand' that regulates the entrance of goods and people into the urban economy also heavily conditions people's livelihoods. In this sense, whoever decides to take an informal job implicitly has to accept this G8 dominance without an official opportunity to rebel or defend her/his rights. For example, when young workers complain about discrimination against them in the workplace, it frequently raises suspicions against them on the basis of their backgrounds (for example, referring to names or accents), their supposed 'rebellious' nature (which implicitly refers to previous militia membership), or other negative social markers. In a context of high labour competition and urban poverty, such suspicions may entail losing work opportunities and being excluded from city life irreversibly in a matter of moments. In the situation of ex-militia recruits, the categorical distinction between insider and outsider or participant and observer of the town's restricted job opportunities operates on a more subtle level than with 'non-violent' displaced youngsters; that is, on the level of suspicion. Whenever difficulties arise at work – for example, if tools get lost or payments do not arrive as promised – young workers find little space to complain or defend their position. Suspicions might be raised that they are Mayi Mayi and hotheads whose 'spirit' still resides in the forest. There have been many occasions when young people in town have been disenfranchised explicitly by the town's leading elites with the justification that they work either as spies or directly for the Mayi Mayi. Such supicion, as already noted, excludes them permanently from a stable social attachment to the city.

This conscious construction of youth as a potential disturbance and as troublemakers serves both as a warrant and a warning that in order to be accepted in the city's economic fabric one had better avoid negative visibility. Former militia recruits who were looking for a job in Butembo found it better to 'stay calm' and stick to themselves (Paul, Pascal, 22 September 2008). This attitude was also deemed beneficial in order to avoid having to return to the bush, where life is harsh and characterized by 'prison-like' conditions. In the words of Pascal '[this situation] really makes me nervous [but] whenever I get angry they will say: "Ah, this one is a Mayi Mayi", so I say to myself, it is better to wait for tomorrow as someone will still bring me food' (Pascal, 22 September 2008).

This difficulty in constructing a proper home is revealed, finally, in the difference youngsters perceive between *having* a home and being *at* home in Butembo. In Swahili, these are two different terms, which respectively translate as *nyumba* (house) and *kwango* (being *at* home). Whereas substantial agreement exists between young displaced people over the necessity to be able to cover one's needs and not depend on others ('*ne pas être sous tutelle*'), a gendered dimension added itself to this discussion during my research in Butembo. Male youth mainly emphasized the need to buy a proper plot of land ('*une parcelle*') so as to build a house and raise a family. On the other hand, girls emphasized the need to find a good environment where they could develop their qualities and eventually raise a family. One girl expressed a seemingly general feeling when she said that

> I think what is best, what is good, is to stay there where you can find a living, find a job [*kazi*], with little difference between remaining here at home, to go somewhere else, or to go back to your family to do nothing. It is good to stay here if you have something on your hands ... if you find a living, regardless the environment, this suits you better [*cela arrange mieux*]. (Masika, 21 September 2008)

As these individual examples make clear, the gradual transformation of Butembo's urban economy from war to post-war crisis has not brought a betterment of young people's condition. On the contrary, increasingly it condemns them to an invisible and vulnerable life in the margins, excluded from stable opportunities. The many youngsters that continue to flee violence and try to make a life in the city mainly survive through precarious jobs that are provided haphazardly to them by a discriminating and unstable job market. As a result, young people who are displaced by the effects of war often feel lost and detached from the city, while they are unable to construct a proper home for themselves. In the next section, I will discuss how this economic disconnectedness further translates into separate and secluded spaces for these youngsters, who continue to move between different places to construct a life and a livelihood.

Secluded spaces

In Congo, the informal economy of the urban poor has often been pictured in terms of bargaining, debt and sacrifice. Theodore Trefon (2004), who did extensive research on the urban poor in Kinshasa, calls it a form of 'despair solidarity'. In the metropole, he says,

> [t]he collective social values and practices characteristic of rural life in Congo have given way to the demands and contradictions of a market economy in which the individual is central. Attitudes and behaviours have evolved due to the degree of crisis and specifically the difficulties in finding cash-earning employment. Always looking for new ways to cope, poverty is psychologically transformed into 'despair solidarity' ... People help each other primarily if they can expect something in return. Debt, whether it be in the form of a loan, a service rendered or a favour, is expected to be redeemed at some point. (Ibid.: 488)

In the aftermath of the Congo war (Vlassenroot and Raeymaekers 2004), this limiting of economic possibilities to individualistic and short-term exchange has wider, important ramifications for the ways in which young people displaced by war succeed in securing a livelihood. At the bottom of the economic ladder, survival is marked by situations of sheer desperation, as one youngster indicated to me during an interview: 'Really, I live here by grace. It happens sometimes to meet with friends from back home. And then automatically, I ask [for money and food]. At that point, I survive' (Petit, 21 September 2008).

Constrained by such desperate exchanges, relationships between young strangers in Butembo often get tied to a straightforward market logic, a tit-for-tat reciprocity that can only be partly redeemed through people's attachment to close-knit social networks. Looking more closely, a kind of haphazardness in fact characterizes the lives of these unattached youngsters, whose home and autonomous social space technically depend on the solidarity expressed by others. As noted previously, most youngsters who arrive in Butembo escaping violence or anguish elsewhere exclusively rely on whatever opportunities they can carve out in the informal economy of the street. The few youngsters who do get hosted by direct acquaintances are expected to pay their host parents for their bed and daily meal in the form of either a regular allowance or household labour. Materially speaking, therefore, it makes little difference whether one spends the night in a private room or with host parents who could be either close family members or distant acquaintances from the youngster's home region. Everything in the household is being calculated and balanced constantly in immediate economic terms. The practical reason that is often cited for this intimate cost–benefit analysis is that in these times of (post-war) crisis, there is no space for free gifts. In this context, host families operate according to fixed hierarchies between their close and more distant kin, while everyone has to contribute to the family's collective survival.

As a result of such implicit family hierarchies, however, household economies often acquire a visibly gendered division of labour, with girls helping out their host mothers in and around the house, while boys bring back the money from their daily labour. Such labour divisions are clearly to the disadvantage of displaced girls, since they have to help in the household and often on the land as well – a form of bonded labour – while boys can concentrate on more independent cash-earning employment. At the same time, the street economy of the urban poor makes little distinction between boys and girls as to the type of labour they carry out. During my stay in Butembo, I witnessed as many displaced boys carrying bags of sand, shovelling and crushing stones as girls who were bearing large bags of charcoal and bananas on their heads and backs to the market. While not all of these activities are remunerated, most of them feed back into the single household economy as some form of allowance and contribution by these hosted youth.

Because their livelihoods often depend on different social spaces, the condition of being displaced in and around Butembo could be described as a kind of pending social situation. Here, partially unstable and incomplete attachments to different environments gradually contribute to the construction of an autonomous social place of their own. I illustrate this through the testimony of a young girl from Biakato, whom I talked to during a meeting with other displaced youngsters in Butembo. She explained to me that she had arrived in Butembo in 2002 together with her mother and father, around the time when the forces of Jean-Pierre Bemba swept across north-eastern Congo with a military campaign code-named '*Effacer le Tableau*' ('erasing the Board').[12] From the moment they arrived in Butembo, however, her parents found it difficult to make a decent living. So they returned to Biakato, leaving their daughter behind in her uncle's house. While the girl continues to live with her uncle in town, she occasionally sends some money home to her parents via a friend or a family member. But she finds the transfer difficult because her messenger sometimes spends the money during the trip. In addition, the supportive capacities of her host family remain limited: 'What I see is that my uncle also has children, so I cannot ask [for support] like them,' she said during our encounter (Masika, 21 September 2008). In order to cope, therefore, she continues to do little jobs in the household, while on market days she hauls agricultural produce from the surrounding fields towards the centre of Butembo.

Both materially and culturally, therefore, these youngsters' life-worlds continue to be located in several places *at the same time*. As Masika explained, her life and livelihood unfold between different sites: the host family, her parents in the village, the city market and its rural hinterland. Rather than sticking to one place, young people like her frequently travel back and forth between these environments, establishing fragile connections in all of them. As I learned during my stay among Butembo's youth, for example, a frequent mobility pattern for displaced youngsters who are still attending school is to combine a more or less permanent residence in town during teaching semesters with regular stays at their parents' place during school holidays, security permitting.

The fact that urban host parents usually ask for some contribution to cover basic needs means that youngsters' savings are usually either non-existent or entirely consumed during these periods. As a result, school holidays usually serve as periods of saving and, occasionally also, luxury spending for these youngsters who have come from the city to their parents' home. In a cultural sense, these periods of vacation in the village also serve as important benchmarks in these youngsters' identity formation as urban and modern, while they do not necessarily experience this as a contradiction to their rural backgrounds. As one boy from Mangina explained, he uses his visits to the village to harvest and sell agricultural produce on the market, which enables him, for example, to buy a nice shirt with his savings (Tembo, 21 September 2008).

The resulting solidarity pattern between these youngsters and their respective (host) parents at 'home' and in the city can thus be described as a kind of give-and-take relationship, in which support and food are shared sequentially. This type of sequential solidarity requires some flexibility on the part of the youngsters' 'encadreurs'. For example, teachers might have to wait months to be paid their weekly school fees, or host parents have to feed hungry mouths in the anticipation of some kind of reward. At the same time, it opens up a modest time frame for these youngsters to allow them to jump-start livelihood options and calculate existing risks. In some cases, their activities in town even permit them to contribute to the livelihoods of relatives and friends. As several youngsters testified during focus group discussions, their 'encadreurs' are generally tolerant towards delays in payments until the support arrives in the form of a letter or a friend. An important prerequisite for the success of these endeavours, therefore, is that youngsters are allowed some level of indebtedness to their teachers and host parents so that they can start building a livelihood of their own.

One crucial asset for displaced youngsters in developing a sustainable livelihood in Butembo, therefore, is to be able to travel between different social spaces. While mobility can often be a constraint instead of an opportunity (in the sense that it is often forced during wartime), the ability to move freely between their respective rural social backgrounds and the street and family life of the city constitutes an important life-making resource. As I have explained, the most important constraint youngsters face in this regard relates not so much to their supposed lack of livelihood assets or social capital – which can be both a burden and an advantage – as to the more subtle practice of being defined as a 'stranger'. In Butembo and its rural surroundings, being a stranger (Swahili: *mukujakuja*) translates primarily into being an outsider to the urban economy of supply and demand. This feeds into the mechanisms of exclusion and social branding one usually associates with the city's destitute and marginalized. The fact that many displaced youngsters find themselves in such a situation today has as much to do with the conscious politics of exclusion on the part of the town's economic elite – who effectively limit access to economic networks to a close circle of family and friends – as with the gradual contraction of social relationships to a market-bound economic logic.

Conclusion

This chapter started from a straightforward but complex question: what is it like to be displaced and young in a post-war environment like the Democratic Republic of Congo (DRC)? This question unfolds on different levels. Materially speaking, the chapter took an inward look into the ways young people who have been physically dislocated by war in the eastern parts of the DRC – and whose wider social and economic environment is concurrently shaped by displacement and war – construct their lives in multiple spaces. Using ethnographic evidence from multiple sites, it elucidates how some of the more invisible dimensions of post-war displacement, involving in particular social exclusion and circular mobility, continue to affect young people's lives in the aftermath of long-term armed conflict.

Young people in eastern Congo face particular difficulties while trying to construct an autonomous living space in the aftermath of protracted warfare and displacement/confinement. This is because they often remain simultaneously displaced-in-place (Hammar and Rodgers 2008) and caught in circular movements between apparently disconnected places, a condition which substantially constrains their access to sustainable livelihoods. The method I use to conceive this squaring of people's movement could be conveniently termed as the spatial construction of the social. Following the work of Doreen Massey (see also Evans, this volume), I find it fruitful to conceive geographical space as being constructed out of interrelations (Massey 1992). What makes the view of these social relations spatial is their *simultaneity*, whereby elements in social systems, and especially moving elements, have spatial relations to each other. Instead of linear journeys from A to B, a more accurate way to conceive of the space through which people move is that of a network of interrelations which places things, people and ideas in a multidimensional relation to each other. Because of their spatial construction, such social relations are by their very nature full of power and symbolism, a complex web of relations of domination and subordination, of solidarity and cooperation, which Massey refers to as power-geometry.

Following people through these networks, it becomes possible to make visible some of the underlying dynamics of power and domination that literally *capture* people's lives and confine their daily choices. In particular in eastern DRC, I have demonstrated how the economy of displacement in the context of the war-affected town of Butembo has taken the shape of a multi-scalar spatial landscape, which connects mechanisms of forced (im)mobility and exclusion in an interconnected social network. It is in this uncertain landscape that the life-worlds of urban displaced youngsters unfold, between rural home regions they have forcibly left behind and urban environments that have not yet become their own, and between material attempts to make a living and the process of imagining a life.

This conclusion echoes the observation, made in the Introduction to this volume, that one needs to consider more closely the ways in which logics of belonging, entitlement and exclusion across space specifically reinforce regimes of management to control things, bodies and borders. In particular, I have taken up this suggestion to reveal dynamics of economic informalization as an active technology and sovereign practice rather than using the residual category of informality, which is often erroneously connected to practices of resistance (see also Bracking, this volume). A great deal of work still needs to be done to concretely expose the constructive interconnection between the economic and the social worlds in situations of enduring distress and physical dislocation.

On a more affective level of *feeling* displaced, I have argued in this chapter that it is important also to acquire a sense of the meanings young displaced people give to their condition, which is primarily expressed as being disconnected and detached from the chance to construct a space of their own. In order to do this, I adopted a phenomenological approach to social action, which is concerned with how human beings articulate their experiences and stories in ways that makes them meaningful to themselves and to others (Finnstrom 2008). As Sverker Finnstrom (ibid.) observes in a similar context (of northern Uganda during and in the aftermath of its long civil war), to live with 'bad surroundings' entails giving meaning to them as existential structures. Through these meaningful expressions, young people affected by long periods of armed conflict continue to connect with and give sense to their material practices of securing a livelihood (that is, of make a *living*) and their potentiality for making a *life* – or having the cultural imagination for constructing a proper life space.

I fully underwrite the broader endeavour of this volume, therefore, to further explore the boundaries between force and choice where displacement is concerned, and between compliance and resistance to sovereign practice and rhetoric. As this chapter clarifies, relationships of authority and citizenship get radically redefined when people are being displaced and 'the economy' is reorganized in different ways. It is only through this 'worm's eye' view (Landau and Monson 2008) of people who seek to construct a proper place in a world that is not of their own making that one can clearly see how such relations of accumulation and authority become intrinsically connected.

Notes

1 I would like to thank the European Commission – in particular through its FP6 programme MICROCON and all its members – for giving me the opportunity to do this research. Additional gratitude goes to my former colleagues in Ghent, Koen Vlassenroot, Karel Arnaut and Anne Walraet, for a collegial and rewarding collaboration.

2 Of the 1.7 million displaced people in 2011, for example, a vast majority had fled since the start of large-scale military operations against armed groups in early 2009. At the end of 2011, however, an estimated 540,000 people were displaced within North Kivu and 520,000 in South Kivu. Because of these recurrent displacements, IDPs often remain dispersed in rural and urban areas, where they either support themselves or rely on the limited resources of host communities (www.internal-displacement.org/countries/drcongo; see below).

3 www.unhcr.org/pages/49e45c366.html.

4 This is more of a fringe group. See congosiasa.blogspot.ch/2012/07/who-are-raia-mutomboki.html. See also a recent Rift Valley Institute report: www.createspace.com/4239650.

5 www.internal-displacement.org/8025708F004CE90B/(httpCountrySummaries)/FE8DB3FD4D9A0D5BC12578FE002BF556?OpenDocument&count=10000.

6 As Hammar suggests in her Introduction, 'those actively displaced often lose not only physical place and property and the means of production or livelihood, but also a sense of their "proper" place in the world'. Such loss may involve abandonment and 'involuntary immobility' (Lubkemann 2008), or forced confinement (Bøås and Bjørkhaug, this volume), but also more subtle mechanisms of preventing access to the means of livelihood.

7 Close to 98 per cent of interviewed people fled their houses because of violent conflict.

8 www.benilubero.com.

9 During a short survey in Butembo and its periphery, around 7 per cent of interviewed displaced youngsters claimed to perform this job, while 6.5 per cent saw it as a potential job in case they lost their current occupations.

10 This partly echoes the 'kiyanomics' that Jeremy Jones argues have come to dominate the lives of the urban 'displaced-in-place' youth in Zimbabwe's chronic crisis (see Jones 2010, and in this volume).

11 Although I don't have the space to develop this here, a strong myth exists in Butembo which directly associates this 'purity' of the city to the designation of Butembo's inhabitants as the 'chosen people'. For an in-depth analysis, see Geenen (2012a).

12 This military campaign provoked serious indignation on the part of local church leaders and international organizations for the sheer brutality in which the Mouvement du Libération du Congo (MLC) and its associated forces skimmed over Kivu's countryside, leaving a trail of destruction and innocent victims in their tracks. In international media, 'Effacer le Tableau' became emblematic of the barbarity of Congo's war as it generated among other things allegations of cannibalism, for which the MLC leader Jean-Pierre Bemba eventually had to stand trial in the International Criminal Court. The brutality and almost carnivalesque manner in which this operation took shape – with commander nicknames such as 'Le Roi des Imbéciles' – caused a flow of refugees and internationally displaced people, mostly from the territory of Beni, where the focal point of this campaign was situated.

References

Åkesson, L. (2004) *Making a Life: Meanings of migration in Cape Verde*, Gothenburg University.

Azarya, V. and N. Chazan (1987) 'Disengagement from the state in Africa: reflections from the experience of Ghana and Guinea', *Comparative Studies in Society and History*, 29(1): 106–31.

Bakewell, O. (2008) 'Research beyond the categories: the importance of policy irrelevant research into forced migration', *Journal of Refugee Studies*, 21(4): 432–53.

Berman, B. J. (1998) 'Ethnicity, patronage and the African state: the politics of uncivil nationalism', *African Affairs*, 97(388): 305–41.

Buur, L., S. Jensen and F. Stepputat (2006) 'The security–development nexus', in L. Buur, S. Jensen and F. Stepputat (eds), *The Security–Development Nexus: Expressions of sovereignty and securitization in Southern Africa*, Uppsala and Cape Town: Nordiska Afrikainstitutet and HSRC Press.

Callaghy, T., R. Kassimir and R. Latham (eds) (2001) *Intervention and Transnationalism in Africa. Global–local networks of power*, Cambridge: Cambridge University Press.

Christiansen, C., M. Utas and H. Vigh (eds) (2006) *Navigating Youth, Generating Adulthood: social becoming in an African context*, Stockholm: Elanders Gotab AB.

Collier, P. (1999) 'Doing well out of war', Paper presented at the conference 'Economic agendas in civil wars', London, 26/27 April.

Collier, P. and A. Hoeffler (2001) 'Greed and grievance in civil war', CEPR Working Paper, Oxford: Centre for the Study of African Economies.

Cramer, C. (2006) *Civil War is Not a Stupid Thing. Accounting for Violence in Developing Countries*, London: Hurst and Co.

De Boeck, F. and M.-F. Plissart (2004) *Kinshasa: Tales of the invisible city*, Ghent: Ludion.

Finnstrom, S. (2008) *Living with Bad Surroundings: War, History, and Everyday Moments in Northern Uganda*, Durham, NC: Duke University Press.

Geenen, K. (2012a) 'How people of Butembo (RDC) were chosen to embody "the New Congo": or what the appearance of a poster in public places can teach about a city's social tissue',

International Journal of Urban and Regional Research, 36(3): 448–61.

— (2012b) 'The pursuit of pleasure in a war-weary city, Butembo, North Kivu, DRC', PhD thesis, Catholic University of Leuven.

Hammar, A. and G. Rodgers (2008) 'Introduction: Notes on political economies of displacement in southern Africa', *Journal of Contemporary African Studies*, 26(4): 355–70.

Honwana, A. and F. Boeck (eds) (2005) *Makers and Breakers: Children and Youth in Postcolonial Africa*, Oxford: James Currey.

Jones, J. L. (2010) '"Nothing is straight in Zimbabwe": the rise of the Kukiya-kiya economy 2000–2008', *Journal of Southern African Studies*, 36(2): 285–99.

Jourdan, L. (2010) *Generazione Kalashnikov. Un antropologo dentro la guerra in Congo*, Rome: Laterza.

Korf, B., T. Hagmann and M. Engeler (2010) 'The geography of warscape', *Third World Quarterly*, 3(3): 385–99.

Landau, L. and T. Monson (2008) 'Displacement, estrangement and sovereignty: reconfiguring state power in urban South Africa', *Government and Opposition*, 43(2): 315–36.

Lindley, A. (2009) 'Leaving Mogadishu: the war on terror and displacement dynamics in Somali region', MICROCON Working Paper, Brighton: Institute of Development Studies.

Lonsdale, J. (1994) 'Moral ethnicity and political tribalism', in P. Kaarsholm and J. Hultin (eds), *Inventions and Boundaries: Historical and anthropological approaches to the study of ethnicity and nationalism*, Roskilde: Institute for Development Studies, Roskilde University, pp. 131–50.

Lubkemann, S. (2008) *Culture in Chaos. An anthropology of the social condition in war*, Chicago, IL, and London: University of Chicago Press.

MacGaffey, J. (1987) *Entrepreneurs and Parasites. The struggle for indigenous capitalism in Zaire*, Cambridge: Cambridge University Press.

Malkki, L. (1995) *Purity and Exile: Violence, Memory, and National Cosmology among Hutu Refugees in Tanzania*, Chicago, IL, and London: University of Chicago Press.

Massey, D. (1992) 'Politics and space/time', *MLR*, 196: 65–84.

Raeymaekers, T. (2009) 'The silent encroachment of the frontier: a politics of transborder trade in the Semliki Valley (Congo–Uganda)', *Political Geography*, 28(1): 55–65.

— (2011) 'Forced displacement and youth employment in the aftermath of the Congo war: from making a living to making a life', MICROCON Research Working Paper 38 (November), Brighton: Institute for Development Studies.

Richards, P. (2005) 'New war: an ethnographic approach', in P. Richards (ed.), *No Peace, No War: An anthropology of contemporary armed conflicts*, Oxford: James Currey.

Richards, P. and J.-P. Chauveau (2007) 'Land, agricultural change and conflict in West Africa: regional issues from Sierra Leone, Liberia and Côte d'Ivoire', Issy-les-Moulineaux: CSAO/SWAC.

Shoumatoff, A. (1988) *African Madness*, New York: Alfred A. Knopf.

Simone, A. (2004) *For the City Yet to Come. Changing African Life in Four Cities*, Durham, NC, and London: Duke University Press.

Sommers, M. (2003) 'Youth, wars, and urban Africa: challenges, misunderstanding, and opportunities', in B. A. Ruble, J. S. Tulchin, D. H. Varat and L. M. Hanley (eds), *Youth Explosion in Developing World Cities. Approaches to Reducing Poverty and Conflict in an Urban Age*, Washington, DC: Woodrow Wilson International Center for Scholars.

— (2006) 'Youth and conflict: a brief review of available literature', USAID & Equip3/Education Development Center.

Stearns, J. (2011) *Dancing in the Glory of Monsters: The Collapse of the Congo and the Great War of Africa*, New York: Public Affairs.

Trefon, T. (ed.) (2004) *Reinventing Order in the Congo: How people respond to state failure in Kinshasa*, London and Kampala: Zed Books and Fountain Publishers.

Turner, S. (2005) 'Suspended spaces – contesting sovereignties in a refugee camp', in T. B. Hansen and F. Stepputat (eds), *Sovereign Bodies: Citizens, Migrants, and States in the Postcolonial World*, Princeton, NJ: Princeton University Press.

— (2006) *The Congo Wars. Conflict, Myth and Reality*, London: Zed Books.

UNICEF/CARE (2008) 'Internal displacement in North Kivu: hosting, camps, and coping mechanisms', 27 April.

Urdal, H. (2004) *The Devil in the Demographics: The Effect of Youth Bulges on Domestic Armed Conflict, 1950–2000*, Washington, DC: World Bank.

Utas, M. (2005) 'Victimcy, girlfriending, soldiering: tactic agency in a young woman's social navigation of the Liberian war zone', *Anthropological Quarterly*, 78(2): 403–30.

Vigh, H. (2006) *Navigating Terrains of War: Youth and soldiering in Guinea-Bissau*, London and New York: Berghahn.

— (2008) 'Crisis and chronicity: anthropological perspectives on continuous conflict and decline', *Ethnos*, 73(1): 5–24.

— (2009) 'Motion squared. A second look at the concept of social navigation', *Anthropological Theory*, 9(4): 419–38.

Vlassenroot, K. (2002) *The Making of a New Order: Dynamics of conflict and dialectics of war in South Kivu (DR Congo)*, PhD thesis, University of Ghent.

Vlassenroot, K. and T. Raeymaekers (2004) *Conflict and Social Transformation in Eastern DR Congo*, Ghent: Academia Press.

About the contributors

Andrea Behrends is an anthropologist, visiting professor at Hamburg University and affiliated as a researcher and lecturer at the Institute for Social and Cultural Anthropology at the Martin Luther University in Halle-Wittenberg, Germany. With a focus on political anthropology, she has studied conflict, displacement, rebellion and creative adaptation in the Chad–Sudan border region. Together with Stephen P. Reyna, she has contributed to the development of an anthropological perspective on African oil production. Her publications include the co-edited volume *Crude Domination. An Anthropology of Oil* (Berghahn, 2011), as well as the forthcoming co-edited volume *Traveling Models in African Conflict Management. Translating Technologies of Social Ordering* (AEGIS, Brill, 2014).

Ingunn Bjørkhaug is a researcher at the Fafo Institute for Applied International Studies (AIS) in Oslo, Norway, and a PhD candidate at the Norwegian University of Life Science in Ås. She has conducted a number of studies in conflict and post-conflict settings on displacement, gender-based violence, children and youth, and ex-combatants, including in Colombia, Liberia and Uganda. She has co-published in the journal *Forum for Development Studies*, and in the MICROCON Research Working Paper series. She contributed to an extensive profiling study of internal displacement in northern Uganda in 2007 and has since continued to follow the post-conflict situation in the area. The focus of her PhD is on displacement economies in Nakivale, Uganda, and on the Liberian side of the Liberian–Ivorian borderlands.

Morten Bøås is a research professor at the Norwegian Institute of International Affairs (NUPI) in Oslo, Norway, which he joined in September 2013. Prior to this he worked for ten years at the Fafo Institute for Applied International Studies (AIS) in Oslo, including as its research director and head of research. He has researched and published extensively on, among other issues, conflict and instability, regionalism and security regimes, and multilateral governance, in Africa. Besides numerous journal articles, his book publications include *African Guerrillas: Raging Against the Machine* (Lynne Rienner, 2007, co-edited with Kevin Dunn), and most recently *The Politics of Origin in Africa* (Zed Books, 2013, co-authored with Kevin Dunn).

Sarah Bracking is professor of international development at the University of Manchester, UK. She is also currently director of the Leverhulme Centre for the Study of Value, a columnist at *Africa Report*, and visiting faculty at the Centre for Civil Society, University of KwaZulu-Natal, South Africa. Her numerous and wide-ranging publications include works on accumulation, corruption, secrecy jurisdictions and democracy, as well as on remittances and poverty, specifically in post-2000 Zimbabwe. She is author of *Money and Power* (Pluto Press, 2009), editor of *Corruption and Development* (Palgrave Macmillan, 2007), and is currently completing a book entitled *The Financialisation of Power in Africa* (Routledge, forthcoming).

Hannah Elliott is a PhD fellow at the Centre of African Studies, University of Copenhagen. She holds previous degrees in anthropology from the University of Manchester and the University of London (School of Oriental and African Studies, SOAS). Her research has focused on displacement, migration, markets and development in eastern Africa, working in various capacities: as a post-graduate student, an attachee with the British Institute in Eastern Africa, and as an independent consultant. She has co-published on the commodification of camel milk in Kenya in the *Journal of Eastern African Studies*. Her current research broadly deals with urban governance and citizenship in Isiolo, a frontier town in northern Kenya.

Martin Evans is a senior lecturer in international development at the University of Chester, UK. He has conducted research for over a decade on economic and political aspects of conflict and 'post-conflict' reconstruction, focusing on the separatist rebellion in Casamance, southern Senegal. He has published widely in such journals as *Africa*, *Journal of Refugee Studies*, *GeoJournal* and the *Canadian Journal of African Studies* on 'war economies', cross-border dynamics, local livelihoods of the displaced, the rebel movement, and the relationship between international aid, insecurity and the local politics of reconstruction. He has also published on the role of home-town associations in local development in Cameroon and Tanzania. His current interests concern the articulation between agro-ecological and social change in Casamance.

Peter Hansen is an independent consultant specializing in migration and development in East Africa. He has a PhD in anthropology from Copenhagen University, and worked for many years at the Danish Institute for International Development (DIIS), Copenhagen. His research and publications over the past decade – in such journals as the *Journal of Ethnic and Migration Studies* and the *Journal of Ethnopharmacology* – have focused on the Somali diaspora in Britain and Denmark, on remittances, on the role of diaspora returnees, and on the role of khat, in the economic, political and socio-economic transformations of Somaliland.

Jeremy L. Jones is assistant professor of anthropology at the College of the Holy Cross in Worcester, Massachusetts, USA. He received a PhD in anthropology from the University of Chicago in 2012. His research and several journal publications – in the *Journal of Southern African Studies* and *Social Dynamics* – focus on the interweaving of economic action and everyday life in contemporary Zimbabwe. He has studied young men working in the urban informal economy, and is currently researching social phenomena associated with Zimbabwe's record-breaking hyperinflation in the mid to later 2000s.

Timothy Raeymaekers teaches political geography and conflict studies at the University of Zurich. He has an MSc from the London School of Economics and a PhD from the University of Ghent, Belgium. His work concentrates on informal economies and the political economy/geography of armed conflict. Completed research projects include the analysis of war economy networks, hybrid governance and cross-border trade in Africa's Great Lakes region, and studies on displacement and borderlands in Africa and Europe. He is co-author with Koen Vlassenroot of *Conflict and Social Transformation in Eastern DRC* (Academia Press, 2004) and co-editor with Benedikt Korf of *Violence on the Margins: States, Conflict and Borderlands* (Palgrave Macmillan, 2013).

Cristina Udelsmann Rodrigues is an associate researcher in African Studies at ISCTE-IUL, University Institute of Lisbon, where she coordinates several research projects. Her main research areas include urban anthropology and sociology, urban transformation, poverty and development and borders in Africa. Most of her research is conducted in Angola, but she has worked in all Lusophone African countries. Her publications in edited books and in journals such as the *Journal of Southern African Studies*, the *Journal of Modern African Studies* and the *Journal of Contemporary African Studies* include works on urban stratification and urban (re)segregation in Angola's cities, entrepreneurship and the state on Angola's southern border, and more recently the growth of diamond mining towns in Angola's Lunda provinces.

Index

displacement economies, 3–32, 57, 145–60, 246; as only economies, 208; as socio-spatial analytical frame, 38; complexity of, 75; concept of, 11, 37, 39, 206–7; in Africa, 11–14; in practice, 18–24; mapping of, 166; necessity of study of, 24; of Somaliland, 158; of Zimbabwe, 161–84; spatial dimension of, 234; use of term, 4, 9

displacement-in-place *see* displacement, in place

disruption, 17–18

division of labour, gendered, 243–4

diya (blood compensation), 135, 137

dollarization of economies, 131, 166, 169, 170; in Zimbabwe, 96

Dubai, 158

Dundo (Angola), 112, 113, 114

Eastleigh Estate (Nairobi), 21, 127–44; as Somali displacement hub, 140

economic ground, concept of, 24

economic opportunities developed by displacement, 47–8

Economic Structural Adjustment Programme (ESAP) (Zimbabwe), 88, 167

economies of rupture and repositioning, 19–20

econoscape, use of term, 221–2

education, free, in Zimbabwe, 86–7

Effacer le Tableau campaign (Congo), 244

elders, deaths of, 69

Elmly Park Farm (Zimbabwe), 92

emplacement, 145, 159

enforced, use of term, 9

enforcement, in displacement, 14–15

environmental disasters, 9

Ethiopia, 156

EUFOR Chad, 42, 43

European Union (EU) Acholi Programme, 189

evacuation of normality, 87

evictions, 166, 198, 209, 212, 214; of Asians from Kenya and Uganda, 163; of Congolese from Angola, 116; of white farmers, 89, 90, 91, 93, 163, 174; urban, 82, 88

exchange rates, in Zimbabwe, 175

exclusion, 81, 83, 212, 240, 246, 247; racialization in, 86; self-exclusion, 240

expulsion, 37

externalization of assets: from Zimbabwe, 22–3, 174–7; practices of, 161–2, 173

extractive economies, 16

family connections, importance of, 156–7

Farchana refugee camp, 38, 45, 49–50, 54

Fast-Track Land Reform Programme (FTLRP) (Zimbabwe), 89–90, 210

fear, production of, 191–5, 203

fending for oneself, 240

financial flows, in Zimbabwe's economy, 161–84

firewood, fetching of, 191, 192

food, role of, in identity construction, 132

food aid: as a means of coping, 197–8; sale of, 198

football pitches, making of, 70

force, use of term, 14

forced labour, 112, 118–19

foreign exchange, 179; dealers in, 94–6

formal sector, 214, 222

fragmentation, use of term, 225

Friedman, J., 133

Fula people, 59

'G8 traders', 236–7

Gambia, 57, 61, 63

garimpo, 108, 111, 113, 114–16, 117, 118, 119, 120–2; networks of, 123

gender, 90; factor in displacement, 18

generation, factor in displacement, 18

generational differentiation, 90

geographies of terror, 59

gift exchange, 132–3; free, no space for, 243; of milk, 136

girls: labour of, 243–4; needs of, 242

Global Political Agreement (Zimbabwe), 96, 211

globalization, 12

gold, panning for, 80

grounding of economic life, 220–2

Guinea-Bissau, 19, 57, 61, 71; border zone, displacement in, 62–4

Guinea-Conakry, 59

Gulu district (Uganda), 189, 190, 192, 194, 195, 196, 198

hairdressing salons, Somali (*coffers*), 149–51

Hargeisa (Somalia), land rush in, 147–9

Hashaba (Darfur), 35, 37, 38, 50–2, 54

hierarchies, 18; of authority, 25

About Zed Books

Zed Books is a critical and dynamic publisher, committed to increasing awareness of important international issues and to promoting diversity, alternative voices and progressive social change. We publish on politics, development, gender, the environment and economics for a global audience of students, academics, activists and general readers. Run as a co-operative, Zed Books aims to operate in an ethical and environmentally sustainable way.

Find out more at:

www.zedbooks.co.uk

For up-to-date news, articles, reviews and events information visit:

http://zed-books.blogspot.com

To subscribe to the monthly Zed Books e-newsletter, send an email headed 'subscribe' to:

marketing@zedbooks.net

We can also be found on **Facebook**, **ZNet**, **Twitter** and **Library Thing**.